VEDIC MYTHOLOGY

BY

A. A. MACDONELL.

VEDIC MYTHOLOGY

BY

A. A. MACDONELL.

I. INTRODUCTION.

§ 1. Religion and mythology. — Religion in its widest sense includes on the one hand the conception which men entertain of the divine or supernatural powers and, on the other, that sense of the dependence of human welfare on those powers which finds its expression in various forms of worship. Mythology is connected with the former side of religion as furnishing the whole body of myths or stories which are told about gods and heroes and which describe their character and origin, their actions and surroundings. Such myths have their source in the attempt of the human mind, in a primitive and unscientific age, to explain the various forces and phenomena of nature with which man is confronted. They represent in fact the conjectural science of a primitive mental condition. For statements which to the highly civilised mind would be merely metaphorical, amount in that early stage to explanations of the phenomena observed. The intellectual difficulties raised by the course of the heavenly bodies, by the incidents of the thunderstorm, by reflexions on the origin and constitution of the outer world, here receive their answers in the form of stories. The basis of these myths is the primitive attitude of mind which regards all nature as an aggregate of animated entities. A myth actually arises when the imagination interprets a natural event as the action of a personified being resembling the human agent. Thus the observation that the moon follows the sun without overtaking it, would have been transformed into a myth by describing the former as a maiden following a man by whom she is rejected. Such an original myth enters on the further stage of poetical embellishment, as soon as it becomes the property of people endowed with creative imagination. Various traits are now added according to the individual fancy of the narrator, as the story passes from mouth to mouth. The natural phenomenon begins to fade out of the picture as its place is taken by a detailed representation of human passions. When the natural basis of the tale is forgotten, new touches totally unconnected with its original significance may be added or even transferred from other myths. When met with at a late stage of its development, a myth may be so far overgrown with secondary accretions unconnected with its original form, that its analysis may be extremely difficult or even impossible. Thus it would be hard indeed to discover the primary naturalistic elements in the characters or actions of the Hellenic gods, if we knew only the highly anthropomorphic deities in the plays of Euripides.

B. DELBRÜCK, ZVP. 1865, pp. 266—99; KUHN, Über Entwicklungsstufen der Mythenbildung, Berliner Ak. der Wissenschaften 1873, pp. 123—51; MAX MÜLLER, Comparative Mythology. Oxford Essays. II; Philosophy of Mythology. Selected

Essays. I; Chips from a German Workship, IV², 155—201; Physical Religion 276–8; SCHWARTZ, Der Ursprung der Mythologie; MANNHARDT, Antike Wald- und Feldkulte, Berlin 1871, Preface; MÜLLENHOFF in preface to MANNHARDT's Mythologische Forschungen, Strassburg 1884; LANG, Mythology. Encyclopaedia Britannica; GRUPPE, Die griechischen Culte und Mythen. Introduction; BLOOMFIELD, JAOS. XV, 135—6; F. B. JEVONS, Mythology. CHAMBERS' Encyclopaedia; Introduction to the History of Religion, London 1896, pp. 23. 32. 249–69.

§ 2. Characteristics of Vedic mythology. — Vedic mythology occupies a very important position in the study of the history of religions. Its oldest source presents to us an earlier stage in the evolution of beliefs based on the personification and worship of natural phenomena, than any other literary monument of the world. To this oldest phase can be traced by uninterrupted development the germs of the religious beliefs of the great majority of the modern Indians, the only branch of the Indo-European race in which its original nature worship has not been entirely supplanted many centuries ago by a foreign monotheistic faith. The earliest stage of Vedic mythology is not so primitive as was at one time supposed[1], but it is sufficiently primitive to enable us to see clearly enough the process of personification by which natural phenomena developed into gods, a process not apparent in other literatures. The mythology, no less than the language, is still transparent enough in many cases to show the connexion both of the god and his name with a physical basis; nay, in several instances the anthropomorphism is only incipient. Thus *uṣas*, the dawn, is also a goddess wearing but a thin veil of personification; and when *agni*, fire, designates the god, the personality of the deity is thoroughly interpenetrated by the physical element.

The foundation on which Vedic mythology rests, is still the belief, surviving from a remote antiquity, that all the objects and phenomena of nature with which man is surrounded, are animate and divine. Everything that impressed the soul with awe or was regarded as capable of exercising a good or evil influence on man, might in the Vedic age still become a direct object not only of adoration but of prayer. Heaven, earth, mountains, rivers, plants might be supplicated as divine powers; the horse, the cow, the bird of omen, and other animals might be invoked; even objects fashioned by the hand of man, weapons, the war-car, the drum, the plough, as well as ritual implements, such as the pressing-stones and the sacrificial post, might be adored.

This lower form of worship, however, occupies but a small space in Vedic religion. The true gods of the Veda are glorified human beings, inspired with human motives and passions, born like men, but immortal. They are almost without exception the deified representatives of the phenomena or agencies of nature[2]. The degree of anthropomorphism to which they have attained, however, varies considerably. When the name of the god is the same as that of his natural basis, the personification has not advanced beyond the rudimentary stage. Such is the case with Dyaus, Heaven, Pṛthivī, Earth, Sūrya, Sun, Uṣas, Dawn, whose names represent the double character of natural phenomena and of the persons presiding over them. Similarly in the case of the two great ritual deities, Agni and Soma, the personifying imagination is held in check by the visible and tangible character of the element of fire and the sacrificial draught, called by the same names, of which they are the divine embodiments. When the name of the deity is different from that of the physical substrate, he tends to become dissociated from the latter, the anthropomorphism being then more developed. Thus the Maruts or Storm-gods are farther removed from their origin than Vāyu, Wind, though the Vedic poets are still conscious of the connexion. Finally, when in addition to the difference in name, the conception of a god dates from a pre-Vedic period, the severance may have become complete. Such is the case with Varuṇa, in whom the connexion can only be inferred from mythological traits surviving from an earlier age. The process of abstraction has here proceeded so far, that Varuṇa's character resembles that of the divine ruler in a monotheistic belief of an exalted type. Personification has, however, nowhere in Vedic mythology attained to the individualized anthropomorphism characteristic of the Hellenic gods. The Vedic deities have but very few distinguishing features, while many attributes and powers are shared by all alike. This is partly due to the fact that the departments of nature which they represent have often much in common, while their anthropomorphism is comparatively undeveloped. Thus the activity of a thunder-god, of the fire-god in his lightning form, and of the storm-gods might easily be described in similar language, their main function in the eyes of the Vedic poets being the discharge of rain. Again, it cannot be doubted that various Vedic deities have started from the same source[3], but have become differentiated by an appellative denoting a particular attribute having gradually assumed an independent character. Such is the case with the solar gods. There is, moreover, often a want of clearness in the statements of the Vedic poets about the deeds of the gods; for owing to the character of the literature, myths are not related but only alluded to. Nor can thorough consistency be expected in such mythological allusions when it is remembered that they are made by a number of different poets, whose productions extend over a prolonged literary period.

[1] BRI. XIII ff.; P. v. BRADKE, Dyaus Asura, Halle 1885, 2—11; ZDMG. 40, 670. — [2] ORV. 591—4. — [3] L. v. SCHROEDER, WZKM. 9, 125—6; cp. BRI. 25.

Works on Vedic Mythology in general: R. ROTH, Die höchsten Götter der arischen Völker, ZDMG. 6, 67—77; 7, 607; BÖHTLINGK and ROTH, Sanskritwörterbuch, 7 vols., St. Petersburg 1852—75; J. MUIR, Original Sanskrit Text on the Origin and History of the People of India, their Religion and Institutions, 5 vols., especially vols. 4² revised (1873) and 5³ (1884); GRASSMANN, Wörterbuch zum Ṛig-Veda, Leipzig 1873; Ṛig-Veda übersetzt und mit kritischen und erläuternden Anmerkungen versehen, 2 vols., Leipzig 1876—7; W. D. WHITNEY, Oriental and Linguistic Studies, 2, 149 ff.; JAOS. 3, 291 ff. 331 ff.; P. WURM, Geschichte der indischen Religion, Basel 1874, pp. 21—54; A. BERGAIGNE, La Religion Védique d'après les Hymnes du Ṛigveda, 3 vols., Paris 1878—83; A. LUDWIG, Der Rigveda oder die heiligen Hymnen der Brāhmaṇa. Zum ersten Male vollständig ins Deutsche übersetzt. Mit Commentar und Einleitung. Prag, Wien, Leipzig 1876—88; F. MAX MÜLLER, Lectures on the Origin and Growth of Religion, London 1878; A. KAEGI, Der Rigveda, 2nd ed., Leipzig 1881; English Translation by R. ARROWSMITH, Boston 1886; A. BARTH, The Religions of India, London 1882; A. KUHN, Mythologische Studien. I²: Die Herabkunft des Feuers und des Göttertranks, Gütersloh 1886; L. v. SCHRÖDER, Indiens Litteratur und Kultur, Leipzig 1887, pp. 45—145; P. D. CHANTEPIE DE LA SAUSSAYE, Lehrbuch der Religionsgeschichte, Freiburg i. B., 1887, 1, pp. 346—69; PISCHEL and GELDNER, Vedische Studien. vol. I, Stuttgart 1889, vol. II, part I 1892; A. HILLEBRANDT, Vedische Mythologie, vol. I, Soma und verwandte Götter, Breslau 1891; P. REGNAUD, Le Rig-Véda et les Origines de la Mythologie indo-européenne, Paris 1892 (the author follows principles of interpretation altogether opposed to those generally accepted). E. HARDY, Die Vedisch-brahmanische Periode der Religion des alten Indiens, Münster i. W. 1893; H. OLDENBERG, Die Religion des Veda, Berlin 1894; P. DEUSSEN, Allgemeine Geschichte der Philosophie mit besonderer Berücksichtigung der Religionen, vol. I, part 1, Philosophie des Veda bis auf die Upanishad's, Leipzig 1894; E. W. HOPKINS, The Religions of India, Boston and London 1895.

§ 3. Sources of Vedic Mythology. — By far the most important source of Vedic Mythology is the oldest literary monument of India, the Rigveda. Its mythology deals with a number of coördinate nature gods of varying importance. This polytheism under the influence of an increasing tendency to abstraction at the end of the Rigvedic period, exhibits in its latest book the beginnings of a kind of monotheism and even signs of pantheism. The hymns of this collection having been composed with a view to the sacrificial ritual, especially that of the Soma offering, furnish a disproportionate presentment of the mythological material of the age. The great gods who occupy an important position at the Soma sacrifice and in the worship of the wealthy, stand forth prominently; but the mythology connected with spirits, with witchcraft, with life after death, is almost a blank, for these spheres of belief have nothing to do with the poetry of the Soma rite. Moreover, while the character of the gods is very completely illustrated in these hymns, which are addressed to them and extol their attributes, their deeds, with the exception of their leading exploits, are far less definitely described. It is only natural that a collection of sacrificial poetry containing very little narrative matter, should supply but a scattered and fragmentary account of this side of mythology. The defective information given by the rest of the RV. regarding spirits, lesser demons, and the future life, is only very partially supplied by its latest book. Thus hardly any reference is made even here to the fate of the wicked after death. Beside and distinguished from the adoration of the gods, the worship of dead ancestors, as well as to some extent the deification of inanimate objects, finds a place in the religion of the Rigveda.

The Sāmaveda, containing but seventy-five verses which do not occur in the RV., is of no importance in the study of Vedic mythology.

The more popular material of the Atharvaveda deals mainly with domestic and magical rites. In the latter portion it is, along with the ritual text of the Kauśika sūtra, a mine of information in regard to the spirit and demon world. On this lower side of religion the Atharvaveda deals with notions of greater antiquity than those of the Rigveda. But on the higher side of religion it represents a more advanced stage. Individual gods exhibit a later phase of development and some new abstractions are deified, while the general character of the religion is pantheistic[1]. Hymns in praise of individual gods are comparatively rare, while the simultaneous invocation of a number of deities, in which their essential nature is hardly touched upon, is characteristic. The deeds of the gods are extolled in the same stereotyped manner as in the RV.; and the AV. can hardly be said to supply any important mythological trait which is not to be found in the older collection.

The Yajurveda represents a still later stage. Its formulas being made for the ritual, are not directly addressed to the gods, who are but shadowy beings having only a very loose connexion with the sacrifice. The most salient features of the mythology of the Yajurveda are the existence of one chief god, Prajāpati, the greater importance of Viṣṇu, and the first appearance of an old god of the Rigveda under the new name of Śiva. Owing, however, to the subordinate position here occupied by the gods in comparison with the ritual, this Veda yields but little mythological material.

Between it and the Brāhmaṇas, the most important of which are the Aitareya and the Śatapatha, there is no essential difference. The sacrifice being the main object of interest, the individual traits of the gods have faded, the general character of certain deities has been modified, and the importance of others increased or reduced. Otherwise the pantheon of the Brāhmaṇas is much the same as that of the RV. and the AV., and the worship of inanimate objects is still recognized. The main difference between the mythology of the RV. and the Brāhmaṇas is the recognized position of Prajāpati or the Father-god as the chief deity in the latter. The pantheism of the

Brāhmaṇas is, moreover, explicit. Thus Prajāpati is said to be the All (ŚB. 1, 3, 5[10]) or the All and everything (ŚB. 1, 6, 4[2]; 4, 5, 7[2]).

The gods having lost their distinctive features, there is apparent a tendency to divide them into groups. Thus it is characteristic of the period that the supernatural powers form the two hostile camps of the Devas or gods on the one hand and the Asuras or demons on the other. The gods are further divided into the three classes of the terrestrial Vasus, the aerial Rudras, and the celestial Ādityas (§ 45). The most significant group is the representative triad of Fire, Wind, and Sun. The formalism of these works further shows itself in the subdivision of individual deities by the personification of their various attributes. Thus they speak of an 'Agni, lord of food', 'Agni, lord of prayer' and so forth[2].

The Brāhmaṇas relate numerous myths in illustration of their main subject-matter. Some of these are not referred to in the Saṃhitās. But where they do occur in the earlier literature, they appear in the Brāhmaṇas only as developments of their older forms, and cannot be said to shed light on their original forms, but only serve as a link between the mythological creations of the oldest Vedic and of the post-Vedic periods.

[1] HRI. 153. — [2] BRI. 42; HRI. 182.

§ 4. Method to be pursued. — Vedic mythology is the product of an age and a country, of social and climatic conditions far removed and widely differing from our own. We have, moreover, here to deal not with direct statements of fact, but with the imaginative creations of poets whose mental attitude towards nature was vastly different from that of the men of to-day. The difficulty involved in dealing with material so complex and representing so early a stage of thought, is further increased by the character of the poetry in which this thought is imbedded. There is thus perhaps no subject capable of scientific treatment, which, in addition to requiring a certain share of poetical insight, demands caution and sobriety of judgment more urgently. Yet the stringency of method which is clearly so necessary, has largely been lacking in the investigation of Vedic mythology. To this defect, no less than to the inherent obscurity of the material, are doubtless in considerable measure due the many and great divergences of opinion prevailing among Vedic scholars on a large number of important mythological questions.

In the earlier period of Vedic studies there was a tendency to begin research at the wrong end. The etymological equations of comparative mythology were then made the starting point. These identifications, though now mostly rejected, have continued to influence unduly the interpretation of the mythological creations of the Veda. But even apart from etymological considerations, theories have frequently been based on general impressions rather than on the careful sifting of evidence, isolated and secondary traits thus sometimes receiving coördinate weight with what is primary. An unmistakable bias has at the same time shown itself in favour of some one particular principle of interpretation[1]. Thus an unduly large number of mythological figures have been explained as derived from dawn, lightning, sun, or moon respectively. An *à priori* bias of this kind leads to an unconsciously partial utilization of the evidence.

Such being the case, it may pove useful to suggest some hints with a view to encourage the student in following more cautious methods. On the principle that scientific investigations should proceed from the better known to the less known, researches which aim at presenting a true picture of the character and actions of the Vedic gods, ought to begin not with the meagre and uncertain conclusions of comparative mythology, but with the information supplied by Indian literature, which contains a practically continuous record of Indian mythology from its most ancient source in the RV. down to modern times[2]. All the material bearing on any deity or myth ought to be collected, grouped, and sifted by the comparison of parallel passages, before any conclusion is drawn[3]. In this process the primary features which form the basis of the personification should be separated from later accretions.

As soon as a person has taken the place of a natural force in the imagination, the poetical fancy begins to weave a web of secondary myth, into which may be introduced in the course of time material that has nothing to do with the original creation, but is borrowed from elsewhere. Primary and essential features, when the material is not too limited, betray themselves by constant iteration. Thus in the Indra myth his fight with Vṛtra, which is essential, is perpetually insisted on, while the isolated statement that he strikes Vṛtra's mother with his bolt (1, 32[9]) is clearly a later touch, added by an individual poet for dramatic effect. Again, the epithet 'Vṛtra-slaying', without doubt originally appropriate to Indra alone, is in the RV. several times applied to the god Soma also. But that it is transferred from the former to the latter deity, is sufficiently plain from the statement that Soma is 'the Vṛtra-slaying intoxicating plant' (6, 17[11]), the juice of which Indra regularly drinks before the fray. The transference of such attributes is particularly easy in the RV. because the poets are fond of celebrating gods in couples, when both share the characteristic exploits and qualities of each other (cp. § 44). Attributes thus acquired must of course be eliminated from the essential features. A similar remark applies to attributes and cosmic powers which are predicated, in about equal degree, of many gods. They can have no cogency as evidence in regard to a particular deity[4]. It is only when such attributes and powers are applied in a predominant manner to an individual god, that they can be adduced with any force. For in such case it is possible they might have started from the god in question and gradually extended to others. The fact must, however, be borne in mind in this connexion, that some gods are celebrated in very many more hymns than others. The frequency of an attribute applied to different deities must therefore be estimated relatively. Thus an epithet connected as often with Varuṇa as with Indra, would in all probability be more essential to the character of the former than of the latter. For Indra is invoked in about ten times as many hymns as Varuṇa. The value of any particular passage as evidence may be affected by the relative antiquity of the hymn in which it occurs. A statement occurring for the first time in a late passage may of course represent an old notion; but if it differs from what has been said on the same point in a chronologically earlier hymn, it most probably furnishes a later development. The tenth and the greater part of the first book of the RV.[5] are therefore more likely to contain later conceptions than the other books. Moreover, the exclusive connexion of the ninth book with Soma Pavamāna may give a different complexion to mythological matter contained in another book. Thus Vivasvat and Trita are here connected with the preparation of Soma in quite a special manner (cp. §§ 18, 23). As regards the Brāhmaṇas, great caution should be exercised in discovering historically primitive notions in them; for they teem with far-fetched fancies, speculations, and identifications[6].

In adducing parallel passages as evidence, due regard should be paid to the context. Their real value can often only be ascertained by a minute and complex consideration of their surroundings and the association of ideas which connects them with what precedes and follows. After a careful estimation of the internal evidence of the Veda, aided by such corroboration as the later phases of Indian literature may afford, further light should be sought from the closely allied mythology of the Iranians. Comparison with it may confirm the results derived from the Indian material, or when the Indian evidence is inconclusive, may enable us either to decide what is old and new or to attain greater definiteness in regard to Vedic conceptions. Thus without the aid of the Avesta, it would be impossible to arrive at anything like certain conclusions about the original nature of the god Mitra.

The further step may now be taken of examining the results of comparative mythology, in order to ascertain if possible, wherein consists the Vedic heritage from the Indo-European period and what is the original significance of that heritage. Finally, the teachings of ethnology cannot be neglected, when it becomes necessary to ascertain what elements survive from a still remoter stage of human development. Recourse to all such evidence beyond the range of the Veda itself must prove a safeguard against on the one hand assuming that various mythological elements are of purely Indian origin, or on the other hand treating the Indo-European period as the very starting point of all mythological notions. The latter view would be as far from the truth as the assumption that the Indo-European language represents the very beginnings of Aryan speech[7].

[1] OLDENBERG, ZDMG. 49, 173. — [2] PVS. XXVI—VIII. — [3] BLOOMFIELD, ZDMG. 48, 542. — [4] HRI. 51. — [5] Cp. OLDENBERG, Die Hymnen des Ṛigveda I, Berlin 1888; E. V. ARNOLD, KZ. 34, 297. 344; HOPKINS, JAOS. 17, 23—92. — [6] HRI. 183. 194; V. SCHRÖDER, WZKM. 9, 120. — [7] ORV. 26—33.

Cp. also LUDWIG, Über Methode bei Interpretation des Ṛgveda, Prag 1890; HILLEBRANDT, Vedainterpretation, Breslau 1895.

§ 5. **The Avesta and Vedic Mythology.** — We have seen that the evidence of the Avesta cannot be ignored by the student of Vedic mythology. The affinity of the oldest form of the Avestan language with the dialect of the Vedas is so great in syntax, vocabulary, diction, metre, and general poetic style, that by the mere application of phonetic laws, whole Avestan stanzas may be translated word for word into Vedic, so as to produce verses correct not only in form but in poetic spirit[1]. The affinity in the domain of mythology is by no means so great. For the religious reform of Zarathuṣtra brought about a very considerable displacement and transformation of mythological conceptions. If therefore we possessed Avestan literature as old as that of the RV., the approximation would have been much greater in this respect. Still, the agreements in detail, in mythology no less than in cult, are surprisingly numerous. Of the many identical terms connected with the ritual it is here only necessary to mention Vedic *yajña* = Avestan *yasna*, sacrifice, *hotṛ* = *zaotar*, priest, *atharvan* = *āthravan*, fire-priest, *ṛta* = *aṣa* order, rite, and above all *soma* = *haoma*, the intoxicating juice of the Soma plant, in both cults offered as the main libation, pressed, purified by a sieve, mixed with milk, and described as the lord of plants, as growing on the mountains, and as brought down by an eagle or eagles (cp. § 37). It is rather with the striking correspondences in mythology that we are concerned. In both religions the term *asura* = *ahura* is applied to the highest gods, who in both are conceived as mighty kings, drawn through the air in their war chariots by swift steeds, and in character benevolent, almost entirely free from guile and immoral traits. Both the Iranians and the Indians observed the cult of fire, though under the different names of *Agni* and *Ātar*. The Waters, *āpaḥ* = *āpo*, were invoked by both, though not frequently[2]. The Vedic Mitra is the Avestan Mithra, the sun god. The Āditya Bhaga corresponds to *bagha*, a god in general; Vāyu, Wind is *vayu*, a genius of air; Apāṃ napāt, the Son of Waters = Apãm napāt; Gandharva = Gandarewa and Kṛśānu = Keresāni are divine beings connected with *soma* = *haoma.* To Trita Āptya correspond two mythical personages named Thrita and Āthwya, and to Indra Vṛtrahan the demon Indra and the genius of victory Verethragna. Yama, son of Vivasvat, ruler of the dead, is identical with Yima, son of Vīvaṅhvant, ruler of paradise. The parallel in character, though not in name, of the god Varuṇa is Ahura Mazda, the wise spirit. The two religions also have in common as designations of evil spirits the terms *druh* = *druj* and *yātu*[3].

[1] Bartholomae in Geiger and Kuhn's Grundriss der iranischen Philologie, vol. 1, p. 1. — [2] Spiegel, Die Arische Periode, Leipzig 1887, p. 155. — [3] Spiegel, op. cit. 225—33; Gruppe, Die griechischen Culte und Mythen, I, 86—97; ORV. 26—33; HRI, 167—8.

§ 6. **Comparative Mythology.** — In regard to the Indo-European period we are on far less certain ground. Many equations of name once made in the first enthusiasm of discovery and generally accepted, have since been rejected and very few of those that remain rest on a firm foundation. Dyaús = Ζεύς is the only one which can be said to be beyond the range of doubt. Varuṇa = Οὐρανός though presenting phonetic difficulties, seems possible. The rain-god Parjanya agrees well in meaning with the Lithuanian thunder-god Perkunas, but the phonetic objections are here still greater. The name of Bhaga is identical with the Slavonic *bogu* as well as the Persian *bagha,* but as the latter two words mean only 'god', the Indo-European word cannot have designated any individual deity. Though the name of Uṣas is radically cognate to Aurora and Ἠώς, the cult of Dawn as a goddess is a specially Indian development. It has been inferred from the identity of mythological traits in the thunder-gods of the various branches of the Indo-European family, that a thunder-god existed in the Indo-European period in spite of the absence of a common name. There are also one or two other not improbable equations based on identity of character only. That the conception of higher gods, whose nature was connected with light ($\sqrt{}$*div*, to shine) and heaven (*div*) had already been arrived at in the Indo-European period, is shown by the common name *deivos* (Skt. *deva-s*, Lith. *deva-s*, Lat. *deu-s*), god. The conception of Earth as a mother (common to Vedic and Greek mythology) and of Heaven as a father (Skt. *Dyaùṣ pitar*, Gk. Ζεῦ πάτερ, Lat. *Jūpiter*) appears to date from a still remoter antiquity. For the idea of Heaven and Earth being universal parents is familiar to the mythology of China and New Zealand and may be traced in that of Egypt[2]. The practice of magical rites and the worship of inanimate objects still surviving in the Veda, doubtless came down from an equally remote stage in the mental development of mankind, though the possibility of a certain influence exercised by the primitive aborigines of India on their Aryan conquerors cannot be altogether excluded.

[1] Gruppe op. cit. I, 97—121; ORV. 33—8; HRI. 168—9. — [2] Tylor, Primitive Culture I, 326; Lang, Mythology. Encyclopaedia Britannica, p. 150—1.

II. VEDIC CONCEPTIONS OF THE WORLD AND ITS ORIGIN.

§ 7. **Cosmology.** — The Universe, the stage on which the actions of the gods are enacted, is regarded by the Vedic poets as divided into the three domains[1] of earth, air or atmosphere, and heaven[2]. The sky when regarded as the whole space above the earth, forms with the latter the entire universe consisting of the upper and the nether world. The vault (*nāka*) of the sky is regarded as the limit dividing the visible upper world from the third or invisible world of heaven, which is the abode of light and the dwelling place of the gods. Heaven, air, and earth form the favourite triad of the RV., constantly spoken of explicitly or implicitly (8, 10[6]. 90[6] &c.). The solar phenomena which appear to take place on the vault of the sky, are referred to heaven, while those of lightning, rain, and wind belong to the atmosphere. But when heaven designates the whole space above the earth both classes of phenomena are spoken of as taking place there. In a passage of the AV. (4, 14[3] = VS. 17, 67) the 'vault of the sky' comes between the triad of earth, air, heaven and the world of light, which thus forms a fourth division[3]. Each of the three worlds is also subdivided. Thus three earths, three atmospheres, three heavens are sometimes mentioned; or when the universe is looked upon as consisting of two halves, we hear of six worlds or spaces (*rajāṃsi*). This subdivision probably arose from the loose use of the word *pṛthivī* 'earth' (1, 108[9. 10]; 7, 104[11])[4] in the plural to denote the three worlds (just as the dual *pitarau*, 'two fathers' regularly denotes 'father and mother').

The earth is variously called *bhūmi*, *kṣam*, *kṣā*, *gmā*, the great (*mahī*), the broad (*pṛthivī* or *urvī*), the extended (*uttānā*), the boundless (*apārā*), or the place here (*idam*) as contrasted with the upper sphere (1, 22[17]. 154[1. 3]).

The conception of the earth being a disc surrounded by an ocean does not appear in the Saṃhitās. But it was naturally regarded as circular, being compared with a wheel (10, 89[4]) and expressly called circular (*parimaṇḍala*) in the ŚB.[6]

The four points of the compass are already mentioned in the RV. in an adverbial form (7, 72[5]; 10, 36[14]. 42[11]) and in the AV. as substantives (AV. 15, 2[1] ff.). Hence 'four quarters' (*pradiśaḥ*) are spoken of (10, 19[8]), a term also used as synonymous with the whole earth (1, 164[42]), and the earth is described as 'four-pointed' (10, 58[3]). Five points are occasionally mentioned (9, 86[29]; AV. 3, 24[3] &c.), when that in the middle (10, 42[11]), where the speaker stands, denotes the fifth. The AV. also refers to six (the zenith being added) and even seven points[5]. The same points may be meant by the seven regions (*diśaḥ*) and the seven places (*dhāma*) of the earth spoken of in the RV. (9, 114[3]; 1, 22[16]).

Heaven or *div* is also commonly termed *vyoman*, sky, or as pervaded with light, the 'luminous space', *rocana* (with or without *divaḥ*). Designations of the dividing firmament besides the 'vault' are the 'summit' (*sānu*), 'surface' (*viṣṭap*), 'ridge' (*pṛṣṭha*), as well as the compound expressions 'ridge of the vault' (1, 125[5] cp. 3, 2[12]) and 'summit of the vault' (8, 92[2])[3]. Even a 'third ridge in the luminous space of heaven' is mentioned (9, 86[27]). When three heavens are distinguished they are very often called the three luminous spaces (*trī rocanā*), a highest (*uttama*), a middle, and a lowest being specified (5, 60[6]). The highest is also termed *uttara* and *pārya* (4, 26[6]; 6, 40[5]). In this third or highest heaven (very often *parame rocane* or *vyoman*) the gods, the fathers, and Soma are conceived as abiding.

Heaven and earth are coupled as a dual conception called by the terms *rodasī*, *kṣoṇī*, *dyāvāpṛthivī* and others (§ 44), and spoken of as the two halves (2, 27[15]). The combination with the semi-spherical sky causes the notion of the earth's shape to be modified, when the two are called 'the two great bowls (*camvā*) turned towards each other' (3, 55[20]). Once they are compared to the wheels at the two ends of an axle (10, 89[4]).

The RV. makes no reference to the supposed distance between heaven and earth, except in such vague phrases as that not even the birds can soar to the abode of Viṣṇu (1, 155[5]). But the AV. (10, 8[18]) says that 'the two wings of the yellow bird (the sun) flying to heaven are 1000 days' journey apart'. A similar notion is found in the AB., where it is remarked (2, 17[8]) that '1000 days' journey for a horse the heavenly world is distant from here'. Another Brāhmaṇa states that the heavenly world is as far from this world as 1000 cows standing on each other (PB. 16, 8[6]; 21, 1[9]).

The air or intermediate space (*antarikṣa*) is hardly susceptible of personification. As the region of mists and cloud, it is also called *rajas* which is described as watery (1, 124[5] cp. 5, 85[2]) and is sometimes thought of as dark, when it is spoken of as 'black' (1, 35[2. 4. 9]; 8, 43[6]). The triple subdivision is referred to as the three spaces or *rajāṃsi* (4, 53[5]; 5, 69[1]). The highest is then spoken of as *uttama* (9, 22[5]), *parama* (3, 30[2]), or *tṛtīya*, the third (9, 74[6]; 10, 45[3]. 123[8]), where the waters and Soma are and the celestial Agni is produced. The two lower spaces are within the range of our perception, but the third belongs to Viṣṇu (7, 99[1] cp. 1, 155[5]). The latter seems to be the 'mysterious' space once referred to elsewhere (10, 105[7]). The twofold subdivision of the atmosphere is commoner. Then the lower (*upara*) or terrestrial (*pārthiva*) is contrasted with the heavenly (*divyam* or *divaḥ*) space (1, 62[5]; 4, 53[3]). The uppermost stratum, as being contiguous with heaven (*div*) in the twofold as well as the triple division, seems often to be loosely employed as synonymous with heaven in the strict sense. Absolute definiteness or consistency in the statements of different poets or even of the same poet could not reasonably be expected in regard to such matters.

The air being above the earth in the threefold division of the universe, its subdivisions, whether two or three, would naturally have been regarded as above it also; and one verse at least (1, 81[5] cp. 90[7]) clearly shows that the 'terrestrial space' is in this position. Three passages, however, of the RV. (6, 9[1]; 7, 80[1]; 5, 81[4]) have been thought to lend themselves to the view[7] that the lower atmosphere was conceived as under the earth, to account for the course of the sun during the night. The least indefinite of these three passages (5, 81[4]) is to the effect that Savitṛ, the sun, goes round night on both sides (*ubhayataḥ*). This may, however, mean nothing more than that night is enclosed between the limits of sunset and sunrise. At any rate, the view advanced in the AB. (3, 44[4]) as to the sun's course during the night is, that the luminary shines upwards at night, while it turns round so as to shine downwards in the daytime. A similar notion may account for the statement of the RV. that the light which the sun's steeds draw is sometimes bright and sometimes dark (1, 115[5]), or that the *rajas* which accompanies the sun to the east is different from the light with which he rises (10, 37[3]).

There being no direct reference to the sun passing below the earth, the balance of probabilities seems to favour the view that the luminary was supposed to return towards the east the way he came, becoming entirely darkened during the return journey. As to what becomes of the stars during the daytime, a doubt is expressed (1, 24[10]), but no conjecture is made.

The atmosphere is often called a sea (*samudra*) as the abode of the celestial waters. It is also assimilated to the earth, inasmuch as it has mountains (1, 32[2] &c.) and seven streams which flow there (1, 32[12] &c.), when the conflict with the demon of drought takes place. Owing to the obvious resemblance the term 'mountain' (*parvata*) thus very often in the RV. refers to clouds[8], the figurative sense being generally clear enough. The word 'rock' (*adri*) is further regularly used in a mythological sense for 'cloud' as enclosing the cows released by Indra and other gods[9].

The rainclouds as containing the waters, as dripping, moving and roaring, are peculiarly liable to theriomorphism as cows[10], whose milk is rain.

The cosmic order or law prevailing in nature is recognised under the name of *ṛta*[11] (properly the 'course' of things), which is considered to be under the guardianship of the highest gods. The same word also designates 'order' in the moral world as truth and 'right', and in the religious world as sacrifice or 'rite'.

[1] Roth, ZDMG. 6, 68. — [2] Cp. Sp.AP. 122; KRV. 34, note 118. — [3] Hopkins, AJP. 4, 189. — [4] Bollensen, ZDMG. 41, 494. — [5] Bloomfield, AJP. 12, 432. — [6] Cp. Weber, IS. 10, 358—64. — [7] AIL. 357—9. — [8] KHF. 178; Delbrück, ZVP. 1865, pp. 284—5. — [9] KHF. 187; Zft. f. deutsche Mythologie, 3, 378. — [10] GW., s. v. *go*; WVB. 1894, p. 13. — [11] Ludwig, Religiöse und philosophische Anschauungen des Veda (1875), p. 15; LRV. 3, 284—5; Harlez, JA. (1878), 11, 105—6; Darmesteter, Ormazd et Ahriman, 13—4; OGR. 198. 243; KRV. 28; BRV. 3, 220; WC. 91—7. 100; Sp.AP. 139; ORV. 195—201; Jackson, Trans. of 10th Or. Congress, 2, 74.

Bruce, Vedic conceptions of the Earth, JRAS. 1862, p. 321 ff.; BRV. I, 1—3; Wallis, Cosmology of the Rigveda (London 1887), 111—17.

§ 8. Cosmogony. — The cosmogonic mythology of the RV. fluctuates between two theories, which are not mutually exclusive, but may be found combined in the same verse. The one regards the universe as the result of mechanical production, the work of the carpenter's and joiner's skill; the other represents it as the result of natural generation.

The poets of the RV. often employ the metaphor of building in its various details, when speaking of the formation of the world. The act of measuring is constantly referred to. Thus Indra measured the six regions, made the wide expanse of earth and the high dome of heaven (6, 47[3.4]). Viṣṇu measured out the terrestrial spaces and made fast the abode on high (1, 154[1]). The measuring instrument, sometimes mentioned (2, 15[3]; 3, 38[3]), is the sun, with which Varuṇa performs the act (5, 85[5]). The Fathers measured the two worlds with measuring rods and made them broad (3, 38[3] cp. 1, 190[2]). The measurement naturally begins in front or the east. Thus Indra measured out as it were a house with measures from the front (2, 15[3] cp. 7, 99[2]). Connected with this idea is that of spreading out the earth, an action attributed to Agni, Indra, the Maruts, and others. As the Vedic house was built of wood, the material is once or twice spoken of as timber. Thus the poet asks: 'What was the wood, what the tree out of which they fashioned heaven and earth?' (10, 31[7] = 10, 81[4]). The answer given to this question in a Brāhmaṇa is that Brahma was the wood and the tree (TB. 2, 8, 9[6]). Heaven and earth are very often described as having been supported (*skabh* or *stabh*) with posts (*skambha* or *skambhana*), but the sky is said to be rafterless (2, 15[2]; 4, 56[3]; 10, 149[1]), and that it never falls is a source of wonder (5, 29[4]; 6, 17[7]; 8, 45[6]). The framework of a door is called *ātā*; in such a frame of heaven Indra fixed the air (1, 56[5]). The doors of the cosmic house are the portals of the east through which the morning light enters (1, 113[4]; 4, 51[2]; 5, 45[1]). Foundations are sometimes alluded to. Thus Savitṛ made fast the earth with bands (10, 149[1]), Viṣṇu fixed it with pegs (7, 99[3]), and Bṛhaspati supports its ends (4, 50[1] cp. 10, 89[1]). The agents in the construction of the world are either the gods in general or various individual gods; but where special professional skill seemed to be required in details, Tvaṣṭṛ, the divine carpenter, or the deft-handed Ṛbhus are mentioned. Little is said as to their motive; but as man builds his house to live in, so of Viṣṇu at least it is indicated that he measured or stretched out the regions as an abode for man (6, 49[13]. 69[5], cp. 1, 155[4]).

The notion of parentage as a creative agency in the universe, chiefly connected with the birth of the sun at dawn and with the production of rain after drought, has three principle applications in the RV. The first is temporal, as involving the idea of priority. One phenomenon preceding another is spoken of as its parent. Thus the dawns generate (*jan*) the sun and the morning sacrifice (7, 78[3]), while Dawn herself is born of Night (1, 123[9]). As the point of view is changed, contradictions with regard to such relationships naturally arise (cp. p. 48). When the rising of the dawn is ascribed to the sacrifice of the Fathers, the explanation is to be found in this notion of priority. Secondly, a local application frequently occurs. The space in which a thing is contained or produced is its father or mother. Illustrations of this are furnished by purely figurative statements. Thus the quiver is called the father of the arrows (6, 75[5]) or the bright steeds of the sun are termed the daughters of his car (1, 50[9]). This idea of local parentage is especially connected with heaven and earth. Paternity is the characteristic feature in the personification of Dyaus (see § 11), and Dawn is constantly called the 'daughter of Heaven'. Similarly the Earth, who produces vegetation on her broad bosom (5, 84[3]), is a mother (1, 89[4] &c.). Heaven and earth are, however, more often found coupled as universal parents, a conception obvious enough from the fact that heaven fertilizes the earth by the descent of moisture and light, and further developed by the observation that both supply nourishment to living beings, the one in the form of rain, the other in that of herbage. They are characteristically the parents of the gods (§ 44). As the latter are often said to have created heaven and earth, we thus arrive at the paradox of the Vedic poets that the children produced their own parents; Indra, for instance, being described as having begotten his father and mother from his own body (1, 159[2]; 10, 54[3]). Again, the raincloud cow is the mother of the lightning calf, or the heavenly waters, as carrying the embryo of the aerial fire, are its mothers, for one of the forms of the fire-god is 'the son of waters' (§ 24). 'Son of the steep' also appears to be a name of lightning in the AV. (1, 13[2. 3]; cp. 26[3] and RV. 10, 142[2]). Thirdly, the notion of parentage arises from a generic point of view: he who is the chief, the most prominent member of a group, becomes their parent. Thus Vāyu, Wind, is father of the Storm-gods (1, 134[4]), Rudra, father of the Maruts or Rudras, Soma, father of plants, while Sarasvatī is mother of rivers.

There are also two minor applications of the idea of paternity in the RV. As in the Semitic languages, an abstract quality is quite frequently employed in a figurative sense (which is sometimes mythologically developed) to represent the parent of sons who possess or bestow that quality in an eminent degree. Thus the gods in general are sons (*sūnavaḥ* or *putrāḥ*) of immortality[1] as well as sons of skill, *dakṣa* (8, 25[5]; cp. § 19). Agni is the 'son of strength' or of 'force' (§ 35). Pūṣan is the 'child of setting free'[2]. Indra is the 'son of truth' (8, 58[4]), the 'child of cow-getting' (4, 32[22]), and the 'son of might' (*śavasaḥ*, 4, 24[1]; 8, 81[14], his mother twice being called *śavasī*, 8, 45[5]. 66[2]). Mitra-Varuṇa are the 'children of great might'. Another application is much less common. As a father transmits his qualities to his son, his name is also occasionally transferred, something like a modern surname. Thus *viśvarupa*, an epithet of Tvaṣṭṛ, becomes the proper name of his son. Analogously the name of Vivasvat is applied to his son Manu in the sense of the patronymic *Vaivasvata* (Vāl. 4[1]).

A mythological account of the origin of the universe, involving neither manufacture nor generation, is given in one of the latest hymns of the RV., the well-known *puruṣa-sūkta* (10, 90). Though several details in this myth point to the most recent period of the RV., the main idea is very primitive, as it accounts for the formation of the world from the body of a giant. With him the gods performed a sacrifice, when his head became the sky, his navel the air, and his feet the earth. From his mind sprang the moon, from his eye the sun, from his mouth Indra and Agni, from his breath, wind. The four castes also arose from him. His mouth became the *brāhmaṇa*, his arms the *rājanya* or warrior, his thighs the *vaiśya*, and his feet the *śūdra*. The interpretation given in the hymn itself is pantheistic, for it is there said (v. 2) that Puruṣa is 'all this, both what has become and what shall be'. In the AV. (10, 17) and the Upaniṣads (Muṇḍ. Up. 2, 1[10]) Puruṣa is also pantheistically interpreted as identical with the universe. He is also identified with Brahma (Chānd. Up. 1, 7[5]). In the SB. (11, 1, 6[1]) he is the same as Prajāpati, the creator.

There are in the last book of the RV. some hymns which treat the origin of the world philosophically rather than mythologically. Various passages show that in the cosmological speculation of the RV. the sun was regarded as an important agent of generation. Thus he is called the soul (*ātmā*) of all that moves and stands (1, 115[1]). Statements such as that he is called by many names though one (1, 164[46]; 10, 114[5] cp. Vāl. 10[2]) indicate that his nature was being tentatively abstracted to that of a supreme god, nearly approaching that of the later conception of Brahmā. In this sense the sun is once glorified as a great power of the universe under the name of the 'golden embryo', *hiraṇya-garbha*, in RV. 10, 121.[3] It is he who measures out space in the air and shines where the sun rises (vv. [5. 6]). In the last verse of this hymn, he is called Prajāpati[4], 'lord of created beings', the name which became that of the chief god of the Brāhmaṇas. It is significant that in the only older passage of the RV. in which it occurs (4, 53[2]), *prajāpati* is an epithet of the solar deity Savitṛ, who in the same hymn (v. [6]) is said to rule over what moves and stands[5].

There are two other cosmogonic hymns which both explain the origin of the universe as a kind of evolution of the existent (*sat*) from the non-existent (*asat*). In 10, 72[6] it is said that Brahmaṇaspati forged together this world like a smith. From the non-existent the existent was produced. Thence in succession arose the earth, the spaces, Aditi with Dakṣa; and after Aditi the gods were born. The gods then brought forward the sun. There were eight sons of Aditi, but the eighth, Mārtāṇḍa, she cast away; she brought him to be born and to die (i. e. to rise and set). Three stages can be distinguished in this hymn: first the world is produced, then the gods, and lastly the sun.

In RV. 10, 129, a more abstract and a very sublime hymn, it is affirmed that nothing existed in the beginning, all being void. Darkness and space enveloped the undifferentiated waters (cp. 10, 82[6]. 121[7], AV. 2, 8). The one primordial substance (*ekam*) was produced by heat. Then desire (*kāma*), the first seed of mind (*manas*) arose. This is the bond between the non-existent and the existent. By this emanation the gods came into being. But here the poet, overcome by his doubts, gives up the riddle of creation as unsolvable. A short hymn of three stanzas (10, 190) forms a sequel to the more general evolution of that just described. Here it is stated that from heat (*tapas*) was produced order (*ṛta*); then night, the ocean, the year; the creator (*dhātā*) produced in succession sun and moon, heaven and earth, air and ether.

In a similar strain to RV. 10, 129 a Brāhmaṇa passage declares that 'formerly nothing existed, neither heaven nor earth nor atmosphere, which being non-existent resolved to come into being' (TB. 2, 2, 9[1] ff.). The regular cosmogonic view of the Brāhmaṇas requires the agency of a creator, who is not, however, always the starting point. The creator here is Prajāpati or the personal Brahmā, who is not only father of gods, men, and demons, but is the All. Prajāpati is here an anthropomorphic representation of the desire which is the first seed spoken of in RV. 10, 129. In all these accounts the starting point is either Prajāpati desiring offspring and creating, or else the primeval waters, on which floated Hiraṇyagarbha the cosmic golden egg, whence is produced the spirit that desires and creates the Universe. This fundamental contradiction as to the priority of Prajāpati or of the waters appears to be the result of combining the theory of evolution with that of creation. Besides this there are many minor conflicts of statement, as, for instance, that the gods create Prajāpati and that Prajāpati creates the gods[7]. The account given in the Chāndogya Brāhmaṇa (5, 19) is that not-being became being; the latter changed into an egg, which after a year by splitting in two became heaven and earth; whatever was produced is the sun, which is Brahma[8] (cp. Ch. Up. 3, 19^{1-4}). Again, in the Bṛhadāraṇyaka Upaniṣad ($5, 6^1$), the order of evolution is thus stated: In the beginning waters were this (universe); they produced the real (*satyam*); from this was produced Brahma, from Brahma Prajāpati, from Prajāpati the gods.

The All-god appears as a creator in the AV. under the new names of Skambha, Support, Prāṇa[9], the personified breath of life (AV. 11, 4), Rohita, as a name of the sun, Kāma, Desire, and various others[10]. The most notable cosmogonic myth of the Brāhmaṇas describes the raising of the submerged earth by a boar, which in post-Vedic mythology developed into an Avatār of Viṣṇu.[11].

[1] OST. 5, 52. — [2] OST. 5, 175, note 271; BRV. 2, 422 ff.; Darmesteter, Haurvatāt et Ameretāt, 83; ORV. 232, note 2. — [3] SPH. 27—8; HRI. 208. — [4] SPH. 29. — [5] OGR. 295; WC. 50—1. — [6] OST. 5, 48. — [7] OST. 4, 20 ff.; HRI. 208—9. — [8] Weber, IS. 1, 261. — [9] SPH. 69—72. — [10] HRI. 209. — [11] Macdonell, JRAS. 1895, pp. 178—89.

Haug, Die Kosmogonie der Inder, Allgemeine Zeitung, 1873, p. 2373 ff.; Weber, IS. 9, 74; Ludwig, Die philosophischen und religiösen Anschauungen des Veda; AIL. 217; BRI. 30—1; Scherman, Philosophische Hymnen aus der Ṛig- und Atharva-veda Saṃhitā, München 1887; Lukas, Die Grundbegriffe in den Kosmogonien der alten Völker, Leipzig 1893, pp. 65—99.

§ 9. **Origin of gods and men.** — As most of the statements contained in the Vedas about the origin of the gods have already been mentioned, only a brief summary need here be added. In the philosophical hymns the origin of the gods is mostly connected with the element of water[1]. In the AV. ($10, 7^{25}$) they are said to have arisen from the non-existent. According to one cosmogonic hymn ($10, 129^6$) they were born after the creation of the universe. Otherwise they are in general described as the children of Heaven and Earth. In one passage ($10, 63^2$) a triple origin, apparently corresponding to the triple division of the universe, is ascribed to the gods, when they are said to have been 'born from Aditi, from the waters, from the earth' (cp. $1, 139^{11}$). According no doubt to a secondary conception, certain individual gods are spoken of as having begotten others. Thus the Dawn is called the mother of the gods ($1, 113^{19}$) and Brahmaṇaspati ($2, 26^3$), as well as Soma ($9, 87^2$), is said to be their father. A group of seven or eight gods, the Ādityas, are regarded as the sons of Aditi. In the AV. some gods are spoken of as fathers, others as sons[2] (AV. $1, 30^2$).

The Vedic conceptions on the subject of the origin of man are rather fluctuating, but the human race appear generally to have been regarded as descended from a first man. The latter is called either Vivasvat's son Manu, who was the first sacrificer ($10, 63^7$) and who is also spoken of as father

Manus (1, 80[16]); or he is Yama Vaivasvata, Vivasvat's son, who with his twin sister Yamī produced the human race. The origin of men, when thought of as going back beyond this first ancestor, seems to have been conceived as celestial. Vivasvat (§ 18) is the father of the primeval twins, while once the celestial Gandharva and the water nymph are designated as their highest kin (10, 10[4]). Men's relationship to the gods is sometimes also alluded to[3]; and men must have been thought of as included among the offspring of Heaven and Earth, the great parents of all that exists. Again, Agni is said to have begotten the offspring of men (1, 96[2.4]), and the Aṅgirases, the semi-divine ancestors of later priestly families, are described as his sons. Various other human families are spoken of as independently descended from the gods through their founders Atri, Kaṇva, and others (1, 139[9]). Vasiṣṭha (7, 33[11]) was miraculously begotten by Mitra and Varuṇa, the divine nymph Urvaśī having been his mother. To quite a different order of ideas belongs the conception of the origin of various classes of men from parts of the world giant Puruṣa[4] (§ 8, p. 13).

[1] SPH. 32. — [2] OST. 5, 13 f., 23 f., 38 f. — [3] BRV. 1, 36. — [4] ORV. 275—7. 125—8.

III. THE VEDIC GODS.

§ 10. **General character and classification.** — Indefiniteness of outline and lack of individuality characterize the Vedic conception of the gods. This is mainly due to the fact that they are nearer to the physical phenomena which they represent, than the gods of any other Indo-European people. Thus the ancient Vedic interpreter Yāska[1] (Nir. 7, 4) speaking of the nature of the gods, remarks that what is seen of them is not anthropomorphic at all, as in the case of the Sun, the Earth, and others. The natural bases of the Vedic gods have, to begin with, but few specific characteristics, while they share some of the attributes of other phenomena belonging to the same domain. Thus Dawn, Sun, Fire have the common features of being luminous, dispelling darkness, appearing in the morning. The absence of distinctiveness must be still greater when several deities have sprung from different aspects of one and the same phenomenon. Hence the character of each Vedic god is made up of only a few essential traits combined with a number of other features common to all the gods, such as brilliance, power, beneficence, and wisdom. Certain great cosmical functions are predicated of nearly every leading deity individually. The action of supporting or establishing heaven and earth is so generally attributed to them, that in the AV. (19, 32) it is even ascribed to a magical bunch of *darbha* grass. Nearly a dozen gods are described as having created the two worlds, and rather more are said to have produced the sun, to have placed it in the sky, or to have prepared a path for it. Four or five are also spoken of as having spread out the earth, the sky, or the two worlds. Several (Sūrya, Savitṛ, Pūṣan, Indra, Prajanya, and the Ādityas) are lords of all that moves and is stationary.

Such common features tend to obscure what is essential, because in hymns of prayer and praise they naturally assume special prominence. Again, gods belonging to different departments, but having prominent functions in common, are apt to be approximated. Thus Agni, primarily the god of terrestrial fire, dispels the demons of darkness with his light, while Indra, the aerial god of the thunderstorm, slays them with his lightning. Into the conception of the fire-god further enters his aspect as lightning in the atmosphere. The assimilation is increased by such gods often being invoked in pairs.

These combinations result in attributes peculiar to the one god attaching themselves to the other, even when the latter appears alone. Thus Agni comes to be called Soma-drinker, Vṛtra-slayer, winner of cows and waters, sun and dawns, attributes all primarily belonging to Indra.

The indefiniteness of outline caused by the possession of so many common attributes, coupled with the tendency to wipe out the few distinctive ones by assigning nearly every power to every god, renders identification of one god with another easy. Such identifications are as a matter of fact frequent in the RV.[1] Thus a poet addressing the fire-god exclaims: 'Thou at thy birth, O Agni, art Varuṇa; when kindled thou becomest Mitra, in thee, O son of strength, all gods are centred; thou art Indra to the worshipper' (5, 3[1]). Reflexions in particular on the nature of Agni, so important a god in the eyes of a priesthood devoted to a fire cult, on his many manifestations as individual fires on earth, and on his other aspects as atmospheric fire in lightning and as celestial fire in the sun, aspects which the Vedic poets are fond of alluding to in riddles, would suggest the idea that various deities are but different forms of a single divine being. This idea is found in more than one passage of the RV. 'The one being priests speak of in many ways; they call it Agni, Yama, Mātariśvan' (1, 164[46]; cp. AV. 10, 8[28]. 13, 4[15]). 'Priests and poets with words make into many the bird (= the sun) that is but one' (10, 114[5]). Thus it appears that by the end of the Rigvedic period a kind of polytheistic monotheism had been arrived at. We find there even the incipient pantheistic conception of a deity representing not only all the gods but nature as well. For the goddess Aditi is identified not only with all the gods, but with men, all that has been and shall be born, air, and heaven (1, 89[10]); and Prajāpati is not only the one god above all gods, but embraces all things (10, 121[8. 10]). This pantheistic view becomes fully developed in the AV. (10, 7[14. 25]) and is explicitly accepted in the later Vedic literature[2].

In the older parts of the RV. individual gods are often invoked as the highest, but this notion is not carried out to its logical conclusion. The fact that the Vedic poets frequently seem to be engrossed in the praise of the particular deity they happen to be invoking, that they exaggerate his attributes to the point of inconsistency, has given rise to the much discussed theory which Max Müller originated and to which he has given the name of Henotheism or Kathenotheism[3]. According to this theory, 'the belief in individual gods alternately regarded as the highest', the Vedic poets attribute to the god they happen to be addressing all the highest traits of divinity, treating him for the moment as if he were an absolutely independent and supreme deity, alone present to the mind. Against this theory it has been urged[4] that Vedic deities are not represented 'as independent of all the rest', since no religion brings its gods into more frequent and varied juxtaposition and combination, and that even the mightiest gods of the Veda are made dependent on others. Thus Varuṇa and Sūrya are subordinate to Indra (1, 101[3]), Varuṇa and the Aśvins submit to the power of Viṣṇu (1, 156[4]), and Indra, Mitra-Varuṇa, Aryaman, Rudra cannot resist the ordinances of Savitṛ (2, 38[9]). It has been further pointed out that in the frequent hymns addressed to the *viśvedevāḥ*, or All-gods, all the deities, even the lesser ones, are praised in succession, and that as the great mass of the Vedic hymns was composed for the ritual of the Soma offering, which included the worship of almost the entire pantheon, the technical priest could not but know the exact relative position of each god in that ritual. Even when a god is spoken of as unique or chief (*eka*), as is natural enough in laudations, such statements rose their temporarily monotheistic force through the modifications or corlections supplied by the context or even by the same verse. Thus a poet says that 'Agni alone, like Varuṇa, is lord of wealth'. It should also be remembered that gods are constantly invoked in pairs, triads, and larger groups, even the exalted Varuṇa being mostly addressed in conjunction with one other god (as in 6, 67) or with several other gods (as in 2, 28). Henotheism is therefore an appearance rather than a reality, an appearance produced by the indefiniteness due to undeveloped anthropomorphism, by the lack of any Vedic god occupying the position of a Zeus as the constant head of the pantheon, by the natural tendency of the priest or singer in extolling a particular god to exaggerate his greatness and to ignore other gods, and by the growing belief in the unity of the gods (cf. the refrain of 3, 55), each of whom might be regarded as a type of the divine. Henotheism might, however, be justified as a term to express the tendency of the RV. towards a kind of monotheism.

The Vedic gods, as has been shown, had a beginning in the view of the Vedic poets, since they are described as the offspring of heaven and earth or sometimes of other gods. This in itself implies different generations of gods, but earlier (*pūrve*) gods are also expressly referred to in several passages (7, 21[7] &c.). An earlier or first age of the gods is also spoken of (10, 72[2. 3]). The AV. (11, 8[10]) speaks of ten gods as having existed before the rest. The gods, too, were originally mortal[5]. This is expressly stated in the AV. (11, 5[19]; 4, 11[6]). The Brāhmaṇas state this both of all the gods (SB. 10, 4, 3[3]) and of the individual gods Indra (AB. 8, 14[4]), Agni (AB. 3, 4), and Prajāpati (SB. 10, 1, 3[1])[6]. That they were originally not immortal is implied in the RV. For immortality was bestowed on them by Savitṛ (4, 54[2] = VS. 33, 54) or by Agni (6, 7[4]; AV. 4, 23[6]). They are also said to have obtained it by drinking Soma (9, 106[8] cp. 109[2. 3]), which is called the principle of immortality (SB. 9, 5, 1[8]). In another passage of the RV. (10, 53[10]), they are said to have acquired immortality, but by what means is not clear. According to a later conception Indra is stated to have conquered heaven by *tapas* or austerity (10, 167[1]). The gods are said to have attained divine rank by the same means (TB. 3, 12, 3[1]), or to have overcome death by continence and austerity (AV. 11, 5[19]) and to have acquired immortality through Rohita (AV. 13, 1[7]). Elsewhere the gods are stated to have overcome death by the performance of a certain ceremony (TS. 7, 4, 2[1]). Indra and several other gods are said to be unaging (3, 46[1] &c.), but whether the immortality of the gods was regarded by the Vedic poets as absolute, there is no evidence to show. According to the post-Vedic view their immortality was only relative, being limited to a cosmic age.

The physical appearance of the gods is anthropomorphic, though only in a shadowy manner; for it often represents only aspects of their natural bases figuratively described to illustrate their activities[7]. Thus head, face, mouth, cheeks, eyes, hair, shoulders, breast, belly, arms, hands, fingers, feet are attributed to various individual gods. Head, breast, arms, and hands are chiefly mentioned in connexion with the warlike equipment of Indra and the Maruts. The arms of the sun are simply his rays, and his eye is intended to represent his physical aspect. The tongue and limbs of Agni merely denote his flames. The fingers of Trita are referred to only in order to illustrate his character as a preparer of Soma, and the belly of Indra only to emphasize his powers of drinking Soma[8]. Two or three gods are spoken of as having or assuming all forms (*viśvarūpa*). It is easy to understand that in the case of deities whose outward shape was so vaguely conceived and whose connexion with natural phenomena was in many instances still clear, no mention of either images (§ 66 c) or temples is found in the RV.

Some of the gods are spoken of as wearing garments. Thus Dawn is described as decked in gay attire. Some of the gods are equipped with armour in the shape of coats of mail or helmets. Indra is regularly armed with a bolt (*vajra*), while to others spears, battle-axes, bows and arrows are assigned. The gods in general are described as driving luminous cars, nearly every individual deity being also said to possess one. The car is usually drawn by steeds, but in the case of Pūṣan by goats, of the Maruts perhaps by spotted deer as well as horses, and of Uṣas, by cows as well as horses.

In their cars the gods are frequently represented as coming to seat themselves on the layer of strewn grass at the sacrifice, which, however, from another point of view, is supposed also to be conveyed to them in heaven by Agni (§ 35). The beverage of the gods is Soma. What they eat is the favourite food of men and is of course represented by what is offered to them at the sacrifice. It consists of milk in its various forms, butter, barley, and (though perhaps not in the oldest Vedic period) rice; cattle, goats, and sheep, with a preference for the animal which in some way is most closely connected with a deity's peculiar qualities. Thus the bull or the buffalo, to which Indra is so often compared, is offered to him and eaten by him, sometimes in extraordinary numbers (§ 22). Analogously, Indra's steeds are supposed to eat grain[9]. The abode of the gods is variously described as heaven, the third heaven, or the highest step of Viṣṇu, where they live a joyous life exhilerated by Soma. The gods on the whole are conceived as dwelling together in harmony and friendship[10]. The only one who ever introduces a note of discord is the warlike and overbearing Indra. He once appears to have fought against the gods in general (4, 30$^{3.5}$)[11]; he slew his own father (§ 22), and shattered the car of Dawn (§ 20). He seems also to have threatened on one occasion to slay his faithful companions the Maruts (§ 29).

The gods representing the chief powers of nature, such as fire, sun, thunderstorm, appeared to the successful and therefore optimistic Vedic Indian as almost exclusively beneficent beings, bestowers of prosperity. The only deity in whom injurious features are at all prominent is Rudra. Evils closely connected with human life, such as disease, proceed from lesser demons, while the greater evils manifested in nature, such as drought and darkness, are produced by powerful demons like Vṛtra. The conquest of these demons brings out the beneficent nature of the gods all the more prominently. The benevolence of the gods resembles that of human beings. They are preëminently the receivers of sacrifice, the hymns to them being recited while the Soma is pressed, the offering is cast in the fire, and priests attend to the intricate details of the ritual[12]. They are therefore the friends of the sacrificer, but are angry with and punish the niggard. This is especially the case with Indra, who at the same time is not altogether free from arbitrariness in the distribution of his favours[13].

The character of the Vedic gods is also moral. All the gods[14] are 'true' and 'not deceitful', being throughout the friends and guardians of honesty and righteousness. It is, however, the Ādityas, especially Varuṇa, who are the chief upholders of the moral law. The gods are angry with the evil-doer, but it is Varuṇa's wrath which is most closely connected with the conception of guilt and sin. Agni also is invoked to free from guilt, but this is only one of many prayers addressed to him, not their chief purport as in the case of Varuṇa. Indra too is a punisher of sin, but this trait is only superficially connected with his character. The standard of divine morality of course reflects only an earlier stage of civilization. Thus even the alliance of Varuṇa with righteousness is not of such a nature as to prevent him from employing craft against the hostile and deceitful man. But towards the good and pious the faithfulness of Varuṇa is unswerving. Indra, however, is occasionally not above practising deceitful wiles even without the justification of a good end[15].

Moral elevation does not, however, occupy so high a position as power among the attributes of the Vedic gods. Epithets such as 'true' and 'not deceitful' are far less prominent than such as 'great' and 'mighty'. The gods can do whatever they will. On them depends the fulfilment of wishes. They have dominion over all creatures; and no one can thwart their ordinances or live beyond the time the gods appoint[16].

The RV. as well as the AV. states the gods to be 33 in number (3, 6^{9} &c.; AV. 10, 7^{13}), this total being several times expressed as 'thrice eleven' (8, 35^{3} &c.). In one passage (1, 139^{11}) eleven of the gods are addressed as being in heaven, eleven on earth, and eleven in the waters (= air). The AV. (10, 9^{12}) similarly divides the gods into dwellers in heaven, air, and earth, but without specifying any number. The aggregate of 33 could not always have been regarded as exhaustive, for in a few passages (1, 34^{11}. 45^{2}; 8, 35^{3}. 39^{9}) other gods are mentioned along with the 33. In one verse (3, 9^{9} = 10, 52^{6} = VS. 33, 7) the number of the gods is by way of a freak stated to be 3339. They are also spoken of in a more general way as forming three troops (6, 51^{2}). A threefold division is implied when the gods are connected with heaven, earth, and waters (7, 35^{11}; 10, 49^{2}. 65^{9}). The Brāhmaṇas also give the number of the gods as 33. The ŚB. and the AB. agree in dividing them into three main groups of 8 Vasus, 11 Rudras, 12 Ādityas, but while the ŚB. adds to these either (4, 5, 7^{2}) Dyaus and Pṛthivī (Prajāpati being here a 34th) or Indra and Prajāpati (11, 6, 3^{5}), the AB. (2, 18^{8}) adds Vaṣaṭkāra and Prajāpati, to make up the total of 33.

Following the triple classification of RV. 1, 139^{11} Yāska (Nir. 7, 5) divides the different deities or forms of the same deity enumerated in the fifth chapter of the Naighaṇṭuka, into the three orders of *pṛthivīsthāna*, terrestrial (Nir. 7, 14—9. 43), *antarikṣasthāna*, *madhyamasthāna*, aerial or intermediate (10, 1—11. 50), and *dyusthāna*, celestial (12, 1—46). He further remarks that in the opinion of his predecessors who expounded the Veda (*nairuktāḥ*) there are only three deities[17], Agni on earth, Vāyu or Indra in air[18], Sūrya in heaven[19]. (This view may be based on such passages as RV. 10, 158^{1}: 'May Sūrya protect us from heaven, Vāta from air, Agni from the earthly regions'.) Each of these he continues has various appellations according to differences of function, just as the same person may act in the capacity of *hotṛ*, *adhvaryu*, *brahman*, *udgātṛ*. Yāska himself does not admit that all the various gods are only forms or manifestations of the three representative deities, though he allows that those forming each of the three orders are allied in sphere and functions. The fifth chapter of the Naighaṇṭuka on which Yāska comments, contains in its enumeration of gods a number of minor deities and deified objects, so that the total far exceeds eleven in each division. It is worthy of note that in this list of gods the names of Tvaṣṭṛ and Pṛthivī appear in all the three spheres, those of Agni and Uṣas in both the terrestrial and the aerial, and those of Varuṇa, Yama, and Savitṛ in the aerial as well as the celestial.

An attempt might be made to classify the various Vedic gods according to their relative greatness. Such a division is in a general way alluded to in the RV. where they are spoken of as great and small, young and old (1, 27[13]). It is probable that this statement represents the settled view of the Vedic poets as to gradation of rank among the gods (cp. pp. 14. 17). It is only a seeming contradiction when in one passage (8, 30[1]) it is said with reference to the gods, 'none of you is small or young; you are all great'; for a poet addressing the gods directly on this point could hardly have expressed himself differently. It is certain that two gods tower above the rest as leading deities about equal in power, Indra as the mighty warrior and Varuṇa as the supreme moral ruler. The older form of Varuṇa became, owing to the predominance of his ethical qualities, the supreme god of Zoroastrianism as Ahura Mazda, while in India Indra developed into the warrior god of the conquering Aryans. Varuṇa appears as preëminent only when the supreme laws of the physical and moral world are contemplated. and cannot be called a popular god. It has been held by various scholars that Varuṇa and the Ādityas were the highest gods of an older period, but were later displaced by Indra (p. 28). There is at any rate no evidence to show that Indra even in the oldest Rigvedic period occupied a subordinate position. It is true that Ahura Mazda is the highest god and Indra only a demon in the Avesta. But even if Indra originally possessed coördinate power with Varuṇa in the Indo-Iranian period, he was necessarily relegated to the background when the reform of the Avestan religion made Ahura Mazda supreme[20] (cp. p. 28). Next to Indra and Varuṇa come the two great ritual deities Agni and Soma. These two along with Indra are, judged by the frequency of the hymns addressed to them, the three most popular deities of the RV. For, roughly speaking, three-fifths of its hymns are dedicated to their praise. The fact that the hymns to Agni and Indra always come first in the family books, while the great majority of the hymns to Soma have a whole book, the ninth, to themselves, confirms this conclusion[21]. Following the number of the hymns dedicated to each of the remaining deities, combined with the frequency with which their names are mentioned in the RV., five classes of gods may be distinguished: 1) Indra, Agni, Soma; 2) Aśvins, Maruts, Varuṇa; 3) Uṣas, Savitṛ, Bṛhaspati, Sūrya, Pūṣan; 4) Vāyu, Dyāvāpṛthivī, Viṣṇu, Rudra; 5) Yama, Parjanya[22]. The statistical standard can of course be only a partial guide. For Varuṇa is celebrated (mostly together with Mitra) in only about thirty hymns, his name being mentioned altogether about 250 times, while the Aśvins can claim over 50 hymns and are named over 400 times. Yet they cannot be said to approach Varuṇa in greatness. Their relative prominence is doubtless owing to their closer connexion with the sacrifice as deities of morning light. Again, the importance of the Maruts is due to their association with Indra. Similar considerations would have to enter into an estimate of the relative greatness of other deities in the list. Such an estimate involves considerable difficulties and doubts. A classification according to gradations of rank would therefore not afford a satisfactory basis for an account of the Vedic gods.

Another but still less satisfactory classification, might take as its basis the relative age of the mythological conception, according as it dates from the period of separate national Indian existence, from the Indo-Iranian, or the Indo-European epoch. Thus Bṛhaspati, Rudra, Viṣṇu may be considered the creations of purely Indian mythology; at least there is no adequate evidence to show that they go back to an earlier age. It has already been indicated (§ 5) that a number of mythological figures date from the Indo-Iranian period. But as to whether any of the Vedic gods besides Dyaus may be traced back to the Indo-European period, considerable doubt is justified.

A classification according to the age of the mythological creation would therefore rest on too uncertain a foundation.

The stage of personification which the various deities represent, might furnish a possible basis of classification. But the task of drawing a clear line of demarcation would involve too many difficulties.

On the whole, the classification of the Vedic deities least open to objection, is that founded on the natural bases which they represent. For though in some cases there may be a doubt as to what the physical substrate really is, and a risk is therefore involved of describing a particular deity in the wrong place, this method offers the advantage of bringing together deities of cognate character and thus facilitating comparison. It has therefore been adopted in the following pages. The various phenomena have been grouped according to the triple division suggested by the RV. itself and adhered to by its oldest commentator.

[1] OST. 5, 219; BRI. 26; BDA. 12—14; ORV. 100. — [2] HRI. 138—40. — [3] MM., ASL. 526. 532. 546; Chips 1, 28; OGR. 266. 285. 298 f. 312 ff.; Science of Religion 52; PhR. 180 ff.; OST. 5. 6 f. 12 f. 125; OO. 3, 449; BÜHLER, OO. 1, 227; LRV. 3, XXVII f.; KRV. 33; note 113; ZIMMER, ZDA. 19(7), 175; HILLEBRANDT, Varuṇa und Mitra, 105; BRI. 26. — [4] WHITNEY, PAOS., Oct. 1881; ORV. 101; HOPKINS, Henotheism in the Rigveda, in Classical studies in honour of H. Drisler (New York 1894), 75—83; HRI. 139 &c. — [5] SVL. 134; cp. ZDMG. 32, 300. — [6] MUIR, JRAS. 20, 41—5; OST. 4, 54—8; 5, 14—17; cp. AV. 3, 22^{3}; 4, 14^{1}; ŚB. 1, 7, 3^{1}; AB. 6, 20^{8}; TS. 1, 7, 1^{3}; 6, 5, 3^{1}; HRI. 187. — [7] NIRUKTA 7, 6. 7. — [8] WC. 9. — [9] ORV. 347. 353. 355. 357—8. — [10] ORV. 93. — [11] OST. 5, 18. — [12] ORV. 238. — [13] BRV. 3, 203—4. — [14] BRV. 3, 199. — [15] ORV. 282. — [16] OST. 5, 18—20; ORV. 97—101; 281—7. 293—301. — [17] KĀTYĀYANA, Sarvānukramaṇī, Introd. § 2, 8; Sāyaṇa on RV. 1, 139^{11}. — [18] 'Indra and Vāyu are closely allied' (TS. 6, 6, 8^{3}). Cp. HRI. 89. — [19] Agni, Vāyu, Sūrya are sons of Prajāpati (MS. 4, 2^{12}). — [20] ORV. 94—8. — [21] HRI. 90. — [22] These classes and the statistics fournished below in the account given of the single gods, are based on data derived from LRV., GW., GRV. (2, 421—3), and AUFRECHT's RV. II^{2}, 668—71.

A. THE CELESTIAL GODS.

§ 11. Dyaus.—By far the most frequent use of the word *dyaus* is as a designation of the concrete 'sky', in which sense it occurs at least 500 times in the RV. It also means 'day'[1] about 50 times. When personified as the god of heaven, Dyaus is generally coupled with Earth in the dual compound *dyāvāpṛthivī*, the universal parents. No single hymn of the RV. is addressed to Dyaus alone. When he is mentioned separately the personification is limited almost entirely to the idea of paternity. The name then nearly always appears in the nominative or genitive case. The latter case, occurring about 50 times, is more frequent than all the other cases together. The genitive is regularly connected with the name of some other deity who is called the son or daughter of Dyaus. In about three-fourths of these instances Uṣas is his daughter, while in the remainder the Aśvins are his offspring (*napātā*), Agni is his son (*sūnu*) or child (*śiśu*), Parjanya, Sūrya, the Ādityas, the Maruts, and the Aṅgirases are his sons (*putra*). Out of its thirty occurrences in the nominative the name appears only eight times alone, being otherwise generally associated with Pṛthivī or mentioned with various deities mostly including Pṛthivī. In these eight passages he is three times styled a father (1, 90^{7}. 164^{33}; 4, 1^{10}), once the father of Indra (4, 72^{3}), once he is spoken of as rich in seed (*suretāḥ*) and as having generated Agni (4, 17^{4}); in the remaining three he is a bull (5, 36^{5}) or a red bull that bellows downwards (5, 58^{6}), and is said to have approved when Vṛtra was slain (6, 72^{3}). In the dative the name is found eight times. In these passages he is mentioned only three times quite alone, once being called the 'great father' (1, 71^{5}), once 'lofty' (1, 54^{3}), and once the 'lofty abode' (5, 47^{7}). In two of the four occurrences in the accusative Dyaus is mentioned with Pṛthivī, once alone and without any distinctive statement (1, 174^{3}), and once (1, 31^{4}) Agni is said to have made him roar for man. Thus it appears that Dyaus is seldom mentioned independently and in only one-sixth of over ninety passages is his paternity not expressly stated or implied by association with Pṛthivī. The only essential feature of the personification in the RV. is in fact his paternity. In a few passages Dyaus is called a bull (1, 160^{3}; 5, 36^{5}) that bellows (5, 58^{6}). Here we have a touch of theriomorphism inasmuch as he is conceived as a roaring animal that fertilizes the earth. Dyaus is once compared with a black steed decked with pearls (10, 68^{11}), an obvious allusion to the nocturnal sky. The statement that Dyaus is furnished with a bolt (*aśanimat*) looks like a touch of anthropomorphism. He is also spoken of as smiling through the clouds (2, 4^{6}), the allusion being doubtless to the lightening sky[2]. Such passages are, however, quite isolated, the conception of Dyaus being practically free from theriomorphism and anthropomorphism, excepting the notion of paternity. As a father he is most usually thought of in combination with Earth as a mother[3]. This is indicated by the fact that his name forms a dual compound with that of Pṛthivī oftener than it is used alone in the singular (§ 44), that in a large proportion of its occurrences in the singular it is accompanied by the name of Pṛthivī, and that when regarded separately he is not sufficiently individualized to have a hymn dedicated to his praise, though in conjunction with Pṛthivī he is celebrated in six. Like nearly all the greater gods[4] Dyaus is sometimes called *asura*[5] (1, 122^{1}. 131^{1}; 8, 20^{17}) and he is once (6, 51^{5}) invoked in the vocative as 'Father Heaven' (*dyauṣ pitar*) along with 'Mother Earth' (*pṛthivi mātar*). In about 20 passages the word *dyaus* is feminine, sometimes even when personified[6]. Dyaus, as has been pointed out (§ 6) goes back to the Indo-European period. There is no reason to assume that the personification in that period was of a more advanced type and that the RV. has in this case relapsed to a more primitive stage. On the contrary there is every ground for supposing the reverse to be the case. Whatever higher gods may have existed in that remote age must have been of a considerably more rudimentary type and can hardly in any instance have been conceived apart from deified natural objects[7]. As the Universal Father who with Mother Earth embraced all other deified objects and phenomena, he would have been the greatest among the deities of a chaotic polytheism. But to speak of him as the supreme god of the Indo-European age is misleading, because this suggests a ruler of the type of Zeus and an incipient monotheism for an extremely remote period, though neither of these conceptions had been arrived at in the earlier Rigvedic times.

The word is derived from the root *div*, to shine, thus meaning 'the bright one' and being allied to *deva*, god[8].

[1] v. SCHRÖDER. WZKM. 8, 126—7. — [2] PVS. 1, 111; SBE. 46, 205. — [3] HRI. 171. — [4] BDA. 119—23. — [5] BDA. 86. — [6] BDA. 114, cf. GW. s. v. *div*; OSTHOFF, IF. 5, 286, n. — [7] BDA. 111. — [8] Cp. KZ. 27, 187; BB. 15, 17; IF. 3, 301.
OST. 5, 21—3; OGR. 209; LRV. 3, 312—3; BRV. 1, 4—5; SP. AP. 160; JAOS. 16, CXLV.

§ 12. Varuṇa.—Varuṇa, as has been shown (p. 20), is by the side of Indra, the greatest of the gods of the RV. The number of hymns dedicated to his praise is not a sufficient criterion of his exalted character. Hardly a dozen hymns celebrate him exclusively. Judged by the statistical standard he would rank only as a third class deity; and even if the two dozen hymns in which he is invoked along with his double Mitra are taken into account, he would only come fifth in order of priority, ranking considerably below the Aśvins and about on an equality with the Maruts (cp. p. 20).

The anthropomorphism of Varuṇa's personality is more fully developed on the moral than the physical side. The descriptions of his person and his equipment are scanty, more stress being laid on his activity. He has a face, an eye, arms, hands, and feet. He moves his arms, walks, drives, sits, eats and drinks. The poet regards the face (*anīkam*) of Varuṇa as that of Agni (7, 88[2] cp. 87[6]). The eye of Mitra and Varuṇa is the sun (1, 115[1]; 6, 51[1]; 7, 61[1]. 63[1]; 10, 37[1]). The fact that this is always mentioned in the first verse of a hymn, suggests that it is one of the first ideas that occur when Mitra and Varuṇa are thought of. The eye with which Varuṇa is said in a hymn to Sūrya (1, 50[6]) to observe mankind, is undoubtedly the sun. Together with Aryaman, Mitra and Varuṇa are called sun-eyed (7, 66[10]), a term applied to other gods also. Varuṇa is far-sighted (1, 25[5. 16]; 8, 90[2]) and thousand-eyed (7, 34[10]). Mitra and Varuṇa stretch out their arms (5, 64[2]; 7, 62[5]) and they drive with the rays of the sun as with arms (8, 90[2]). Like Savitṛ and Tvaṣṭṛ they are beautiful-handed (*supāṇi*). Mitra and Varuṇa hasten up with their feet (5, 64[7]), and Varuṇa treads down wiles with shining foot (8, 41[8]). He sits on the strewn grass at the sacrifice (1, 26[4]; 5, 72[2]), and like other gods he and Mitra drink Soma (4, 41[3] &c.). Varuṇa wears a golden mantle (*drāpi*) and puts on a shining robe (1, 25[13]). But the shining robe of ghee with which he and Mitra are clothed (5, 62[4]; 7, 64[1]) is only a figurative allusion to the sacrificial offering of melted butter. The glistening garments which they wear (1, 152[1]) probably mean the same thing. In the SB. (13, 3, 6[5]) Varuṇa is represented as a fair, bald, yellow-eyed old man[1]. The only part of Varuṇa's equipment which is at all prominent is his car. It is described as shining like the sun (1, 122[15]), as having thongs for a pole (ibid.), a car-seat and a whip (5, 62[7]), and as drawn by well-yoked steeds (5, 62[4]). Mitra and Varuṇa mount their car in the highest heaven (5, 63[1]). The poet prays that he may see Varuṇa's car on the earth (1, 25[18]).

Mitra and Varuṇa's abode is golden and situated in heaven (5, 67[2]; 1, 136[2]) and Varuṇa sits in his mansions (*pastyāsu*) looking on all deeds (1, 25[10. 11]). His and Mitra's seat (*sadas*) is great, very lofty, firm with a thousand columns (5, 68[5]; 2, 41[5]) and their house has a thousand doors (7, 88[5]). The all-seeing sun rising from his abode, goes to the dwellings of Mitra and Varuṇa to report the deeds of men (7, 60[1. 3]), and enters their dear dwelling (1, 152[4]). It is in the highest heaven that the Fathers behold Varuṇa (10, 14[8]). According to the SB. (11, 6, 1) Varuṇa, conceived as the lord of the Universe, is seated in the midst of heaven, from which he surveys the places of punishment situated all around him[1].

The spies (*spaśaḥ*) of Varuṇa are sometimes mentioned. They sit down around him (1, 24[13]). They behold the two worlds; acquainted with sacrifice they stimulate prayer (7, 87[3]). Mitra's and Varuṇa's spies whom they send separately into houses (7, 61[3]), are undeceived and wise (6, 67[5]). In the AV. (4, 16[4]) it is said that Varuṇa's messengers descending from heaven, traverse the world; thousand-eyed they look across the whole world. The natural basis of these spies is usually assumed to be the stars; but the RV. yields no evidence in support of this view. The stars are there never said to watch, nor are the spies connected with night. The conception may very well have been suggested by the spies with whom a strict ruler on earth is surrounded[2]. Nor are spies peculiar to Varuṇa and Mitra, for they are also attributed to Agni (4, 4[3]), to Soma (9, 73[4. 7], here perhaps suggested by the previous mention of Varuṇa), to demons combated by Indra (1, 33[8]), and to the gods in general (10, 10[8]). In one passage the Ādityas are said to look down like spies from a height (8, 47[11]). That these spies were primarily connected with Mitra and Varuṇa is to be inferred from the fact that the Iranian Mithra also has spies, who are, moreover, called by the same name (*spaś*) as in the Veda[3]. The golden-winged messenger (*dūta*) of Varuṇa once mentioned in the RV. (10, 123[6]), is doubtless the sun.

Varuṇa alone, or conjointly with Mitra, is often called a king (*rājā*), like the other leading deities and Yama (1, 24[7.8] &c.)[4]. He is king of all, both gods and men (10, 132[4]; 2, 27[10]), of the whole world (5, 85[3]), and of all that exists (7, 87[6]). Varuṇa is also a self-dependent ruler (2, 28[1]), a term generally applied to Indra. Much more frequently Varuṇa, alone or mostly in association with Mitra, is called a universal monarch (*samrāj*). This term is also applied to Agni a few times and oftener to Indra. Counting the passages in which Varuṇa and Mitra together are so called, it is connected with Varuṇa nearly twice as often as with Indra. Considering that for every eight or ten hymns celebrating Indra only one is dedicated to Varuṇa in the RV., the epithet may be considered peculiarly appropriate to Varuṇa.

The attribute of sovereignty (*kṣatra*) is in a predominant manner appropriated to Varuṇa, generally with Mitra and twice with Aryaman also. Otherwise it is applied only once respectively to Agni, Bṛhaspati, and the Aśvins. Similarly the term 'ruler' (*kṣatriya*) in four of its five occurrences refers to Varuṇa or the Ādityas and once only to the gods in general. The epithet ***asura*** (§ 67) is connected with Varuṇa, alone or accompanied by Mitra, oftener than with Indra and Agni; and, taking account of the proportion of hymns, it may be said to be specially applicable to Varuṇa[5]. Mitra and Varuṇa are also called the mysterious and noble lords (*asurā aryā*) among the gods (7, 65[2]).

The divine dominion of Varuṇa and Mitra is often referred to with the word *māyā*[6]. This term signifies occult power, applicable in a good sense to gods or in a bad sense to demons. It has an almost exact parallel in the English word 'craft', which in its old signification meant 'occult power, magic', then 'skilfulness, art' on the one hand and 'deceitful skill, wile' on the other. The good sense of *māyā*, like that of *asura* (which might be rendered by 'mysterious being') is mainly connected with Varuṇa and Mitra, while its bad sense is reserved for demons. By occult power Varuṇa standing in the air measures out the earth with the sun as with a measure (5, 85[5]), Varuṇa and Mitra send the dawns (3, 61[7]), make the sun to cross the sky and obscure it with cloud and rain, while the honied drops fall (5, 63[4]); or (ibid. [3.7]) they cause heaven to rain and they uphold the ordinances by the occult power of the Asura (here = Dyaus or Parjanya)[7]. And so the epithet *māyin*, 'crafty', is chiefly applied to Varuṇa among the gods (6, 48[14]; 7, 28[4]; 10, 99[10]. 147[5]).

In marked contrast with Indra, Varuṇa has no myths related of him, while much is said about him (and Mitra) as upholder of physical and moral order. Varuṇa is a great lord of the laws of nature. He established heaven and earth and dwells in all the worlds (8, 42[1]). The three heavens and the three earths are deposited within him (7, 87[5]). He and Mitra rule over the whole world (5, 63[7]) or encompass the two worlds (7, 61[4]). They are the guardians of the whole world (2, 27[4] &c.). By the law of Varuṇa heaven and earth are held apart (6, 70[1]; 7, 86[1]; 8, 41[10]). With Mitra he supports earth and heaven (5, 62[3]), or heaven, earth, and air (5, 69[1.4]). He made the golden swing (the sun) to shine in heaven (7, 87[5]). He placed fire in the waters, the sun in the sky, Soma on the rock (5, 85^{2}). He has made a wide path for the sun (1, 24^{8}; 7, 87^{1}). Varuṇa, Mitra, and Aryaman open paths for the sun (7, 60^{4}). The order (*ṛta*) of Mitra and Varuṇa is established where the steeds of the sun are loosed (5, 62^{1}). The wind which resounds through the air is Varuṇa's breath (7, 87^{2}).

By Varuṇa's ordinances (*vratāni*) the moon shining brightly moves at night, and the stars placed up on high are seen at night but disappear by day (1, 24^{10}). In another passage (8, 41^{3}) it is said that Varuṇa has embraced (*pari ṣasvaje*) the nights, and by his occult power has established the mornings or days (*usraḥ*). This can hardly indicate a closer connexion with night than that he regulates or divides night and day (cp. 7, 66^{11}). In fact it is the sun that is usually mentioned with him, and not the moon or night. Thus in the oldest Veda Varuṇa is the lord of light both by day and by night, while Mitra, as far as can be judged, appears as the god of the celestial light of day only.

In the later Vedic period of the Brāhmaṇas Varuṇa comes to be specially connected with the nocturnal heaven[8]. Thus Mitra is said to have produced the day and Varuṇa the night (TS. 6, 4, 8^{3}); and the day is said to belong to Mitra and the night to Varuṇa (TS. 2, 1, 7^{4})[9]. This view may have arisen from a desire to contrast Mitra, who was still felt to be related to the sun, with Varuṇa whose natural basis was more obscure. The antithesis between the two is differently expressed by the ŚB. (12, 9, 2^{12}), which asserts that this world is Mitra, that (the celestial) world is Varuṇa.

Varuṇa is sometimes referred to as regulating the seasons. He knows the twelve months (1, 25^{8})[10]; and the kings Mitra, Varuṇa, and Aryaman are said to have disposed the autumn, the month, day and night (7, 66^{11}).

Even in the RV. Varuṇa is often spoken of as a regulator of the waters. He caused the rivers to flow; they stream unceasingly according to his ordinance (2, 28^{4}). By his occult power the rivers swiftly pouring into the ocean do not fill it with water (5, 85^{6}). Varuṇa and Mitra are lords of rivers (7, 64^{2}). Varuṇa is already found connected with the sea in the RV., but very rarely, perhaps owing to its unimportance in that collection. Varuṇa going in the oceanic waters is contrasted with the Maruts in the sky, Agni on earth, and Vāta in air (1, 161^{14})[11]. The statement that the seven rivers flow into the jaws of Varuṇa as into a surging abyss (8, 58^{12}), may refer to the ocean[12]. Varuṇa is said to descend into the sea (*sindhum*) like Dyaus (7, 87^{6})[13]. It is rather the aerial waters that he is ordinarily connected with. Varuṇa ascends to heaven as a hidden ocean (8, 41^{8}). Beholding the truth and falsehood of men, he moves in the midst of the waters which drop sweetness and are clear (7, 49^{3}). Varuṇa clothes himself in the waters (9, 90^{2} cp. 8, $69^{11.12}$). He and Mitra are among the gods most frequently thought of and prayed to as bestowers of rain. Varuṇa makes the inverted cask (of the cloud) to pour its waters on heaven, earth, and air, and to moisten the ground, the mountains then being enveloped in cloud (5, $85^{3.4}$). Mitra and Varuṇa have kine yielding refreshment and streams flowing with honey (5, 69^{2}). They have rainy skies and streaming waters (5, 68^{5}). They bedew the pasturage with ghee (= rain) and the spaces with honey (3, 62^{16}). They send rain and refreshment from the sky (7, 64^{2}). Rain abounding in heavenly water comes from them (8, 25^{6}). Indeed, one entire hymn (5, 63) dwells on their powers of bestowing rain. It is probably owing to his connexion with the waters and rain, that in the fifth chapter of the Naighaṇṭuka Varuṇa is enumerated among the deities of the atmospheric as well as those of the celestial world. In the Brāhmaṇas Mitra and Varuṇa are also gods of rain[14]. In the AV. Varuṇa appears divested of his powers as a universal ruler, retaining only the control of the department of waters. He is connected with the waters as Soma with the mountains (AV. 3, 3^{5}). As a divine father he sheds rain-waters (AV. 4, 15^{14}). His golden house is in the waters (AV. 7, 83^{1}). He is the overlord of waters, he and Mitra are lords of rain (AV. 5, 24$^{4.5}$). In the YV. he is spoken of as the child (*śiśu*) of waters, making his abode within the most motherly waters (VS. 10, 7). The waters are wives of Varuṇa (TS. 5, 5, 4^{1}). Mitra and Varuṇa are the leaders of waters (TS. 6, 4, 3^{2}).

Varuṇa's ordinances are constantly said to be fixed, the epithet *dhṛta-vrata* being preëminently applicable to him, sometimes conjointly with Mitra. The gods themselves follow Varuṇa's ordinances (8, 41^{7}) or those of Varuṇa, Mitra, and Savitṛ (10, 36^{13}). Even the immortal gods cannot obstruct the fixed ordinances of Mitra and Varuṇa (5, 69^{4} cp. 5, 63^{7}). Mitra and Varuṇa are lords of order (*ṛta*) and light, who by means of order are the upholders of order (1, 23^{5}). The latter epithet is mostly applied either to them and sometimes the Ādityas or to the gods in general. They are cherishers of order or right (1, 2^{8}). Varuṇa or the Ādityas are sometimes called guardians of order (*ṛtasya gopā*), but this term is also applied to Agni and Soma. The epithet 'observer of order' (*ṛtāvan*), predominantly used of Agni, is also several times connected with Varuṇa and Mitra.

Varuṇa's power is so great that neither the birds as they fly nor the rivers as they flow, can reach the limit of his dominion, his might, and his wrath (1, 24^{6}). Neither the skies nor the rivers have reached (the limit of) the godhead of Mitra and Varuṇa (1, 151^{9}). He embraces the All and the abodes of all beings (8, 41$^{1.7}$). The three heavens and the three earths are deposited in him (7, 87^{5}). Varuṇa is omniscient. He knows the flight of birds in the sky, the path of ships in the ocean, the course of the far-travelling wind, and beholds all the secret things that have been or shall be done (1, 25$^{7.9.11}$). He witnesses men's truth and falsehood (7, 49^{3}). No creature can even wink without him (2, 28^{6}). The winkings of men's eyes are all numbered by Varuṇa, and whatever man does, thinks, or devises, Varuṇa knows (AV. 4, 16$^{2.5}$). He perceives all that exists within heaven and earth, and all that is beyond: a man could not escape from Varuṇa by fleeing far beyond the sky (AV. 4, 16$^{4.5}$). That Varuṇa's omniscience is typical is indicated by the fact that Agni is compared with him in this respect (10, 11^{1}).

As a moral governor Varuṇa stands far above any other deity. His wrath is roused by sin, the infringement of his ordinances, which he severely punishes (7, 86$^{3.4}$). The fetters (*pāśāḥ*) with which he binds sinners, are often mentioned (1, 24^{15}. 25^{21}; 6, 74^{4}; 10, 85^{24}). They are cast sevenfold and threefold, ensnaring the man who tells lies, passing by him who speaks truth (AV. 4, 16^{6}). Mitra and Varuṇa are barriers, furnished with many fetters, against falsehood (7, 65^{3}). Once Varuṇa, coupled with Indra, is said to tie with bonds not formed of rope (7, 84^{2}). The term *pāśa* is only once used in connexion with another god, Agni, who is implored to loosen the fetters of his worshippers (5, 2^{7}). It is therefore distinctive of Varuṇa. According to BERGAIGNE the conception of Varuṇa's fetters is based on the tying up of the waters, according to HILLEBRANDT on the fetters of night[15]. But is seems to be sufficiently accounted for by the figurative application of the fetters of criminals to moral guilt. Together with Mitra, Varuṇa is said to be a dispeller, hater, and punisher of falsehood (1, 152^{1}; 7, 60^{5}. 66^{13}). They afflict with disease[16] those who neglect their worship (1, 122^{9}). On the other hand, Varuṇa is gracious to the penitent. He unties like a rope and removes sin

(2, 28^{5}; 5, 85$^{7.8}$). He releases not only from the sins which men themselves commit, but from those committed by their fathers (7, 86^{5}). He spares the suppliant who daily transgresses his laws (1, 25^{1}) and is gracious to those who have broken his laws by thoughtlessness (7, 89^{5}). There is in fact no hymn to Varuṇa (and the Ādityas) in which the prayer for forgiveness of guilt does not occur, as in the hymns to other deities the prayer for worldly goods.

Varuṇa has a hundred, a thousand remedies, and drives away death as well as releases from sin (1, 24^{9}). He can take away or prolong life (1, 24^{11}. 25^{12}; 7, 88^{4}. 89^{1}). He is a wise guardian of immortality (8, 42^{2}), and the righteous hope to see in the next world Varuṇa and Yama, the two kings who reign in bliss (10, 14^{7}).

Varuṇa is on a footing of friendship with his worshipper (7, 88$^{4-6}$), who communes with him in his celestial abode and sometimes sees him with the mental eye (1, 25^{18}; 7, 88^{2}).

What conclusions as to the natural basis of Varuṇa can be drawn from the Vedic evidence which has been adduced? It is clear from this evidence, in combination with what is said below about Mitra (§ 13), that Varuṇa and Mitra are closely connected with the sun, but that the former is the much more important deity. Mitra has in fact been so closely assimilated to the greater god that he has hardly an independent trait left. Mitra must have lost his individuality through the predominant characteristics of the god with whom he is almost invariably associated. Now, chiefly on the evidence of the Avesta, Mitra has been almost unanimously acknowledged to be a solar deity (§ 13). Varuṇa must therefore have originally represented a different phenomenon. This according to the generally received opinion, is the encompassing sky. The vault of heaven presents a phenomenon far more vast to the eye of the observer than the sun, which occupies but an extremely small portion of that expanse during its daily course. The sky would therefore appear to the imagination as the greater deity. The sun might very naturally become associated with the sky as the space which it traverses every day and apart from which it is never seen. The conception of the sun as the eye of heaven is sufficiently obvious. It could not very appropriately be termed the eye of Mitra till the original character of the latter had become obscured and absorbed in that of Varuṇa. Yet even the eye of Sūrya is several times spoken of in the RV. (p. 30). The attribute of 'far-seeing', appropriate to the sun, is also appropriate to the sky, which might naturally be conceived as seeing not only by day but even at night by means of the moon and stars. No real difficulty is presented by the notion of Varuṇa, who has become quite separate from his physical basis[17], mounting a car in the height of heaven with Mitra. For such a conception is easily explicable from his association with a solar deity; besides every leading deity in the RV. drives in a car. On the other hand, the palace of Varuṇa in the highest heavens and his connexion with rain are particularly appropriate to a deity originally representing the vault of heaven. Finally, no natural phenomenon would be so likely to develope into a sovereign ruler, as the sky. For the personification of its vast expanse, which encompasses and rises far above the earth and on which the most striking phenomena of regular recurrence, the movements of the luminaries, are enacted, would naturally be conceived as watching by night and day all the deeds of men and as being the guardian of unswerving law. This development has indeed actually taken place in the case of the Zeus (= Dyaus) of Hellenic mythology. What was at first only an appellative of the sky has here become the supreme ruler of the gods dwelling in the serene heights of heaven, who gathers the clouds, who wields the thunderbolt, and whose will is law.

The phenomena with which the two greatest gods of the RV. were originally connected, largely accounts for the difference in their personality. Varuṇa as concerned with the regularly recurring phenomena of celestial light, is the supreme upholder of law in the moral as well as the physical world. His character as such afforded no scope for the development of myths. Indra as the god fighting in the strife of the elements, was conceived by the militant Vedic Indian as a sovereign of the warrior type. Owing to his close connexion with the meteorological phenomena of the thunderstorm, which are so irregular in time and diversified in feature, the character of Indra on the one hand shows traits of capriciousness, while on the other he becomes the centre of more myths than any other deity of the RV. The theory of ROTH as to the supersession of Varuṇa by Indra in the Rigvedic period, is dealt with below (§ 22).

With the growth of the conception of Prajāpati (§ 39) as a supreme deity, the characteristics of Varuṇa as a sovereign god naturally faded away, and the dominion of the waters, only a part of his original sphere, alone remained to him. Thus he ultimately became in post-Vedic mythology an Indian Neptune, god of the Sea.

The hypothesis recently advanced by OLDENBERG[18] that Varuṇa primarily represented the moon, cannot be passed over here. Starting from the assertion that the characteristic number of the Ādityas was seven and that their identity with the Ameṣaspentas of the Avesta is an assured fact, he believes that Varuṇa and Mitra were the moon and sun, the lesser Ādityas representing the five planets, and that they were not Indo-European deities, but were borrowed during the Indo-Iranian period from a Semitic people more skilled in astronomy than the Aryans. The character of Varuṇa when borrowed must further have lost much of its original significance and have already possessed a highly ethical aspect. For otherwise a distinctly lunar deity could hardly have thrown Mitra, who was clearly understood to be the sun, into the shade in the Indo-Iranian period, or have developed so highly abstract a character as to account for the supreme position, as a moral ruler, of Ahura Mazda in the Avesta and of Varuṇa in the Veda. This hypothesis does not seem to account at all well for the actual characteristics of Varuṇa in the RV. It also requires the absolute rejection of any connection between Varuṇa and οὐρανός[19].

It has already been mentioned that Varuṇa goes back to the Indo-Iranian period (§ 5), for the Ahura Mazda of the Avesta agrees with him in character[20] though not in name. The name of *Váruṇa* may even be Indo-European. At least, the long accepted identification of the word with the Greek οὐρανός, though presenting phonetic difficulties, has not been rejected by some recent authorities on comparative philology[21].

But whether the word is Indo-European or the formation of a later period[22], it is probably derived from the root *var*, to cover[23], thus meaning 'the encompasser'. Sāyaṇa (on RV. 1, 89[3]) connects it with this root in the sense of enveloping or confining the wicked with his bonds[24], or commenting on TS. 1, 8, 16[1], in that of enveloping 'like darkness' (cp. TS. 2, 1, 7[4]). If the word is Indo-European, it may have been an attribute of *dyaus*, the ordinary name of 'sky', later becoming the regular appellative of sky in Greece, but an exalted god of the sky in India[25].

1 WEBER, ZDMG. 9, 242; 18, 268. — 2 ORV. 286, n. 2. — 3 Cp. ROTH, ZDMG. 6, 72; EGGERS, Mitra 54—7; OLDENBERG, ZDMG. 50, 48. — 4 OST. 5, 60.

— 5 BDA. 120—1; ORV. 163. — 6 BRV. 3, 81; v. BRADKE, ZDMG. 48, 499—501; ORV. 163. 294. — 7 Cf. BDA. 55. 60. — 8 OST. 5, 70; ROTH, PW. s. v. Varuṇa; BRV. 3, 116 ff.; v. SCHROEDER, WZKM. 9, 119. — 9 Cf. TB. 1, 7, 10[1]; Sāyaṇa on RV. 1, 89[3]; 2, 38[8]; 7, 87[1]; TS. 1, 8, 16[1]. — 10 Cp. WVB. 1894, p. 38. — 11 BOLLENSEN, OO. 2, 467. — 12 ROTH, Nirukta, Erl. 70—1. — 13 Cp. ROTH, ZDMG. 6, 73. — 14 HILLEBRANDT, Varuṇa und Mitra 67, note. — 15 Cp. HRI. 68. — 16 Varuṇa's later connexion with dropsy is traced by HILLEBRANDT, p. 63 f. and ORV. 203 even in the RV., a view opposed by BRV. 3, 155. — 17 Cp. OLDENBERG, ZDMG. 50, 61. — 18 ORV. 285—98. — 19 Cp. v. SCHROEDER, WZKM. 9, 116—28; MACDONELL, JRAS. 27, 947—9. — 20 ROTH, ZDMG. 6, 69 ff. (cp. OST. 5, 72); WHITNEY, JAOS. 3, 327; but WINDISCHMANN (Zoroastrische Studien p. 122) held Ahura Mazda to be purely Iranian, and SPIEGEL, Av. Transl. 3, introd. iii., sees no similarity between Ahura Mazda and Varuṇa; cp. SP.AP. 181. — 21 BRUGMANN, Grundriss 2, 154; PRELLWITZ, Etym. Wörterbuch d. gr. Spr. — 22 Cp. v. SCHROEDER, WZKM. 9, 127. — 23 HILLEBRANDT 9—14; v. SCHROEDER, WZKM. 9, 118, n. 1; HRI. 66, note; 70; cp. also SONNE, KZ. 12, 364—6; ZDMG. 32, 716 f.; BOLLENSEN, ZDMG. 41, 504 f.; GELDNER, BB. 11, 329; MM., Chips 4[2], xxiii f. — 24 Cp. GVS. 2, 22, note; OLDENBERG, ZDMG. 50, 60. — 25 MACDONELL, JRAS. 26, 628.

ROTH, ZDMG. 6, 70—4; 7, 607; JAOS. 3, 341—2. WEBER, IS. 17, 212 f.; OST. 5, 58—75; LRV. 3, 314—6; GRV. 1, 34; HILLEBRANDT, Varuṇa und Mitra, Breslau 1877; BRV. 3, 110—49; MM., India 197—200; BRI. 16—9; GPVS. I, 142. 188; WC. 98—103; KERBAKER, Varuṇa e gli Aditya, Napoli 1889; BOHNENBERGER, Der altindische Gott Varuṇa, Tübingen 1893; ORV. 189—95. 202—3. 293—8. 336, n. 1; ZDMG. 50, 43—68; HRI. 61—72; JAOS. 16, CXLVIII ff.; 17, 81, note; FOY, Die königliche Gewalt, Leipzig 1895, p. 80—6 (Die Späher Varuṇa's).

§ 13. **Mitra.** — The association of Mitra with Varuṇa is so predominant that only one single hymn of the RV. (3, 59) is addressed to him alone. The praise of the god is there rather indefinite, but the first verse at least contains something distinctive about him. Uttering his voice (*bruvāṇaḥ*) he brings men together (*yātayati*) and watches the tillers with unwinking eye (*animiṣā*, said also of Mitra-Varuṇa in 7, 60[6]).

In another passage (7, 36[2]) almost the same words are applied to Mitra who 'brings men together, uttering his voice', in contrast with Varuṇa who is here called 'a mighty, infallible guide'. This seems a tolerably clear reference to Mitra's solar character, if we compare with it another verse (5, 82[9]) where it is said that the sun-god Savitṛ 'causes all creatures to hear him and impels them'. In the fifth verse of the hymn to Mitra the god is spoken of as the great Āditya 'bringing men together'. This epithet (*yātayaj-jana*) is found in only three other passages of the RV. In one of these it is applied to Mitra-Varuṇa in the dual (5, 72[2]), in another to Mitra, Varuṇa, and Aryaman (1, 136[3]), and in the third (8, 91[12]) to Agni, who 'brings men together like Mitra'. The attribute therefore seems to have properly belonged to Mitra. The hymn to Mitra further adds that he supports heaven and earth, that the five tribes of men obey him, and that he sustains all the gods. Savitṛ is once (5, 81[4]) identified with Mitra because of his laws, and elsewhere (Vāl. 4[3]) Viṣṇu is said to take his three steps by the laws of Mitra. These two passages appear to indicate that Mitra regulates the course of the sun. Agni who goes at the head of the dawns produces Mitra for himself (10, 8[4]); Agni when kindled is Mitra (3, 5[4]); Agni when born is Varuṇa, when kindled is Mitra[1] (5, 3[1]). In the AV. (13, 3[13]) Mitra at sunrise is contrasted with Varuṇa in the evening, and (AV. 9, 3[18]) Mitra is asked to uncover in the morning what has been covered up by Varuṇa[2]. These passages point to the beginning of the view prevailing in the Brāhmaṇas, that Mitra is connected with day and Varuṇa with night. That view must have arisen from Mitra having been predominantly conceived as allied to the sun, Varuṇa by antithesis becoming god of night[3]. The same contrast between Mitra as god of day and Varuṇa as god of night is implied in the ritual literature, when it is prescribed that Mitra should receive a white and Varuṇa a dark victim at the sacrificial post (TS. 2, 1, 7^{1}. 9^{1}; MS. 2, 5^{7})[4]. The somewhat scanty evidence of the Veda showing that Mitra is a solar deity, is corroborated by the Avesta and Persian religion in general. Here Mithra is undoubtedly a sun-god or a god of light specially connected with the sun[5].

The etymology of the name is uncertain[6]. However, as the word also often means 'friend' in the RV. and the kindly nature of the god is often referred to in the Veda, Mitra even appearing as a god of peace (TS. 2, 1, 8^{4})[7], while in the Avesta Mithra is on the ethical side of his character the guardian of faithfulness[8], it must have originally signified 'ally' or 'friend' and have been applied to the sun-god in his aspect of a beneficent power of nature.

1 Eggers 16—19. — 2 Hillebrandt 67. — 3 Oldenberg thinks that the special connexion of Varuṇa with night is old: ZDMG. 50, 64—5. — 4 Hillebrandt 67. 90; ORV. 192, note. — 5 Sp.AP. 183; ORV. 48. 190; Eggers 6—13. 6 Hillebrandt 113—4; Eggers 70. — 7 Eggers 42—3. — 8 Eggers 53—6.

KHF. 13; Roth, ZDMG. 6, 70 ff.; PW.; OST. 5, 69—71; Windischmann, Mithra, Leipzig 1859; GW. s. v. Mitra; Hillebrandt, Varuṇa und Mitra 111—36; BRV. 3, 110—29; Bollensen, ZDMG. 41, 503—4; Weber, IS. 17, 212; BRI. 17; ORV. 190—2; Bohnenberger 85; A. Eggers, Der arische Gott Mitra, Dorpat 1894 (Dissertation); v. Schroeder, WZKM. 9, 118; HRI. 71; Oldenberg, SBE. 46, 241. 287.

§ 14. **Sūrya.** — Ten entire hymns of the RV. may be said to be devoted to the celebration of Sūrya specifically. It is impossible to say how often the name of the god occurs, it being in many cases doubtful whether only the natural phenomenon is meant or its personification. Since his name designates the orb of the sun as well, Sūrya is the most concrete of the solar deities, his connexion with the luminary never being lost sight of. The adorable light of Sūrya in the sky is as the face (*anīka*) of great Agni (10, 7^{3}). The eye of Sūrya is mentioned several times (5, 40^{8} &c.), but he is himself equally often called the eye of Mitra and Varuṇa (p. 23) or of Agni as well (1, 115^{1}); and once (7, 77^{3}) Dawn is said to bring the eye of the gods. The affinity of the eye and the sun is indicated in a passage where the eye of the dead man is conceived as going to Sūrya (10, 16^{3} cp. 90^{3}. $158^{3.4}$). In the AV. he is called the 'lord of eyes' (AV. 5, 24^{9}) and is said to be the one eye of created beings and to see beyond the sky, the earth, and the waters (AV. 13, 1^{45}). He is far-seeing (7, 35^{8}; 10, 37^{1}), all-seeing (1, 50^{2}), is the spy (*spaś*) of the whole world (4, 13^{3}), beholds all beings and the good and bad deeds of mortals (1, 50^{7}; 6, 51^{2}; 7, 60^{2}. 61^{1}. $63^{1.4}$). Aroused by Sūrya men pursue their objects and perform their work (7, 63^{4}). Common to all men, he rises as their rouser (7, $63^{2.3}$). He is the soul or the guardian of all that moves or is stationary (1, 115^{1}; 7, 60^{2}). He has a car which is drawn by one steed, called *etaśa* (7, 63^{2}), or by an indefinite number of steeds (1, 115^{3}; 10, 37^{3}. 49^{7}) or mares (5, 29^{5}) or by seven horses (5, 45^{9}) or mares called *haritaḥ* (1, $50^{8.9}$; 7, 60^{3}) or by seven swift mares (4, 13^{3}).

Sūrya's path is prepared for him by Varuṇa (1, 24^{8}; 7, 87^{1}) or by the Ādityas Mitra, Varuṇa, Aryaman (7, 60^{4}). Pūṣan is his messenger (6, 58^{3}). The Dawn or Dawns reveal or produce Sūrya as well as Agni and the sacrifice (7, 80^{2}. 78^{3}). He shines forth from the lap of the dawns (7, 63^{3}). But from another point of view Dawn is Sūrya's wife (7, 75^{5}).

He also bears the metronymic Āditya, son of Aditi (1, 50^{12}. 191^{9}; 8, 90^{11}) or Āditeya (10, 88^{11}), but he is elsewhere distinguished from the Ādityas (8, 35^{13-15}). His father is Dyaus (10, 37^{1}). He is god-born (ibid.). The gods raised him who had been hidden in the ocean (10, 72^{7}). As a form of Agni he was placed by the gods in heaven (10, 88^{11}). According to another order of ideas he is said to have arisen from the eye of the world-giant Puruṣa (10, 90^{13}). In the AV. (4, 10^{5}) the sun (*divākara*) is even described as having sprung from Vṛtra.

Various individual gods are said to have produced the sun. Indra generated him (2, 12^{7} &c.), caused him to shine or raised him to heaven (3, 44^{2}; 8, 78^{7}). Indra-Viṣṇu generated him (7, 99^{4}). Indra-Soma brought up Sūrya with light (6, 72^{2}); Indra-Varuṇa raised him to heaven (7, 82^{3}). Mitra-Varuṇa raised or placed him in heaven (4, 13^{2}; 5, $63^{4, 7}$). Soma placed light in the Sun (6, 44^{23}; 9, 97^{41}), generated Sūrya (9, 96^{5}. 110^{5}), caused him to shine (9, 63^{7}), or raised him in heaven (9, 107^{7}). Agni establishes the brightness of the sun on high (10, 3^{2}) and caused him to ascend to heaven (10, 156^{4}). Dhātṛ, the creator, fashioned the sun as well as the moon (10, 190^{3}). The Aṅgirases by their rites caused him to ascend the sky (10, 62^{3}). In all these passages referring to the generation of Sūrya the notion of the simple luminary doubtless predominates.

In various passages Sūrya is conceived as a bird traversing space. He is a bird (10, $177^{1, 2}$), or a ruddy bird (5, 47^{3}), is represented as flying (1, 191^{9}), is compared with a flying eagle (7, 63^{5}) and seems to be directly called an eagle (5, 45^{9})[1]. He is in one passage called a bull as well as a bird (5, 47^{3}) and in another a mottled bull[2] (10, 189^{1} cp. 5, 47^{3}). He is once alluded to as a white and brilliant steed[3] brought by Uṣas (7, 77^{3}). Sūrya's horses represent his rays (which are seven in number: 8, 61^{16}), for the latter (*ketavaḥ*), it is said, bring (*vahanti*) him. His seven mares are called the daughters of his car (1, 50^{9}).

Elsewhere Sūrya is occasionally spoken of as an inanimate object. He is a gem of the sky (7, 63^{4} cp. 6, 51^{1}) and is alluded to as the variegated stone placed in the midst of heaven (5, 47^{3} cp. ŚB. 6, 1, 2^{3}). He is a brilliant weapon (*āyudha*) which Mitra-Varuṇa conceal with cloud and rain (5, 63^{4}), he is the felly (*pavi*) of Mitra-Varuṇa (5, 62^{2}), or a brilliant car placed in heaven by Mitra-Varuṇa (5, 63^{7}). The sun is also called a wheel (1, 175^{4}; 4, 30^{4}) or the 'wheel of the sun' is spoken of (4, 28^{2}; 5, 29^{10}).

Sūrya shines for all the world (7, 63^{1}), for men and gods (1, 50^{5}). He dispels the darkness with his light (10, 37^{4}). He rolls up the darkness as a skin (7, 63^{1}). His rays throw off the darkness as a skin into the waters (4, 13^{4}). He triumphs over beings of darkness and witches (1, $191^{8, 9}$ cp. 7, 104^{24}). There are only two or three allusions to the sun's burning heat (7, 34^{19}; 9, 107^{20}); for in the RV. the sun is not a maleficent power[4], and for this aspect of the luminary only passages from the AV. and the literature of the Brāhmaṇas can be quoted[5].

Sūrya measures the days (1, 50^{7}) and prolongs the days of life (8, 48^{7}). He drives away sickness, disease, and every evil dream (10, 37^{4}). To live is to see the Sun rise (4, 25^{4}; 6, 52^{5}). All creatures depend on Sūrya (1, 164^{14}). and the sky is upheld by him (10, 85^{1}). The epithet 'all-creating' (*viśva-karman*) is also applied to him (10, 170^{4}; cp. § 39). By his greatness he is the divine priest (*asuryaḥ purohitaḥ*) of the gods (8, 90^{12}). At his rising he is prayed to declare men sinless to Mitra-Varuṇa and other gods (7, 60^{1}. 62^{2}). He is said, when rising, to go to the Vṛtra-slayer Indra and is even styled a Vṛtra-slayer himself when invoked with Indra (8, $82^{1, 2, 4}$).

The only myth told about Sūrya is that Indra vanquished him (10, 43^{5}) and stole his wheel (1, 175^{4}; 4, 30^{4}). This may allude to the obscuration of the sun by a thunderstorm.

In the Avesta, the sun, *hvare* (= Vedic *svar*, of which *sūrya*[6] is a derivative and to which Gk. ἥλιος[7] is allied) has swift horses, like Sūrya, and is called the eye of Ahura Mazda[8].

1 Cp. ZDMG. 7, 475—6. — 2 Otherwise HVM. 1, 345, note 3. — 3 Cp. ZDMG. 2, 223; 7, 82. — 4 BRV. 1, 6; 2, 2. — 5 EHNI, Yama 134. — 6 KZ. 12, 358; J. SCHMIDT, KZ. 26, 9. — 7 BRUGMANN, Grundriss 1, 218. — 8 Sp.AP. 1, 190—1; cp. OLDENBERG, ZDMG. 50, 49.

Nirukta 12, 14—16; OST. 5, 151—61; GKR. 55—6; BRI. 20; KRV. 54—5. 145; BRV. 1, 7; HVM. 1, 45; HVBP. 29—30; ORV. 240—1; HRI. 40—6.

§ 15. Savitṛ. — Savitṛ is celebrated in eleven whole hymns of the RV. and in parts of others, his name being mentioned about 170 times. Eight or nine of these are in the family books, while all but three of those to Sūrya are in the first and tenth. Savitṛ is preëminently a golden deity, nearly all his members and his equipment being described by that epithet. He is golden-eyed (1, 35^{8}), golden-handed (1, $35^{9.10}$), golden-tongued (6, 71^{3}), all these epithets being peculiar to him. He has golden arms (6, $71^{1.5}$; 7, 45^{2}), and is broad-handed (2, 38^{2}) or beautiful-handed (3, 33^{6}). He is also pleasant-tongued (6, 71^{4}) or beautiful-tongued (3, 54^{11}), and is once called iron-jawed (6, 71^{4}). He is yellow-haired (10, 139^{1}), an attribute of Agni and Indra also. He puts on a tawny garment (4, 53^{2}). He has a golden car with a golden pole (1, $35^{2.5}$), which is omniform (1, 35^{3}), just as he himself assumes all forms (5, 81^{2}). His car is drawn by two radiant steeds or by two or more brown, white-footed horses (1, $35^{2.5}$; 7, 45^{1}).

Mighty splendour (*amati*) is preëminently attributed to Savitṛ, and mighty golden splendour to him only (3, 38^{8}; 7, 38^{1}). This splendour he stretches out or diffuses. He illumines the air, heaven and earth, the world, the spaces of the earth, the vault of heaven (1, $35^{7.8}$; 4, 14^{2}. 53^{4}; 5, 81^{2}). He raises aloft his strong golden arms, with which he blesses and arouses all beings and which extend to the ends of the earth (2, 38^{2}; 4, $53^{3.4}$; 6, $71^{1.5}$; 7, 45^{2}). The raising of his arms is characteristic, for the action of other gods is compared with it. Agni is said to raise his arms like Savitṛ (1, 95^{7}); the dawns extend light as Savitṛ his arms (7, 79^{2}), and Bṛhaspati is implored to raise hymns of praise as Savitṛ his arms (1, 190^{3}). He moves in his golden car, seeing all creatures, on a downward and an upward path (1, $35^{2.3}$). He impels the car of the Aśvins before dawn (1, 34^{10}). He shines after the path of the dawn (5, 81^{2}). He has measured out the earthly spaces, he goes to the three bright realms of heaven and is united with the rays of the sun (5, $81^{3.4}$). The only time the epithet *sūrya-raśmi* is used in the RV. it is applied to Savitṛ: 'Shining with the rays of the sun, yellow-haired, Savitṛ raises up his light continually from the east' (10, 139^{1}). He thrice surrounds the air, the three spaces, the three bright realms of heaven (4, 53^{5}: cp. Viṣṇu, § 17). His ancient paths in the air are dustless and easy to traverse, on them he is besought to protect his worshippers (1, 35^{11}). He is prayed to convey the departed spirit to where the righteous dwell (10, 17^{4}). He bestows immortality on the gods as well as length of life on man (4, 54^{2}). He also bestowed immortality on the Ṛbhus, who by the greatness of their deeds went to his house (1, $110^{2.3}$). Like Sūrya, he is implored to remove evil dreams (5, 82^{4}) and to make men sinless (4, 54^{3}). He drives away evil spirits and sorcerers (1, 35^{10}; 7, 38^{7}).

Like many other gods Savitṛ is called *asura* (4, 53^{1}). He observes fixed laws (4, 53^{4}; 10, 34^{8}. 139^{3}). The waters and the wind are subject to his ordinance (2, 38^{2}). He leads the waters and by his propulsion they flow broadly (3, 33^{6} cp. Nir. 2, 26). The other gods follow his lead (5, 81^{3}). No being, not even Indra, Varuṇa, Mitra, Aryaman, Rudra, can resist his will and independent dominion (2, 38[7. 9]; 5, 82[2]). His praises are celebrated by the Vasus, Aditi, Varuṇa, Mitra and Aryaman (7, 38[3. 4]). Like Pūṣan and Sūrya, he is lord of that which moves and is stationary (4, 53[6]). He is lord of all desirable things, and sends blessings from heaven, air, earth (1, 24[3]; 2, 38[11]). He is twice (1, 123[3]; 6, 71[4]) even spoken of as 'domestic' (*damūnas)*, an epithet otherwise almost entirely limited to Agni. Like other gods, he is a supporter of the sky (4, 53[2]; 10, 149[4]). He supports the whole world (4, 54[4]). He fixed the earth with bonds and made firm the sky in the rafterless space (10, 149[1]).

Savitṛ is at least once (1, 22[6]) called 'child of Waters' (*apāṃ napāt)*, an epithet otherwise exclusively belonging to Agni. It is probably also applied to him in 10, 149[2]. Yāska (Nir. 10, 32) commenting on this verse regards Savitṛ here as belonging to the middle region (or atmosphere) because he causes rain, adding that the sun (*Āditya*, who is in heaven) is also called Savitṛ[3]. It is probably owing to this epithet and because Savitṛ's paths are once (1, 35[11]) said to be in the atmosphere, that this deity occurs among the gods of the middle region as well as among those of heaven in the Naighaṇṭuka. Savitṛ is once called the *prajāpati* of the world (4, 53[2]). In the ŚB. (12, 3, 5[1]) people are said to identify Savitṛ with Prajāpati; and in the TB. (1, 6, 4[1]) it is stated that Prajāpati becoming Savitṛ created living beings[4]. Savitṛ is alone lord of vivifying power and by his movements (*yāmabhiḥ*) becomes Pūṣan (5, 82[5]). In his vivifying power Pūṣan marches, beholding all beings as a guardian (10, 139[1]). In two consecutive verses (3, 62[9. 10]) Pūṣan and Savitṛ are thought of as connected. In the first the favour of Pūṣan who sees all beings is invoked, and in the second, Savitṛ is besought to stimultae (cp. Pūṣan, p. 36) the thoughts of worshippers who desire to think of the excellent brilliance of god Savitṛ. The latter verse is the celebrated *Sâvitrī*, with which Savitṛ was in later times invoked at the beginning of Vedic study[5]. Savitṛ is also said to become Mitra by reason of his laws (5, 81[4]). Savitṛ seems sometimes (5, 82[1. 3]; 7, 38[1. 6]) to be identified with Bhaga also, unless the latter word is here only an epithet of Savitṛ. The name of Bhaga (the good god bestowing benefits) is indeed often added to that of Savitṛ so as to form the single expression *Savitā Bhagaḥ* or *Bhagaḥ Savitā*[6]. In other texts, however, Savitṛ is distinguished from Mitra, Pūṣan, and Bhaga. In several passages Savitṛ and Sūrya appear to be spoken of indiscriminately to denote the same deity. Thus a poet says: 'God Savitṛ has raised aloft his brilliance, making light for the whole world; Sūrya shining brightly has filled heaven and earth and air with his rays' (4, 14[2]). In another hymn (7, 63) Sūrya is (in verses 1. 2. 4) spoken of in terms (e. g. *prasavitṛ*, vivifier) usually applied to Savitṛ, and in the third verse Savitṛ is apparently mentioned as the same god. In other hymns also (10, 158[1-4]; 1, 35[1-11]. 124[1]) it is hardly possible to keep the two deities apart. In passages such as the following, Savitṛ is, however, distinguished from Sūrya. 'Savitṛ moves between both heaven and earth, drives away disease, impels (*veti*) the sun' (1, 35[9]). Savitṛ declares men sinless to the sun (1, 123[3]). He combines with the rays of the sun (5,81[4]) or shines with the rays of the sun (10,139[1] cp. 181[3]; 1, 157[1]; 7, 35[8. 10]). With Mitra, Aryaman, Bhaga, Savitṛ is besought to vivify the worshipper when the sun has risen (7, 66[4]).

According to Yāska (Nir. 12, 12), the time of Savitṛ's appearance is when darkness has been removed. Sāyaṇa (on RV. 5, 81[4]) remarks that before his rising the sun is called Savitṛ, but from his rising to his setting, Sūrya. But Savitṛ is also sometimes spoken of as sending to sleep (4,53[6];7,45[1]), and must therefore be connected with evening as well as morning. He is, indeed, extolled as the setting sun in one hymn (2, 38); and there are indications that most of the hymns addressed to him are meant for either a morning or an evening sacrifice[7]. He brings all two-footed and four-footed beings to rest and awakens them (6, 71[4] cp. 4, 53[3]; 7, 45[1]). He unyokes his steeds, brings the wanderer to rest; at his command night comes; the weaver rolls up her web and the skilful man lays down his unfinished work (2, 38[3. 4]). Later the west was wont to be assigned to him (ŚB. 3, 2, 3[18]), as the east to Agni and the south to Soma.

The name Savitṛ has all the appearance of being a word of purely Indian formation. This is borne out by the fact that the root *sū*, from which it is derived, is continually used along with it in a manner which is unique in the RV. Some other verb would nearly always be used to express the same action in connexion with any other god. In the case of Savitṛ not only is the root itself used, but also several derivatives (such as *prasavitṛ* and *prasava*) constituting a perpetual play on the name[8]. These frequent combinations show clearly that the root has the sense of stimulating, arousing, vivifying. A few examples may here be given in illustration of this peculiar usage. 'God Savitṛ has aroused (*prāsāvīt*) each moving thing' (1, 157[1]). 'Thou alone art the lord of stimulation' (*prasavasya*: 5, 81[5]). 'Savitṛ bestowed (*āsuvat*) that immortality on you' (1, 110[3]). 'God Savitṛ has arisen to arouse (*savāya*) us' (2, 38[1]). 'Thrice a day Savitṛ sends down (*soṣavīti*) boons from the sky' (3, 56[6]). 'Do thou, o Savitṛ, constitute (*suvatāt*) us sinless' (4, 54[3]). 'May we being sinless towards Aditi through the influence (*save*) of Savitṛ possess all boons' (5, 82[6]). 'Send away (*parā sava*) evil dream, send away all calamities, bestow (*āsuva*) what is good (ib. [4. 5]). 'May Savitṛ remove (*apa sāviṣat*) sickness' (10, 100[8]). With this verb Savitṛ is specially often besought to bestow wealth (2, 56[6] &c.). This use of *sū* is almost peculiar to Savitṛ; but it is two or three times applied to Sūrya (7, 63[2. 4]; 10, 37[4]). It also occurs with Uṣas (7, 77[1]), with Varuṇa (2, 28[9]), with the Ādityas (8, 18[1]), and with Mitra, Aryaman coupled with Savitṛ (7, 66[4]). This employment being so frequent, Yāska (Nir. 10, 31) defines Savitṛ as *sarvasya prasavitā*, 'the stimulator of everything'.

The fact that in nearly half its occurrences the name is accompanied by *deva*, god, seems to show that is has not yet lost the nature of an epithet, meaning 'the stimulator god'. At any rate, the word appears to be an epithet of Tvaṣṭṛ in two passages (3, 55[10]; 10, 10[5]), where the juxtaposition of the words *devas tvaṣṭā savitā viśvarūpa* and the collocation with *deva* indicate that Savitṛ is here identical with Tvaṣṭṛ.

We may therefore conclude that Savitṛ was originally an epithet of Indian origin applied to the sun as the great stimulator of life and motion in the world, representing the most important movement which dominates all others in the universe, but that as differentiated from Sūrya he is a more abstract deity. He is in the eyes of the Vedic poets the divine power of the sun personified, while Sūrya is the more concrete deity, in the conception of whom the outward form of the sun-body is never absent owing to the identity of his name with that of the orb (cp. 1, 35[9]. 124[1]).

Oldenberg[9], reversing the order of development generally recognized, thinks that Savitṛ represents an abstraction of the idea of stimulation and that the notion of the sun, or of the sun in a particular direction, is only secondary in his character[10].

1 HRI. 44. — 2 Cp. v. Bradke, ZDMG. 40. 355; HRI. 48. — 3 Cp. Roth, Nirukta Erl. 143; OST. 4, 96. 111. — 4 Weber, Omina und Portenta 386. 392. — 5 Whitney in Colebrooke's essays. rev. ed. 2, 111. — 6 BRV. 3, 39. — 7 HRI.

46. — [8] ROTH, op. cit. 76. — [9] ORV. 64—5. — [10] MACDONELL, JRAS. 27, 951—2; v. SCHROEDER, WZKM. 9, 125.

WHITNEY, JAOS. 3, 324; OST. 5, 162—70; ROTH, PW.; ZDMG. 24, 306—8; GRV. I, 49; GW. s. v.; KRV. 56; BRV. 3, 38—64; HVBP. 33.

§ 16. **Pūṣan.** — The name of Pūṣan is mentioned about 120 times in the RV. and he is celebrated in eight hymns (five of them occurring in the sixth, two in the first, and one in the tenth book). He is also lauded as a dual divinity in one hymn (6, 57) with Indra and in another with Soma (2, 40). Thus statistically he occupies a somewhat higher position than Viṣṇu (§ 17). In the later Vedic and the post-Vedic periods his name is mentioned with increasing rareness. His individuality is indistinct and his anthropomorphic traits are scanty. His foot is referred to when he is asked to trample on the brand of the wicked. His right hand is also mentioned (6, 54^{10}). He has (like Rudra) braided hair (6, 55^{2}) and a beard (10, 26^{7}). He wields a golden spear (1, 42^{6}) and carries an awl (6, $53^{5.6.8}$) or a goad (53^{9}. 58^{2}). The wheel, the felly, and the seat of his car (6, 54^{3}) are spoken of and he is called the best charioteer (6, $56^{2.3}$). His car is drawn by goats[1] (*ajāśva*) instead of horses (1, 38^{4}; 6, $55^{3.4}$). He eats, for his food is gruel (6, 56^{1} cp. 3, 52^{7}). It is probably for this reason that he is said to be toothless in the SB. (1, 7, 4^{7}).

Pūṣan sees all creatures clearly and at once (3, 62^{9}), these identical words being applied to Agni also (10, 187^{4}). He is 'the lord of all things moving and stationary' almost the same words with which Sūrya is described (1, 115^{1}; 7, 60^{2}). He is the wooer of his mother (6, 55^{5}) or the lover of his sister (ib. $^{4.5}$), similar expressions being used of Sūrya (1, 115^{2}) and of Agni (10, 3^{3}). The gods are said to have given him, subdued by love, to the sun-maiden Sūryā in marriage (6, 58^{4}). Probably as the husband of Sūryā, Pūṣan is connected with the marriage ceremonial in the wedding hymn (10, 85), being besought to take the bride's hand and lead her away and to bless her in her conjugal relation[2] (v. 37). In another passage (9, 67^{10}) he is besought to give his worshippers their share of maidens. With his golden ships which move in the aerial ocean, subdued by love he acts as the messenger[3] of Sūrya (6, 58^{3}). He moves onward beholding the universe (2, 40^{5}; 6, 58^{2}) and makes his abode in heaven (2, 40^{4}). He is a guardian, who goes at the instigation of Savitṛ, knowing and beholding all creatures. In a hymn devoted to his praise, Pūṣan is said as best of charioteers to have driven downwards the golden wheel of the sun (6, 56^{3}), but the connexion is obscure (cp. Nir. 2, 6). A frequent and exclusive epithet of Pūṣan is 'glowing' (*āghṛṇi*). He is once termed *agohya*, 'not to be concealed', an attribute almost peculiar to Savitṛ.

Pūṣan is born on the far path of paths, on the far path of heaven and of earth; he goes to and returns from both the beloved abodes, knowing them (6, 17^{6}). Owing to this familiarity he conducts the dead on the far path to the Fathers, as Agni and Savitṛ take them to where the righteous have gone and where they and the gods abide, and leads his worshippers thither in safety, showing them the way (10, 17^{3-5}). The AV. also speaks of Pūṣan as conducting to the world of the righteous, the beautiful world of the gods (AV. 16, 9^{2}; 18, 2^{53}). So Pūṣan's goat conducts the sacrificial horse (1, $162^{2.3}$). Perhaps to Pūṣan's familiarity with the (steep) paths is due the notion that his car is drawn by the sure-footed goat.

As knower of paths, Pūṣan is conceived as a guardian of roads. He is besought to remove dangers, the wolf, the waylayer, from the path (1, 42^{1-3}). In this connexion he is called *vimuco napāt*, 'son of deliverance'[4]. The same epithet is applied to him in another passage (6, 55[1]) and he is twice (8, 4[15.16]) called *vimocana*, 'deliverer'. As *vimuco napāt* he is invoked to deliver from sin' (AV. 6, 112[3]). Pūṣan is prayed to disperse foes and make the paths lead to booty (6, 53[4]), to remove foes, to make the paths good, and to lead to good pasture (1, 42[7.8]). He is invoked to protect from harm on his path (6, 54[9]) and to grant an auspicious path (10, 59[7]). He is the guardian of every path (6, 49[8]) and lord of the road (6, 53[1]). He is a guide (*prapathya*) on roads (VS. 22, 20). So in the Sūtras, whoever is starting on a journey makes an offering to Pūṣan, the road-maker, while reciting RV. 6, 53; and whoever loses his way, turns to Pūṣan (AGS. 3, 7[8.9]; ŚŚS. 3, 4[9]). Moreover, in the morning and evening offerings to all gods and beings, Pūṣan the road-maker receives his on the threshold of the house (ŚGS. 2, 14[9]).

As knower of ways he can make hidden goods manifest and easy to find (6, 48[15]). He is in one passage (1, 23[14.15] cp. TS. 3, 3, 9[1]) said to have found the king who was lost and hidden in secret (probably Soma), and asked to bring him like a lost beast. So in the Sūtras, Pūṣan is sacrificed to when anything lost is sought (AGS. 3, 7[9]). Similarly, it is characteristic of Pūṣan that he follows and protects cattle (6, 54[5.6.10]. 58[2] cp. 10, 26[3]). He preserves them from injury by falling into a pit, brings them home unhurt, and drives back the lost (6, 54[7.10]). His goad directs cattle straight (6, 53[9]). Perhaps connected with the idea of guiding straight is the notion that he directs the furrow (4, 57[7]). Pūṣan also protects horses (6, 54[5]) and weaves and smooths the clothing of sheep (10, 26[6]). Hence beasts are said to be sacred to Pūṣan (1, 5[1.2]), and he is called the producer of cattle (MS. 4, 3[7]; TB. 1, 7, 2[4]). In the Sūtras verses to Pūṣan are prescribed to be recited when cows are driven to pasture or stray (ŚGS. 3, 9).

Pūṣan has various attributes in common with other gods. He is called *asura* (5, 51[11]). He is strong (5, 43[9]), vigorous (8, 4[15]), nimble (6, 54[8]), powerful (1, 138[1]), resistless (6, 48[15]). He transcends mortals and is equal to the gods in glory (6, 48[19]). He is a ruler of heroes (1, 106[4]), an unconquerable protector and defender (1, 89[5]), and assists in battle (6, 48[19]). He is a protector of the world (10, 17[3] cp. 2, 40[1]). He is a seer, a protecting friend of the priest, the unshaken friend born of old, of every suppliant (10, 26[5.8]). He is wise (1, 42[5]) and liberal[5] (2, 31[4]). His bounty is particularly often mentioned. He possesses all wealth (1, 89[6]), abounds in wealth (8, 4[15]), gives increase of wealth (1, 89[5]), is beneficent (1, 138[2]), bountiful (6, 58[4]; 8, 4[18]), and bestows all blessings (1, 42[6]). He is the strong friend of abundance, the strong lord and increaser of nourishment (10, 26[7.8]). The term *dasra*, 'wonder-working', distinctive of the Aśvins, is a few times (1, 42[5]; 6, 56[4]) applied to him, as well as *dasma*, 'wondrous' (1, 42[10]. 138[4]) and *dasma-varcas*, 'of wondrous splendour' (6, 58[4]), usually said of Agni and Indra. He is also twice (1, 106[4]; 10, 64[3]) called Narāśaṃsa 'praised of men', an epithet otherwise exclusively limited to Agni. He is once spoken of as 'all-pervading' (2, 40[6]). He is termed 'devotion-stimulating' (9, 88[3]), is invoked to quicken devotion (2, 40[6]), and his awl is spoken of as 'prayer-instigating' (6, 53[8]; cp. Savitṛ, p. 33).

The epithets exclusively connected with Pūṣan are *āghṛṇi, ajāśva, vimocana, vimuco napāt*, and once each *puṣṭimbhara*, 'bringing prosperity', *anaṣṭapaśu*, 'losing no cattle', *anaṣṭavedas*, 'losing no goods', *karambhād*, 'eating gruel'. The latter attribute seems to have been a cause for despising Pūṣan by some (cp. 6, 56[1]; 1, 138[4])[6]. *Karambha*, mentioned three times in the RV., is Pūṣan's distinctive food, being contrasted with Soma as Indra's (6, 57[2]). Indra, however, shares it (3, 52[7]), and in the only two passages in which the adjective *karambhin* 'mixed with gruel' occurs, it applies to the libation of Indra (3, 52^1; 8, 80^2). Pūṣan is the only god who receives the epithet *paśupā*, 'protector of cattle' (6, 58^2) directly (and not in comparisons).

The only deities with whom Pūṣan is invoked conjointly in the dual are Soma (2, 40) and Indra (6, 57), whose brother he is once called (6, 55^5). Next to these two, Pūṣan is most frequently addressed with Bhaga (1, 90^4; 4, 30^{24}; 5, 41^4. 46^2; 10, 125^2; cp. ŚB. 11, 4, 3^3; KSS. 5, 13^1) and Viṣṇu (1, 90^5; 5, 46^3; 6, 21^9; 7, 44^1; 10, 66^5), his name in all these passages of the RV. being in juxtaposition with theirs. He is occasionally addressed with various other deities also.

The evidence adduced does not show clearly that Pūṣan represents a phenomenon of nature. But a large number of passages quoted at the beginning point to his being closely connected with the sun. Yāska, too, (Nir. 7, 9) explains Pūṣan to be 'the sun (*Āditya*), the preserver of all beings', and in post-Vedic literature Pūṣan occasionally occurs as a name of the sun. The path of the sun which leads from earth to heaven, the abode of the gods and the pious dead, might account for a solar deity being both a conductor of departed souls (like Savitṛ) and a guardian of paths in general. The latter aspect of his character would explain his special bucolic features as a guide and protector of cattle, which form a part of his general nature as a promoter of prosperity. Mithra, the solar deity of the Avesta, has the bucolic traits of increasing cattle and bringing back beasts that have strayed[7].

Etymologically the word means 'prosperer' as derived from the root *puṣ*, 'to cause to thrive'. This side of his character is conspicuous both in his epithets *viśvavedas, anaṣṭavedas, purūvasu, puṣṭimbhara*, and in the frequent invocations to him to bestow wealth and protection (6, 48^{15} &c.). He is lord of great wealth, a stream of wealth, a heap of riches (6, $55^{2.3}$). But the prosperitiy he confers is not, as in the case of Indra, Parjanya, and the Maruts, connected with rain, but with light, which is emphasized by his exclusive epithet 'glowing'. The welfare which he bestows results from the protection he extends to men and cattle on earth, and from his guidance of men to the abodes of bliss in the next world. Thus the conception which seems to underlie the character of Pūṣan, is the beneficent power of the sun manifested chiefly as a pastoral deity.

[1] KRV. note 120. — [2] IS. 5, 186. 190. — [3] GGA. 1889, p. 8. — [4] OST. 5, 175; GW.; LRV. 4, 444; HVBP. 34, and BRV. (who explains the original meaning differently); 'Sohn der Einkehr' (= unyoking): ROTH, FW. und ORV. 232; 'Son of the cloud': Sāyaṇa and GRIFFITH on RV. 1, 42^1. — [5] *Puraṃdhi* according to HILLEBRANDT, WZKM. 3, 192—3, means 'active, zealous'. — [6] HRI. 51. — [7] Sp.AP. 184.

WHITNEY, JAOS. 3, 325; OST. 5, 171—80; GUBERNATIS, Letture 82; BRV. 2, 420—30; KRV. 55; PVS. 1, 11; HVM. 1, 456; HVBP. 34; ORV. 230—3 (cp. WZKM. 9, 252); PERRY, Drisler Memorial 241—3; HRI. 50—3.

§ 17. Viṣṇu. — Viṣṇu, though a deity of capital importance in the mythology of the Brāhmaṇas, occupies but a subordinate position in the RV. His personality is at the same time more important there than would appear from the statistical standard alone. According to that he would be a deity only of the fourth rank, for he is celebrated in not more than five whole hymns and in part of another, while his name occurs only about 100 times altogether in the RV. The only anthropomorphic traits of Viṣṇu are the frequently mentioned strides which he takes, and his being a youth vast in body, who is no longer a child (1, 155^6). The essential feature of his character is that he takes (generally expressed by *vi-kram*) three strides, which are referred to about a dozen times. His epithets *urugāya*, 'wide-going' and *urukrama*, 'wide-striding', which also occur about a dozen times, allude to the same action. With these three steps Viṣṇu is described as traversing the earth or the terrestrial spaces. Two of these steps or spaces are visible to men, but the third or highest step is beyond the flight of birds or mortal ken (1, 155^{5}; 7, 99^{2}). The same notion seems to be mystically expressed (1, 155^{3}) when he is said to bear his third name in the bright realm of heaven. The highest place of Viṣṇu is regarded as identical with the highest place of Agni, for Viṣṇu guards the highest, the third place of Agni (10, 1^{3}) and Agni with the loftiest station of Viṣṇu guards the mysterious cows (probably = clouds: 5, 3^{3}). The highest step of Viṣṇu is seen by the liberal like an eye fixed in heaven (1, 22^{20}). It is his dear abode, where pious men rejoice and where there is a well of honey (1, 154^{5}), and where the gods rejoice (8, 29^{7}). This highest step[1] shines down brightly and is the dwelling of Indra and Viṣṇu, where are the many-horned swiftly moving cows[2] (probably = clouds), and which the singer desires to attain (1, 154^{6}). Within these three footsteps all beings dwell (1, 154^{2}), and they are full of honey (1, 154^{4}), probably because the third and most important is full of it[3]. Viṣṇu guards the highest abode (*pāthas*)[4], which implies his favourite dwelling-place (3, 55^{10}) and is elsewhere expressly stated to be so (1, 154^{5}). In another passage (7, 100^{5}) Viṣṇu is less definitely said to dwell far from this space. He is once spoken of (1, 156^{5}) as having three abodes, *triṣadhastha*, an epithet primarily appropriate to Agni (§ 35).

The opinion that Viṣṇu's three steps refer to the course of the sun is almost unanimous. But what did they originally represent? The purely naturalistic interpretation favoured by most European scholars[5] and by Yāska's predecessor Aurṇavābha (Nir. 12, 19) takes the three steps to mean the rising, culminating, and setting of the sun. The alternative view, which prevails throughout the younger Vedas, the Brāhmaṇas, as well as post-Vedic literature, and was supported by Yāska's predecessor Śākapūṇi and is favoured by BERGAIGNE and the present writer[8], interprets the three steps as the course of the solar deity through the three divisions of the universe. With the former interpretation is at variance the fact that the third step of Viṣṇu shows no trace of being connected with sunset, but on the contrary is identical with the highest step. The alternative view does not conflict with what evidence the RV. itself supplies, and is supported by the practically unvarying tradition in India beginning with the later Vedas.

That the idea of motion is characteristic of Viṣṇu is shown by other expressions besides the three steps. The epithets 'wide-going' and 'wide-striding' are almost entirely limited to Viṣṇu, as well as the verb *vi-kram*. The latter is also employed in allusion to the sun, spoken of as the variegated stone placed in the midst of heaven, which took strides (5, 47^{3}). Viṣṇu is also swift *eṣa* (otherwise said only once of Bṛhaspati) or 'swift-going' *evayā*, *evayāvan* (otherwise connected only with the Maruts). Coupled with the constant idea of swift and far-extending motion is that of regularity. In taking his three strides Viṣṇu observes laws (1, 22^{18}). Like other deities typical of regular recurrence (Agni, Soma, Sūrya, Uṣas), Viṣṇu is the 'ancient germ of order', and an ordainer, who (like Agni, Sūrya, Uṣas) is both ancient and recent (1, 156^{2-4}). In the same words as the sun-god Savitṛ (5, 81^{3}), he is said (1, 154^{1}; 6, 49^{13}) to have measured out the earthly spaces. With this may also be compared the statement that Varuṇa measured out the spaces with the sun (p. 11). Viṣṇu is in one passage (1, 155^{6} cp. 1, $164^{4 \cdot 48}$) described as setting in motion like a revolving wheel his 90 steeds (= days) with their four names (= seasons). This can hardly refer to anything but the solar year of 360 days. In the AV. (5, 26[7]) Viṣṇu is besought to bestow heat on the sacrifice. In the Brāhmaṇas Viṣṇu's head when cut off becomes the sun. In post-Vedic literature one of Viṣṇu's weapons is a rolling wheel[8] which is represented like the sun (cp. RV. 5, 63[4]), and his vehicle is Garuḍa, chief of birds, who is of brilliant lustre like Agni, and is also called *garutmat* and *suparṇa*, two terms already applied to the sun-bird in the RV. Finally the post-Vedic *kaustubha* or breast-jewel of Viṣṇu has been explained as the sun by KUHN[9]. Thus though Viṣṇu is no longer clearly connected with a natural phenomenon, the evidence appears to justify the inference that he was originally conceived as the sun, not in his general character, but as the personified swiftly moving luminary, which with vast strides traverses the whole universe. This explanation would be borne out by the derivation from the root *viṣ*[10], which is used tolerably often in the RV. and primarily means 'to be active' (PW.). According to this, Viṣṇu would be the 'active one' as representing solar motion. OLDENBERG, however, thinks that every definite trace of solar character is lacking in Viṣṇu, that he was from the beginning conceived only as a traverser of wide space, and that no concrete natural conception corresponded to the three steps. The number of the steps he attributes simply to the fondness for triads in mythology.

Viṣṇu's highest step, as has been indicated, is conceived as his distinctive abode. The sun would naturally be thought of as stationary in the meridian rather than anywhere else. So we find the name of the zenith in Yāska to be *viṣṇupada*, the step or place of Viṣṇu. Probably connected with the same range of ideas are the epithets 'mountain-dwelling' (*girikṣit*) and 'mountain-abiding' (*giriṣṭhā*) applied to Viṣṇu in the same hymn (1, 154[2. 3]); for in the next hymn (1, 155[1]) Viṣṇu and Indra are conjointly called 'the two undeceivable ones, who have stood on the summit (*sānuni*) of the mountains, as it were with an unerring steed'. This would allude to the sun looking down from the height of the cloud mountains[12] (cp. 5, 87[4]). It is probably owing to such expressions in the RV. that Viṣṇu is later called 'lord of mountains' (TS. 3, 4, 5[1]).

The reason why Viṣṇu took his three steps is a secondary trait. He thrice traversed the earthly spaces for man in distress (6, 49[13]); he traversed the earth to bestow it on man for a dwelling (7, 100[4]); he traversed the earthly spaces for wide-stepping existence (1, 155[4]); with Indra he took vast strides and stretched out the worlds for our existence (6, 69[5. 6]). To this feature in the RV. may ultimately be traced the myth of Viṣṇu's dwarf incarnation which appears in the Epic and the Purāṇas. The intermediate stage is found in the Brāhmaṇas (ŚB. 1, 2, 5[5]; TS. 2, 1, 3[1]; TB. 1, 6, 1[5]), where Viṣṇu already assumes the form of a dwarf, in order by artifice to recover the earth for the gods from the Asuras by taking his three strides[13].

The most prominent secondary characteristic of Viṣṇu is his friendship for Indra, with whom he is frequently allied in the fight with Vṛtra. This is indicated by the fact that one whole hymn (6, 69) is dedicated to the two deities conjointly, and that Indra's name is coupled with that of Viṣṇu in the dual as often as with that of Soma, though the name of the latter occurs vastly oftener in the RV. The closeness of their alliance is also indicated by the fact that in hymns extolling Viṣṇu alone, Indra is the only other deity incidentally associated with him either explicitly (7, 99[5. 6]; 1, 155[2]) or implicitly (7, 99[4]; 1, 154[6]. 155[1]; cp. 1, 61[7])[14]. Viṣṇu strode his three steps by tha energy (*ojasā*) of Indra (8, 12[27]), who in the preceding verse is described as slaying Vṛtra, or for Indra (Vāl. 4[3]). Indra about to slay Vṛtra says, 'friend Viṣṇu, stride out vastly' (4, 18[11]). In company with Viṣṇu, Indra slew Vṛtra

(6, 20^{2}). Viṣṇu and Indra together triumphed over the Dāsa, destroyed Śambara's 99 castles and conquered the hosts of Varcin (7, 99$^{4.5}$). Viṣṇu is Indra's intimate friend (1, 22^{19}). Viṣṇu accompanied by his friend opens the cows' stall (1, 156^{4}). In the ŚB. (5, 5, 5^{1}) Indra is described as shooting the thunderbolt at Vṛtra, while Viṣṇu follows him (cp. TS. 6, 5, 1^{1}). Viṣṇu is also invoked with Indra in various single verses (4, 2^{4}. 55^{4}; 8, 10^{2}; 10, 66^{4}). When associated with Indra as a dual divinity, Viṣṇu shares Indra's powers of drinking Soma (6,69) as well as his victories (7, 99$^{4-6}$), Indra conversely participating in Viṣṇu's power of striding (6, 69^{5}; 7, 99^{6}). To both conjointly is attributed the action of creating the wide air and of spreading out the spaces (6, 69^{5}) and of producing Sūrya, Uṣas, and Agni (7, 99^{4}). Owing to this friendship Indra drinks Soma beside Viṣṇu (8, 3^{8}. 12^{16}) and thereby increases his strength (8, 3^{8}; 10, 113^{2}). Indra drank the Soma pressed by Viṣṇu in three cups (2, 22^{1} cp. 6, 17^{11}), which recall Viṣṇu's three footsteps filled with honey (1,154^{4}). Viṣṇu also cooks for Indra 100 buffaloes (6,17^{11}) or 100 buffaloes and a brew of milk (8, 66^{10} cp. 1, 61^{7}). Along with Mitra, Varuṇa, and the Maruts, Viṣṇu celebrates Indra with songs (8, 15^{9}).

Indra's constant attendants in the Vṛtra-fight, the Maruts, are also drawn into association with Viṣṇu. When Viṣṇu favoured the exhilerating Soma, the Maruts like birds sat down on their beloved altar (1,85^{7})[15]. The Maruts are invoked at the offering of the swift Viṣṇu (2, 34^{11} cp. 7, 40^{5}). They are the bountiful ones of the swift Viṣṇu (8,20^{3}). The Maruts supported Indra, while Pūṣan Viṣṇu cooked 100 buffaloes for him (6, 17^{11}). Viṣṇu is the ordainer associated with the Maruts (*māruta*), whose will Varuṇa and the Aśvins follow (1, 156^{4}). Throughout one hymn (5, 87, especially verses $^{4.5}$) he is associated with the Maruts, with whom, when he starts, he speeds along[16].

Among stray references to Viṣṇu in the RV. may be mentioned one (7, 100^{6}) in which different forms of Viṣṇu are spoken of: 'Do not conceal from us this form, since thou didst assume another form in battle'. He is further said to be a protector of embryos (7,36^{9}) and is invoked along with other deities to promote conception (10, 184^{1}). In the third verse of the *Khila* after 10, 184[17], Viṣṇu is, according to one reading, called upon to place in the womb a male child with a most beautiful form, or, according to another, a male child with Viṣṇu's most beautiful form is prayed for[18].

Other traits of Viṣṇu are applicable to the gods in general. He is beneficent (1, 156^{5}), is innocuous and bountiful (8, 25^{12}), liberal (7, 40^{5}), a guardian (3, 55^{10}), who is undeceivable (1, 22^{18}), and an innoxious and generous deliverer (1,155^{4}). He alone sustains the threefold (world), heaven and earth, and all beings (1, 154^{4}). He fastened the world all about with pegs (7,99^{3}). He is an ordainer (1, 156^{4}).

In the Brāhmaṇas Viṣṇu is conceived as taking his three steps in earth, air, and heaven (ŚB. 1, 9, 3^{9}; TB. 3, 1, 2^{7}). These three strides are imitated by the sacrificer, who takes three Viṣṇu strides beginning with earth and ending with heaven[19], for that is the goal, the safe refuge, which is the sun (ŚB. 1, 9, 3$^{10.15}$). The three steps of the Amṣaspands taken from earth to the sphere of the sun, are similarly imitated in the ritual of the Avesta[20]. A special feature of the Brāhmaṇas is the constant identification of Viṣṇu with the sacrifice.

Two myths connected with Viṣṇu, the source of which can be traced to the RV., are further developed in the Brāhmaṇas. Viṣṇu in alliance with Indra is in the RV. described as vanquishing demons. In the Brāhmaṇas the gods and demons commonly appear as two hostile hosts, the former not, as in the RV., uniformly victorious, but often worsted. They therefore have recourse to artifice, in order to recover the supremacy. In the AB. (6, 15) it is related that Indra and Viṣṇu, engaged in conflict with the Asuras, agreed with the latter that as much as Viṣṇu could stride over in three steps should belong to the two deities. Viṣṇu accordingly strode over these worlds, the Vedas, and speech. The ŚB. (1, 2, 5) tells how the Asuras having overcome the gods began dividing the earth. The gods placing Viṣṇu, the sacrifice, at their head, came and asked for a share in the earth. The Asuras agreed to give up as much as Viṣṇu, who was a dwarf, could lie on. Then the gods by sacrificing with Viṣṇu, who was equal in size to sacrifice, gained the whole earth. The three steps are not mentioned here, but in another passage (ŚB. 1, 9, 3⁹), Viṣṇu is said to have acquired for the gods the all-pervading power which they now possess, by striding through the three worlds. It is further stated in TS. 2, 1, 3¹, that Viṣṇu, by assuming the form of a dwarf whom he had seen, conquered the three worlds (cp. TB. 1, 6, 1⁵). The introduction of the dwarf as a disguise of Viṣṇu is naturally to be accounted for as a stratagem to avert the suspicion of the Asuras[21]. This Brāhmaṇa story forms the transition to the myth of Viṣṇu's Dwarf Incarnation in post-Vedic literature[22].

Another myth of the Brāhmaṇas has its origin in two passages of the RV. (1, 61⁷; 8, 66¹⁰). Their purport is that Viṣṇu having drunk Soma and being urged by Indra, carried off 100 buffaloes and a brew of milk belonging to the boar (= Vṛtra), while Indra shooting across the (cloud) mountain, slew the fierce (*emuṣam*) boar. This myth is in the TS. (6, 2, 4²·³) developed as follows. A boar, the plunderer of wealth, kept the goods of the Asuras on the other side of seven hills. Indra plucking up a bunch of *kuśa* grass and piercing through these hills, slew the boar. Viṣṇu, the sacrifice, carried the boar off as a sacrifice for the gods. So the gods obtained the goods of the Asuras. In the corresponding passage of the Kāṭhaka (IS. XI. p. 161) the boar is called Emūṣa. The same story with slight variations is told in the Caraka Brāhmaṇa (quoted by Sāyaṇa on RV. 8,66¹⁰). This boar appears in a cosmogonic character in the ŚB. (14, 1, 2¹¹) where under the name of Emūṣa he is stated to have raised up the earth from the waters. In the TS. (7, 1, 5¹) this cosmogonic boar, which raised the earth from the primeval waters, is described as a form of Prajāpati. This modification of the myth is further expanded in the TB. (1, 1, 3⁵). In the post-Vedic mythology of the Rāmāyaṇa and the Purāṇas, the boar which raises the earth, has become one of the Avatārs of Viṣṇu.

The germs of two other Avatārs of Viṣṇu are to be found in the Brāhmaṇas, but not as yet connected with Viṣṇu. The fish which in the ŚB. (1, 8, 1¹) delivers Manu from the flood, appears in the Mahābhārata as a form of Prajāpati, becoming in the Purāṇas an incarnation of Viṣṇu. In the ŚB. (7, 5, 1⁵, cp. TA. 1, 23³) Prajāpati about to create offspring becomes a tortoise moving in the primeval waters. In the Purāṇas this tortoise is an Avatār of Viṣṇu, who assumes this form to recover various objects lost in the deluge[23].

The ŚB. (14, 1, 1) tells a myth of how Viṣṇu, the sacrifice, by first comprehending the issue of the sacrifice, became the most eminent among the gods, and how his head, by his bow starting asunder, was cut off and became the sun (*āditya*). To this story the TA. (5, 1, 1—7) adds the trait that the Aśvins as physicians replaced the head of the sacrifice and that the gods now able to offer it in its complete form conquered heaven (cp. PB. 7, 5⁶).

In the AB. (1, 1) Viṣṇu as the locally highest of the gods is contrasted with Agni the lowest, all the other deities being placed between them. The same Brāhmaṇa (1, 30) in quoting RV. 1, 156[4], where 'Viṣṇu accompanied by his friend opens the stall', states that Viṣṇu is the doorkeeper of the gods.

[1] The moon according to HVBP. 33. — [2] Stars according to PW., HVBP. and others. — [3] Cp. BRV. 2, 416. — [4] Otherwise SIEG in FaW. (Leipzig 1896), 97—100. — [5] WHITNEY, MAX MÜLLER, HAUG, KAEGI, DEUSSEN, and others. — [6] BRV. 2, 414—5. — [7] MACDONELL, JRAS. 27, 170—5. — [8] KHF. 222. — [9] Entwicklungsstufen, 116. — [10] Other derivations in ORV. 229, HRI. 580, BB. 21, 205. — [11] ORV. 228—30. — [12] Cp. ORV. 230, note 2; MACDONELL, JRAS. 27, p. 174, note 2. — [13] JRAS. 27, 188—9. — [14] Ibid. 184. — [15] BERGAIGNE, JA. 1884, p. 472. — [16] MM., SBE. 32, p. 127. 133—7. — [17] AUFRECHT, RV. II², 687. — [18] WINTERNITZ, JRAS. 27, 150—1. — [19] HILLEBRANDT, Neu- und Vollmondsopfer, 171 f. — [20] DARMESTETER, French Tr. of the Avesta 1, 401; ORV. 227. — [21] Otherwise A. KUHN, Entwicklungsstufen der Mythenbildung, 128. — [22] JRAS. 27, 168—177. — [23] Ibid. 166—8.

WHITNEY, JAOS. 3, 325; OST. 4, 63—98. 121—9. 298; WEBER, IStr. 2, 226 f.; Omina und Portenta 338; BRV. 2, 414—8; ORV. 227—30; HOPKINS, PAOS. 1894, CXLVII f.; HRI. 56 f.

§ 18. **Vivasvat**.—Vivasvat is not celebrated in any single hymn of the RV., but his name occurs there about thirty times, generally as Vivásvat, five times also as Vívasvat. He is the father of the Aśvins (10, 17[2]) and of Yama (10, 14[5]. 17[1]). As in post-Vedic literature he is already also in the Vedas the father of Manu (§ 50), the ancestor of the human race, who is once (Vāl. 4[1]) called Vivasvat (= Vaivasvata, p. 12) and receives the patronymic Vaivasvata in the AV. and the SB. Men are also directly stated to be the progeny of Vivasvān Ādityaḥ (TS. 6, 5, 6[2]; ŚB. 3, 1, 3[4]). The gods are also once spoken of as the offspring (*janimā*) of Vivasvat (10, 63[1]). Vivasvat's wife is Saraṇyū, daughter of Tvaṣṭṛ (10, 17[1.2]).

It was to Vivasvat as well as Mātariśvan that Agni was first manifested (1, 31[3]). Vivasvat's messenger is once (6, 8[4]) stated to be Mātariśvan, but is otherwise Agni (1, 58[1]; 4, 7[4]; 8, 39[3]; 10, 21[5]). Agni is once said to be produced from his parents (the fire-sticks) as the sage of Vivasvat (5, 11[3]).

The seat (*sadana*) of Vivasvat is mentioned five times. The gods (10, 12[7]) and Indra delight in it (3, 51[3]) and there singers extol the greatness of Indra (1, 53[1]; 3, 34[7]) or of the waters (10, 75[1]). Perhaps the same notion is referred to when a new hymn is said (1, 139[1]) to be placed in Vivasvat as a centre (*nābhā*).

Indra is connected with Vivasvat in several passages of the RV. He rejoices in the prayer of Vivasvat (8, 6[39]) and placed his treasure beside Vivasvat (2, 13[6]). With the ten[1] (fingers) of Vivasvat Indra pours out the pail from heaven (8, 61[8], cp. 5, 53[6]). Indra being so closely associated with the abode of Vivasvat, Soma is likely to be there. And indeed Soma is in the ninth book brought into intimate relation to Vivasvat. Soma dwells with Vivasvat (9, 26[4]) and is cleansed by the daughters (= fingers) of Vivasvat (9, 14[5]). The prayers of Vivasvat urge the tawny Soma to flow (9, 99[2]). The seven sisters (= waters) urge the wise Soma on the course of Vivasvat (9, 66[8]). The streams of Soma flow through the sieve having obtained (the blessing) of Vivasvat and producing the blessing (*bhagam*) of dawn (9, 10[5]).

The Aśvins who dwell with Vivasvat are besought to come to the offering (1, 46[13]). At the yoking of the Aśvins' car the daughter of the sky is born and the two bright days (probably day and night) of Vivasvat (10, 39[12]; cp. SB. 10, 5, 2[4]).

Vivasvat is also mentioned along with Varuṇa and the gods as an object of worship (10, 65[6]). In one passage Vivasvat shows a hostile trait, when the worshippers of the Ādityas pray that the missile, the well-wrought arrow of Vivasvat, may not slay them before old age[2] (8, 56[20], cp. AV. 19, 9[7]). On the other hand, Vivasvat preserves from Yama (AV. 18, 3[62]).

The word *vivasvat* occurs a few times as an adjective meaning 'brilliant' in connexion with Agni and Uṣas. Agni is said to have produced the children of men and by brilliant sheen heaven and the waters (1, 96[2]). Agni is the wise, boundless, brilliant sage who shines at the beginning of dawn (7, 9[3]). Agni is besought to bring the brilliant gift of dawn (1, 44[1]), and men desire to see the shining face of brilliant dawn (3, 30[13]). The etymological meaning 'shining forth' (*vi* + √ *vas*) is peculiarly appropriate in relation to Uṣas, whose name is derived from the same root and in connexion with whom the words *viuṣ* and *viuṣṭi*, 'shining forth, dawning' are nearly always used. The derivation is given in the ŚB. where it is said that Āditya Vivasvat illumines (*vi-vaste*) night and day (ŚB. 10, 5, 2[4]).

In the YV. (VS. 8, 5; MS. 1, 6[12]) and the Brāhmaṇas Vivasvat is called Āditya and in the post-Vedic literature is a common name of the sun.

He goes back to the Indo-Iranian period, being identical with Vivañhvant (the father of Yima), who is described as the first man that prepared Haoma, Āthwya being the second, and Thrita the third (Yasna, 9, 10). The first and third of these are found connected in the RV. also (Vāl. 4[1]), where Indra is said to have drunk Soma beside Manu Vivasvat and Trita.

As a mythological figure Vivasvat seems to have faded by the time of the RV. like Trita[3]. Considering the etymology, the connexion with the Aśvins, Agni, and Soma, the fact that his seat is the place of sacrifice[4], the most probable interpretation of Vivasvat seems to be that he originally represented the rising sun[5]. Most scholars[6] explain him simply as the sun. Some take him to be the god of the bright sky[7] or the heaven of the sun[8]. BERGAIGNE (1, 88) thinks that Agni alone, of whom the sun is a form, can be responsible for the character of a sacrificer which is prominent in Vivasvat. OLDENBERG[9] comparing the Avestan Vīvañhvant, the first mortal that prepared Haoma, believes that the reasons for considering Vivasvat a god of light, are insufficient and that he represents simply the first sacrificer, the ancestor of the human race.

1 Cp. LRV. 4, 386. — 2 SVL. 148. — 3 ROTH, ZDMG. 4, 424. — 4 PW., BRV. 1, 87, ORV. 275; PVS. I, 242 ('chapel of V.'); FOY, KZ. 34, 228. — 5 The later view of ROTH, PW. ('Morgensonne'); cp. ZDMG. 4, 425 ('das Licht der Himmelshöhe'). — 6 A. KUHN, Sp.AP. 248 ff., HVM. 1, 488, HRI. 128. 130, and others. — 7 LRV. 3, 333; 5, 392; EHNI, Yama, 19. 24. — 8 BRI. 9—10. — 9 ORV. 122, ZDMG. 49, 173, SBE. 46, 392. Cp. also ROTH, ZDMG. 4, 432; BRV. 1, 86—8; HVM. 1, 474—88; BLOOMFIELD, JAOS. 15, 176—7.

§ 19. **Ādityas.**—The group of gods called Ādityas is celebrated in six whole hymns and in parts of two others in the RV. It is rather indefinite both as to the names of the gods it includes and as to their number. Not more than six are anywhere enumerated and that only once: Mitra, Aryaman, Bhaga, Varuṇa, Dakṣa, Aṃśa (2, 27[1]). In the last books of the RV. the number is once (9, 114[3]) stated to be seven and once (10, 72[8]) eight, Aditi at first presenting only seven to the gods and bringing the eighth, Mārtāṇḍa[1], afterwards (ibid. [9]). The names of the Ādityas are not specified in either of these passages. The AV. states that Aditi had eight sons (8, 9[21]), and the TB. (1, 1, 9[1]) mentions these eight by name as Mitra, Varuṇa, Aryaman, Aṃśa, Bhaga, Dhātṛ, Indra, Vivasvat (the first five occur in RV. 2, 27[1]), and the same list is quoted by Sāyaṇa (on RV. 2, 27[1]) as found in another passage of the Taittirīya branch of the Veda. The ŚB. in one passage speaks of the Ādityas as having become eight by the addition of Mārtāṇḍa, while in two others (6, 1, 2[8]; 11, 6, 3[8]) they are said to be twelve in number and are identified with the twelve months. In post-Vedic literature they are regularly twelve sun-gods, evidently connected with the twelve months, Viṣṇu being one of them and the greatest[2]. In addition to the six Ādityas mentioned in RV. 2, 27[1], Sūrya is a few times termed an Āditya (p. 30), which is a common name for the sun in the Brāhmaṇas and later. Under the name of Āditya, identified with Agni, Sūrya is said to have been placed by the gods in the sky (10, 88[11]). Savitṛ is also once mentioned in an enumeration with the four Ādityas Bhaga, Varuṇa, Mitra, Aryaman (8, 18[3]). If therefore the number of the Ādityas was regarded by the poets of the RV. to have been definitely seven, the sun must have been the seventh, the eighth Mārtāṇḍa whom Aditi throws away and brings back (10, 72[8. 9]) probably being the setting sun. In the AV. (13, 2[9. 37]) the sun is called the son of Aditi, the sun and moon Ādityas (8, 2[15]), and Viṣṇu is invoked in an enumeration containing gods who in the RV. are Ādityas: Varuṇa, Mitra, Viṣṇu, Bhaga, Aṃśa besides Vivasvat (11, 6[2]). The mother of the Ādityas is here once (9, 1[4]) said to be not Aditi but the golden-hued Madhukaśā, daughter of the Vasus.

Indra is, however, in the RV. once coupled in the dual as an Āditya with Varuṇa the chief of the Ādityas (7, 85[4]), and in Vāl. 4[7] he is directly invoked as the fourth Āditya. In MS. 2, 1[12] Indra is a son of Aditi, but in the ŚB. (11, 6, 3[5]) he is distinguished from the 12 Ādityas. When one god alone is mentioned as an Āditya, it is generally Varuṇa, their chief; but in the hymn in which Mitra is celebrated alone (3, 59), that deity is called an Āditya, as well as Sūrya. When two are mentioned, they are Varuṇa and Mitra, once Varuṇa and Indra; when three, Varuṇa, Mitra, and Aryaman[3]; when five, which is only once the case, the same three together with Savitṛ and Bhaga. Dakṣa occurs only in the enumeration of six mentioned above. The Ādityas are often invoked as a group, the names of Mitra and Varuṇa being generally mentioned at the same time. They also appear frequently along with other groups (§ 45) Vasus, Rudras, Maruts, Aṅgirases, Ṛbhus, Viśvedevas. The term Ādityas seems not infrequently to be used in a wider sense, as an equivalent for the gods generally[4]. Their nature as a class in fact resembles that of the gods in general, not being specifically characterized like that of their two chiefs, Mitra and Varuṇa. In the aggregate sense they are the gods of celestial light, without representing any particular manifestation of that light, such as sun, moon, and stars, or dawn. The hypothesis of OLDENBERG that the Ādityas originally represented sun, moon, and the five planets, is based on their abstract nature and names (such as Bhaga, Aṃśa, Dakṣa) and the supposition that their characteristic number is seven[5], which is also the number of the Iranian Ameṣaspentas[6]. It is here to be noted that the two groups have not a single name in common, even Mithra not being an Ameṣaspenta; that the belief in the Ādityas being seven in number is not distinctly characteristic and old[7]; and that though the identity of the Ādityas and Ameṣaspentas has been generally accepted since ROTH's essay[8], it is rejected by some distinguished Avestan scholars[9].

In some of the hymns of the RV. in which the Ādityas are celebrated (especially in 2, 27), only the three most frequently mentioned together, Mitra, Varuṇa, and Aryaman, seem to be meant. What is distant is near to them; they support all that moves and is stationary, as gods who protect the universe (2, 27[3. 4]). They see what is good and evil in men's hearts and distinguish the honest man from the deceitful (2, 27[3]; 8, 18[15]). They are haters of falsehood and punish sin (2, 27[4]; 7, 52[2]. 60[5]. 66[13]). They are besought to forgive sin (2, 27[14]. 29[5]), to avert its consequences or to transfer them to Trita Āptya (5, 52[2]; 8, 47[8]). They spread fetters for their enemies (2, 27[16]), but protect their worshippers as birds spread their wings over their young (8, 47[4]). Their servants are protected as with armour, so that no shaft can strike them (ib. [7, 8]). They ward off sickness and distress (8, 18[10]), and bestow various boons such as light, long life, offspring, guidance (2, 27; 8, 18[22]. 56[15, 20]).

The epithets which describe them are: bright (*śuci*), golden (*hiraṇyaya*), many-eyed (*bhūryakṣa*), unwinking (*animiṣa*), sleepless (*asvapnaj*), far-observing (*dīrghadhī*). They are kings, mighty (*kṣatriya*), vast (*uru*), deep (*gabhīra*), inviolable (*ariṣṭa*), having fixed ordinances (*dhṛtavrata*), blameless (*anavadya*), sinless (*avṛjina*), pure (*dhārapūta*), holy (*ṛtāvan*).

The name is clearly a metronymic formation from that of their mother Aditi, with whom they are naturally often invoked. This is also one of the three derivations given by Yāska (Nir. 2, 13, cp. TA. 1, 14[1]).

The greater gods belonging to the group have already been dealt with separately, but the lesser Ādityas having hardly any individuality may best be described here in succession.

Aryaman[10] though mentioned about 100 times in the RV. is so destitute of individual characteristics, that in the Naighaṇṭuka he is passed over in the list of gods. Except in two passages, he is always mentioned with other deities, in the great majority of cases with Mitra and Varuṇa. In less than a dozen passages the word has only the appellative senses of 'comrade' and 'groomsman', which are occasionally also connected with the god. Thus Agni is once addressed with the words: 'Thou art Aryaman when (the wooer) of maidens' (5, 3[2]). The derivative adjective *aryamya*, 'relating to a comrade', once occurs as a parallel to *mitrya*, 'relating to a friend' (5, 85[7]). Thus the conception of Aryaman seems to have differed but little from that of the greater Āditya Mitra, 'the Friend'. The name goes back to the Indo-Iranian period, as it occurs in the Avesta.

One hymn of the RV. (7, 41) is devoted chiefly to the praise of Bhaga[11], though some other deities are invoked in it as well; and the name of the god occurs over sixty times. The word means 'dispenser, giver' and appears to be used in this sense more than a score of times attributively, in several cases with the name of Savitṛ[12]. The god is also regularly conceived in the Vedic hymns as a distributor of wealth, comparisons with Bhaga being generally intended to express glorification of Indra's and Agni's bounty. The word *bhaga* also occurs about twenty times in the RV. with the sense of 'bounty, wealth, fortune', and the ambiguity is sometimes played upon. Thus in one passage (7, 41[2]) where Bhaga is called the distributor (*vidhartā*), it is stated that men say of the god, 'May I share in Bhaga' (*bhagaṃ bhakṣi*). In another verse (5, 46[6]) in which he is termed the 'dispenser' (*vibhaktā*, derived from the same root *bhaj*), he is invoked to be full of bounty (*bhagavān*) to his worshippers.

Dawn is Bhaga's sister (1, 123[5]). Bhaga's eye is adorned with rays (1, 136[2]), and hymns rise up to Viṣṇu as on Bhaga's path (3, 54[14]). Yāska describes Bhaga as presiding over the forenoon (Nir. 12, 13). The Iranian form of the name is *bagha*, 'god', which occurs as an epithet of Ahura Mazda. The word is even Indo-European[13], since it occurs in Old Church Slavonic as *bogŭ* in the sense of 'god'. There is no reason to suppose that it designated any individual god in the Indo-European period, for it cannot have attained a more specialized sense than 'bountiful god', if indeed it meant more than merely 'bountiful giver'.

The word Aṃśa, which occurs less than a dozen times in the RV., is almost synonymous with *bhaga*, expressing both the concrete sense of 'share, portion' and that of 'apportioner'. It is found but three times as the name of a god[14], only one of these passages stating anything about him besides his name. Agni is here said to be Aṃśa, a bountiful (*bhājayu*) god at the feast' (2, 1[4]).

Dakṣa[15] is mentioned hardly more than half a dozen times in the RV. as the name of a god. The word occurs more frequently as an adjective meaning 'dexterous, strong, clever, intelligent', applied to Agni (3, 14[7]) and Soma (9, 61[18] &c.), or as a substantive in the sense of 'dexterity, strength, cleverness, understanding'. The name of the personification therefore appears to mean the 'dexterous' or 'clever' god. Excepting the verse (2, 27[1]) which enumerates the six Ādityas, he is mentioned only in the first and tenth books. In one passage (1, 89[3]) he is referred to with other Ādityas, and in another (10, 64[5]) with Mitra, Varuṇa, and Aryaman, Aditi also being spoken of in connexion with his birth. In a cosmogonic hymn (10, 72[4. 5]) Dakṣa is said to have sprung from Aditi, when it is immediately added that Aditi sprang from him and is his daughter, the gods being born afterwards. In another verse (10, 5[7]) it is stated that the existent and non-existent were in the womb of Aditi, in the birthplace of Dakṣa. Thus the last two passages seem to regard Aditi and Dakṣa as universal parents. The paradox of children producing their own parents has been shown (p. 12) to be not unfamiliar to the poets of the RV. The manner in which it came to be applied in this particular case seems to be as follows. The Ādityas are spoken of as 'gods who have intelligence for their father' (6, 50[2]), the epithet (*dakṣapitarā*) being also applied to Mitra-Varuṇa, who in the same verse (7, 66[2]) are called 'very intelligent' (*sudakṣa*). The expression is made clearer by another passage (8, 25[5]), where Mitra-Varuṇa are termed 'sons of intelligence' (*sūnū dakṣasya*) as well as 'children of great might' (*napātā śavaso mahaḥ*). The juxtaposition of the latter epithets shows that *dakṣa* is here not a personification but the abstract word used as in Agni's epithets 'father of skill' (*dakṣasya pitṛ:* 3, 27[9]) or 'son of strength' (§§ 8, 35). This conclusion is confirmed by the fact that ordinary human sacrificers are called *dakṣápitaraḥ*, 'having skill for their father' (8, 52[10]). Such expressions probably brought about the personification of Dakṣa as the father of the Ādityas and his association with Aditi. In the TS. the gods in general are called *dakṣapitaraḥ*, and in the ŚB. (2, 4, 4[2]) Dakṣa is identified with the creator Prajāpati.

1 Bloomfield, JAOS. 15, 176 note; SPH. 31. — 2 OST. 4, 117—21. — 3 Bollensen, ZDMG. 41, 503. — 4 Cp. GW., s. v. Āditya. — 5 Cp. v. Schroeder, WZKM. 9, 122. — 6 On the Ameṣaspentaṣ see Darmesteter, Haurvatāṭ et Ameretāṭ (Paris 1875), 1 f.; Bartholomae, AF. 3, 26. — 7 Cp. Macdonell, JRAS. 27, 948. — 8 ZDMG. 6, 69 f. — 9 Sp.AP. 199; Harlez, JA. 1878 (11), 129 ff. — 10 Roth, ZDMG. 6, 74; Bollensen, ibid. 41, 503; HVBP. 55—6. — 11 Roth, l. c.; WC. 11—12; Baynes, The Biography of Bhaga. Transactions of the 8th Oriental Congress, II, 1, 85—9; HRI. 53—6. — 12 Cp. GW. s. v. *bhaga*. — 13 v. Schroeder, WZKM. 9, 127. — 14 Roth, ZDMG. 6, 75; BRI. 19. — 15 OST. 5, 51—2; BRV. 3, 93. 99; WC. 45.

Whitney, JAOS. 3, 323—6; OST. 5, 54—7; MM., SBE. 32, 252—4; ORV. 185—9. 286—7; ZDMG. 49, 177—8; 50, 50—4; SBE. 48, 190; Hopkins, JAOS. 17, 28; IF. 6, 116.

§ 20. **Uṣas.**—Uṣas, goddess of Dawn, is celebrated in about 20 hymns of the RV. and mentioned more than 300 times. Owing to the identity of name, the personification is but slight, the physical phenomenon of dawn never being absent from the poet's mind, when the goddess is addressed. Uṣas is the most graceful creation of Vedic poetry and there is no more charming figure in the descriptive religious lyrics of any other literature. The brightness of her form has not been obscured by priestly speculation nor has the imagery as a rule been marred by references to the sacrifice. Arraying herself in gay attire, like a dancer, she displays her bosom (1, 92[4], cp. 6, 64[2]). Like a maiden decked by her mother she shows her form (1, 123[11]). Clothed in light the maiden appears in the east, and unveils her charms (1, 124[3. 4]). Effulgent in peerless beauty she withholds her light from neither small nor great (ib. [6]). Rising resplendent as from a bath, showing her charms she comes with light, driving away the darkness (5, 80[5. 6]). She is young, being born again and again, though ancient; shining with an uniform hue, she wastes away the life of mortals (1, 92[10]). As she has shone in former days, so she shines now and will shine in future, never aging, immortal (1, 113[13. 15]). The maiden coming again awakes before all the world (1, 123[2]). Ever shortening the ages of men, she shines forth, the last of the dawns that have always gone, the first of those to come[1] (1, 124[2]). Like a wheel she revolves ever anew (3, 61[3]). She awakens creatures that have feet and makes the birds to fly up: she is the breath and life of everything (1, 48[5. 10]. 49[3]). She awakens every living being to motion (1, 92[9]; 7, 77[1]). The Dawns waken the sleeping and urge the living, the two-footed and the four-footed, to motion (4, 51[5]). When Uṣas shines forth, the birds fly up from their nests, and men seek nourishment (1, 124[12]). She reveals the paths of men, wakening the five tribes (7, 79[1]). She manifests all beings and bestows new life (7, 80[1. 2]). She drives away evil dreams to Trita Āptya (8, 47[14. 16]). She removes the black robe of night (1, 113[14]). She dispels the darkness (6, 64[3]. 65[2]). She wards off evil spirits and the hated darkness (7, 75[1]). She discloses the treasures concealed by darkness and distributes them bountifully (1, 123[4. 6]). She illumines the ends of the sky when she awakes (1, 92[11]). She opens the gates of heaven (1, 48[15]. 113[4]). She opens the doors of darkness as the cows their stall (1, 92[4]). Her radiant beams appear like herds of cattle (4, 52[2–4]). She is visible afar, spreading out cattle (*paśūn*) as it were (1, 92[12]). The ruddy beams fly up, the ruddy cows yoke themselves, the ruddy dawns weave their web (of light) as of old (ib. [2]). Thus Uṣas comes to be called 'mother of kine'[2] (4, 52[2. 3]; 7, 77[2]).

Day by day appearing at the appointed place, she never infringes the ordinance of order and of the gods (1, 92[12]. 123[9]. 124[2]; 7, 76[5]); she goes straight along the path of order, knowing the way she never loses her direction (5, 80[4]). She renders good service to the gods by causing all worshippers to awake and the sacrificial fires to be kindled (1, 113[9]). She is besought to arouse only the devout and liberal worshipper, leaving the ungodly niggard to sleep on (1, 124[10]; 4, 51[3]). Worshippers are however sometimes spoken of as wakening her instead of being awakened by her (4, 52[4] &c.), and the Vasiṣṭhas claim to have first wakened her with their hymns (7, 80[1]). She is once asked not to delay, that the sun may not scorch her as a thief or an enemy (5, 79[9]). She is besought to bring the gods to drink Soma (1, 48[12]). Hence probably, the gods are often described as 'waking with Uṣas' (1, 14[9] &c.).

Uṣas is borne on a car which is shining (7, 78[1]), brilliant (1, 23[7]), bright (3, 61[2]), well-adorned (1, 49[2]), all-adorning (7, 75[6]), massive (1, 48[10] &c.), and spontaneously-yoked (7, 78[4]). She is also said to arrive on a hundred chariots (1, 48[7]). She is drawn by steeds which are ruddy (7, 75[6] &c.), easily guided (3, 61[2]), regularly-yoked (4, 51[5]), or is said to be resplendent with steeds (5, 79[1–10]). She is also described as being drawn by ruddy kine or bulls (*go:* 1, 92[2]. 124[11]; 5, 80[3]). Both the horses and the cows probably represent the ruddy rays of morning light[3]; but the cows are generally explained as the red morning clouds. The distance the dawns traverse in a day is 30 *yojanas* (1, 123[8]).

As is to be expected, Uṣas is closely associated with the sun. She has opened paths for Sūrya to travel (1, 113[16]). She brings the eye of the gods and leads on the beautiful white horse (7, 77[3]). She shines with the light of the sun (1, 113[9]), with the light of her lover (1, 92[11]). Savitṛ shines after the path of Uṣas (5, 81[2]). Sūrya follows her as a young man a maiden (1, 115[2]). She meets the god who desires her (1, 123[10]). She is the wife of Sūrya (7, 75[5]); the Dawns are the wives of the Sun (4, 5[13]). Thus as followed in space by the sun, she is conceived as his wife or mistress. But as preceding the sun in time she is occasionally thought of as his mother (cp. p. 35). She has generated Sūrya, sacrifice, Agni (7, 78[3]). She has been produced (*prasūtā*) for the production (*savāya*) of Savitṛ, and arrives with a bright child (1, 113[1. 2]). Uṣas is the sister of the Āditya Bhaga (1, 123[5]; cp. p. 45) and the kinswoman (*jāmi*) of Varuṇa (1, 123[5]). She is also the sister (1, 113[2. 3]; 10, 127[3]) or the elder sister (1, 124[8]) of Night; and the names of Dawn and Night are often conjoined as a dual compound (*uṣāsā-naktā* or *naktoṣāsā*). Uṣas is born in the sky (7, 75[1]); and the place of her birth suggests the relationship most frequently mentioned in the RV.: she is constantly called the daughter of heaven (1, 30[22] &c.)[4]. She is once also spoken of as the beloved (*priyā*) of heaven (1, 46[1]).

The sacrificial fire being regularly kindled at dawn, Agni is naturally often associated with Uṣas in this connexion, sometimes not without a side-glance at the sun, the manifestation of Agni which appears simultaneously with the kindling of the sacrificial fire (1, 124[1. 11] &c.)[5]. Agni appears with or before the Dawn. Uṣas causes Agni to be kindled (1, 113[9]). He is thus like the sun sometimes called her lover (1, 69[1]; 7, 10[1], cp. 10, 3[3]). He goes to meet the shining Uṣas as she comes, asking her for fair riches (3, 61[6]). Uṣas is naturally also often connected with the twin gods of the early morning, the Aśvins (1, 44[2] &c.). They accompany her (1, 183[2]) and she is their friend (4, 52[2. 3]). She is invoked to arouse them (8, 9[17]), and her hymn is said to have awakened them (3, 58[1]). When the Aśvins' car is yoked, the daughter of the sky is born (10, 39[12]). Uṣas is once associated with the moon, which being born ever anew goes before the dawns as harbinger of day (10, 85[19]).

Various gods are described as having produced or discovered the dawns. Indra who is characteristically a winner of light, is said to have generated or lighted up Uṣas (2, 12[7] &c.). But he is sometimes also hostile to her, being described as shattering her wain (§ 22). Soma made the dawns bright at their birth (6, 39[3]) and constituted them the wives of a good husband (6, 44[23]), as Agni does (7, 6[5]). Bṛhaspati discovered the Dawn, the sky (*svar*), and Agni, repelling the darkness with light (10, 68[9]). The ancient Fathers, companions of the gods, by efficacious hymns discovered the hidden light and generated Uṣas (7, 76[4]).

The goddess is often implored to dawn on the worshipper or bring to him wealth and children, to bestow protection and long life (1, 30[22]. 48[1] &c.), to confer renown and glory on all the liberal benefactors of the poet (5, 79[6], cp. 1, 48[4]). Her adorers ask from her riches and desire to be to her as sons to a mother (7, 81[4]). The soul of the dead man goes to the sun and to Uṣas (10, 58[8]), and by the ruddy ones in whose lap the Fathers are said to be seated, the Dawns are doubtless meant (10, 15[7]).

Besides the sixteen enumerated in the Naighaṇṭuka (1, 8) Uṣas has many other epithets. She is resplendent, shining, bright, white, ruddy, golden-hued, of brilliant bounty, born in law, most Indra-like, divine,[1] immortal[2]. She is characteristically bountiful (*maghonī*: ZDMG. 50, 440).

The name of Uṣas is derived from the root *vas* to shine and is radically cognate to Aurora and Ἠώς (p. 8)[7].

[1] GVS. 1, 265—6. — [2] Cp. KUHN, Entwicklungsstufen, 131. — [3] See the passages quoted above, where the rays of dawn are compared with cattle or cows. — [4] OST. 5, 190; cp. above p. 21. — [5] Ibid. 191. — [6] Ibid. 193—4. — [7] SONNE, KZ. 10, 416.
WHITNEY, JAOS. 3, 321—2; OST. 5, 181—98; MM., LSL. 2, 583—4; GKR. 35—6; KRV. 52—4; BRV. 1, 241—50; BRANDES, Uṣas (Copenhagen 1879, pp. 123).

§ 21. Aśvins.—Next to Indra, Agni, and Soma, the twin deities named the **Aśvins** are the most prominent in the RV. judged by the frequency with which they are invoked. They are celebrated in more than fifty entire hymns and in parts of several others, while their name occurs more than 400 times. Though they hold a distinct position among the deities of light and their appellation is Indian, their connexion with any definite phenomenon of light is so obscure, that their original nature has been a puzzle to Vedic interpreters from the earliest times. This obscurity makes it probable that the origin of these gods is to be sought in a pre-Vedic period. They are twins (3, 39^{3}; 10, 17^{2}) and inseparable. The sole purpose of one hymn (2, 39) is to compare them with different twin objects such as eyes, hands, feet, wings, or with animals and birds going in pairs, such as dogs and goats or swans and eagles (cp. 5, 78^{1-3}; 8, 35^{7-9}; 10, 106^{2-10}). There are, however, a few passages which may perhaps point to their originally having been separate. Thus they are spoken of as born separately (*nānā:* 5, 73^{4}) and as born here and there (*iheha*), one being called a victorious prince, and the other the son of heaven (1, 181^{4}). Yāska also quotes a passage stating that 'one is called the son of night, the other the son of dawn' (Nir. 12, 2). The RV., moreover, in another passage (4, 3^{6}) mentions alone 'the encompassing Nāsatya', a frequent epithet otherwise only designating both Aśvins in the dual.

The Aśvins are young (7, 67^{10}), the TS. (7, 2, 7^{2}) even describing them as the youngest of the gods. They are at the same time ancient (7, 62^{5}). They are bright (7, 68^{1}), lords of lustre (8, 22^{14}; 10, 93^{6}), of golden brilliancy (8, 8^{2}), and honey-hued (8, 26^{6}). They possess many forms (1, 117^{9}). They are beautiful (6, 62^{5}. 63^{1}) and wear lotus-garlands (10, 184^{2}; AV. 3, 22^{4}; ŚB. 4, 1, 5^{16}). They are agile (6, 63^{5}), fleet as thought (8, 22^{16}), or as an eagle (5, 78^{4}). They are strong (10, 24^{4}), very mighty (6, 62^{5}), and are several times called 'red'[1] (*rudrā,* 5, 75^{3} &c.). They possess profound wisdom (8, 8^{2}) and occult power (6, 63^{5}; 10, 93^{7}). The two most distinctive and frequent epithets of the Aśvins are *dasra,* 'wondrous', which is almost entirely limited to them, and *nāsatya,* which is generally explained to mean 'not untrue' (*na-asatya*), but other etymologies[2], such as 'the savers' have been proposed. The latter word occurs as the name of a demon in the Avesta[3], which, however, sheds no further light on it. These two epithets in later times became the separate proper names of the Aśvins[4]. The attribute *rudravartani* 'having a red path'[5] is peculiar to them, and they are the only gods called 'golden-pathed' (*hiraṇyavartani*), an epithet otherwise only used (twice) of rivers.[6]

Of all the gods[7] the Aśvins are most closely connected with honey (*madhu*), with which they are mentioned in many passages. They have a skin filled with honey, and the birds which draw them abound in it (4, $45^{3.4}$). They poured out 100 jars of honey (1, 117^{6}). Their honey-goad (1, 122^{3}. 157^{4}) with which they bestrew the sacrifice and the worshipper[8], is peculiar to them. Only the car of the Aśvins is described as honey-hued (*madhuvarṇa*) or 'honey-bearing' (*madhu-vāhana*). They only are said to be fond of honey (*madhūyu, mādhvī*) or drinkers of it (*madhupā*). The priest to whom they are invited to come is called honey-handed (10, 41[3]). They give honey to the bee (1, 112[21] cp. 10, 40[6]) and are compared with bees (10, 106[10]). They are, however, like other gods, fond of Soma (3, 58[7. 9] &c.) and are invited to drink it with Uṣas and Sūrya (8, 35[1]). Hillebrandt (VM. 1, 241), however, finds traces showing that the Aśvins were at first excluded from the circle of the Soma-worshipped gods.

The car of the Aśvins is sun-like (8, 8[2]) or golden (4, 44[4. 5]), and all its parts, such as wheels, axle, fellies, reins are golden (1, 180[1]; 8, 5[29]. 22[5]). It has a thousand rays (1, 119[1]) or ornaments (8, 8[11. 14]). It is peculiar in construction, being threefold, having three wheels, three fellies, and some other parts triple (1, 118[1. 2] &c.). It moves lightly (8, 9[8]), is swifter than thought (1, 117[2] &c.) or than the twinkling of an eye (8, 62[2]). It was fashioned by the Ṛbhus (10, 39[12]). The Aśvins' car is the only one which is three-wheeled. One of its wheels is said to have been lost when the Aśvins came to the wedding of Sūryā (10, 85[15]; cp. § 37).

The Aśvins' name implies only the possession of horses, there being no evidence to show that they are so called because they ride on horses[10]. Their car is drawn by horses (1, 117[2] &c.), more commonly by birds (*vi,* 6, 63[6] &c. or *patatrin,* 10, 143[5]), swans (4, 45[4]), eagles (1, 118[4]), bird steeds (6, 63[7]) or eagle steeds (8, 5[7]). It is sometimes described as drawn by a buffalo (*kakuha*) or buffaloes (5, 73[7]; 1, 184[3] &c.) or by a single ass (*rāsabha:* 1, 34[9]. 116[2]; 8, 74[7]). In the AB. (4, 7—9) the Aśvins are said at the marriage of Soma and Sūryā to have won a race in a car drawn by asses[11] (cp. RV. 1, 116[7] and Sāyaṇa's comm.). Their car touches the ends of heaven and extends over the five countries (7, 63[2. 3]). It moves round heaven (1, 180[10]). It traverses heaven and earth in a single day (3, 58[8]), as the car of the sun (1, 115[3]) and that of Uṣas (4, 51[5]) are also said to do. It goes round the sun in the distance (1, 112[13]). Frequent mention is also made of their course (*vartis*), a word which with one exception is applicable to them only. The word *parijman,* 'going round' is several times connected with the Aśvins or their car, as it is also with Vāta, Agni, and Sūrya.

The locality of the Aśvins is variously described. They come from afar (8, 5[30]), from heaven (8, 8[7]), heaven and earth (1, 44[5]), from heaven and air (8, 8[4]. 9[2]), from air (8, 8[3]), earth, heaven, and ocean (8, 10[1]), from the air, from far and near (5, 73[1]). They abide in the sea of heaven (8, 26[17]), in the floods of heaven, plants, houses, the mountain top (7, 70[3]). They come from behind, before, below, above (7, 72[5]). Sometimes their locality is inquired about as if unknown[12] (5, 74[2. 3]; 6, 63[1]; 8, 62[4]). They are once (8, 8[23]) said to have three places (*padāni*), possibly because invoked three times a day.

The time of their appearance is often said to be the early dawn[13], when 'darkness still stands among the ruddy cows' (10, 61[4]) and they yoke their car to descend to earth and receive the offerings of worshippers (1, 22[2] &c.). Uṣas awakes them (8, 9[17]). They follow after Uṣas in their car (8, 5[2]). At the yoking of their car Uṣas is born (10, 39[12]). Thus their relative time seems to have been between dawn and sunrise. But Savitṛ is once said to set their car in motion before the dawn (1, 34[10]). Occasionally the appearance of the Aśvins[14], the kindling of the sacrificial fire, the break of dawn, and sunrise seem to be spoken of as simultaneous (1, 157[1]; 7, 72[4]). The Aśvins are invoked to come to the offering not only at their natural time, but also in the evening (8, 22[14]) or at morning, noon, and sunset (5, 76[3]). The appearance of the Aśvins at the three daily sacrifices may have been the starting-point of the continual play on the word 'three' in the whole of a hymn devoted to their praise (1, 34). As deities of the morning, the Aśvins dispel darkness (3, 39^{3}) and are sometimes said to chase away evil spirits (7, 73^{4}; 8, 35^{16}). In the AB. (2, 15), the Aśvins as well as Uṣas and Agni are stated to be gods of dawn; and in the Vedic ritual they are connected with sunrise[15]. In the ŚB. (5, 5, 4^{1}) the Aśvins are described as red-white in colour and therefore a red-white goat is offered to them[16].

The Aśvins are children of Heaven (1, 182^{1}. 184^{1}; 10, 61^{4}), one of them alone being once said to be a son of Heaven (1, 184^{4}). They are once (1, 46^{2}) said to have the ocean as their mother (*sindhumātarā*). Otherwise they are in one passage (10, 17^{2}) said to be the twin sons of Vivasvat and Tvaṣṭṛ's daughter Saraṇyū (p. 42), who appear to represent the rising sun and dawn. On the other hand the solar deity Pūṣan claims them as his fathers (10, 85^{14})[17]. By their sister (1, 180^{2}) Dawn seems to be meant (cp. p. 48). They are, as male deities of morning light, often associated with the sun conceived as a female called either Sūryā or more commonly the 'daughter of Sūrya'. They are Sūryā's two husbands (4, 43^{6} cp. 1, 119^{5}), whom she chose (7, 69^{4}). Sūryā (5, 73^{5}) or the maiden (8, 8^{10}) ascended their car. The daughter of the sun mounts their car (1, 34^{5}. 116^{17}. 118^{5}; 6, 63^{5}) or chose it (1, 117^{13}; 4, 43^{2}). They possess Sūryā as their own (7, 68^{3}), and the fact that Sūryā accompanies them on their car is characteristic (8, 29^{8}). She must be meant by the goddess called Aśvinī and mentioned with others in 5, 46^{8}. In a late hymn (10, 85^{9}) it is said that when Savitṛ gave Sūryā to her husband (*patye*) Soma was wooer (*vadhūyu*) while the Aśvins were groomsmen (*varā*). In another passage (6, 58^{4}) the gods are said to have given Pūṣan to Sūryā. Owing to their connexion with Sūryā the Aśvins are invoked to conduct the bride home on their chariot (10, 85^{26}). They are also besought along with several other deities to bestow fertility on the bride (10, 184^{2}). They give the wife of the eunuch a child and make the barren cow yield milk (1, 112^{3}). They give a husband to the old maid (10, 39^{3}) and bestowed a wife on one of their favourites (1, 116^{1} &c.). In the AV. (2, 30^{2} &c.) they are said to bring lovers together[18].

The Aśvins may originally have been conceived as finding and restoring or rescuing the vanished light of the sun[19]. In the RV. they have come to be typically succouring divinities. They are the speediest helpers and deliverers from distress in general (1, 112^{2}. 118^{3}). They are constantly praised for such deeds. In particular, they rescue from the ocean in a ship or ships. They are also invoked to bring treasures from the ocean or from heaven (1, 47^{6}) and their car approaches from the ocean (4, 43^{5}); here, however, the celestial ocean appears to be intended. Their rescue from all kinds of distress is a peaceful manifestation of divine grace, not a deliverance from foes in battle, as is generally the case with Indra (with whom, however, they are once associated in fight, even receiving the epithet of Vṛtra-slayers)[20]. They are thus also characteristically divine physicians (8, 18^{8} &c.), who heal diseases with their remedies (8, 22^{10} &c.), restoring sight (1, 116^{16}), curing the blind, sick, and maimed (10, 39^{3}). They are the physicians of the gods and guardians of immortality, who ward off death from the worshipper (AV. 7, 53^{1}; TB. 3, 1, 2^{11}). Apart from their character as helpers, healers, and wonder-workers, their general beneficence is often praised. They bring their worshipper to old age with seeing eye and reward him with riches and abundance of children (1, 116^{25}; 8, 8^{13} &c.).

Quite a number of legends illustrating the succouring power of the Aśvins are referred to in the RV. The sage Cyavāna, grown old and deserted, they released from his decrepit body; they prolonged his life, restored him to youth, rendered him desirable to his wife and made him the husband of maidens (1, 116[10] &c.: OST. 5, 143). A detailed story of how Cyavāna was restored to youth by the Aśvins is given in the ŚB. (4, 1, 5)[21]. They also renewed the youth of the aged Kali (10, 39[8]) and befriended him when he had taken a wife (1, 112[15]). They brought on a car to the youthful Vimada wives (1, 112[19]) or a wife (1, 116[1]) named Kamadyū (10, 65[12]), who seems to have been the beautiful spouse of Purumitra (1. 117[20]; 10, 39[7]). They restored Viṣṇāpū, like a lost animal, to the sight of their worshipper Viśvaka, son of Kṛṣṇa (1, 116[23]. 117[7]; 10, 65[12]), who according to the commentator was his father. The story most often referred to is that of the rescue of Bhujyu, son of Tugra, who was abandoned in the midst of the ocean (*samudre*) or in the water-cloud (*udameghe*) and who tossed about in darkness invoked the aid of the youthful heroes. In the ocean which is without support they took him home in a hundred-oared ship. They rescued him with animated, water-tight ships, which traversed the air, with four ships, with an animated winged boat, with three flying cars having a hundred feet and six horses, with their headlong flying steeds, with their well-yoked chariot swift as thought. In one passage Bhujyu is described as clinging to a log (*vṛkṣa*) for support in the midst of the waves[22]. The sage Rebha, stabbed, bound, hidden by the malignant, overwhelmed in the waters for ten nights and nine days, abandoned as dead, was by the Aśvins revived and drawn out as Soma is raised with a ladle[23]. They delivered Vandana from calamity and restored him to the light of the sun (1, 112[5]. 116[11]. 117[5]. 118[6]), raising him up from a pit in which he lay hidden away as one dead (10, 39[8]) or restoring him from decrepitude (1, 119[6. 7])[24]. They succoured the sage Atri Saptavadhri who along with his companions was plunged in a burning pit by the wiles of a demon. They brought him a cooling and refreshing draught, protected him from the flames, and finally released him in youthful strength. They are also said to have delivered him from darkness. When Agni is spoken of as having rescued Atri from heat (10, 80[3]), the meaning probably is that Agni spared him through the intervention of the Aśvins[25]. The Aśvins even rescued from the jaws of a wolf a quail which invoked their aid[26].

To Rijrāśva who had been blinded by his father for killing one hundred and one sheep and giving them to a she-wolf to devour, they restored his eyesight at the prayer of the she-wolf (1, 116[16]. 117[17. 18]); and cured Parāvṛj of blindness and lameness (1, 112[8]). When Viśpalā's leg had been cut off in battle like the wing of a bird, the Aśvins gave her an iron one instead[27]. They befriended Ghoṣā when she was growing old in her father's house by giving her a husband (1, 117[7]; 10, 39[3. 6]. 40[5]). To the wife of a eunuch they gave a son called Hiraṇyahasta (1, 116[13]. 117[24]; 6, 62[7]; 10, 39[7]), who is, however, once called Syāva (10, 65[12]). The cow of Sayu, which had left off bearing they caused to give milk (1, 116[22] &c.). They gave to Pedu a swift, strong, white, incomparable, dragon-slaying steed impelled by Indra, which won him unbounded spoils (1, 116[6] &c.). To Kakṣīvat of the family of Pajra they granted blessings in abundance, causing a hundred jars of wine (*surā*) or of honey to flow from a strong horse's hoof, as from a sieve (1, 116[7]. 117[6])[28]. Another miraculous deed of theirs is connected with honey or mead. They placed a horse's head on Dadhyañc, son of Atharvan, who then told them where was the mead (*madhu*) of Tvaṣṭṛ (§ 53)[29]. Besides the persons referred to above, many others are mentioned as having been succoured or befriended by the Aśvins in RV. 1, 112 and 116—19. These may be largely the names of actual persons who were saved or cured in a remarkable manner. Their rescue or cure would easily have been attributed to the Aśvins, who having acquired the character of divine deliverers and healers, naturally attracted to themselves all stories connected with such miraculous powers. The opinion of BERGAIGNE and others that the various miracles attributed to the Aśvins are anthropomorphized forms of solar phenomena (the healing of the blind man thus meaning the release of the sun from darkness), seems to lack probability[30]. At the same time the legend of Atri (cp. § 56) may be a reminiscence of a myth explaining the restoration of the vanished sun.

As to the physical basis of the Aśvins, the language of the Ṛṣis is so vague that they themselves do not seem to have understood what phenomenon these deities represented. The other gods of the morning, the night-dispelling Agni, the man-waking Uṣas, and the rising Sūrya are much more vividly addressed. They may be called possessors of horses, because the latter are symbolical of rays of light, especially the sun's. But what they actually represented puzzled even the oldest commentators mentioned by Yāska. That scholar remarks (Nir. 12, 1) that some regarded them as Heaven and Earth (as does also the ŚB. 4, 1, 5[16]), others, as Day and Night, others, as sun and moon, while the 'legendary writers' took them to be 'two kings, performers of holy acts'.

Yāska's own opinion is obscure.. ROTH thinks he means Indra and the sun, GOLDSTÜCKER, that he means the transition from darkness to light, which represents an inseparable duality corresponding to their twin nature, and agrees with this view. This is also the opinion of MYRIANTHEUS as well as of HOPKINS, who considers it probable that the inseparable twins represent the twin-lights or twilight before dawn, half dark, half light, so that one of them could be spoken of alone as the son of Dyaus, the bright sky. Other scholars[31] favour the identification of the Aśvins with sun and moon. OLDENBERG following MANNHARDT[32] and BOLLENSEN (ZDMG. 41, 496) believes the natural basis of the Aśvins must be the morning star, that being the only morning light beside fire, dawn, and sun. The time, the luminous nature, and the course of the Aśvins round the heavens suit, but not their duality.

The morning star would indeed naturally be thought of in connexion with the evening star, but they are eternally separate, while the Aśvins are joined. The latter are, however, in one or two passages of the RV. spoken of separately; and though the morning in Vedic worship is so important, while sunset plays no part (5, 77[2]), the Aśvins are nevertheless sometimes (8, 22[14]; 10, 39[1]. 40[4]) invoked morning and evening[33]. The Aśvins, sons of Dyaus, who drive across the sky with their steeds and possess a sister, have a parallel in the two famous horsemen of Greek mythology, sons of Zeus (Διὸς κοῦροι)[34], brothers of Helena, and in the two Lettic God's sons who come riding on their steeds to woo the daughter of the sun, either for themselves or the moon. In the Lettic myth the morning star is said to have come to look at the daughter of the sun[35]. As the two Aśvins wed the one Sūryā, so the two Lettic god-sons wed the one daughter of the sun; they too are (like the Διόσκουροι) rescuers from the ocean, delivering the daughter of the sun or the sun himself[36]. If this theory is correct, the character of the Aśvins as rescuers may have been derived from the idea of the morning star being a harbinger of deliverance from the distress of darkness. WEBER is also of opinion that the Aśvins represent two stars, the twin constellation of the Gemini[37]. Finally GELDNER thinks that the Aśvins do not represent any natural phenomenon, but are simply succouring saints (Notheilige) of purely Indian origin[38].

The twilight and the morning star theory seem the most probable. In any case, it appears not unlikely that the Aśvins date from the Indo-European period in character though not in name.

[1] According to PVS. 1, 56—8; variously interpreted by others; cp. BRV. 3, 38 note. — [2] BRUNNHOFER, ('savers' from √nas in Gothic nasyan), Vom Aral bis zur Gangā, p. 99; BRV. 2, 434; HRI. 83. — [3] SP.AP. 207; COLINET, BOR. 3, 193. — [4] KRV. note 172. — [5] PVS. 1, 55. — [6] PVS. 56—7, gives a list of the epithets of the Aśvins. — [7] HVM. 1, 237. — [8] According to OLDENBERG, this refers to morning dew; cp. BRV. 2, 433. — [9] HAUG, GGA. 1875, p. 93. — [10] BOLLENSEN, ZDMG. 41, 496; HRI. 80. — [11] On the car and steeds of the Aśvins cp. HOPKINS, JAOS. 15, 269—71. — [12] PVS. 2, 105. — [13] OST. 5, 238—9; HRI. 82. — [14] BRV. 2, 432. — [15] ORV. 208. — [16] HRI. 83. — [17] Cp. IS. 5, 183. 187; EHNI, ZDMG. 33, 168—70. — [18] WEBER, IS. 5. 218. 227. 234. — [19] v. SCHRÖDER, WZKM. 9, 131; HRI. 83. — [20] OST. 5, 248—9. — [21] OST. 5, 250—3; SBE. XXVI, 273ff; BENFEY, OO. 3, 160; MYRIANTHEUS p. 93 (= sun which has set restored in the morning); HVBP. 112. — [22] References in OST. 5, 244—5; SONNE, KZ. 10, 335—6; BENFEY, OO. 3, 159; MYRIANTHEUS 158; HVBP. 112. — [23] OST. 5, 246; BENFEY, OO. 3, 162. 164; MYRIANTHEUS 174; BAUNACK, ZDMG. 50, 264—6. — [24] BAUNACK, ibid. 263—4. — [25] Ibid. 268; SONNE, KZ. 10, 331 (Atri = sun); OST, 5, 247; cp. v. BRADKE, ZDMG. 45, 482—4. — [26] MM, LSL. 2, 525—6; OST. 5, 248; MYRIANTHEUS 78—81. — [27] OST. 5, 245; MYRIANTHEUS 100—12; PVS. 1, 171—3 (Viśpalā, name of a racing mare). Viśpalā is variously interpreted. — [28] MYRIANTHEUS 149f.; KRV. note 185. — [29] BENFEY, OO. 2, 245; MYRIANTHEUS 142—3; HVBP. 113. — [30] OST. 5, 248; HVBP. 112. — [31] LRV. 3, 334; HVM. 1, 535 (against ZIMMER, Archiv f. slav. Philol. 2, 669 ff.); HVBP. 47—9. — [32] Zft. f. Ethnologie 7, 312f. — [33] BRV. 2, 500. — [34] HRI. 78. 80; JRAS. 27, 953—4. — [35] ORV. 212 n. 3. — [36] v. SCHRÖDER, WZKM. 9, 130—1. — [37] WEBER, IS. 5, 234; Rājasūya 100. — [38] GVS. 2, 31 cp. 1. xxvii.

ROTH, ZDMG, 4, 425; WHITNEY, JAOS. 3, 322; MAX MÜLLER, LSL, 2, 607—9; BENFEY, OO. 2, 245; OST. 5, 234—54: GOLDSTÜCKER, ibid. 255—7; GRV. 1, 150; MYRIANTHEUS, Die Aśvins oder Arischen Dioskuren, München 1876; BRV. 2, 431—510; KRV. 49—52, notes 171. 179. 180; HVBP. 47—49. 111—13; ORV. 209—15; HRI. 80—6.

B. THE ATMOSPHERIC GODS.

§ 22. **Indra.** — Indra is the favourite national god of the Vedic Indians. His importance is indicated by the fact that about 250 hymns celebrate his greatness, more than those devoted to any other god and very nearly one-fourth of the total number of hymns in the RV. If the hymns in parts of which he is praised or in which he is associated with other gods, are taken into account, the aggregate is brought up to at least 300. As the name, which dates from the Indo-Iranian period and is of uncertain meaning, does not designate any phenomenon of nature, the figure of Indra has become very anthropomorphic and much surrounded by mythological imagery, more so indeed than that of any other god in the Veda. The significance of his character is, however, sufficiently clear. He is primarily the thunder-god, the conquest of the demons of drought or darkness and the consequent liberation of the waters or the winning of light forming his mythological essence. Secondarily Indra is the god of battle, who aids the victorious Aryan in the conquest of the aboriginal inhabitants of India.

He is the dominant deity of the middle region. He pervades the air (1, 51^2). He occurs among the gods of the air alone in the Naighaṇṭuka (5, 4), and is the representative of the air in the triad Agni, Indra (or Vāyu), Sūrya.

Many of Indra's physical features are mentioned. He has a body, a head, arms, and hands (2, 16^2; 8, 85^3). His belly is often spoken of in connexion with his powers of drinking Soma (2, 16^2 &c.). It is compared when full of Soma to a lake (3, 36^{8}). His lips (the probable meaning of *śiprā*) are often referred to, the frequent attributes *suśipra* or *śiprin*, 'fair-lipped', being almost peculiar to him. He agitates his jaws after drinking Soma (8, 65^{10}). His beard is violently agitated when he is exhilerated or puts himself in motion (2, 11^{17}; 10, 23^{1}). He is tawny-haired (10, $96^{5.8}$) and tawny-bearded (10, 23^{4}). His whole appearance is tawny, the changes being rung on that word (*hari*) in every verse of an entire hymn (10, 96) with reference to Indra. He is a few times described as golden (1, 7^{2}; 8, 55^{3}), an attribute distinctive of Savitṛ (p. 32), as golden-armed (7, 34^{4}), and as iron-like (1, 56^{3}; 10, $96^{4.8}$). His arms as wielding the thunderbolt are mentioned particularly often. They are long, far-extended, great (6, 19^{3}; 8. 32^{10}. 70^{1}), strong and well-shaped (SV. 2, 1219). Indra assumes the most beautiful forms and the ruddy brightness of the sun (10, 112^{3}) and takes many different forms at will (3, 48^{4}. 53^{8}; 6, 47^{18}).

The thunderbolt (*vajra*)[1] is the weapon exclusively appropriate to Indra. It is the regular mythological name of the lightning stroke (cp. p. 59). It is generally described as fashioned for him by Tvaṣṭṛ (1, 32^{2} &c.), but Kāvya Uśanā is also said to have made it and given it to him (1, 121^{12}; 5, 34^{2}). In the AB. (4, 1) it is the gods who are said to have provided Indra with his bolt. It lies in the ocean enveloped in water (8, 89^{9}). Its place is below that of the sun (10, 27^{21}). It is generally described as *āyasa* or metallic (1, 52^{8} &c.), but sometimes as golden (1, 57^{2} &c.), tawny (3, 44^{4}; 10, 96^{3}) or bright (3, 44^{5}). It is four-angled (4, 22^{2}), hundred-angled (4, 17^{10}), hundred-jointed (8, 6^{6} &c.), and thousand-pointed (1, 80^{12} &c.). It is sharp (7, 18^{18} &c.). Indra whets it like a knife or as a bull his horns[2] (1, 130^{4}. 55^{1}). It is spoken of as a stone (*aśman*) or rock (*parvata*: 7, 104^{19}). The bolt in Indra's hand is compared with the sun in the sky (8, 59^{2}). Epithets derived from or compounded with *vajra*, some of which are very frequent, are almost entirely limited to Indra. *Vajrabhṛt*, 'bearing the bolt', *vajrivat*, 'armed with the bolt', and *vajradakṣiṇa*, 'holding the bolt in his right hand' are applied to him exclusively, while *vajrabāhu* or *-hasta*, 'holding the bolt in his arm or hand', and the commonest derivative *vajrin*, 'armed with the bolt', otherwise occur as attributes of Rudra, the Maruts, and Manyu only once each respectively.

Indra is sometimes said to be armed with a bow and arrows (8, 45^{4}. $66^{6.11}$; 10, $103^{2.3}$). The latter are golden, hundred-pointed, and winged with a thousand feathers (8, $66^{7.11}$). He also carries a hook (*aṅkuśa*) with which he bestows wealth (8, 17^{10}; AV. 6, 82^{3}) or which he uses as a weapon (10, 44^{9}). A net with which he overwhelms all his foes is also attributed to him (AV. 8, 8^{5-8}).

Indra is borne on a car which is golden (6, 29^{2} &c.) and is swifter than thought (10, 112^{2}). The epithet 'car-fighter' (*ratheṣṭhā*) is exclusively appropriated to Indra. His car is drawn by two tawny steeds (*harī*)[3], a term very frequently used and in the great majority of instances referring to Indra's horses. In a few passages a greater number than two, up to a hundred and even a thousand or eleven hundred are mentioned (2, 18^{4-7}; 4. 46^{3}; 6, 47^{18}; 8, $1^{9.24}$). These steeds are sun-eyed (1, $16^{1.2}$). They snort and neigh (1, 30^{16}). They have flowing manes (1, 10^{3} &c.) or golden manes (8, 32^{29}. 82^{24}). Their hair is like peacocks' feathers or tails (3, 45^{1}; 8, 1^{25}). They swiftly traverse vast distances and Indra is transported by them as an eagle is borne by its wings (2, 16^{3}; 8, 34^{9}). They are yoked by prayer (2, 18^{3} &c.), which doubtless means that invocations bring Indra to the sacrifice. Indra is a few times said to be drawn by the horses of Sūrya (10, 49^{7}) or by those of Vāta (10, 22^{4-6}), and Vāyu has Indra for his charioteer (4, 46^{2}. 48^{2}) or his car-companion (7, 91^{6}). Indra's car and his steeds were fashioned by the Ṛbhus (1, 111^{1}; 5, 31^{4}). Indra is once said to be provided with a golden goad (*kaśā*: 8, 33^{11}).

Though the gods in general are fond of Soma (8, 2^{18}. 58^{11}), Indra is preëminently addicted to it (1, 104^{9} &c.). He even stole it in order to drink it (3, 48^{4}; 8, 4^{4}). He is the one Soma-drinker among gods and men (8, 2^{4}), only Vāyu, his companion, coming near him in this respect[4]. It is his favourite nutriment (8, 4^{12}). The frequent epithet 'Soma-drinker' (*soma-pā, -pāvan*) is characteristic of him, being otherwise only applied a few times to Agni and Bṛhaspati when associated with Indra, and once besides to Vāyu alone.

Soma is sometimes said to stimulate Indra to perform great cosmic actions such as supporting earth and sky or spreading out the earth (2, 15^{2}). But it characteristically exhilerates him to carry out his warlike deeds, the slaughter of the dragon or Vṛtra (2, 15^{1}. 19^{2}; 6, $47^{1.2}$) or the conquest of foes (6, 27; 7, 22^{2}; 8, 81^{6}). So essential is Soma to Indra that his mother gave it to him or he drank it on the very day of his birth (3, $48^{2.3}$. $32^{9.10}$; 6, 40^{2}; 7, 98^{3}). For the slaughter of Vṛtra he drank three lakes[5] of Soma (5, 29^{7} cp. 6, 17^{11}), and he is even said to have drunk at a single draught thirty lakes of the beverage (8, 66^{4}). One entire hymn (10, 119) consists of a monologue in which Indra describes his sensations after a draught of Soma. But just as too much Soma is said to produce disease in men, so Indra himself is described as suffering from excessive indulgence in it and having to be cured by the gods with the Sautrāmaṇī ceremony[6]. Indra also drinks milk mixed with honey[7] (8, 4^{8}).

He at the same time eats the flesh of bulls (10, 28^{3}), of one (10, 27^{2}), of twenty (10, 86^{14}), or of a hundred buffaloes (6, 17^{11}; 8, 66^{10}), or 300 buffaloes roasted by Agni (5, 29^{7}). At the sacrifice he also eats an offering of cake (3, $52^{7.8}$), as well as of grain (3, 35^{3}. 43^{4}; 1, 16^{2}), and the latter his steeds are supposed to eat as well (3, 35^{7}. 52^{7}).

Indra is often spoken of as having been born. Two whole hymns (3, 48; 4, 18) deal with the subject of his birth. Once (4, $18^{1.2}$) he is represented as wishing to be born in an unnatural way through the side of his mother[8]. This trait may possibly be derived from the notion of lightning breaking from the side of the storm-cloud. On being born he illuminates the sky (3, 44^{4}). Scarcely born he set the wheel of the sun in motion (1, 130^{9}). He was a warrior as soon as born (3, 51^{8}; 5, 30^{5}; 8, 45^{4}. 66^{1}; 10, 113^{4}) and was irresistible from birth (1, 102^{8}; 10, 133^{2}). Through fear of him when he is born, the firm mountains, heaven and earth are agitated (1, 61^{14}). At his birth heaven and earth trembled through fear of his wrath (4, 17^{2}) and all the gods feared him (5, 30^{5})[9]. His mother is often mentioned (3, $48^{2.3}$ &c.)[10]. She is once (4, 18^{10}) spoken of as a cow (*gṛṣṭi*), he being her calf; and he is spoken (10, 111^{2}) of as a bull, the offspring of a cow (*gārṣṭeya*). He is once (10, 101^{12}) called the son of Niṣṭigrī, whom Sāyaṇa regards as synonymous with Aditi (cp. § 41). According to the AV. (3, $10^{12.13}$) Indra's (and Agni's) mother is Ekāṣṭakā, daughter of Prajāpati. Indra has the same father as Agni (6, 59^{2}), who is the son of Dyaus and Pṛthivī (§ 35). According to one interpretation of a verse in a hymn (4, 17^{4}) in which his father is twice mentioned, the latter is Dyaus. A similar inference may be drawn from a verse in an Indra hymn (10, 120^{1}) where it is said that 'among the worlds that was the highest from which this fierce (god) was born', and from a few other passages (cp. 6, 30^{5}; 8, 36^{4} with 10, 54^{3}, and 10, 138^{5} with 1, 164^{11}). His father is said to have made his thunderbolt (2, 17^{6}), which is elsewhere generally described as fashioned by Tvaṣṭṛ (§ 38). Indra drank Soma in the house of his father, where it was given to him by his mother (3, 48^{2}). He drank Soma in the house of Tvaṣṭṛ (4, 18^{3}), Indra having at his birth overcome Tvaṣṭṛ and having stolen the Soma, drank it in the cups (3, 48^{4}). Indra seizing his father by the foot crushed him, and he is asked in the same verse who made his mother a widow (4, 18^{12}). From these passages it is clearly to be inferred that Indra's father whom he slays in order to obtain the Soma, is Tvaṣṭṛ[11] (cp. 1, 80^{14}). The hostility of the gods, who in one passage (4, 30^{3}) are said to have fought against him, is perhaps connected with the notion of his trying to obtain Soma forcibly.[12].

A few different accounts are given of the origin of Indra. He is said to have been generated by the gods as a destroyer of fiends (3, 49^{1}), but the verb *jan* is here no doubt only used in the figurative sense of 'to constitute' (cp. 2, 13^{5}; 3, 51^{8}). Soma is once spoken of as the generator of Indra and some other gods (9, 96^{5}). In the Puruṣa hymn Indra and Agni are said to have sprung from the mouth of the world-giant (10, 90^{13}). According to the SB. (11, 1, 6^{14}) Indra, as well as Agni, Soma, and Parameṣṭhin, is said to have been created from Prajāpati. The TB. (2, 2, 10^{1}) states that Prajāpati created Indra last of the gods.

Agni is Indra's twin brother (6, 59^{2}) and Pūṣan is also his brother (6, 55^{5}). The sons of Indra's brother are once mentioned (10, 55^{1}), but who are meant by them is uncertain.

Indra's wife is several times referred to (1, 82$^{5.6}$; 3, 53$^{4.6}$; 10, 86$^{9.10}$). Her name is Indrāṇī in a hymn in which she is represented as conversing with Indra (10, 86$^{11.12}$) and occurs in a few other passages which contain enumerations of goddesses (1, 22^{12}; 2, 32^{8}; 5, 46^{8}). The SB. expressly states Indrāṇī to be Indra's wife (14, 2, 1^{8}). The AB. (3, 22^{7}), however, mentions Prāsahā and Senā as Indra's wives[13]. These two are identified with Indrāṇī (TB. 2, 4, 2$^{7.8}$; MS. 3, 8^{4}; 4, 12^{1})[14]. PISCHEL (VS. 2, 52) thinks that Śacī is the Proper name of Indra's wife in the RV. as well as in post-Vedic literature[15]. The AV. (7, 38^{2}) refers to an Asura female who drew Indra down from among the gods; and the Kāṭhaka (IS. 3, 479) states that Indra enamoured of a Dānavī named Vilistengā, went to live among the Asuras, assuming the form of a female among females and of a male among males.

Indra is associated with various other gods. His chief friends and allies are the Maruts, who in innumerable passages are described as assisting him in his warlike exploits (§ 29). His connexion with these deities is so close that the epithet *marutvat*, 'accompanied by the Maruts', though sometimes applied to other gods, is characteristic of Indra, this epithet, as well as *marudgaṇa* 'attended by the Marut host', being sufficient to designate him (5, 42^{6}; 9, 65^{10}). With Agni Indra is more frequently coupled as a dual divinity than with any other god (§ 44)[16]. This is natural, as lightning is a form of fire. Indra is also said to have produced Agni between two stones (2, 12^{3}) or to have found Agni hidden in the waters (10, 32^{6}). Indra is further often coupled with Varuṇa and Vāyu, less frequently with Soma, Bṛhaspati, Pūṣan, and Viṣṇu (§ 44). The latter is a faithful friend of Indra and sometimes attends him in his conflict with the demons (§§ 17. 44)[17].

Indra is in three or four passages more or less distinctly identified with Sūrya[18]. Speaking in the first person (4, 26^{1}) Indra asserts that he was once Manu and Sūrya. He is once directly called Sūrya (10, 89^{2}); and Sūrya and Indra are both invoked in another verse (8, 82^{4}) as if they were the same person. In one passage Indra receives the epithet Savitṛ (2, 30^{1}). The SB. (1, 6, 4^{18}), too, once identifies Indra with the sun, Vṛtra being the moon.

The gigantic size of Indra is dwelt upon in many passages. When Indra grasped the two boundless worlds, they were but a handful to him (3, 30[5]). He surpasses in greatness heaven, earth, and air (3, 46[3]). The two worlds are but equal to the half of him (6, 30[1]; 10, 119[7]). Heaven and earth do not suffice for his girdle (1, 173[6]). If the earth were ten times as large, Indra would be equal to it (1, 52[11]). If Indra had a hundred heavens and a hundred earths, a thousand suns would not equal him nor both worlds (8, 59[5]).

His greatness and power are lauded in the most unstinted terms. He has no parallel among those born or to be born (4, 18[4]). No one, celestial or terrestrial, has been born or shall be born, like to him (7, 32[23]). No one, god or man, either surpasses or equals him (6, 30[4]). Neither former, later, nor recent beings have attained to his valour (5, 42[6]). Neither gods nor men nor waters have attained to the limit of his might (1, 100[15]). No one like him is known among the gods; no one born, past or present, can rival him (1, 165[9]). He surpasses the gods (3, 46[3]). All the gods yield to him in might and strength (8, 51[7]). Even the former gods subordinated their powers to his divine glory and kingly dignity (7, 21[7]). All the gods are unable to frustrate his deeds and counsels (2, 32[4]). Even Varuṇa and Sūrya are subject to his command (1, 101[3] cp. 2, 38[9] p. 16). He is besought to destroy the foes of Mitra, Aryaman, and Varuṇa (10, 89[8. 9]) and is said to have acquired by battle ample space for the gods (7, 98[3]). Indra alone is king of the whole world (3, 46[2]). He is the lord of all that moves and breathes (1, 101[5]). He is the king of things moving and of men (5, 30[5]); he is the eye of all that moves and sees (10, 102[12]). He is the leader of human races and divine (3, 34[2]). He is several times called a universal monarch (4, 19[2] &c.) and still oftener a self-dependent sovereign (3, 46[1] &c.; cp. p. 24). He is also said to rule alone (*eka*) by his might as an ancient seer (8, 6[41]). A few times he receives the epithet *asura* (1, 174[1]; 8, 79[6]). Indra bears several characteristic attributes expressive of power. *Śakra* 'mighty' applies to Indra about 40 times and only about five times to other gods. *Śacīvat*, 'possessed of might' describes Indra some fifteen times and other deities only twice. The epithet *śacīpati* 'lord of might', occurring eleven times in the RV. belongs to Indra with only one exception (7, 67[5]), when the Aśvins as 'lords of might' are besought to strengthen their worshippers with might (*śacībhiḥ*). In one of these passages (10, 24[2]) Indra is pleonastically invoked as 'mighty lord of might' (*śacīpate śacīnām*). This epithet survives in post-Vedic literature as a designation of Indra in the sense of 'husband of Śacī' (a sense claimed for it by Pischel even in the RV.). The very frequent attribute *śatakratu*, 'having a hundred powers', occurring some 60 times in the RV. is with two exceptions entirely limited to Indra. In the great majority of instances *satpati*, 'strong lord' is appropriated to Indra. Indra's strength and valour are also described with various other epithets. He is strong (*tavas*), nimble (*nṛtu*), victorious (*tura*), heroic (*śūra*), of unbounded force (1, 11[4]. 102[6]), of irresistible might (1, 84[2]). He is clothed in might like the elephant and bears weapons like the terrible lion (4, 16[14]). He is also young (1, 11[4] &c.) and unaging (*ajara*), as well as ancient (*pūrvya*).

Having dealt with Indra's personal traits and his character, we now come to the great myth which is the basis of his nature. Exhilerated by Soma and generally escorted by the Maruts he enters upon the fray with the chief demon of drought, most frequently called by the name of Vṛtra, the Obstructor (§ 68) and also very often styled *ahi* the 'Serpent' or 'Dragon' (§ 64). The conflict is terrible. Heaven and earth tremble with fear when Indra strikes Vṛtra with his bolt (1, 80[11]; 2, 11[9. 10]; 6, 17[9]); even Tvaṣṭṛ who forged the bolt trembles at Indra's anger (1, 80[14]). Indra shatters Vṛtra with his bolt (1, 32[5]. 61[10]; 10, 89[7]). He strikes Vṛtra with his bolt on his back (1, 32[7]. 80[5]), strikes his face with his pointed weapon (1, 52[15]), and finds his vulnerable parts (3, 32[4]; 5, 32[5]). He smote Vṛtra who encompassed the waters (6, 20[2] &c.) or the dragon that lay around (*pariśayānam*) the waters (4, 19[2]); he overcame the dragon lying on the waters (5, 30[6]). He slew the dragon hidden in the waters and obstructing the waters and the sky (2, 11[5]), and smote Vṛtra, who enclosed the waters, like a tree with the bolt (2, 14[2]). Thus 'conquering in the waters' (*apsujit*) is his exclusive attribute. Indra being frequently described as slaying Vṛtra in the present or being invoked to do so, is regarded as constantly renewing the combat, which mythically represents the constant renewal of the natural phenomena. For many dawns and autumns Indra has let loose the streams after slaying Vṛtra (4, 19[8]) or he is invoked to do so in the future (8, 78[4]). He cleaves the mountain, making the streams flow or taking the cows (1, 57[6]; 10, 89[7]), even with the sound of his bolt (6, 27[4]). When he laid open the great mountain, he let loose the torrents and slew the Dānava, he set free the pent up springs, the udder of the mountain (5, 32[1.2]). He slew the Dānava, shattered the great mountain, broke open the well, set free the pent up waters (1, 57[6]; 5, 33[1]). He releases the streams which are like imprisoned cows (1, 61[10]) or which, like lowing cows, flow to the ocean (1, 32[2]). He won the cows and Soma and made the seven rivers to flow (1, 32[12]; 2, 12[12]). He releases the imprisoned waters (1, 57[6]. 103[2]), released the streams pent up by the dragon (2, 11[2]), dug out channels for the streams with his bolt (2, 15[3]), let the flood of waters flow in the sea (2, 19[3]), caused the waters pent up by Vṛtra to flow (3, 26[6]; 4, 17[1]). Having slain Vṛtra, he opened the orifice of the waters which had been closed (1, 32[11]). His bolts are dispersed over ninety rivers (1, 80[8]). References to this conflict with Vṛtra and the release of the waters are extremely frequent in the RV. The changes on the myth are rung throughout the whole of one hymn (1, 80). Another deals with the details of the Vṛtra fight (1, 32). That this exploit is Indra's chief characteristic, is shown by the manner in which the poet epitomizes the myth in the two first verses of the latter hymn: 'I will proclaim the heroic deeds of Indra, which the wielder of the bolt first performed: he slew the dragon lying on the mountain, released the waters, pierced the belly of the mountains'. The physical elements are nearly always indicated by the stereotyped figurative terms 'bolt', 'mountain', 'waters or rivers', while lightning, thunder, cloud, rain (*vṛṣṭi, varṣa*, or the verb *vṛṣ*) are seldom directly named (1, 52[5. 6. 14] &c.)[19]. The rivers caused to flow are of course often terrestrial (BRV. 2, 184), but it cannot be doubted that waters and rivers are in the RV. very often conceived as aerial or celestial (1, 10[8]; 2, 20[8]. 22[4] cp. BRV. 2, 187). Apart from a desire to express the Vṛtra myth in phraseology differing from that applied to other gods, the large stores of water (cp. *arṇas*, flood) released by Indra would encourage the use of words like 'streams' rather than 'rain'. The 'cows' released by Indra may in many cases refer to the waters, for we have seen that the latter are occasionally compared with lowing cows. Thus Indra is said to have found the cows for man when he slew the dragon (5, 29[3] cp. 1, 52[8]). The context seems to shew that the waters are meant when Indra is described as having, with his bolt for an ally, extracted the cows with light from darkness (1, 33[10]). But the cows may also in other cases be conceived as connected with Indra's winning of light, for the ruddy beams of dawn issuing from the blackness of night are compared with cattle coming out of their dark stalls (p. 47). Again, though clouds play no great part in the RV.[20] under their literal name (*abhra* &c.) it can hardly be denied that, as containing the waters, they figure mythologically to a considerable extent under the name of cow (*go*: § 61), as well as udder (*ūdhar*), spring (*utsa*), cask (*kavandha*), pail (*kośa*) and others. Thus the rain-clouds are probably meant when it is said that the cows roared at the birth of Indra (8, 59^{1}).

It is however rather as mountains (*parvata, giri*: p. 10) that they appear in the Indra myth. They are the mountains (1, 32^{1}) on which the demons dwell (1, 32^{2}; 2, 12^{11}), or from which he casts them down (1, 130^{7}; 4, 30^{14}; 6, 26^{5}). Indra shoots forth his well-aimed arrow from these mountains (8, 66^{6}). He cleft wide the mountain to release the cows (8, 45^{30}). Or the cloud is a rock (*adri*) which encompasses the cows and which Indra moves from its place (6, 17^{5}). He loosened the rock and made the cows easy to obtain (10, 112^{8}). He released the cows which were fast within the stone (6, 43^{3} cp. 5, 30^{4}). The cloud rocks or mountains would seem to represent the stationary rainless clouds seen during drought, while the cloud cows would rather be the moving and roaring rain-cloud (p. 10). OLDENBERG (ORV. 140 f.) thinks that to the poets of the RV. the mountains as well as the rivers in the Vṛtra-myth are terrestrial, though he admits that they were originally aerial and at a later period also were understood as such.

In the mythical imagery of the thunderstorm the clouds also very frequently become the fortresses (*puraḥ*)[21] of the aerial demons. They are spoken of as ninety, ninety-nine, or a hundred in number (2, 14^{6}. 19^{6}; 8, 17^{14}. 87^{6}). These fortresses are 'moving' (8, 1^{28}), autumnal (1, 130^{7}. 131^{4}. 174^{2}; 6, 20^{10}), made of metal (2, 20^{8}) or stone (4, 30^{20})[22]. Indra shatters them (1, 51^{5} &c.), and so the epithet 'fort-shatterer' (*pūrbhid*) is peculiar to him. In one verse (10, 111^{10}) he is spoken of as a fort-shatterer and lover of waters at the same time. In another the various features of the myth are mentioned together: he slew Vṛtra, broke the castles, made a channel for the rivers, pierced the mountain, and made over the cows to his friends (10, 89^{7}).

Owing to the importance of the Vṛtra-myth the chief and specific epithet of Indra is *Vṛtrahan*, 'Vṛtra-slayer'[23]. It is applied about 70 times to him in the RV. The only other deity who receives it with any frequency is Agni; but this is due to Agni's frequent association with Indra as a dual divinity. The few applications of the epithet to Soma are also clearly secondary (§ 37)[24]. Though Indra is sometimes expressly stated to have slain Vṛtra by his own might alone (1, 165^{8}; 7, 21^{6}; 10, 138^{6}) other deities are very often associated with him in the conflict. The gods in general are said to have placed him in the van for action or battle (1, 55^{3}; 6, 17^{8}) or the slaughter of Vṛtra (8, 12^{22}). They are also said to have increased his vigour for the fray with Vṛtra (10, 113^{8}), or to have infused might or valour into him (1, 80^{15}; 6, 20^{2}; 10, 48^{3}. 120^{3}), or to have placed the bolt in his hands (2, 20^{8}). But most frequently he is urged on and fortified by the Maruts (3, 32^{4}; 10, $73^{1.2}$ &c. § 29). Even when the other gods terrified by Vṛtra fled away (8, 85^{7} cp. 4, 18^{11}; AB. 3, 20), they stood by him; but the Maruts themselves are in one passage said to have deserted him (8, 7^{31}). Agni, Soma, and Viṣṇu are often also allied with Indra in the fight with Vṛtra. Even priests on earth sometimes associate themselves with Indra in his combats (5, 30^{8}; 8, 51^{11}; 10, 44^{9}). The worshipper (*jaritā*) is said to have placed the bolt in Indra's hands (1, 63^{2}), and the sacrifice is spoken of as having assisted the bolt at the slaughter of the dragon (3, 32^{12}). Hymns, prayers, and worship, as well as Soma, are also often described as increasing ($\sqrt{}$*vṛdh*) the vigour of Indra[25].

Besides Vṛtra, Indra engages in conflict with many minor demons also

(§ 69). One of these, Urana, mentioned only once (2, 14^{4}) is described as having 99 arms, while another, Viśvarūpa, is three-headed and six-eyed (10, 99^{6}). He does not always slay them with his bolt. Thus one of them, Arbuda, he crushes with his foot or pierces with ice (1, 51^{6}; 8, 32^{26}). Sometimes Indra is described as destroying demons in general. Thus he is said to sweep away the Asuras with his wheel (8, 85^{9}), to consume the Rakṣases with his bolt as fire a dry forest (6, 18^{10}) and to overcome the *druhaḥ* or malignant spirits (4, 23^{7}. 28^{2}).

With the liberation of the waters is connected the winning of light, sun, and dawn. Indra won light and the divine waters (3, 34^{8}). The god is invoked to slay Vṛtra and win the light (8, 78^{4}). When Indra had slain the dragon Vṛtra with his metallic bolt, releasing the waters for man, he placed the sun visibly in the heavens (1, 51^{4}. 52^{8}). Indra, the dragon-slayer, set in motion the flood of waters to the sea, generated the sun, and found the cows (2, 19^{3}). He gained the sun and the waters after slaying the demons (3, $34^{8.\,9}$). When Indra slew the chief of the dragons and released the waters from the mountain, he generated the sun, the sky and the dawn (1, 32^{4}; 6, 30^{5}). The sun shone forth when Indra blew the dragon from the air (8, 3^{20}). Though the sun is usually the prize of the conflict, it also appears as Indra's weapon, for he burns the demon with the rays of the sun (8, 12^{9}). Without any reference to the Vṛtra fight, Indra is said to find the light (3, 34^{4}; 8, 15^{5}; 10, 43^{4}) in the darkness (1, 108^{8}; 4, 16^{4}). Indra is the generator of the sun (3, 49^{4}). He placed the sun, the brilliant light, in the sky (8, 12^{30}). He made the sun to shine (8, 3^{6}. 87^{2}), and made it mount in the sky (1, 7^{3}). He gained the sun (1, $100^{6.\,18}$; 3, 34^{9}) or found it in the darkness in which it abode (3, 39^{5}) and made a path for it (10, 111^{3}).

Indra produces the dawn as well as the sun (2, 12^{7}. 21^{4}; 3, 31^{15}; 32^{8}. 49^{4}). He has made the dawns and the sun to shine (3, 44^{2}). He has opened the darkness with the dawn and the sun (1, 62^{5}). He steals the dawn with the sun (2, 20^{5}). The cows which are mentioned along with sun and dawn (1, 62^{5}; 2, 12^{7}; 6, 17^{5}) or with the sun alone (1, 7^{3}; 2, 19^{3}; 3, 34^{9}; 6, 17^{3}. 32^{2}; 10, 138^{2}) as found, delivered, or won by Indra, probably do not so much represent the waters[23] or rainclouds, as the morning beams (§ 61) or, according to BERGAIGNE (BRV. 1, 245) and others, the red clouds of dawn. The waters are probably meant by the ruddy watery (*apyā*) cows (9, 108^{6}), but the morning beams or clouds in the following passages. The dawns on seeing Indra went to meet him, when he became the lord of the cows (3, 31^{4}). When he overcame Vṛtra he made visible the cows (*dhenāḥ*) of the nights (3, 34^{3} cp. BRV. 2, 200). Dawn is in some passages spoken of in expressions reminding of the winning of the cows. Thus 'Dawn opens the darkness as cows their stall' (1, 92^{4}). Dawn opens the doors of the firm rock (7, 79^{4}). The cows low towards the dawns (7, 75^{7}). The Aṅgirases burst open the cowstalls of Uṣas on the heights (6, 65^{5}). The dawn is sometimes said to have been produced along with the sun in the same passages in which the conquest of the waters is celebrated (1, $32^{1.\,2.\,4}$; 6, 30^{5}; 10, $138^{1.\,2}$). Thus there appears to be a confusion between the notion of the restoration of the sun after the darkness of the thunderstorm and the recovery of the sun from the darkness of night at dawn. The latter trait is in the Indra myth most probably only an extension of the former.

Indra's activity in the thunderstorm is sometimes more directly expressed. Thus he is said to have created the lightnings of heaven (2, 13^{7}) and to have directed the action of the waters downwards (2, 17^{5}).

With the Vṛtra fight, with the winning of the cows and of the sun, is also connected that of Soma. When Indra drove the dragon from the air, fires, the sun, and Soma, Indra's juice, shone forth (8, 3^{20}). After his victory over the demon, he chose Soma for his drink (3, 36^{8}). After he conquered the demons, Soma became his own property (7, 98^{5}); he became the king of the Soma mead (6, 20^{3}). Indra disclosed the juice pressed with stones and drove out the cows (3, 44^{5}). He won Soma at the same time as the cows (1, 32^{12}). He found in heaven the hidden nectar (6, 44^{23}). He found the honey accumulated in the ruddy cow (*usriyāyām*: 3, 39^{6}). The raw cow goes with ripe milk, in the ruddy cow is accumulated all sweetness, which Indra placed there for enjoyment (3, 30^{14}). Indra places ripe milk in the cows (8, 32^{25}), which are raw (8, 78^{7}) black or red (1, 62^{9}), and for which he opens the gates (6, 17^{6}). These passages seem to have primarily at least a mythological reference to rainclouds, as the context in most cases describes the great cosmical actions of Indra.

Indra is said to have settled the quaking mountains and plains (2, 12^{2}; 10, 44^{8}). In a later text Indra is said to have cut off the wings of the mountains, which originally alighted wherever they pleased and thus made the earth unsteady. The wings became the thunder clouds (MS. 1, 10^{13}). This is a favourite myth in post-Vedic literature. PISCHEL (VS. 1, 174) traces its origin to a verse of the RV. (4, 54^{5}). Indra also fixed the bright realms of the sky (8, 14^{9}). He supported the earth and propped the sky (2, 17^{5} &c.). He holds asunder heaven and earth as two wheels are kept apart by the axle (10, 89^{4}). He stretches out heaven and earth (8, 3^{6}) like a hide (8, 6^{5}). He is the generator of heaven and earth (8, 36^{4} cp. 6, 47^{4}). He generated that which is and shall be by his great secret name (10, 55^{2}) and made the non-existent into the existent in a moment (6, 24^{5}). The separation and supporting of heaven and earth are sometimes described as the result of Indra's victory over a demon (5, 29^{4}), who held them together (8, 6^{17}). When he was born for the Vṛtra fight, Indra spread out the earth and fixed the sky (8, 78^{5}). The dragon-slayer made earth visible to heaven, when he opened a path for the streams (2, 13^{5}). Similarly he is said to have found heaven and earth which were hidden (8, 85^{10}) or to have won them along with light and waters (3, 34^{8}). Possibly the effect of light extending the range of vision and seeming to separate heaven and earth apparently pressed together by darkness, may have been the starting point of such conceptions.

Indra, the wielder of the thunderbolt, who destroys the aerial demons in battle, is constantly invoked by warriors (4, 24^{3} &c.). As the great god of battle he is more frequently called upon than any other deity as the helper of the Aryans in their conflicts with earthly enemies. He protects the Aryan colour and subjects the black skin (3, 34^{9}; 1, 130^{8}). He dispersed 50000 of the black race and rent their citadels (4, 16^{13}). He subjected the Dasyus to the Aryan (6, 18^{3}) and gave land to the Aryan (4, 26^{2}). He turns away from the Ārya the weapon of the Dasyu in the land of the seven rivers (8, 24^{27}). Other deities are only occasionally referred to as protectors of the Āryas, as the Aśvins (1, 117^{21}), Agni (8, 92^{1}), or the gods in general (6, 21^{11}).

More generally Indra is spoken of as the one compassionate helper (1, 84^{19}; 8, 55^{13}. 69^{1}), as the deliverer and advocate of his worshippers (8, 85^{20}), as their strength (7, 31^{5}), and as a wall of defence (8, 69^{7}). His friend is never slain or conquered (10, 152^{1}). Indra is very often called the friend of his worshippers[27], sometimes even a brother (3, 53^{5}), a father (4, 17^{17}; 10, 48^{1}) or a father and mother in one (8, 87^{11}). He was also the friend of the fathers in the olden time (6, 21^{8} cp. 7, 33^{1}), and the epithet Kauśika which he once receives (1, 10^{11}), implies that he particularly favoured the family of the Kuśikas[28]. Indra does not desire the friendship of him who offers no libations (10, 42^{4}). But he bestows goods and wealth on the pious man (2, 19^{4}. 22^{3}; 7, 27^{3}), and is implored not to be diverted by other worshippers (2, 18^{3} &c.)[29]. All men share his benefits (8, 54^{7}). Both his hands are full of riches (7, 37^{5}). He is a treasury filled with wealth (10, 42^{2}). He can shower satisfying wealth on his worshippers as a man with a hook shakes down ripe fruit from a tree (3, 45^{4}). Gods and mortals can no more stop him wishing to give than a terrific bull (8, 70^{3}). He is an ocean of riches (1, 51^{1}), and all the paths of wealth lead to him as the rivers to the sea (6, 19^{5}). One entire hymn in particular (10, 47) dwells on the manifold wealth which Indra bestows. Cows and horses are the goods which Indra, like other gods, is most often asked to bestow (1, 16^{9}. 101^{4} &c.), and it is chiefly to him that the epithet *gopati*, 'lord of cows' is applied. His combats are frequently called *gaviṣṭi*, literally 'desire of cows' (8, 24^{5} &c.) and his gifts are considered the result of victories (4, 17$^{10.11}$ &c.: cp. BRV. 2, 178). Indra also bestows wives (4, 17^{16}) and male children (1, 53^{5} &c.). His liberality is so characteristic that the very frequent attribute ***maghavan***, 'bountiful' is almost entirely monopolized by him in the RV. (cp. p. 48) and in post-Vedic literature remains his exclusive epithet. The epithet ***vasupati***, 'lord of wealth', is also predominantly applicable to Indra.

Though the main myth concerning Indra is his combat with Vṛtra, various other stories attached themselves to him as the performer of heroic deeds. Some passages describe Indra as coming into conflict with Uṣas. He struck down the wain (*anas*) of Dawn (10, 73^{6}). He shattered the wain of Uṣas with his bolt and rent her slow (steeds) with his swift (mares: 2, 15^{6}). Terrified at the bolt of Indra, Uṣas abandoned her wain (10, 138^{5}). Indra performed the heroic manly exploit of striking and crushing the female meditating evil, Uṣas, the daughter of the sky; her wain lay shattered in the river Vipāś and Uṣas fled away in terror (4, 30$^{8-11}$). The obscuration of the dawn by a thunderstorm is usually regarded as the basis of this myth. Against such an interpretation BERGAIGNE urges that it is not Indra who obscures the sky but a demon, and that the application of the bolt, Indra's characteristic weapon, need not be restricted to the Vṛtra-fight. He concludes that the sunrise overcoming the delaying dawn (cp. 2, 15^{6}; 5, 79^{9}) is here conceived as a victory of Indra bringing the sun[30].

Indra comes in conflict with the sun in the obscure myth about a race run between the swift steed Etaśa, who draws a car, and the sun drawn by his yellow steeds. The sun being ahead is hindered by Indra. His car loses a wheel, a loss which in some way seems to have been caused by Indra (§ 60D). With this myth is probably connected the statement that Indra stopped the tawny steeds of the sun (10, 92^{8}). Indra is also associated with the myth of the rape of Soma. For it is to him that the eagle brings the draught of immortality (§ 37). Another myth which is not often mentioned and the details of which chiefly occur in a single hymn (10, 108) is that of the capture by Indra of the cows of the Paṇis (§ 67). These demons, who here seem to be the mythical representatives of the niggards who withhold cows from the pious sacrificer, possess herds of cows which they keep hidden in a cave far away beyond the Rasā, a mythical river. Saramā, Indra's messenger, tracks the cows and asks for them in Indra's name, but is mocked by the Paṇis. In another passage (6, 39^{2}) Indra desiring the cows around the rock is said to have pierced Vala's unbroken ridge and to have overcome the Paṇis. Elsewhere the cows are spoken of as confined by the demon

Vala without reference to the Paṇis, and driven out by Indra (2, 12[3]; 3, 30[10]). In various passages the Aṅgirases are associated with Indra in piercing Vala, shattering his strongholds, and releasing the cows (§ 54).

Fragmentary references, often in enumerations, are frequently made to the victory of Indra over Dāsas or Dasyus. These are primarily human foes whose skin is black (1, 130[8] cp. 2, 20[7]), who are noseless (5, 29[10]), are godless and do not sacrifice. Though mythological elements are no doubt largely mingled in the account of his victory over individual Dāsas, the foundation of these myths seems to be terrestrial and human. For while Vṛtra is slain for the good of man in general, individual human beings are mentioned for whom or with whom Indra overcame the Dāsa or Dāsas. These *protégés* of Indra are not as a rule ancestors of priests but are princes or warriors who seem to have been historical. Thus Divodāsa Atithigva[31] is the father of the famous king Sudās, his Dāsa foe being Śambara, the son of Kulitara (§ 69 B). But when the term *dāsa* is applied to the dragon (*ahi*), from whom Indra wrests the waters (2, 11[2]) or to the three-headed six-eyed monster whom Trita combats (10, 99[6]) or to Vyaṃsa who struck off Indra's jaws (4, 18[9]), it unmistakably designates regular demons. An account of Namuci and other Dāsas vanquished by Indra will be found in the chapter on demons.

A myth which seems to have no general significance but to be simply the invention of a later poet of the RV., is that of Indra and Vṛṣākapi, the details of which are given somewhat obscurely in RV. 10, 86. This hymn describes a dispute between Indra and his wife Indrāṇī about the monkey Vṛṣākapi, who is the favourite of the former and has damaged the property of the latter. Vṛṣākapi is soundly threshed and escapes, but afterwards returns, when a reconciliation takes place. v. Bradke considers the story a satire, in which under the names of Indra and Indrāṇī a certain prince and his wife are intended[32].

Among stories preserving historical traits is that of Indra having safely brought Turvaśa and Yadu across the rivers (1, 174[9] &c.). They are the eponymous heroes of two closely connected Aryan tribes, which are, however, sometimes mentioned by the poets in a hostile sense. This varying attitude is a tolerably sure indication of historical matter. Here the national warrior god appears as the patron of Aryan migrations. In another passage Indra is said with Suśravas to have crushed twenty chiefs and their 60099 warriors with fatal chariot wheel. The accounts of the conflicts of king Sudās have all the appearence of a historical character. Thus Indra is said to have helped him in the battle of the ten kings (7, 33[3]), to have aided him in answer to the prayers of his priests the Tṛtsus (among whom Vasiṣṭha is prominent), and to have drowned his foes in the river Paruṣṇī (7, 18[9. 13]).

Finally, a hymn of the RV. (8, 80) relates how a maiden named Apālā having found Soma beside a river and having pressed it with her teeth, dedicates it to Indra who approaches and from whom she receives as a reward the fulfilment of certain desires[33].

Regarded as a whole the attributes of Indra are chiefly those of physical superiority and of dominion over the physical world. Energetic action is characteristic of him, while passive sway is distinctive of Varuṇa. Indra is a universal monarch, not as the applier of the eternal laws of the universe nor as a moral ruler, but as an irresistible warrior whose mighty arm wins victory, whose inexhaustible liberality bestows the highest goods on mankind, and who delighting in the exhileration of magnificent Soma sacrifices, confers rich rewards on the hosts of priests officiating in his worship. The numerous hymns which celebrate him dwell on these features in more or less stereotyped terms and are seldom free from references to the Soma offering. He is not usually described as possessing the moral elevation and grandeur of Varuṇa. There are, however, several passages which ascribe to Indra actions characteristic of Varuṇa[34]. There are also a few, mostly in the later books, in which an ethical character is attributed to him and faith in him is confessed or enjoined (1, 55[5] &c.), faith in the reality of his existence being sometimes expressed as against the disbelief of sceptics (2, 12[5] &c.)[35]. Once he is said in a late passage of the RV. to have attained heaven by austere fervour (10, 167[1] cp. 159[4]).

To the more intense anthropomorphism of Indra's nature are doubtless due certain sensual and immoral traits which are at variance with the moral perfection elsewhere attributed to him and essential to the character of the Vedic gods. This incongruity cannot be accounted for by different passages representing chronologically different stages in the development of his character, for it is apparent in the words of the same poet, sometimes even in the same verse. It is chiefly connected with his excessive fondness for Soma. In one passage (8, 67[5. 6]) he is said to hear and see everything, viewing the zeal of mortals, and in the next verse his belly is described as full of the vigorous draught. One entire hymn (10, 119) consists of a monologue in which Indra is intoxicated with Soma, boasting of his greatness and capricious power. It is even indicated that he once suffered from the effects of excessive drinking (§ 69). His love of Soma is even represented as having driven him to parricide (4, 18[12]). In judging morally of Indra's immoderate indulgence in Soma, it must be borne in mind that the exhilaration of Soma partook of a religious character in the eyes of the Vedic poets and that the intoxicating influence of Soma itself led to its being regarded as the drink of immortality. It is probably from the latter point of view that Indra is conceived as having performed his grandest cosmical feats, such as fixing heaven and earth, under the influence of Soma (2, 15[2]). And the evident sympathy of the poets with the effect of Soma on the god but reflects the moral standard to the age. Amorous adventures, on the other hand, are entirely absent from the exploits of Indra in the RV. and there is hardly a trace of such even in the Brāhmaṇas, except that he is spoken of as the paramour of Ahalyā the wife of Gautama[36]. It is only natural that the poetry of the Soma offering should have dwelt on the thirsty aspect of his nature.

It has been maintained by ROTH[37] followed by WHITNEY (JAOS. 3, 327) that the preeminence of Varuṇa as belonging to an older order of gods was in the course of the Rigvedic period transferred to Indra. This view is based partly on the fact that not a single entire hymn in the tenth book is addressed to Varuṇa, while Indra is celebrated in forty-five. There are, however, two hymns (126, 185) of book X, in which Varuṇa is lauded with two other Ādityas, and in many single verses of that book Varuṇa is invoked or referred to along with other deities. The argument from the number of hymns is not very cogent, as in all the earlier books of the RV. far more hymns are addressed to Indra than to Varuṇa. In book III no hymn is devoted to Varuṇa but 22 to Indra, and in book II there is only one to Varuṇa and 23 to Indra. Moreover, these two books added together are considerably shorter than the tenth alone. It is, however, true that Varuṇa is much less frequently mentioned in the last book than in the earlier books of the RV. Beyond this fact there seems to be no direct and decisive proof of the supersession of Varuṇa by Indra during the composition of the RV. One hymn (4, 42) of the earlier part, describing in the form of a dialogue the rivalry between Indra and Varuṇa has, however, been regarded (GKR. 27) as characteristically indicating a transition from an older period in the relative importance of the two gods. The conclusion is perhaps hardly justified by the statements of another (cp. GRV. 2, 401) of the last book (10, 124)[38]. At the same time it must be remembered that on the one hand Varuṇa seems to have occupied a more important position than Indra in the Indo-Iranian period, while on the other, Indra in the Brāhmaṇas (AB. 8, 12) and in the epics has become chief of the Indian heaven and even maintains this position under the Purāṇic triad Brahmā-Viṣṇu-Śiva, though of course subordinate to them[39]. Varuṇa meanwhile had become divested of his supreme powers by the time of the AV. (p. 26). Thus there must have been at least a gradually increasing popularity of Indra even in the Rigvedic age. By Benfey (OO. 1, 48) and Bréal (Hercule et Cacus 101) Indra in the Vedas is considered rather to have superseded the ancient Dyaus. This may perhaps with greater probability be maintained with regard to the Indo-Iranian Trita Āptya. For Trita though rarely mentioned in the RV. is there described as performing the same exploits as Indra, occasionally appearing even as the more important personage in the myth (§ 23).

The name of Indra occurs only twice in the Avesta[40]. Beyond the fact of his being no god, but only a demon, his character there is uncertain[41]. Indra's distinctive Vedic epithet *vṛtrahan* also occurs in the Avesta in the form of *verethraghna*, which is, however, unconnected with Indra or the thunderstorm myth, designating merely the God of Victory[42]. Thus it is probable that the Indo-Iranian period possessed a god approaching to the Vedic form of the Vṛtra-slaying Indra. It is even possible that beside the thundering god of heaven, the Indo-European period may have known as a distinct conception a thundergod gigantic in size, a mighty eater and drinker, who slays the dragon with his lightning bolt[43]. The etymology[44] of Indra is doubtful, but that the root is connected with that in *indu*, drop, seems likely.

[1] ZDMG. 32, 296—7; WZKM. 9, 232. — [2] HVM. 1, 44, note. — [3] ZDMG. 1, 67. — [4] HVM. 1, 119. — [5] Roth on Nir. 5, 11; KHF. 138—9. — [6] SB. 5, 5, 4[9]; 12, 7, 1[11]; TS. 2, 3, 2, cp. HVM. 1, 266; Zimmer, AIL. 275. — [7] HVM. 238. — [8] PVS. 2, 242—53; Lang, Myth, Ritual and Religion 1, 183; 2, 113 f. 244. — [9] PVS. 2, 249. — [10] Ibid. 2, 51—4; Macdonell, JRAS. 27, 183. — [11] BRV. 3, 58—62; PVS. 1, 44. — [12] Ibid. 1, 211. — [13] Cp. ibid. 2, 38, note 1. — [14] Bloomfield, ZDMG. 48, 549—51. — [15] Ibid. 548. — [16] Macdonell, JRAS. 25, 470—1; 27, 175. — [17] Ibid. 27, 175. — [18] HRI. 92. — [19] Other passages 1, 80[4. 14]; 2, 13[4]; 4, 26[2]; 8, 3[19. 20]. 6[1]; 10, 92[8]. 124[9]; AV. 13, 4[41]. — [20] HVM. 1, 313. — [21] Zimmer, AIL 42. — [22] Also Kāṭhaka IS. 12, 161; JRAS. 27, 181. — [23] ZDMG. 8, 460. — [24] Macdonell, JRAS. 25, 472. — [25] OST. 5, 91—2. — [26] Aufrecht, ZDMG. 13, 497; BRV. 1, 259; KRV. 42 (raincloud). — [27] OST. 5, 104—5. — [28] OST. 5, 348—9. [29] OST. 5, 106—7. — [30] BRV. 2, 193; cp. Sonne, KZ. 10, 416—7; MM. Chips 2, 91 f.; ORV. 169; HRI. 77, note. — [31] BRV. 2, 209; HVM. 1, 96. 107. — [32] ZDMG. 46, 465 cp. ORV. 172—4. — [33] Aufrecht, IS. 4, 1—8; Oldenberg, ZDMG. 39, 76—7. — [34] BRV. 3, 143. — [35] OST. 5, 103—4. — [36] Weber, Sitzungsberichte der Berliner Akad. 1887, p. 903. — [37] ZDMG. 6, 73; PW.; cp. BRI. 27. — [38] ORV. 95—7; OST. 5, 121—6. — [39] ZDMG. 6, 77; 25, 31. — [40] Spiegel, Av. Tr. III, lxxxi; Sp.AP. 195; OST. 5, 121, note 212. — [41] Darmesteter, SBE. IV[2], lxxii; Hillebrandt, ZDMG. 48, 422. — [42] Sp.AP. 195. — [43] ORV. 34, note 1; 134; v. Schröder, WZKM. 9, 230. — [44] YN. 10, 8; Sāyaṇa on RV. 1, 34; Benfey, OO. 1, 49; Roth, PW.; MM., LSL. (1891) 2, 543, note; OGR. 218; AR. 396; OST. 5, 119, note. 208; GW.; BB. 1, 342; BRV. 2, 166; Bollensen, ZDMG. 41, 505—7; Jacobi, KZ. 31, 316; IF. 3, 235.

KHF. 8; Roth, ZDMG. 1, 72; Whitney, JAOS. 3, 319—21; Delbrück, ZVP. 1865, 277—9; OST. 5, 77—139; 4, 99—108; LRV. 3, 317; KRV. 40—7; BRI. 12—3; BRV. 2, 159—96; Perry, Indra in the Rigveda, JAOS. 11, 117—208; Hillebrandt, Literaturblatt f. Or. Philol. 1884—5, p. 108; Die Sonnwendfeste in Altindien (1889), 16; Sp. AP. 194—7; HVBP. 60—80; ORV. 134—75; ZDMG. 49, 174—5; HRI. 91—6; v. Schröder, WZKM. 9, 230—4.

§ 23. **Trita Āptya.** — Trita Āptya is not celebrated in any entire hymn of the RV. but is only incidentally mentioned there in forty passages occurring in twenty-nine hymns. The epithet Āptya accompanies or alternates with Trita seven times in four hymns of the RV. (1, 109; 5, 41; 8, 47; 10, 8). He is oftenest mentioned or associated with Indra; he is seven times connected or identified with Agni, is several times spoken of with the Maruts, and ten times with Soma either as the beverage or the deity. Trita is mentioned alone as having rent Vṛtra by the power of the Soma draught (1, 187^{1}).

The Maruts aided Trita and Indra in the victory over Vṛtra (8, 7^{24}). Such action must have been regarded as characteristic of Trita, for it is mentioned as an illustration. When Indra in the Vṛtra fight strove against the withholder of rain, he cleft him as Trita cleaves the fences of Vala (1, $52^{4.5}$). So again the man who is aided by Indra-Agni, pierces rich strongholds like Trita (5, 86^{1}). Trita Āptya knowing his paternal weapons and urged by Indra fought against and slew the three-headed son of Tvaṣṭṛ and released the cows (10, 8^{8}). In the following stanza Indra performs exactly the same feat; for he strikes off the three heads of Viśvarūpa the son of Tvaṣṭṛ and takes possession of the cows. Indra (or perhaps Agni) subdued the loudly roaring three-headed six-eyed demon and Trita strengthened by his might slew the boar (i. e. the demon, cp. 1, 121^{11}) with iron-pointed bolt (10,99^{6}). Here the feat performed by the two gods is again identical. Indra produced cows for Trita from the dragon (10, 48^{2}). Indra delivered over Viśvarūpa the son of Tvaṣṭṛ to Trita (2, 11^{19}). Indra strengthened by the Soma-pressing Trita, cast down Arbuda and with the Aṅgirases rent Vala (2, 11^{20}). When the mighty Maruts go forth and the lightnings flash, Trita thunders and the waters roar (5, 54^{2}). In two obscure passages of a Marut hymn (2, 34) the bright path of the Maruts is said to shine forth when Trita appears (v. 10) and Trita seems to be conceived as bringing the Maruts on his car (v. 14). In an Agni hymn the winds are said to have found Trita, instructing him to help them (10, 115^{4}). The flames of Agni rise when Trita in the sky blows upon him like a smelter and sharpens him as in a smelting furnace (5,9^{5}). Trita eagerly seeking him (Agni) found him on the head of the cow; he when born in houses becomes as a youth the centre of brightness, establishing himself in dwellings. Trita enveloped (in flames) seated himself within his place (10,$46^{3.6}$). Trita is spoken of as in heaven (5,9^{5}). His abode is secret (9, 102^{2}). It is remote; for the Ādityas and Uṣas are prayed to remove ill deeds and evil dreams to Trita Āptya (8, 47^{13-7}). It seems to be in the region of the sun. For the poet says: 'Where those seven rays are, there my origin is extended; Trita Āptya knows that; he speaks for kinship': which seems to mean that he claims kinship with it (1, 105^{9}). In the same hymn (v. 17) Trita is described as buried in a well (*kūpe*) and praying to the gods for help; Bṛhaspati heard him and released him from his distress. In another passage (10, 8^{7}) Trita within a pit (*vavre*) prays to his father and goes forth claiming his paternal weapons; and in the next stanza (10, 8^{8}) he fights with Viśvarūpa. Indra is said to drink Soma beside Viṣṇu, Trita Āptya, or the Maruts (8, 12^{16}) and to delight in a hymn of praise beside Trita (Vāl. 4^{1}). In the ninth book, doubtless owing to its peculiar character, Trita appears in the special capacity of a preparer of Soma, a feature alluded to only once in the rest of the RV. (2, 11^{20}). Soma is purified by Trita (9, 34^{4}). Trita's maidens (the fingers) urge the tawny drop with stones for Indra to drink (9, 32^{2}. 38^{2}). Soma occupies the secret place near the two pressing stones of Trita (9, 102^{2}) and is besought to bring wealth in a stream on the ridges (*pṛṣṭheṣu*) of Trita (9, 102[3]). Soma caused the sun along with the sisters to shine on the summit (*sānu*) of Trita (9, 37[4]). They press out the stalk, the bull that dwells on the mountains, who, like a buffalo, is purified on the summit; hymns accompany him as he roars; Trita cherishes (him who is like) Varuṇa in the ocean (9, 95[4]). When Soma pours the mead, he calls up the name of Trita (9, 86[20]).

There are several passages from which little or nothing can be gathered as to Trita's original nature. Thus his name occurs in some enumerations which furnish no information (2, 31[6]; 5, 41[4]; 10, 64[3]). In two other verses (5, 41[9. 10]) the interpretation is uncertain, as the text seems to be corrupt. In one passage in the middle of a Varuṇa hymn Trita is described as one in whom all wisdom is centred, as the nave in the wheel (8, 41[6]). In another passage Trita is said to have harnessed a celestial steed fashioned from the sun and given by Yama, this steed being in the following stanza said to be identical with Yama, the Sun, and with Trita 'by secret operation' (1, 163[2. 3]). The half dozen passages of the AV.[1] which mention Trita, add no definite information about him. They suggest only the idea of a remote god, to whom guilt or dream is transferred (1, 113[1. 3]; 19, 56[4]). The TS. (1, 8, 10[2]) describes Trita as a bestower of long life. This is no doubt a secondary trait[2] accruing to Trita as the preparer of Soma, the draught of immortality. The Brāhmaṇas speak of Trita as one of three deities, the other two being Ekata and Dvita, sons of Agni and born from the waters (ŚB. 1, 2, 3[1. 2]; TB. 3, 2, 8[10. 11]). Sāyaṇa on RV. 1, 105 quotes a story of the Śāṭyāyanins, in which the same three brothers are Ṛṣis, Trita being cast into a well by the other two. It is clear that here the three names have a numerical sense. Dvita already occurs in the RV., once along with Trita (8, 47[16]) and once alone in an Agni hymn (5, 18[2]) and apparently identified with Agni. The name of Trita is not mentioned in the list of deities in the Naighaṇṭuka. Yāska (Nir. 4, 6) explains the word to mean 'very proficient in wisdom' (deriving it from √*tṛ*), or as a numeral referring to the three brothers Ekata, Dvita, Trita. In another passage (Nir. 9, 25) he explains Trita as 'Indra in three abodes' (i. e. heaven, earth, air).

In examining the evidence of the RV. we find that Indra and Trita in three or four passages perform the same feat, that of slaying a demon. Trita in one is impelled by Indra, while in another Indra is inspired by Trita; and twice Indra is said to have acted for Trita. Further, Trita is associated with the Maruts in the thunderstorm. Moreover, he finds Agni, kindles Agni in heaven, and takes up his abode in human dwellings, clearly as a form of Agni. His abode is remote and hidden, and Soma is there. In the ninth book Trita as the preparer of Soma diverges more from Indra, who is only a drinker of Soma. Corresponding to Trita in the Avesta we find Thrita, who is a man (as Trita becomes in the Indian Epic). He is once (Yasna 9, 10) described as the third man who prepared Haoma (= Soma) for the corporeal world (Āthwya = Āptya being the second) and once (Vend. 20, 2) as the first healer who received from Ahura Mazda ten thousand healing plants which grow round the white Haoma, the tree of immortality. Thrita is also called the son of Sāyuzhdri in two passages (Yasht 5, 72; 13, 113) in one of which he is said to have dwelt in Apām napāṭ (as a locality on earth)[3]. This shows that Trita was connected with Soma as early as the Indo-Iranian period. The other side of Trita's activity, the slaughter of the three-headed six-eyed demon or dragon we find in the Avesta transferred to a cognate personage, Thraetaona, who slays the fiendish serpent (*Azi dahāka*), the three-mouthed, three-headed, six-eyed demon. It is noteworthy that Thraetaona in his expedition against Dahāka is accompanied by two brothers who seek to slay him on the way[4]. The word *tritá* phonetically corresponds to the Greek τρίτος[5], the third. That it was felt to have the meaning of 'the third', is shown by the occurrence beside it of Dvita in the RV. and by the invention of Ekata beside these two in the Brāhmaṇas. The collocation of *trīṇi*, three, with Trita (RV. 9, 102^{3}; AV. 5, 1^{1}) points in the same direction. Finally, it is highly probable that in one passage of the RV. (6, 44^{23})[6] the word *trita* in the plural means 'third'.

Trita's regular epithet Āptya seems to be derived from *āp*, water, and hence to be practically equivalent in sense to Apāṃ napāt[7]. Sāyaṇa (on RV. 8, 47^{15}) explains it as 'son (*putra*) of waters'. Another epithet of Trita, *vaibhūvasa*, which is formed like a patronymic and only occurs once (10, 46^{3}) may be connected with Soma[8].

The above evidence may perhaps justify the conclusion that Trita was a god of lightning, the third or aerial form of fire, originally the middle member of the triad Agni, Vāyu or Indra, Sūrya. By a process of natural selection Indra seems to have ousted this god originally almost identical in character with himself, with the result that Trita occupies but an obscure position even in the RV. If this interpretation be correct, Trita's original connexion with Soma would signify the bringing of Soma from heaven by lightning (as in the Soma-eagle myth: § 37). The paucity of the evidence has led to many divergent views[9]. Only some of these need be mentioned here. ROTH (ZDMG. 2, 224) considered Trita a water and wind god. HILLEBRANDT[10] regards him as a deity of the bright sky. PERRY believes him to be a god of the storm, older than Indra[11]. PISCHEL who formerly (PVS. 1, 186) thought him to be 'a god of the sea and of the waters' has recently (GGA. 1894, p. 428) expressed the opinion that Trita was originally a human healer who was later deified. HARDY thinks Trita is a moon god[12].

1 See WHITNEY's AV. Index verborum, s. v. Tṛta. — 2 Otherwise PISCHEL, GGA. 1894, p. 427. — 3 SP. AP. 193. — 4 SP. AP. 271. — 5 BRUGMANN, Grundriss 2, 229; according to FICK, Vergleichendes Wörterbuch 14, 63. 229, Trita originally meant sea. — 6 ORV. 183, n.; cp. POTT, KZ. 4, 441. — 7 Cp. JOHANSSON, IF. 4, 136. 143. — 8 JRAS. 25, 450. — 9 Stated up to date in JRAS. 25, 4, 19—23. — 10 Varuṇa und Mitra 94—5. — 11 JAOS. 11, 142—5. — 12 HVBP. 35—8.

MACDONELL, The god Trita; JRAS. 25, 419—96. To the authorities here quoted may be added: LRV. 3, 355—7; KRV. 33, note 112 d; BRI. 11; BDA. 82, n. 3; SP. AP. 262—71; BLOOMFIELD, AJP. 11, 341; PAOS. 1894, cxix—cxxiii; LUDWIG, Ṛgveda-Forschung 117—9; FAY, PAOS. 1894, clxxiv; AJP. 17, 13; ORV. 143; SBE. 46, 406; HRI. 104; OERTEL, JAOS. 18, 18—20.

§ 24. **Apāṃ napāt.** — The deity called Apāṃ napāt is celebrated in one whole hymn (2, 35), is invoked in two verses of a hymn to the waters (10, $30^{3.4}$), and is mentioned by name nearly thirty times altogether in the RV. The waters stood around the brilliant Son of waters; the youthful waters go around him the youthful; three divine females desire to give food to him the divine; he sucks the milk of the first mothers (2, 35^{3-5}). He, the bull, engendered the embryo in them; he the child, sucks and they kiss him (v. ^{13}); the Son of waters growing strong within the waters, shines forth (v. ^{7}). He shines without fuel in the waters (v. ^{4}; 10, 30^{4}). Clothed in lightning the Son of waters has mounted upright the lap of the slanting (waters); carrying him the swift (waters) golden in colour go around him (v. ^{9}; cp. Agni in 1, $95^{4.5}$). The Son of waters is golden in form, appearance and colour; coming from a golden womb he sits down and gives food to his worshipper (v. ^{10}). Standing in the highest place he always shines with undimmed (splendour); the swift waters carrying ghee as food to their son, fly around with their garments (v. ^{14}). The face of the Son of waters, whom the maidens kindle, whose colour is golden, and whose food is ghee, increases in secret (v. ^{11}). He has a cow which in his own house gives good milk (v. ^{7}). Steeds (*vṛṣaṇaḥ*) swift as thought carry the son of waters (1, 186^{5}). The son of waters is connected with rivers (*nadya*: v. ^{1}). The son of waters has engendered all beings, who are merely branches of him (v. $^{2.8}$). In the last stanza of the Apāṃ napāt hymn, the deity is invoked as Agni and must be identified with him. Conversely Agni is in some hymns addressed to him, spoken of as Apāṃ napāt (cp. VS. 8, 24). Agni is the Son of waters (3,9^{1}). He is the Son of waters who sat down on earth as a dear priest (1, 143^{1}). But they are also distinguished. Agni, accordant with the Son of waters, confers victory over Vṛtra (6, 13^{3}). The Son of waters unites here with the body of another as it were (2,35^{13}). The epithet *āśuheman*, 'swiftly speeding'[1], applied three times to Apāṃ napāt, is in its only other occurrence used of Agni.

Apāṃ napāt is mentioned in various enumerations, especially with Aja ekapād (2, 31^{6}; 7, 35^{13}), Ahi budhnya (1, 186^{5}; 2, 31^{6}; 7, 35^{13}), and Savitṛ (2, 31^{6}; 6, 50^{13}). The epithet is directly applied to Savitṛ at least once (p. 33), perhaps because Savitṛ represents another fertilizing form of Agni.

Apāṃ napāt, who is golden, is clothed in lightning, dwells in the highest place, grows in concealment, shines forth, is the offspring of the waters, comes down to earth, and is identified with Agni, appears to represent the lightning form of Agni which is concealed in the cloud. For Agni, besides being directly called Apāṃ napāt, is also termed the embryo (*garbha*) of the waters (7, 9^{3}; 1, 70^{3}). As such he has been deposited in human dwellings (3, 5^{3}), his abode is in the waters (8, 43^{9}) and the two fire-sticks engender Agni who is the embryo both of plants and of waters (3, 1^{13}). Agni is also called the 'son of the rock' (10, 20^{7} cp. 6, 48^{5}), which can hardly refer to anything but the lightning which issues from the cloud mountain. As contrasted with his celestial and terrestrial forms, the third form of Agni is described as kindled in the waters, the ocean, the udder of heaven, the lap of the waters (10,45$^{1-3}$). In fact the abode of the celestial Agni in the waters is one of the best established points in Vedic mythology[2]. The term Āptya applied to Trita appears to bear a similar interpretation (§ 23).

Apāṃ napāt is not a creation of Indian mythology, but goes back to the Indo-Iranian period. In the Avesta Apām napāt is a spirit of the waters, who lives in their depths, is surrounded by females and is often invoked with them, drives with swift steeds, and is said to have seized the brightness in the depth of the ocean[3]. SPIEGEL[4] thinks this deity shows indications of an igneous nature in the Avesta, and DARMESTETER considers him to be the fire-god as born from the cloud in lightning[5]. L. v. SCHROEDER agrees with this view[6]; some scholars, however, dissent from it. OLDENBERG[7] is of opinion that Apāṃ napāt was originally a water genius pure and simple, who became confused with the water-born Agni, a totally different being. His grounds are, that one of the two hymns in which he is celebrated (10, 30), is connected in the ritual with ceremonies exclusively concerned with water, while even in 2, 35 his aqueous nature predominates[8]. HILLEBRANDT[9], on the other hand, followed by HARDY[10], thinks Apāṃ napāt is the moon, and MAX MÜLLER[11] that he is the sun or lightning.

1 WINDISCH, FaR. 144. — 2 Cp. especially RV. 3, 1 (GVS. 1, 157—70); also 5, 85^{2}; 7, 49^{4}; 10, 9^{6}. — 3 Cp. HVM. 1, 377—8. — 4 Sp.AP. 192—3. — 5 SBE. 4^{2}, LXiii; l'Avesta traduit 2, 630, note, 3, 82 (cp. Ormazd et Ahriman 34); but see HILLEBRANDT, ZDMG. 48, 422. — 6 WZKM. 9, 227—8. — 7 ORV. 118—20, cp.

357. — [8] Cp. v. SCHROEDER, WZKM. l. c.; MACDONELL, JRAS. 27, 955—6. — [9] HVM. 1, 365—80; ZDMG. 48, 422 f. — [10] HVBP. 38 f. — [11] Chips, 4[2], 410; NR. 500.
RIALLE, Revue de Ling. 3, 49 ff.; WINDISCHMANN in SPIEGEL's Zoroastrische Studien 177—86; SPIEGEL, Avesta Tr. 3, xix. LIV; GRV. I, 45; BRV. 2, 17—19. 36—7; 3, 45; Manuel pour étudier le Sanscrit védique, s. v. apāṃ napāt; LRV. 4, 181; GRUPPE, Die griech. Culte 1, 89; BDA. 82, note 2; LRF. 93; MACDONELL, JRAS. 25, 475—6; HRI. 106.

§ 25. **Mātariśvan.** — Mātariśvan is not celebrated in any hymn of the RV., and the name is found there only twenty-seven times, occurring twenty-one times in the latest portions of that Veda and otherwise only five times in the third and once in the sixth book. In these six older passages Mātariśvan is always either identified with Agni or is the producer of fire. Though the myth of Mātariśvan is based on the distinction between fire and a personification which produces it, the analysis of the myth shows these two to be identical. Nothing even in any of the later books of the RV., can be said to show clearly that the conception of Mātariśvan prevailing in the other Vedas and in the post-Vedic period, had begun to appear in that Veda.

Mātariśvan is a name of Agni in three passages (3, 5[9]. 26[2]; 1, 96[4]). This is probably also the case where the name occurs in the vocative at the end of an Agni hymn (9, 88[19]). In another verse, where an etymological explanation of the name is given, he is spoken of as one of the forms of Agni: 'As heavenly germ he is called Tanūnapāt, he becomes Narāśaṃsa when he is born; when as Mātariśvan he was fashioned in his mother (*ami mīta mātari*: cp. 1, 141[5]), he became the swift flight of wind' (3, 29[11]). It is further said elsewhere: 'One being the wise call variously: they speak of Agni, Yama, Mātariśvan' (1, 164[46]). Once Mātariśvan is also a form of Bṛhaspati, who is several times identified with Agni (§ 36): 'That Bṛhaspati appeared (*sam abhavat*) at the rite as Mātariśvan' (1, 190[2]).

Elsewhere Mātariśvan is distinguished from Agni. 'He (Agni) being born in the highest heavens appeared to Mātariśvan' (1, 143[2]). 'Agni first appeared to Mātariśvan and Vivasvat; the two worlds trembled at the choosing of the priest' (1, 31[3]). 'Agni being the highest of the luminaries has supported with his flame the firmament, when Mātariśvan kindled the oblation-bearer who was concealed' (3, 5[10]). This verse follows one in which Agni is directly called Mātariśvan. The only explanation of such a discrepancy in contiguous verses of the same hymn, seems to be that the name of a specific personification of Agni in the latter verse is used as an epithet of the generic Agni in the former. Mātariśvan brought to Bhṛgu as a gift the glorious offerer, the banner of the sacrificial gathering, the messenger who has two births (1, 60[1]). Mātariśvan brought the one (Agni) from the sky, the eagle wrested the other (Soma) from the rock (1, 93[6]). Mātariśvan brought Agni the adorable priest, the dweller in heaven (3, 2[13]). Mātariśvan (and) the gods fashioned Agni, whom the Bhṛgus produced, as the first adorable (priest) for man (10, 46[9]). Him, the god, Mātariśvan has brought from afar for man (1, 128[2]). Mātariśvan, the messenger of Vivasvat, brought hither from afar Agni Vaiśvānara, whom the mighty seized in the lap of the waters (6, 8[4]). Mātariśvan brought from afar the hidden Agni, produced by friction, from the gods (3, 9[5]). Mātariśvan produced by friction the hidden Agni (1, 141[3]). Agni was produced with friction by Mātariśvan and was set up in human abodes (1, 71[4]. 148[1]). Indra produced cows for Trita from the dragon and delivered the cowstalls to Dadhyañc (and) Mātariśvan (10, 48[2]).

There are a few obscure passages in late hymns which hardly shed any further light on the character of Mātariśvan. In two of these he seems to be regarded as purifying and enjoying Soma (9, 67[31]; 10, 114[1]); and in another, he is mentioned in an enumeration of Fathers beside whom Indra drank Soma (Vāl. 4[2]). Indra is once compared with him as with a skilful artificer (10, 105[6]), probably in allusion to Mātariśvan's skill in producing Agni (cp. 10, 46[9], where the same verb *takṣ* is used). This notion of skill is probably also present in a verse of the wedding hymn (10, 85[47]), where Mātariśvan is invoked along with other deities to join the hearts of two lovers (cp. Tvaṣṭṛ, § 38). Finally, in a very obscure verse (10, 109[1]) Mātariśvan is spoken of as 'boundless' and 'wandering' (*salila*, an adjective several times used with *vāta* in the AV.), attributes which possibly already represent the conception of Mātariśvan to be found in later times.

Mātariśvan would thus appear to be a personification of a celestial form of Agni, who at the same time is thought of as having like Prometheus brought down the hidden fire from heaven to earth. Hardly anything but lightning can be his natural basis. This would account for his being the messenger of Vivasvat from heaven to earth (6, 8[4]), just as Agni himself is a messenger of Vivasvat (§ 35) between the two worlds[1]. In the AV. Mātariśvan is still found as a mystic name of Agni (AV. 10, 8[39. 40]); but generally in that (AV. 12, 1[51] &c.) and other Saṃhitās, the Brāhmaṇas and all the subsequent literature, the name is a designation of wind. The transition to this conception is to be found in a passage already quoted (3, 29[11]): 'Agni, when as Mātariśvan he was formed in his mother, became the swift flight of wind'[2], and Agni in the air as a raging serpent is elsewhere compared with the rushing wind (1, 79[1]). Such a statement might easily have been taken later to interpret Mātariśvan as the wind.

The word *mātariśvan*, which is without a cognate in any other Indo-European language, has every appearance of being a purely Indian compound (like *mātaríbhvarī, ṛjiśvan, durgṛbhiśvan*). The Rigvedic poet's explanation of the name as 'he who is formed in his mother' can hardly be dismissed as an etymological conceit, since the word in all likelihood dates from a contemporary phase of language. It probably means 'growing in his mother' (√*śū*, to swell, from which we have *śiśu*, child, and other derivatives)[3], Agni being also said to grow (√*vṛdh*) in his mothers (1, 141[5]). There is a change of accent from the second to the third syllable, probably due to the influence of numerous words in *-van* (like *prātarítvan*). By the mother either the lower *araṇī* or the thundercloud might be meant; but the latter is the more probable, as Mātariśvan comes from heaven. Yāska (Nir. 7, 26), who regards Mātariśvan as a designation of Vāyu, analyzes the compound into *mātari* (= *antarikṣe*) and *śvan* (from *śvas* to breathe or *āśu an* to breathe quickly), so as to mean the wind that breathes in the air.

[1] ORV. 122, n. 1 thinks the frequently expressed opinion that Mātariśvan is nothing but a form of Agni, has no sure foundation, and regards Mātariśvan simply as the Prometheus of the RV.; cp. ORV. 108, n. 1, and SBE. 46, 123. — [2] Cp. BRV. 1, 27; BDA. 51; OLDENBERG, SBE. 46, 306. — [3] Cp. WHITNEY, Sanskrit Roots p. 176; ROTH, Nirukta 111—3; WEBER, IS. 1, 416; REUTER, KZ. 31, 544—5.

KHF. 8.14; MUIR, JRAS. 20, 416, note; OST. 5, 204, note; SCHWARTZ, KZ. 20, 210; GW. s. v.; BRV. 1, 52—7; BRI. 9; KRV. 35; HVBP. 110; EGGELING, SBE. 12, 186, note 2; ORV. 122—3.

§ 26. Ahi budhnya. — The serpent of the Deep, Ahi budhnya, whose name is mentioned solely in hymns to the Viśvedevas, is spoken of only twelve times in the RV. and hardly ever alone. He is associated five times with Aja ekapād, three times with Apāṃ napāt, three times with the ocean (*samudra*), and twice with Savitṛ. There are only three verses (5, 41[16];

7, 34[16, 17]) in which he is invoked alone. When only one other deity is referred to with him, it is either Apāṃ napāt (1, 186[5]) or Aja ekapād (10, 64[4]). When Ahi budhnya and Aja ekapād are mentioned together in the same verse, they are always (with the slight exception of 10, 66[11]) in juxtaposition. The most characteristic enumerations in which the name is invoked are: Aja ekapād, Ahi budhnya, the ocean, Apāṃ napāt, Pṛśni (7, 35[13]); Ahi budhnya, Aja ekapād, Trita, Ṛbhukṣan, Savitṛ, Apāṃ napāt (2, 31[6]); the ocean, the stream, the space (*rajas*), the air, Aja ekapād, the thundering flood, Ahi budhnya, and all the gods (10, 66[11]). Judged by these associates Ahi budhnya would seem to be an atmospheric deity, and he is enumerated in the Naighaṇṭuka (5, 4) among the divinities of the middle or aerial region. But it is only where he is mentioned alone that anything more definite than this can be gathered. In the verse which gives most information about him, the poet exclaims: 'I praise with songs the serpent born in water (*abjām*), sitting in the bottom (*budhne*) of the streams in the spaces' (7, 34[16]; cp. 10, 93[5]). This indicates that he dwells in the atmospheric ocean, and Yāska explains *budhna* as air (Nir. 10, 44). In the verse immediately following he is besought not to give his worshippers over to injury, and these identical words are addressed to him in another passage also (5, 41[16]). This suggests that there is something hurtful in his nature. Ahi is otherwise a term commonly applied to Vṛtra (§ 68), and Vṛtra enclosing the waters is described as overflowed by the waters or lying in them (ibid.) or at the bottom (*budhna*) of the air (1, 52[6]). Agni in the space of air is called a raging *ahi* (1, 79[1]) and is also said to have been produced in the depth (*budhne*) of the great space (4, 11[1]). Thus it may be surmised that Ahi budhnya was originally not different from Ahi Vṛtra, though he is invoked as a divine being, who resembles Apāṃ napāt, his baleful aspect only being hinted at. In later Vedic texts Ahi budhnya is allegorically connected with Agni Gārhapatya (VS. 5, 33; AB. 3, 36; TB. 1, 1, 10[3]). In post-Vedic literature Ahi budhnya is the name of a Rudra as well as an epithet of Śiva.

WEBER, IS. 1, 96; ROTH, PW. s. v. *budhnya*; OST. 5, 336; BRV. 2, 205—6. 401; 3, 24—5; HVBP. 41 (as a name of the moon).

§ 27. **Aja ekapād.** — This being is closely connected with Ahi budhnya, his name occurring five times in juxtaposition with that of the latter and only once unaccompanied by it (10, 65[13]). The deities invoked in the latter passage, 'the thundering Pāvīravī ('daughter of lightning': PW.), Ekapād aja, the supporter of the sky, the stream, the oceanic waters, all the gods, Sarasvatī', are, however, almost identical with those enumerated in the following hymn: 'the ocean, the stream, the aerial space, Aja ekapād, the thundering flood, Ahi budhnya, and all the gods' (10, 66[11]). These two passages suggest that Aja ekapād is an aerial deity. He is, however, enumerated in the Naighaṇṭuka (5, 6) among the deities of the celestial region. In the AV. Aja ekapāda is said to have made firm the two worlds (AV. 13, 1[6]). The TB. (3, 1, 2[8]) speaks of Aja ekapād as having risen in the east. The commentator on his passage defines Aja ekapād as a kind of Agni, and Durga on Nirukta 12, 29 interprets him as the sun. Yāska himself does not express an opinion as to what Aja ekapād represents, merely explaining *Aja* as *ajana*, driving, and *ekapad* as 'he who has one foot' or 'he who protects or drinks with one foot'. Though hardly any longer an independent deity, Aja ekapād as well as Ahi budhnya receives a libation in the domestic ritual (Pārask. 2, 15[2]). In the Epic Ajaikapād is both the name of one of the eleven Rudras and an epithet of Śiva.

ROTH[1], with whom GRASSMANN agrees[2], regards Aja ekapād as a genius of the storm, translating the name as the 'one-footed Driver or Stormer'. BLOOMFIELD[3] and VICTOR HENRY[4] think he represents a solar deity. HARDY[5] believes that 'the goat who goes alone' is the moon. BERGAIGNE[6], interpreting the name as 'the unborn (*a-ja*) who has only one foot', thinks this means he who inhabits the one isolated mysterious world. If another conjecture may be added, the name, meaning 'the one-footed goat'[7], was originally a figurative designation of lightning, the 'goat' alluding to its agile swiftness in the cloud-mountains, and the one foot to the single streak which strikes the earth.

1 PW. s. v. *aja*; Nirukta, Erl. 165—6 (cp. OST. 5, 336). — 2 GW. s. v. 1 *aja*; cp. FAY, AJP. 17, 24—5. — 3 AJP. 12, 443; SBE. 42, 664. — 4 Les hymnes Rohita, Paris 1891, p. 24. — 5 HVBP. 41—2. — 6 BRV. 3, 23. — 7 ORV. 71—2; cp. BRI. 24. WEBER, IS. 1, 96.

§ 28. **Rudra.** — This god occupies a subordinate position in the RV., being celebrated in only three entire hymns, in part of another, and in one conjointly with Soma, while his name occurs about 75 times.

His physical features in the RV. are the following. He has a hand (2, 33^7 &c.), arms (2, 33^3; VS. 16, 1), and firm limbs (2, 33^{11}). He has beautiful lips (2, 33^5) and (like Pūṣan) wears braided hair (1, $114^{1.5}$). His colour is brown (*babhru*: 2, 33^5 &c.). His shape is dazzling (1, 114^5), and he is multiform (2, 33^9). He shines like the brilliant sun, like gold (1, 43^5). He is arrayed with golden ornaments (2, 33^9) and wears a glorious multiform necklace[1] (*niṣka*: 2, 33^{10}). He sits on a car-seat (2, 33^4). The later Saṃhitās (especially VS. 16) add a number of other traits. He is thousand-eyed (AV. 11, $2^{3.7}$, VS. 16, 7). He has a belly, a mouth, a tongue, and teeth (AV. 11, 2^6). His belly is black and his back red (AV. 15, $1^{7.8}$). He is blue-necked (VS. 16, 7) and blue-tufted (AV. 2, 27^6). He is copper-coloured and red (VS. 16, 7). He is clothed in a skin (VS. 3, 61; 16, 51) and dwells in mountains (VS. 16, 2—4).

The RV. often mentions Rudra's weapons of offence. He is once said to hold the thunderbolt in his arm (2, 33^3). His lightning shaft (*didyut*) discharged from the sky traverses the earth (7, 46^3). He is usually said to be armed with a bow and arrows (2, $33^{10.11}$; 5, 42^{11}; 10, 125^6), which are strong and swift (7, 46^1). He is invoked with Kṛśānu (§ 48) and the archers (10, 64^8); and seems to be intended when Indra is compared with the archer on the car-seat (6, 20^9, cp. 2, 33^{11}). In the AV. he is also called an archer (1, 28^1; 6, 93^1; 15, 5^{1-7}). In that and other later Vedic texts his bow, arrow, weapon, bolt, or club are frequently referred to (AV. 1, 28^5 &c.; ŚB. 9, 1, 1^6).

One of the points most frequently mentioned about Rudra is his relationship to the Maruts. He is their father (1, $114^{6.9}$; 2, 33^1); or they are more frequently spoken of as his sons and are also several times called Rudras or Rudriyas[2]. He is said to have generated them from the shining udder of Pṛśni (2, 34^2)[3]. But Rudra is never associated, as Indra is, with the warlike exploits of the Maruts, for he does not engage in conflict with the demons. *Tryambaka*, a common epithet of Śiva in post-Vedic literature, is already applied to Rudra in Vedic texts (VS. 3, 58; ŚB. 2, 6, 2^9) and seems to refer to him once even in the RV. (7, 59^{12}). The meaning appears to be 'he who has three mothers' (cp. 3, 56^5) in allusion to the threefold division of the universe (cp. GRV. 1, 555). Ambikā, a post-Vedic name of Śiva's wife, is mentioned for the first time in VS. 3, 5, appearing here, however, not as Rudra's wife, but as his sister. Umā and Pārvatī, regular names of Śiva's wife, seem first to occur in the TA. and the Kena Upaniṣad.

In a passage of the RV. (2, 1^6) Rudra is one of several deities identified with Agni. He is also identified with Agni in the AV. (7, 87^{1}), in the TS. (5, 4, 3^{1}; 5, 5, 7^{4}), and the ŚB. (6, 1, 3^{10}, cp. 9, 1, 1^{1}). The word *rudra* often occurs as an adjective, in several cases as an attribute of Agni[4] (though rather oftener as an attribute of the Aśvins (§ 21). Śarva and Bhava are, among several others, two new names assigned to Rudra in VS. (16, 18. 28). These two also occur in the AV. where their destructive arrows and lightnings are referred to (2, 27^{6}; 6, 93^{1}; 10, 1^{23}; 11, $2^{1.\,12}$); but they seem here to have been regarded as deities distinct from one another and from Rudra. Bhava and Śarva are in a Sūtra passage spoken of as sons of Rudra and are compared with wolves eager for prey (ŚSS. 4, 20^{1}). In VS. 39,8 Agni, Aśani, Paśupati, Bhava, Śarva, Īśāna, Mahādeva, Ugradeva, and others are enumerated as gods or forms of one god. Rudra, Śarva, Paśupati, Ugra, Aśani, Bhava, Mahān devaḥ are names given to represent eight different forms of Agni (ŚB. 6, 1, 3^{7}; cp. Śāṅkh. Br. 6, 1 &c.), and Śarva, Bhava, Paśupati, and Rudra are said to be all names of Agni (ŚB. 1, 7, 3^{8}). Aśani, one of the above names assigned to Agni Kumāra in the ŚB. (6, 1, 3^{10}), is there explained to mean lightning (*vidyut*) but in the Śāṅkh. Br. it is interpreted as Indra. The epithet *paśupati*, 'lord of beasts', which Rudra often receives in the VS., AV., and later, is doubtless assigned to him because unhoused cattle are peculiarly exposed to his attacks and are therefore especially consigned to his care.

Rudra is described in the RV. as fierce (2, $33^{9.\,11}$; 10, 126^{5}) and destructive like a terrible beast (2, 33^{11}). He is the ruddy[5] (*aruṣa*) boar of heaven (1, 114^{5}). He is a bull (2, $33^{7.\,8.\,15}$). He is exalted (7, 10^{4}), strong (1,43^{1}. 114^{1}), strongest of the strong (2, 33^{3}), unassailable (7, 46^{1}), unsurpassed in might (2, 33^{10}), rapid (10, 92^{5}), and swift (1, 114^{4}). He is young (2, 33^{1}; 5, 60^{5}) and unaging (6, 49^{10}). He is called *asura* (5, 42^{11}) or the great *asura* of heaven[6] (2, 1^{6}). He is self-glorious (1, 129^{3}; 10, 92^{9}), rules heroes (1, $114^{1.\,2}$ &c.), and is a lord (*īśāna*) of this vast world (2, 33^{9}) and father of the world (6, 49^{10}). He is an ordainer (6, 46^{1}), and by his rule and universal dominion he is aware of the doings of men and gods (7, 46^{2}). He makes the streams flow over the earth and, roaring, moistens everything (10, 92^{5}). He is intelligent (1, 43^{1}), wise (1, 114^{4}), and beneficent (2, 33^{7}; 6, 49^{10}). He is several times called 'bountiful', *mīḍhvas* (1, 114^{3}), and in the later Vedas the comparative and superlative of this word have only been found in connexion with Rudra[7]. He is easily invoked (2, 33^{6}) and is auspicious, *śiva* (10, 92^{9}), an epithet which is not even in the AV. as yet peculiar to any particular deity.

Malevolence is frequently attributed to Rudra in the RV.; for the hymns addressed to him chiefly express fear of his terrible shafts and deprecation of his wrath. He is implored not to slay or injure, in his anger, his worshippers, their parents, children, men, cattle, or horses (1, $114^{7.\,8}$), but to spare their horses (2, 33^{1}), to avert his great malevolence and his bolt from his worshippers, and to prostrate others with them (2, $33^{11.\,14}$). He is besought to avert his bolt when he is incensed and not to injure his adorers, their children, and their cows (6, 28^{7}. 46^{2-4}), and to keep from them his cow-slaying, man-slaying missile (2, 33^{1}). His ill-will and anger are deprecated (2, $33^{4-6.\,15}$), and he is besought to be merciful to the walking food (10, 169^{1}). His worshippers pray that they may be unharmed and obtain his favour (2, $33^{1.\,6}$). He once even receives the epithet 'man-slaying' (4, 3^{6}), and in a Sūtra passage it is said that this god seeks to slay men (AG. 4, 8^{32}). Rudra's malevolence is still more prominent in the later Vedic texts. His wrath is frequently deprecated (VS. 3,61 &c.; AV. 1,28^{5} &c.). He is invoked not to assail his worshippers with celestial fire and to cause the lightning to descend elsewhere (AV. 11, 2[26]; 10, 1[23]). He is even said to assail with fever, cough, and poison[8] (AV. 11, 2[22. 26]; 6, 90 cp. 93). Rudra's wide-mouthed, howling dogs, who swallow their prey unchewed, are also spoken of (AV. 10, 1[30], cp. VS. 16, 28). Even the gods were afraid of the strung bow and the arrows of Rudra, lest he should destroy them (ŚB. 9, 1, 1[1. 6]). Under the name of Mahādeva he is said to slay cattle (TMB. 6, 9[7]). In another Brāhmaṇa passage he is said to have been formed of a compound of all the most terrible substances (AB. 3, 33[1]). It is probably owing to his formidable characteristics that in the Brāhmaṇas and Sūtras Rudra is regarded as isolated from the other gods. When the gods attained heaven, Rudra remained behind (ŚB. 1, 7, 3[1]). In the Vedic ritual after offerings to other gods, a remainder is not uncommonly assigned to Rudra (Gobh. GS. 1, 8[28]; Āp. Dh. S. 2, 4[23]). His hosts, which attack man and beast with disease and death, receive the bloody entrails of the victim (ŚŚS. 4, 19[8]), just as blood is poured out to demons as their peculiar share of the sacrifice[9] (AB. 2, 7[1]). The abode of Rudra in these later texts is commonly regarded as in the north[10], while that of the other gods is in the east. It is perhaps due to his formidable nature that in the RV. Rudra only appears once associated with another deity (Soma: § 44) as a dual divinity in one short hymn of four stanzas.

In the VS., besides many other epithets too numerous to repeat, several disgraceful attributes of Rudra are mentioned. Thus he is called a 'robber, cheat, deceiver, lord of pilferers and robbers' (16, 20—1). In fact, his character as shown by the various epithets occurring here, approximates to the fierce, terrific, impure, and repulsive nature of the post-Vedic Śiva.

Rudra is, however, not purely maleficent like a demon. He is also supplicated in the RV. to avert the anger or the evil that comes from the gods (1, 114[4]; 2, 33[7]). He is besought not only to preserve from calamity (5, 51[13]), but to bestow blessings (1, 114[1. 2]; 2, 33[6]), and produce welfare for man and beast (1, 43[6]). His healing powers are mentioned with especial frequency. He grants remedies (2, 33[12]), he commands every remedy (5, 42[11]), and has a thousand remedies (7, 46[3]). He carries in his hand choice remedies (1, 114[5]), and his hand is restorative and healing (2, 33[7]). He raises up heroes by his remedies, for he is the greatest physician of physicians (2, 33[4]), and by his auspicious remedies his worshipper hopes to live a hundred winters (2, 33[2]). He is besought to remove sickness from his worshippers' offspring (7, 46[2]) and to be favourable to man and beast, that all in the village may be well-fed and free from disease (1, 114[1]). In this connexion Rudra has two epithets which are peculiar to him, *jalāṣa*, (perhaps) 'healing' and *jalāṣa-bheṣaja*, 'possessing healing remedies (1, 43[4]; AV. 2, 27[6]). These medicines against sickness are probably rains[11] (cp. 5, 53[14]; 10, 59[9]). That this attribute was essential to his nature, appears from a verse of a hymn in which various deities are characterized without being named (8, 29[5]): 'One bright, fierce, possessing healing remedies, holds a sharp weapon in his hand'. Rudra's lightning and his remedies are also mentioned together in another verse (7, 46[3]). The healing Rudra with the Rudras is invoked to be favourable (7. 35[6]). The Maruts are also in another verse associated with Rudra as possessing pure and beneficent remedies (2, 33[13]). The healing power of Rudra is sometimes referred to in the other Saṃhitās (VS. 3, 59; 16, 5. 49; AV. 2, 27[6]); but much less frequently than his destructive activity. In the Sūtras, sacrifices to him are prescribed for removing or preventing disease in cattle (AG. 4, 8[40]; Kauś. S. 51, 7 &c.).

The evidence of the RV. does not distinctly show with what physical basis Rudra is connected. He is generally regarded as a storm-god. But his missile is maleficent, unlike that of Indra, which is directed only against the enemies of his worshippers. Rudra appears therefore to have originally represented not the storm pure and simple, but rather its baleful side in the destructive agency of lightning[12]. This would account for his deadly shafts and for his being the father or chief of the Maruts or Storm-gods, who are armed with lightning and who are said to have been born 'from the laughter of lightning' (1, 23^{12}). His beneficent and healing powers would be based partly on the fertilizing and purifying action of the thunderstorm and partly on the indirect action of sparing those whom he might slay. Thus the deprecations of his wrath gave rise to the euphemistic epithet 'auspicious' (*śiva*), which became the regular name of Rudra's historical successor in post-Vedic mythology. This explanation would also account for Rudra's close connexion with Agni in the RV.

WEBER[13] expresses the view that this deity in the earliest period specially designated the howling of the Storm (the plural therefore meaning the Maruts), but that as the roaring of fire is analogous, Storm and Fire combined to form a god of rage and destruction, the epithets of the Śatarudriya being derived partly from Rudra = Storm and partly from Agni = Fire. H. H. WILSON thought that Rudra was 'evidently a form of either Agni or Indra'[14]. L. v. SCHROEDER[15] regards Rudra as originally the chief of the souls of the dead conceived as storming along in the wind (cp. p. 81). OLDENBERG is of opinion that Rudra probably represented in his origin a god of mountain and forest, whence the shafts of disease attack mankind[16].

The etymology of the word *rudra* is somewhat uncertain as regards the meaning. It is generally derived from the root *rud*, to cry, and interpreted as the Howler[17]. This is the Indian derivation[18]. By GRASSMANN[19] it is connected with a root *rud* having the conjectural meaning of 'to shine' or, according to PISCHEL, 'to be ruddy'[20]. Rudra would thus mean the 'bright' or the 'red one'[21].

[1] Cp. PISCHEL, ZDMG. 40, 120—1. — [2] 1, $64^{2.12}$. 85^{11}; 5, 42^{15}; 6, 50^{4}. 66^{11}; 8, 20^{17} (cp. 5, 59^{8}; 7, 56^{1}. 58^{5}). — [3] Vāyu is once said to have generated the Maruts from the sky (1, 134^{4}) and Vāta is approximated to Rudra in 10, 169^{1}. — [4] 1, 27^{10} (cp. Nir. 10, 8; Erl. 136); 3, 2^{5}; 4, 3^{1}; 5, 3^{3}; 8, 61^{3}. — [5] Cp. BLOOMFIELD, AJP. 12, 429; PVS. 1, 57; ORV. 359, note 4. — [6] Cp. BDA. 46. 54; GELDNER, FaW. 20. — [7] BLOOMFIELD, AJP. 12, 428—9. — [8] Cp. BLOOMFIELD's explanation (AJP. 7, 469—72) of AV. 1, 12 as a prayer to lightning conceived as the cause of fever, headache, and coughs (otherwise WEBER, IS. 4, 405). — [9] HRI. 250, note 2; cp. ORV. 488. 302—3. 334—5. 458. — [10] Cp. ORV. 335, note 3. — [11] The remedy is explained by BRV. 3, 32 as Soma, the draught of immortality, and by BLOOMFIELD (AJP. 12, 425—9) followed by HVBP. 83—4, and HOPKINS, PAOS. Dec. 1894, CL ff., as rain (*jalāṣa* = the *mūtra* of Rudra). — [12] MACDONELL, JRAS. 27, 957; HOPKINS, PAOS. Dec. 1894, p. CLI; HRI. 112; cp. KRV. 38, note 133. — [13] IS. 2, 19—22. — [14] Translation of the RV., introductions to vol. 1, 26—7. 37—8; cp. vol. 2, 9—10. — [15] WZKM. 9, 248. — [16] ORV. 216—24 (cp. HOPKINS, PAOS. l. c.). — [17] KUHN, Herabkunft 177; KZ. 2, 278; 3, 335; WEBER, IS. 2, 19—22; MM., OGR. 216; otherwise v. BRADKE, ZDMG. 40, 359—61. — [18] TS. 1, 5, 1^{1}; ŚB. 6, 1, 3^{10}; YN. 10, 5; Sāyaṇa on RV. 1, 114^{1}. — [19] GW. — [20] PVS. 1, 57; ZDMG. 40, 120. — [21] Cp. BRI. 14; HVBP. 83.

ROTH, ZDMG. 2, 222; WHITNEY, JAOS. 3, 318—9; Oriental and Linguistic Studies 1873, p. 34—5; OST. 4, 299—363. 420—3; LRV. 3, 320—2; BRV. 3, 31—8. 152—4; v. SCHROEDER, WZKM. 9, 233—8. 248—52; HRI. 99. 578.

§ 29. **The Maruts.** — These are prominent deities in the RV., thirty-three hymns being dedicated to them alone, seven at least to them conjointly with Indra, and one each to them with Agni and Pūṣan. They form a troop, *gaṇa* (a word generally used in connexion with them) or *śardhas* (1, $37^{1.5}$ &c.),

of deities mentioned only in the plural. Their number is thrice sixty (8, 85^{8}) or thrice seven (1, 133^{6}; AV. 13, 1^{13}). Their birth is often referred to (5, 57^{5} &c.). They are the sons of Rudra (p. 74), being also often called Rudras (1, $39^{4.7}$ &c.) and sometimes Rudriyas (1, 38^{7}; 2, 34^{10} &c.), and of Pṛśni (2, 34^{2}; 5, 52^{16}. 60^{5}; 6, 66^{3}), often also receiving the epithet *pṛśnimātaraḥ*, 'having Pṛśni for their mother' (1, 23^{10} &c.; AV. 5, 21^{11}). The cow Pṛśni (5, 52^{16}), or simply a cow is their mother (8, 83^{1}) and they bear the epithet *gomātaraḥ*, 'having a cow for their mother' (1, 85^{3}, cp. 8, 20^{8}). This cow presumably represents the mottled storm-cloud (§§ 43. 61 B.); and the flaming cows having distended udders with whom they come (2, 34^{5}), can hardly refer to anything but the clouds charged with rain and lightning. When born from Pṛśni the Maruts are compared with fires (6, 66^{1-3}). They are also said to have been born from the laughter of lightning (1, 23^{12}, cp. 38^{8}). Agni is said to have fashioned or begotten them (6, 3^{8}; 1, 71^{8}). Vāyu is once said to have engendered them in the wombs of heaven (1, 134^{4}), and once they are called the sons of heaven (10, 77^{2}), being also referred to as the heroes (*vīrāḥ*) of heaven (1, 64^{4}. 122^{1}; 5, 54^{10}) or as the males (*maryāḥ*) of heaven (3, 54^{13}; 5, 59^{6}). Once they are said to have the ocean for their mother, *sindhumātaraḥ* (10, 78^{6} cp. p. 51). Elsewhere they are said to be self-born (1, 168^{2}; 5, 87^{2}).

They are brothers among whom none is eldest or youngest (5, 59^{6}. 60^{5}), for they are equal in age (1, 165^{1}). They have grown together (5, 56^{5}; 7, 58^{1}) and are of one mind (8, $20^{1.21}$). They have the same birthplace (5, 53^{3}) and the same abode (1, 165^{1}; 7, 56^{1}). They are spoken of as having grown on earth, in air, and heaven (5, 55^{7}) or as dwelling in the three heavens (5, 60^{6}). They are also once described as dwelling in the mountains (8, $83^{1.2}$).

They are associated with the goddess Indrāṇī, who is their friend (10, 86^{9}), and with Sarasvatī (7, 96^{2}, cp. 39^{5}). Their connexion is, however, closest with the goddess Rodasī, who is described as standing with them on their car bringing enjoyments (5, 56^{8}) or simply as standing beside them (6, 66^{6}). In all the five passages in which her name occurs, she is mentioned with them (cp. 1, $167^{4.5}$). She therefore appears to have been regarded as their bride (like Sūryā as the bride of the Aśvins). It is probably to this connexion that they owe the epithet *bhadrajānayaḥ*, 'having a beautiful wife' (5, 61^{4}) and their comparison with bridegrooms (5, 60^{4}) or youthful wooers (10, 78^{6}).

The brilliance of the Maruts is constantly referred to. They are golden, of sun-like brightness, like blazing fires, of ruddy aspect (6, 66^{2}; 7, 59^{11}; 8, 7^{7}). They shine like tongues of fire (10, 78^{3}). They have the form or the brilliance of Agni (10, 84^{1}; 3, 26^{5}), with whom they are compared in brightness (10, 78^{2}). They are like fires (2, 34^{1}) or kindled fires (6, 66^{2}) and are expressly called fires (3, 26^{4}). They have the brilliance of serpents (*ahibhānavaḥ*: 1, 172^{1}). They shine in the mountains (8, 7^{1}). They are self-luminous (1,37^{2} &c.), an epithet almost exclusively applied to them. They are frequently spoken of in a more general way as shining and brilliant (1, 165^{12} &c.).

They are particularly often associated with lightning, *vidyut* (5, $54^{2.3.11}$; 1, 64^{5}). The lightnings smile down on earth when the Maruts shed their ghee (1, 168^{8}, cp. 5, 52^{6}). The lightning lows like a cow, as a mother following her calf, when they shed their rain (1, 38^{8}). They are like lightnings shining with rain (7, 56^{13}). Lightning is so characteristic of them that all the five compounds of *vidyut* in the RV. are connected with the Maruts and, excepting a single instance, with them only. They hold lightnings in their hands (8, 7^{25}; 5, 54^{11}), they delight in lightnings and cast a stone (5, 54^{3}). Their lances (*ṛṣṭi*) are often mentioned, and that these represent the lightning is shown by their epithet *ṛṣṭividyut*, 'lightning-speared' (1, 168^{5}; 5, 52^{13}). Less frequently they are spoken of as having axes (1, 37^{2}. 88^{3}; 5, 33^{4}. 57^{2}; 8, 20^{4}), which are golden (8, 7^{32}). Once (ibid.) they are said to bear the bolt (*vajra*), Indra's peculiar weapon, in their hands. Sometimes they are said to be armed with bows and arrows (5, 53^{4}. 57^{2}; 8, $20^{4.\,12}$), once being termed archers shooting an arrow; but as this trait is rare in the numerous hymns addressed to them, it may be borrowed from their father Rudra. The Maruts are decorated with garlands and other ornaments (5, 53^{4}). They wear golden mantles (5, 55^{6}). Like rich wooers they deck their bodies with golden ornaments (5, 60^{4}). Armlets or anklets (*khādi*) are an ornament peculiar to them. With these they shine like the sky with stars and glitter like showers from the clouds (2, 34^{2}). One verse describes their appearance more fully than usual. They have spears on their shoulders, anklets on their feet, golden ornaments on their breasts, fiery lightnings in their hands, golden helmets upon their heads (5, 54^{11}).

The Maruts ride on cars which gleam with lightning (1, 88^{1}; 3, 54^{13}), which are golden (5, 57^{1}), which have golden wheels or fellies (1, 64^{11}. 88^{5}), in which are weapons (5, 57^{6}), and which have buckets standing in them (1, 87^{2}). The coursers which draw their cars are ruddy or tawny (1, 88^{2}; 5, 57^{4}), golden-footed (8, 7^{27}), and swift as thought (1, 85^{4}). These coursers are spotted, as appears from the epithet *pṛṣadaśva*, 'having spotted steeds', which is several times and exclusively connected with the Maruts. More frequently the animals which draw their car are spoken of in the feminine as *pṛṣatīḥ* (1, 39^{6} &c.). These are in two passages (5, 55^{6}. 58^{6}), mentioned with the masculine *aśvāḥ*. The Maruts are also described as having yoked the winds as steeds to their pole (5, 58^{7}).

The Maruts are great as the sky (5, 57^{4}), they surpass heaven and earth (10, 77^{3}), are immeasurable in greatness (5, 58^{2}), and no others can reach the limit of their might (1, 167^{9}). The Maruts are young (1, 64^{2}. 165^{2}; 5, 42^{15}) and unaging (1, 64^{3}). They are divine (*asura*), vigorous, impetuous, without soil (1, $64^{2.\,12}$) and dustless (6, 66^{2}). They are fierce (1, 19^{4}), irascible (7, 56^{8}), terrible (5, $56^{2.\,3}$; 7, 58^{2}), of terrible aspect (5, 56^{2}), of fearful form (1, 19^{5}. 64^{2}), and are terrible like wild beasts (2, 34^{1}; cp. p. 75). They are playful like children or calves (1, 166^{2}; 7, 56^{16}; 10, 78^{6}). They are like black-backed swans (7, 59^{7}). They are iron-tusked boars (1, 88^{5}); they are like lions (1, 64^{8}).

The noise which they make is often referred to (1, 169^{7} &c.) and is expressly called thunder (1, 23^{11}); but it is also the roaring of the winds (7, 56^{3}). At their coming heaven as it were roars with fear (8, 7^{26}). They are often described as causing the mountains to quake as well as making the earth or the two worlds tremble[1]. With the fellies of their cars they rend the mountains or the rock (1, 64^{11}; 5, 52^{9}). It is when they come with the winds that they cause the mountains to quake (8, 7^{4}). They rend trees and like wild elephants devour the forests (1, 39^{5}. 64^{7}). The forests bow down before them through fear (5, 60^{2}). Resistless as mountains they cast down terrestrial and celestial creatures (1, 64^{3}). All creatures are afraid of them (1, 85^{8}). They speed like boisterous winds (10, 78^{3}) and whirl up dust (1, 64^{12}). They make the winds or the noise of the winds (7, 56^{3}). They come with the winds (8, $7^{3.\,4.\,17}$) and take them as their steeds (5, 58^{7}).

One of the main functions of the Maruts is to shed rain. They are clothed with rain (5, 57[4]). They rise from the ocean and shed rain (1, 38[9]). Milking the unfailing well, they blow through the two worlds with rain (1, 64[6]; 8, 7[16]). Rain follows them (5, 53[10]). They bring water and impel rain (5, 58[3]). They obscure their brilliance with rain (5, 59[1]). They cover the eye of the sun with rain (5, 59[5]). They create darkness with the cloud when they shed rain (1, 38[9]). They scatter mist when they speed with winds (8, 7[4]). They cause the heavenly pail (5, 53[6]. 59[8]) and the streams of the mountains to pour (5, 59[7]). When they hurry on, the waters flow (5, 58[6]). A terrestrial river receives its name, Marudvṛddhā, 'swelled by the Maruts' (10, 75[5]), from this action. The sweat of the sons of Rudra became rain (5, 58[7]). The rain shed by the Maruts is also figuratively referred to as milk (1, 166[3]), ghee (1, 85[3]; 10, 78[4]), milk and ghee (1, 64[6]); or they are said to pour out the spring (1, 85[11]) or to wet the earth with honey (5, 54[8])[2]. They raise waters from sea to sky and discharge them from the sky upon the earth (AV. 4, 27[4]). The waters which they shed are often clearly connected with the thunderstorm. Desiring to give water, whirling hail, violent, they rush on with thunder (5, 54[3]). They cause winds and lightnings with their might, milk heavenly gifts from the udder, and fill the earth with milk (1, 64[5]). The spring which they milk, thunders (1, 64[6]). The sky, the ruddy bull, bellows when they shed the waters (5, 58[6]). They cause the stallion to make water (1, 64[6]). They bestow the rain of heaven and shed abundantly the streams of the stallion (5, 83[6]). They assume a golden colour when they make water with the steed (2, 34[13]). The streams resound with the fellies of the Maruts, when they raise the voice of the cloud (1, 168[8]). The waters which Indra sheds are called *marutvatīḥ*, 'attended by the Maruts' (1, 80[4]). In connexion with their character as shedders of rain, the Maruts receive the epithets *purudrapsāḥ* (5, 57[5]) or *drapsinaḥ* (1, 64[2]) 'abounding in drops' and the frequent *sudānavaḥ*, 'dripping well'. They also avert heat (5, 54[1]). But they likewise dispel darkness (7, 56[20]), produce light (1, 86[10]), and prepare a path for the sun (8, 7[8]). They are also said to have measured out the air (5, 55[2]), stretched out the terrestrial regions as well as the bright realms of heaven, and held apart the two worlds (8, 83[9. 11]).

Doubtless in allusion to the sound of the wind, the Maruts are several times called singers (5, 52[1]. 60[8]; 7, 35[9]). They are the singers of heaven (5, 57[5]). They sing a song (1, 19[4]. 166[7]). While singing they made the sun to shine (8, 29[10]) and while blowing their pipe they cleft the mountain (1, 85[10]). For Indra when he slew the dragon, they sang a song and pressed Soma (5, 29[2]. 30[6]). In singing a song they created Indra-might (1, 85[2]). Though their song must primarily have represented the sound of the winds (cp. 4, 22[4]), it is also conceived as a hymn of praise (3, 14[4]). Thus they come to be addressed as priests when in the company of Indra (5, 29[3]), and are compared with priests (10, 78[1]). They were the first to perform the sacrifice as Daśagvas (2, 36[2]), and they purified Agni in the house of the pious, while the Bhṛgus kindled him (10, 122[5]). Like the other gods they are several times also spoken of as drinkers of Soma (2, 36[2]; 8, 83[9–12] &c.).

Being identified with the phenomena of the thunderstorm, the Maruts are naturally intimate associates of Indra, appearing as his friends and allies in innumerable passages. They increase his strength and prowess (3, 35[9]; 6, 17[11]), with their prayers, hymns, and songs[3] (1, 165[11] &c.). They generally assist Indra in the Vṛtra fight (8, 65[2. 3]; 10, 113[3]). They help Trita as well as Indra in slaying Vṛtra (8, 7[24]). They are besought to sing a Vṛtra-slaying hymn (8, 78[1–3]). They helped Indra in the conflict with the dragon and with Śambara (3, 47[3. 4]). With them Indra gains the light (8, 65[4]), found the cows (1, 6[5]) and supported the sky (7, 47[5]). In fact Indra accomplishes all his celestial exploits in their company (1, 100. 101. 165; 10, 65). Sometimes the Maruts appear more independent in these exploits. Thus they strike Vṛtra, assisted by Indra (1, 23[9]) and are even spoken of alone as having rent Vṛtra joint from joint (8, 7[23]) or as having disclosed the cows (2, 34[1]). They (like the gods in general) have Indra as their chief (1, 23[8] &c.) and are accompanied by Indra (10, 128[2]). They are like sons to Indra (1, 100[5]) and are called his brothers (1, 170[2]). The Maruts are, however two or three times said to have left Indra in the lurch. They involved him alone in the fight with the dragon (1, 165[6]) and they abandoned him (8, 7[31]). One verse even gives evidence of hostility between Indra and the Maruts, when the latter say to him: 'Why dost thou seek to kill us, Indra? Do not kill us in the fray' (1, 170[2] cp. 171[6])[4]. A Brāhmaṇa passage (TB. 2, 7, 11[1]) also refers to a conflict between the Maruts and Indra.

When not associated with Indra, the Maruts occasionally exhibit malevolent traits. They then to some extent participate in the maleficent nature of their father Rudra. They are implored to ward off the lightning from their worshippers nor to let their ill-will reach them (7, 56[9]), and are besought to avert their arrow and the stone which they hurl (1, 172[2]), their lightning (7, 57[4]), and their cow- and man-slaying bolt (7, 56[17]). Evil can come from them (1, 39[8]), their anger is deprecated (1, 171[1]; 7, 58[5]), and they are said to have the wrath of the serpent (1, 64[8.9]). But like their father Rudra, the Maruts are supplicated to bring healing remedies, which abide in the Sindhu, the Asiknī, the seas, and mountains (8, 20[25–26]), and once they are associated with Rudra in the possession of pure, salutary, and beneficent remedies (2, 33[13]). The remedies appear to be the waters, for the Maruts bestow medicine by raining (5, 53[14]). Like Agni, they are several times also said to be pure or purifying, *pāvaka* (7, 56[12] &c.).

From the constant association of the Maruts with lightning, thunder, wind, and rain, as well as from other traits mentioned above, it seems clear that they are Storm-gods in the RV. According to the native interpreters the Maruts represent the winds, and the post-Vedic meaning of the word is simply 'wind'. But in the RV. they hardly represent the winds pure and simple, as some of their attributes are borrowed from cloud and lightning as well. A. KUHN and BENFEY[5] held the Maruts to be personifications of the souls of the dead (cp. p. 77), and with this view MEYER[6] and v. SCHROEDER[7] substantially agree. This origin is historically possible, but the RV. furnishes no evidence in support of it. The etymology[8] being uncertain can throw no additional light on the beginnings of the conception. The root appears to be *mar*, but whether in the sense of 'to die', 'to crush', or 'to shine', it is hard to decide. The latter meaning, however, seems to accord best with the description given of the Maruts in the RV.

[1] PVS. 2, 73. — [2] On the various names for rain in the RV. see BOHNENBERGER, op. cit. 43–4. — [3] BRV. 2, 391. — [4] PVS. 1, 59. — [5] OO. on RV. 1, 64. — [6] Indogermanische Mythen 1, 218. — [7] WZKM. 9, 248—9. — [8] Nirukta 11, 13; GRASSMANN, KZ. 16, 161—4; BDA. 112—3; ZDMG. 40, 349—60; KRV. note 136; MM., Vedic Hymns, SBE. 32, xxiv—xxv; HRI. 97.

ROTH, ZDMG. 2, 222; WHITNEY, JAOS. 3, 319; OST. 5, 147—54; GRV. 1, 44; BRV. 2, 369—402; BRI. 14; KRV. 39; MMPhR. 317—20; HVBP. 83—5; V. BRADKE, FaR. 117—25; ORV. 224—5. 283; HRI. 96—9.

§ 30. Vāyu-Vāta. — Each of the two names of wind Vāyu and Vāta is used to express both the physical phenomenon and its divine personification. But Vāyu is chiefly the god and Vāta the element. Vāyu is celebrated alone in one whole hymn besides parts of others, and in about half a dozen others conjointly with Indra. Vāta is invoked only in two short hymns (168 and 186) at the end of the tenth book of the RV. The names of both sometimes occur in the same verse (6, 50[12]; 10, 92[13]). The difference between the two is illustrated by the fact that Vāyu alone is as a god associated with Indra, the two deities being then often invoked as Indravāyū. This couple was regarded as so closely connected by the ancient native interpreters, that either of them might represent the deities of the atmospheric region in the Vedic triad (Nir. 7, 5). Vāta on the other hand, being less fully personified, is only associated with Parjanya (§ 31), whose connexion with the thunderstorm is much more vivid than that of Indra. Different sets of epithets are applied to the two wind-gods, those belonging to Vāta being chiefly expressive of the physical attributes of swiftness and violence.

Few references are made to Vāyu's origin. The two worlds are said to have generated him for wealth (7, 90[3]). He is once spoken of as the son-in-law of Tvaṣṭṛ (8, 26[21-2]), though his wife's name is not mentioned (cp. § 38). In the Puruṣa hymn he is said to have sprung from the breath of the world-giant (10, 90[13]). Vāyu is rarely connected with the Maruts. He is, however, once said to have generated them from the wombs of heaven (1, 134[4]) and to be accompanied by them (1, 142[12]) as well as by Pūṣan and the Viśvedevas. His personal attributes are rather indefinite. He is beautiful (1, 2[1]) and with Indra is spoken of as touching the sky, swift as thought, and thousand-eyed (1, 23[2, 3]). He is once said to have roaring velocity (10, 100[2]). Vāyu has a shining car drawn by a team or by a pair of red (*rohita*) or ruddy (*aruṇa*) steeds. His team consists of 99 (4, 48[4]), 100 or even 1000 (4, 46[3]) horses yoked by his will. The attribute *niyutvat*, 'drawn by a team', often occurs with reference to Vāyu or his car, being otherwise used only once or twice in each case with reference to Indra, Agni, Pūṣan, or the Maruts. Vāyu's car, in which Indra is his companion (4, 46[2]. 48[2]; 7, 91[5]), has a golden seat and touches the sky (4, 46[4]). Like the other gods, Vāyu is fond of Soma, to which he is often invited to come with his teams and the first draught of which he obtains as his share[1] (also in company with Indra: 1, 135[4]), for he is the swiftest of the gods (ŚB. 13, 1, 2[7] &c.)[2]. The AB. (2, 25) tells a story of how in a race which the gods ran for the first draught of Soma, Vāyu reached the goal first and Indra second. He is in the RV. also called a protector of Soma (10, 85[5]) and has the characteristic epithet *śucipā*, 'drinking the clear (Soma draught)', an epithet which Indra once shares with him. He is also once connected with the 'nectar-yielding' (*sabardughā*) cow[3] (1, 134[4]). Vāyu grants fame, offspring, wealth in steeds, oxen, and gold (7, 90[2. 6]). He disperses foes (4, 48[2]) and is invoked for protection by the weak (1, 134[5]).

Vāta, as the ordinary name of wind, is celebrated in a more concrete manner. His name is frequently connected with the root *vā*, to blow, from which it is derived. One of the hymns devoted to his praise (10, 168) describes him as follows. Shattering everything and thundering, his din presses on; he goes along whirling up the dust of the earth; he wanders in the air on his paths; he does not rest even a day. Firstborn, he is a friend of the waters; but the place of his birth is unknown. This deity wanders where he lists; one hears his roaring, but his form one does not see (cp. 1, 164[44]). He is the breath of the gods (cp. 7, 87[2]; 10, 92[13]) and is worshipped with oblations.

Vāta, like Rudra, also wafts healing and prolongs life, for he has the treasure of immortality in his house (10, 186). This healing power of wind doubtless represents its purifying character (cp. p. 77). The activity of wind is chiefly mentioned in connexion with the thunderstorm (4, 17[11]; 5, 83[4]; 10, 168[1. 2]). Blasts of wind being coincident with the appearance of lightnings and preceding the reappearance of the sun, Vāta is spoken of as producing ruddy lights (10, 168[1]) and of making the dawns to shine (1, 134[3]). The swiftness of wind often supplies a comparison for the speed of the gods (4, 17[12]; 5, 41[3]; 9, 97[52]) or of mythical steeds (1, 163[11]; 4, 38[3]). Its noise is also frequently mentioned (4, 22[4]; 8, 91[3]; 10, 168[1. 4]). The name of Vāta has been identified with that of the Germanic god of storm and battle, Odhin or Wodan[4], which is explained as formed with a derivative suffix from the cognate base. But this identification seems to be very doubtful[5].

[1] 1, 134[1]. 135[1]; 4, 46[1]; 5, 43[3]; 7, 92[1]; 8, 89[4]. — [2] OLDENBERG, ZDMG. 39, 55, note 1; HVM. 1, 260. — [3] Cp. OLDENBERG, SBE. 46, 244. — [4] GROHMANN, KZ. 10, 274; ZIMMER, ZDA. 19, 170–2. 179–80; MANNHARDT, ibid. 22, 4; MOGK in PAUL's Grundriss 1075; STOKES, BB. 19, 74; MACDONELL, JRAS. 25, 488; v. SCHROEDER, WZKM. 9, 239. — [5] Cp. BDA. p. x; IF. 5, 272.

OST. 5, 143–6; KRV. 38; BRV. 1, 24–8; SP.AP. 156–8; HVBP. 82–3; ORV. 225–6.

§ 31. Parjanya. — This god plays a very subordinate part among the deities of the RV., being celebrated in only three hymns, while the name is mentioned less than thirty times. His praises are also sung in one hymn of the AV. (4, 15), which, however, chiefly consists of verses from the RV. In the following passages the word *parjanya* can only have the appellative sense of 'rain-cloud'. 'This same water rises and descends day by day; the rain-clouds (*parjanyāḥ*) quicken the earth, the fires quicken heaven' (1, 164[51]). The Maruts 'even during the day cause darkness by the water-carrying rain-cloud, when they inundate the earth' (1, 38[9]); 'they poured out the pail of heaven, they discharge the raincloud through the two worlds, the rain pervades the dry places' (5, 53[6]). Bṛhaspati is besought to cause the cloud to rain and to send the rain-charged (*vṛṣṭimantam*) cloud (10, 98[1. 8]). Soma flows 'like the rain-charged cloud' (9, 2[9]) and the drops of Soma speed 'like the rains of the cloud' (9, 22[2]). In the AV. the rain-shedding cow Vaśā is thus addressed: 'The rain-cloud is thy udder, o excellent goddess, the lightnings are thy teats, O Vaśā' (AV. 10, 10[7]). In all such passages the native commentators explain *parjanya* by *megha*, 'cloud'. On the other hand, *parjanya* is used to explain *dyaus* in VS. 12, 6 and *stanayitnu*, 'thunder' in ŚB. (14, 5, 5[10])[1]. In some cases it is hard to say whether we have the appellative or the personified meaning. Thus the might of Agni is said to resound like *parjanya* (8, 91[5]); and the frogs are spoken of as uttering their voices when roused by *parjanya* (7, 103[1]). In most passages, however, the word clearly represents the personification which presides over the rain-cloud, while generally retaining the attributes belonging to the phenomenon. The latter then becomes an udder, a pail (*kośa*) or water-skin (*dṛti*: 5, 83[8. 9]; 7, 101[4]). The personification is to a considerable extent theriomorphic, Parjanya being often spoken of as a bull, though with a certain confusion of gender (probably because clouds are otherwise cows). He is a roaring bull with swift-flowing drops, who places his seed in the plants as a germ (5, 83[1], cp. [7. 9]; AV. 4, 15[1]). The clouds (*abhrāṇi*) impelled by the wind come together, and the roaring waters of the great bellowing aqueous (*nabhasvataḥ*) bull delight the earth (AV. 4, 15[1]). Sometimes Parjanya is like a barren cow, sometimes he is productive, disposing of his body according to his wish (7, 101[3]).

The shedding of rain is his most prominent characteristic. He flies around with a watery car and loosens and draws downwards the water-skin (5, 83[7]). Like a charioteer urging on his horses, he displays his rainy messengers; when he sheds rain water, the roar of the lion resounds from afar;

with thunder he comes shedding rain-water as our divine (*asura*) father (5, $83^{3.6}$). He is besought for rains (7, 101^{5}) and is implored to withhold rain after shedding it (5, 83^{10}). It is, however, implied that the action of Parjanya, as well as of the Maruts, in shedding rain is subordinate to that of Mitra and Varuṇa (5, 63^{3-6}). He is several times said to thunder (5, 83). Thundering he strikes down trees, demons, evil-doers; the whole world is terrified at his mighty weapon (5, 83^{2}). He and Vāta are the wielders of mighty thunder (10, 66^{10}). Parjanya is also associated with lightning, though less frequently than with thunder. The winds blow forth, the lightnings fall, when Parjanya quickens the earth with his seed (5, 83^{4}). Parjanya thunders with lightning in the (aerial) ocean (AV. 19, 30^{5}). He also appears to be meant, in a hymn of the RV. to the Viśvedevas, by the god who thunders and roars, rich in clouds and water, who with lightning excites the two worlds, besprinkling them (5, 42^{14}).

As the shedder of rain Parjanya is naturally in a special degree the producer and nourisher of vegetation. When he quickens the earth with his seed, the plants spring up; in his activity are plants of every form; he has produced plants for nourishment (5, $83^{4.5.10}$, cp. 6, 52^{6}; AV. 4, $15^{2.3.15}$; 8, 7^{21}). He is the fructifier and increaser of plants; protected by the god they bear good fruit (7, $101^{1.5}$). Reeds and grass are produced by his action (7, 102^{1}, cp. 5, 75^{15}; AV. 1, 2^{1}. 3^{1}; 19, 30^{5}). Parjanya places the germ not only in plants but in cows, mares, and women (7, 102^{2}), and is invoked to bestow fertility (5, 83^{7} cp. 6, 52^{16}). He is the bull that impregnates everything: in him is the soul of what moves and stands (7, 101^{6}; cp. 1, 115^{1}). He is even described as self-dependent sovereign, who rules over the whole world, in whom all beings and the three heavens are established, and in whom the threefold waters flow (7, $101^{2.4.5}$). Owing to his generative activity Parjanya several times receives the epithet of 'father' (7, 101^{3}; 9, 82^{3}; AV. 4, 15^{12}; 12, 1^{12}). He is once called 'our divine (*asura*) father' (5, 83^{6}); and in another passage 'the occult power of the Asura' (5, $63^{3.7}$) perhaps refers to him.

His wife is by implication the Earth (5, 83^{4}; 7, 101^{3}, cp. 1, 160^{3}). The AV. (12, 1^{12}) states that Earth is the mother, Parjanya the father[2], but elsewhere explicitly calls Vaśā his wife (10, 10^{6}). In these respects as well as the theriomorphic conception of him as a bull, his relation to thunder, lightning, and rain, he approximates to the character of Dyaus (cp. 10, 45^{4}; 2, 4^{6}. 27^{15}) whose son he is once called (7, 102^{1}). Parjanya himself is said to produce a calf (*vatsam*), the germ of plants (7, 101^{1}, cp. v. 3; 5, 83^{1}), who perhaps represents lightning. Soma may, however, be meant, for his father is once (9, 82^{3}) said to be Parjanya[3], and he is spoken of as 'increased by Parjanya' (9, 113^{3}).

Parjanya is associated with various other deities. His connexion is closest with Vāta, who, with the single exception of Agni in one passage, is the only god forming a dual divinity with him (§ 44). The Maruts are also a few times invoked with Parjanya (5, 63^{6}. 83^{5}) and are called upon to sing his praises (AV. 4, 15^{4}). Agni is celebrated with him in two verses of one hymn (6, $52^{6.16}$; cp. § 44). Indra has much in common with the 'rainy' Parjanya, being compared with him in this respect (8, 6^{1}). The two gods have in fact much the same natural basis, the connexion with which is, however, much clearer in the case of Parjanya (cp. p. 82).

Parjanya's name is of uncertain derivation. But it is still usually identified, owing to the similarity of character, with that of the Lithuanian thundergod Perkúnas[4], though the phonetic difficulties of the identification cannot be explained. The freshness of the conception in the RV. renders it probable that if the two names are really connected, their Indo-European form was still an appellative. It seems clear that in the RV. the word is an appellative of the thundering rain-cloud as well as the proper name of its personification, the god who actually sheds the rain. The senses of rain-cloud and rain-god both survive through the Brāhmaṇas into the later language. The native dictionaries explain the appellative as 'thunder-cloud' (*garjanmegha* &c.), while the deity is sometimes found identified with Indra in the Mahābhārata.

[1] Cp. OO. 1, 223. — [2] The TA. 1, 10, 1[4] says that Bhūmi or Earth is the wife and Vyoman or Sky is the husband. — [3] Cp. BLOOMFIELD, FaR. 153. — [4] OO. 1, 223; ZIMMER, ZDA. 19, 164 f., cp. AIL. 42 f.; LRV. 3, 322 f.; ZDMG. 32, 314 f.; KRV. note 139; HIRT, IF. 1, 481—2.

BÜHLER, OO. 1, 214—20; DELBRÜCK, ZVP. 1865, p. 275 f.; ROTH, ZDMG. 24, 302—5 (on RV. 1, 165); OST. 5, 140—2; BRV. 3, 25—30; KRV. 40; BRL 14; WC. 56 f.; HVBP. 80—2; ORV. 226; SBE. 46, 105; HRI. 103—4.

§ 32. Āpaḥ. — The Waters, Āpaḥ, are lauded in four hymns of the RV. (7, 47. 49; 10, 9. 30), as well as in a few scattered verses. They are also invoked in many detached verses along with other deities. The personification is only incipient, hardly extending beyond the notion of their being mothers, young wives, and goddesses who bestow boons and come to the sacrifice. They are goddesses who follow the path of the gods (7, 47^{3}). Indra armed with the bolt dug out a channel for them (7, 47^{4}. 49^{1}), and they never infringe his ordinances (7, 47^{3}). They are also said to be under the commands of Savitṛ (p. 32). They are celestial, as well as flowing in channels, and have the sea for their goal (7, 49^{2}). It is implied that they abide where the gods are and the seat of Mitra and Varuṇa is (10, 30^{1}). They are beside the sun and the sun is with them (1, 23^{17}). King Varuṇa moves in their midst, looking down on the truth and falsehood of men (7, 49^{3}). In such passages at least, the rain-waters must be meant (HRI. 99). But the Naighaṇṭuka (5, 3) enumerates the waters among the terrestrial deities only (cp. YN. 9, 26).

Agni is often described as dwelling in the waters (p 92). He is said to have entered into them (7, 49^{4}). As mothers they produce Agni (10, 91^{6}, cp. 2^{7}; AV. 1, 33^{1}), one of whose forms is called 'Son of Waters' (§ 24). The waters are mothers (10, 17^{10}; 1, 23^{16}), who are the wives of the world, equal in age and origin (10, 30^{10}). They are besought to give their auspicious fluid like loving mothers (10, 9^{2}). They are most motherly, the producers of all that is fixed and moves (6, 50^{7}).

The waters cleanse and purify; these goddesses bear away defilement; the worshipper comes up out of them pure and cleansed (10, 17^{10}). They are even invoked to cleanse from moral guilt, the sins of violence, cursing, and lying (1, 23^{22} = 10, 9^{8}). They are remedial (6, 50^{7}), bestowing remedies and long life, for all remedies, immortality and healing are contained in them (10, 9^{5-7}; 1, 23^{19-21}). They watch over man's health in the house (HGS. 2, 4^{5}). They dispose of boons and wealth and bestow excellent strength and immortality (10, 9^{5}. 30^{12}). Their blessing and aid is often implored (7, 47^{4}. 49^{1-4}; 10, 9. 30^{11}), and they are invited to seat themselves along with the Son of waters on the sacrificial grass at the offering of the soma-priest (10, $30^{14.15}$).

The waters are several times associated with honey. As mothers they mix their milk with honey (1, 23^{16}). The wave of the waters is rich in honey; dripping with ghee it became the drink of Indra, whom it exhilerated (7, $47^{1.2}$). Apāṃ napāt is besought to give waters rich in honey, by which Indra grew to heroic strength (10, 30^{4}). The waters are invoked to pour the wave, rich in honey and gladdening the gods, for Indra who released them from confinement; the wave which intoxicates, the draught of Indra, which is produced in the sky (10, 30⁷⁻⁹). These passages appear to show that sometimes at least the celestial waters were regarded as containing or identical with the heavenly Soma, the beverage of Indra. In other passages the waters used in preparing the terrestrial Soma seem to be meant. When they appear bearing ghee, milk, and honey, they are accordant with the priests, bearing well-pressed Soma for Indra (10, 30^{13}). Soma delights in them as a young man in lovely maidens; he approaches them as a lover; they are maidens who bow down before the youth (10, 30^{5-6}).

OST. 5, 24, note. 343. 345; BRV. 1, 260; DARMESTETER, Haurvataṭ et Ameretaṭ 73—4; WC. 56; SP.AP. 153—5; ORV. 242.

C. TERRESTRIAL GODS.

§ 33. **Rivers.** — Beside the divine Waters, deified rivers occupy a not unimportant position in the RV. The whole of one hymn (10,75) celebrates the Sindhu or Indus with the exception of the fifth verse, in which several of its tributaries are invoked besides other streams, while in the sixth verse a number of other rivers are mentioned as affluents of the Indus. Another entire hymn (3, 33), is devoted to the invocation and praise of the sister streams Vipāś and Śutudrī.

The Sarasvatī is, however, more greatly celebrated than any other river. But though the personification in this case goes much further than in the others, the connexion of the goddess with the river is in the RV. always present to the minds of the poets. Sarasvatī is lauded in three hymns of the RV. and in numerous detached verses. Sarasvatī, Sarayu, and Sindhu are invoked as great streams (10, 64^{9}) and elsewhere (10, 75^{5}) Gaṅgā, Yamunā, Sarasvatī, Śutudrī, Paruṣṇī, and others known and unknown, altogether twenty-one, are addressed. Kings and peoples living on the banks of the Sarasvatī are referred to (7, 96^{2}; 8, 21^{18}). Sarasvatī, an iron fort, flows with fertile flood, a stream (*sindhu*) surpassing all other waters in greatness; she alone of rivers appeared pure, flowing from the mountains, from[1] the (celestial) ocean (7, $95^{1.2}$, cp. 5, 43^{11}). She tears away with her mighty waves the peaks of mountains, and her immense and impetuous flood moves roaring (6, $61^{2.8}$). She is distinguished by greatness among the great, she is the most active of the active, and is implored not to withhold her milk (6, 61^{13}). The poet prays that he may not be removed from her to fields which are strange (6, 61^{14}). She has seven sisters and is sevenfold (6, $61^{10.12}$). She is one of seven, a mother of streams[2] (7, 36^{6}). She is the best of mothers, of rivers, and of goddesses (2, 41^{16}). She is called *pāvīravī*, an epithet (applied also to *tanyatu*, 'thunder', in 10, 65^{13}) probably meaning 'daughter of lightning'[3], and is said (6, 49^{7}) to be the wife of a hero (probably Sarasvat). She fills the terrestrial regions and the wide atmospheric space and occupies three abodes (6, $61^{11.12}$). She is invoked to descend from the sky, from the great mountain, to the sacrifice (5, 43^{11}). The last three passages (cp. also 7, 95^{2}) seem to allude to the notion of a celestial origin, like that of Gaṅgā in post-Vedic mythology. She is once called *asuryā* or divine (7, 96^{1}). The goddess comes to the sacrifice on the same chariot as the Fathers and seats herself on the sacrificial grass (10, $17^{8.9}$). Even here she must be conceived as the river goddess, for in the following two verses the waters are invoked to cleanse from defilement.

She herself is a purifier (1, 3^{10}). She is besought to come 'swelling with streams' (6, 52^{6}) and, along with the waters, the bestowers of wealth, progeny, and immortality, to grant vitality (10, 30[12]). She bestows vitality and offspring (2, 41[17]) and is associated with deities who assist procreation (10, 184[2]). She is also said to have given a son named Divodāsa to Vadhryaśva (6, 61[1]). Her unfailing breast (cp. AB. 4, 1) yields riches of every kind (1, 164[49]). She is often said to bestow wealth, plenty, and nourishment (7, 95[2]; 8, 21[17]; 9, 67[32]; 10, 17[8. 9]), and several times receives the epithet *subhaga*, 'bountiful' (1, 89[3]; 7, 95[4. 6]; 8, 21[17]). As a mother (*ambā*) she grants reputation to the unrenowned (2, 41[16]). She stimulates, directs, and prospers the devotions of her worshippers (1, 3[10. 11]; 2, 3[8]; 6, 61[4]). She is invoked along with the goddesses of prayer (7, 37[11]; 10, 65[13]). She destroys the revilers of the gods, is terrible, and a Vṛtra-slayer (6, 61[3. 7]). But to her worshippers she affords protection and conquers their enemies (7, 95[4. 5]; 2, 30[8]; 6, 49[7]).

Sarasvatī is often invoked with other deities. Besides Pūṣan and Indra, she is particularly associated with the Maruts (3, 54[13]; 7, 9[5]. 39[5]. 40[3]) and is said to be accompanied by them (2, 30[8]) or to have them as her friends[4] (7, 96[2]). She is also once in the RV. connected with the Aśvins. When the latter aided Indra, Sarasvatī is said to have refreshed him (10, 131[5]). With reference to the same myth the VS. (19, 12) states that when the gods celebrated a healing sacrifice, the Aśvins as physicians and Sarasvatī through speech (*vācā*) communicated vigour to Indra[5]. The VS. even speaks of Sarasvatī as the wife of the Aśvins (19, 94). Sarasvatī is several times associated in the eighth and ninth verses of the *āprī* and *āpra* hymns with the sacrificial goddesses Iḍā and Bhāratī (with whom she forms a triad), and sometimes also with Mahī and Hotrā. This association may have been due to the sacred character of the river. Allusion is made to Agni being kindled for sacrifice on the banks of the Sarasvatī and Dṛṣadvatī (3, 23[4])[6]; and the AB. (2, 19) refers to a sacrifice performed by Ṛṣis on the Sarasvatī. Hence on the banks of the Sarasvatī there were perhaps places of worship of the Bharatas; in that case, Bhāratī, the personified offering of the Bharatas, would naturally find a fixed place along with Sarasvatī in the Āpri litany which accompanied the animal sacrifice[7].

Though there is nothing to show distinctly (cp. 7, 35[11]) that Sarasvatī is ever anything more in the RV. than a river goddess, we find her identified in the Brāhmaṇas (ŚB. 3. 9, 1[7]; AB. 3, 1[10]), with Vāc, Speech, and in post-Vedic mythology she has become goddess of eloquence and wisdom, invoked as a muse and regarded as the wife of Brahmā[8]. The transition from the older to the later conception is perhaps to be found in passages like VS. 19, 12 quoted above.

There has been much controversy as to the identity of the stream of which the goddess Sarasvatī is a personification. The name is identical with that of the Avestan river Haraqaiti in Afghanistan[9], and it may have been the latter river which was first lauded as the Sarasvatī[10]. But ROTH (PW.), GRASSMANN (GW.), LUDWIG[11], and ZIMMER (AIL. 10) are of opinion, that in the RV. Sarasvatī usually and originally meant a mighty stream, probably the Indus (Sarasvatī being the sacred and Sindhu the secular name), but that it occasionally designates the small stream in Madhyadeśa, to which both its name and its sacred character were in later times transferred. MAX MÜLLER[12] believes it to be identical with this small river Sarasvatī, which with the Dṛṣadvatī formed the boundaries of the sacred region Brahmāvarta and which loses itself in the sands of the desert, but in Vedic times reached the sea. According to OLDHAM[13] a survey of ancient river-beds affords evidence that the Sarasvatī was originally a tributary of the Śutudrī (the modern Sutlej)[14], and that when the latter left its old bed and joined the Vipāś, the Sarasvatī continued to flow in the old bed of the Sutudrī.

Sarasvatī has a male correlative named Sarasvat, who after the praises of the river goddess have been sung in three verses of one hymn (7, 96), is invoked in the next three by worshippers desiring wives and offspring, protection and plenty. Here his fertilizing waters and even his exuberant breast are referred to. In another passage (1, 164^{52}), Sarasvat, here apparently a name of the bird Agni[15], is spoken of as refreshing with rain. Roth (PW.) regards him as a guardian of the celestial waters who bestows fertility. Hillebrandt[16] identifies Sarasvat with Apāṃ napāt (= Soma, the moon) and Hardy[17] expresses a similar view.

[1] Cp. BRV. 1, 326. — [2] According to Bergaigne (ibid.) 'having the (celestial) ocean for her mother', owing to the accent. — [3] Roth, Nir. 165f.; PW.; BRV. 1, 327. — [4] Cp. Marudvṛddhā as the name of a river (10, 75^5). — [5] Cp. ŚB. 12, 7, 3^1; OST. 5, 94 note. — [6] Cp. Mānavadharmaśāstra II, 17f.; Oldenberg, Buddha 413f. — [7] ORV. 243. — [8] Cp. ZDMG. 1, 84; 27, 705. — [9] SP.AP. 105f. — [10] HRI. 31. [11] Nachrichten des RV. und AV. über Geographie etc., Prag 1875—6, p. 13; cp. PVS. 2, 86. — [12] Vedic Hymns SBE., 32, 60. — [13] JRAS. 25, 49—76. — [14] OST. 2, 345. — [15] BRV. 1, 144; 2, 47. — [16] HVM. 1, 380—2. — [17] HVBP. 42—3.

OST. 5, 337—43; BRV. 1, 325—8; Bollensen, ZDMG. 41, 499; HVM. 1, 382—3 (celestial Sarasvatī = milky way); HVBP. 98; ORV. 243.

§ 34. **Pṛthivī.** — The Earth, Pṛthivī, being, as has been shown (p. 22), generally celebrated conjointly with Dyaus, is lauded alone in only one short hymn of three stanzas in the RV. (5, 84) and in a long and beautiful one in the AV. (12, 1). The personification is but slight, the attributes of the goddess being chiefly those of the physical earth. According to the RV. she abounds in heights, bears the burden of the mountains, and supports the trees of the forest in the ground (*kṣmā*). She quickens the soil, for she scatters rain, and the showers of heaven are shed from the lightning of her cloud. She is great (*mahī*), firm (*dṛḷhā*) and shining (*arjunī*).

The meaning of Pṛthivī is 'the broad one'; and a poet of the RV. (2, 15^2) alludes to the etymology when he says that Indra upheld the earth (*pṛthivī*) and spread it out (*paprathat*). The TS. (7, 1, 5) and TB. (1, 1, 3^5) in describing the origin of the earth, expressly derive the name of Pṛthivī from the root *prath*, to extend, because she is extended.

Pṛthivī is spoken of as 'kindly Mother Earth', to whom the dead man in a funeral hymn (10, 18^{10}), is exhorted to go. When mentioned wirh Dyaus, Pṛthivī frequently receives the epithet of 'mother' (cp. §§ 11. 44).

Bruce, JRAS. 1862, p. 321; OST. 5, 21—2; BRV. 1, 4—5; BDA. 48; Bollensen, ZDMG. 41, 494—5; HVBP. 25—6; Thurneysen, IF. 4, 84.

§ 35. **Agni.** — The chief terrestrial deity is Agni, being naturally of primary importance as the personification of the sacrificial fire, which is the centre of the ritual poetry of the Veda. Next to Indra he is the most prominent of the Vedic gods. He is celebrated in at least 200 hymns of the RV., and in several besides he is invoked conjointly with other deities.

As his name is also the regular designation of fire, the anthropomorphism of his physical appearance is only rudimentary, his bodily parts having a clear reference to the phenomena of terrestrial fire mainly in its sacrificial aspect. He is butter-backed (5, 4^3 &c.), butter-faced (3, 1^{18} &c.) and beautiful-tongued (1, 14^7). He is butter-haired (8, 49^2), flame-haired (1, 45^6 &c.) or tawny-haired (3, 2^{13}), and has a tawny beard (5, 7^7). He has sharp (8, 49^3 &c.) or burning jaws (1, 58^5 &c.), golden (5, 2^3) or shining teeth (5, 7^4) and iron grinders (10, 87^2). He is once described as footless and headless (4, 1^{11}), but elsewhere he is said to have a burning head (7, 3^{1}) or three heads and seven rays (1, 146^{1}; 2, 5^{3}). He faces in all directions (2, 3^{1} &c.). His tongue is often mentioned (8, 61^{18} &c.). He is also said to have three tongues (3, 20^{2}) or seven (VS. 17, 79), his steeds also being seven-tongued (3, 6^{2}). A name was later given to each of these seven tongues[1]. Butter is Agni's eye (3, 26^{7}); he is four-eyed (1, 31^{13}), thousand-eyed (1, 79^{12}), and thousand-horned (6, 1^{8}). In his hand he bears many gifts for men (1, 72^{1}). Like Indra, he has the epithet *sahasra-muṣka* (8, 19^{32}). He is called an archer (4, 4^{1}) or is compared with an archer (1, 70^{11}), who sharpens his flame like a blade of iron (6, 3^{5}).

He is often likened to various animals, in most cases doubtless with a view to indicating his functions rather than representing his personal form. He is frequently called a bull (1, 58^{5} &c.). He is a strong bull with a mighty neck (5, 2^{12}). As such he bellows (10, 8^{1}), abounds in seed (4, 5^{3}), and is provided with horns (5, 1^{8}; 6, 16^{39}), which he sharpens (8, 49^{13}), which he shakes, and which make him difficult to seize (1, 140^{6}). He is many times spoken of or alluded to when born as a calf (*vatsa*). He is also often compared with (1, 58^{2} &c.) or directly called a steed (1, 149^{3}; 6, 12^{6})[2]. The tail which he agitates like a horse (2, 4^{4}) is doubtless his flame. When purified by sacrificers he is compared with a groomed horse (1, 60^{5} &c.). Sacrificers lead (3, 2^{7}), excite, and set him in motion like a horse (7, 7^{1} &c.). He is the horse they seek to tame and direct (2, 5^{1}; 3, 27^{3}). He is kindled like a horse that brings the gods (3, 27^{14}). He is attached to the pole at places of sacrifice (2, 2^{1}) or to the pole of the rite (1, 143^{7}). He is yoked in order to waft the sacrifice to the gods (10, 51^{7}). He is also compared with (3, 26^{3}) or directly called a neighing steed (1, 36^{8}). He is further likened to a horse as conquering (8, 91^{12}) or causing to escape from dangers (4, 2^{8}). Agni is, moreover, like a bird. He is the eagle of the sky (7, 15^{4}) and a divine bird (1, 164^{52}). As dwelling in the waters he resembles the aquatic bird *haṃsa* (1, 65^{9}). He takes possession of the wood as a bird perches on a tree (1, 66^{2}; 6, 3^{5}; 10, 91^{2}). He is winged (1, 58^{5}; 2, 2^{4}), his course is a flight (6, 3^{7}. 4^{6} &c.), and he darts with rapid flight to the gods (10, 6^{4}). He is once described as a raging serpent (1, 79^{1}).

Agni is besides frequently compared with inanimate objects. Like the sun, he resembles gold (2, 2^{4}; 7, 3^{6}). When he stretches out his tongue (6, 3^{4}) he is like a hatchet, to which he is elsewhere also several times compared (1, 127^{3} &c.). He resembles (1, 141^{8} &c.) or is directly called a car (3, 11^{5}), as bringing riches (1, 58^{3}; 3, 15^{5}) or as being formidable in battle (1, 66^{6}). He seems to be thought of as a car directed by others, for he is conducted to the sacrifice like a laden car (10, 176^{3}). He is even compared to wealth (1, 58^{6}. 60^{1}) or to wealth acquired by inheritance (1, 73^{1}).

Wood (2, 7^{6}) or ghee (7, 3^{1}) is his food, melted butter is his beverage (2, 7^{6}; 10, 69^{2}). He is nourished by ghee poured into his mouth (3, 21^{1}; 5, 11^{3} &c.) and is an eater of oil (AV. 1, 7^{2}). He eats and chews the forests with sharp tooth (1, 143^{5}) or eats and blackens them with his tongue (6, 60^{10}; 10, 79^{2}). He is all-devouring (8, 44^{26}). He is nourished three times a day (4, 12^{1}, cp. 1, 140^{2}; 7, 11^{3}). He is sometimes spoken of as the mouth and the tongue by which the gods eat the sacrifice (2, $1^{13.14}$); and his flames are spoons with which he besprinkles or honours the gods (1, 76^{5}; 10, 6^{4}). But he is more frequently asked to eat the offerings himself (3, 21^{1-4}. 28^{1-6}). With upright, god-ward form he strives after the ghee that is offered (1, 127^{1}). Though the regular offering to him is fuel or butter[3], he is sometimes, and then nearly always with other gods, invited to drink the Soma juice (1, 14^{10}.

19^{9}. 21$^{1.3}$; 2, 36^{4}). In one hymn he is called *somagopā*, 'guardian of Soma' (10, 45$^{5.12}$). He is invited to come to the sacrifice (10, 98^{9}) and is often spoken of as sitting down on the sacrificial grass along with the gods (3, 14^{2}; 5, 11^{2}. 26^{5}; 7, 11^{2}, cp. 43^{3}).

Agni's brightness is naturally much dwelt upon. He is of brilliant lustre (2, 10^{2} &c.), brilliant-flamed (6, 10^{3}), bright-flamed (7, 15^{10} &c.), clear-flamed (8, 43^{31}), and bright-coloured (1, 140^{1}; 5, 2^{3}). He has a golden form (4, 3^{1} 10, 20^{9}). He shines like the sun (1, 149^{3}; 7, 3^{6}). His lustre is like the rays of the dawn and the sun and like the lightnings of the rain-cloud (10, 91$^{4.5}$). He shines even at night (5, 7^{4}). Like the sun he dispels the darkness with his rays (8, 43^{32}). He is a destroyer of darkness and sees through the gloom of the night (1, 94^{5}; 7, 9^{3}). Kindled he opens the gates of darkness (3, 5^{1}). The earth enveloped in darkness and the sky become visible when Agni is born (10, 88^{2}). For he is kindled at dawn and is the only individual god who is described as 'waking at dawn', *uṣarbudh* (though the gods collectively sometimes receive this epithet).

On the other hand, Agni's course, path, or track, and his fellies are black (1, 141^{7}; 2, 4$^{6.7}$; 6, 6^{1}; 7, 8^{2}; 8, 23^{19}), and his steeds make black furrows (1, 140^{4}). Driven by the wind he rushes through the wood (1, 58$^{4.5}$), invades the forests and shears the hairs of the earth (1, 65^{8}), shaving the earth as a barber a beard (10, 142^{4}).

His flames are like the roaring waves of the sea (1, 44^{12}). His sound is like the Wind or the thunder of Heaven (5, 25^{8}; 7, 3^{6}). He roars like the thundering Dyaus (10, 45^{4}), or Parjanya (8, 91^{5}), or a lion (3, 2^{11}). He bellows like a bull when he invades the forest trees, and the birds are terrified at the noise when his grass-devouring sparks arise (1, 94$^{10.11}$). He cannot be checked any more than the sound of the Maruts, an army let loose, or the bolt of heaven (1, 143^{5}).

Agni flames upwards (6, 15^{2}). Driven by the wind his flames shoot into the sky (8, 43^{4}). His smoke wavers and his flame cannot be seized (8, 23^{1}). His red smoke rises up to heaven (7, 3^{3}. 16^{3}). His smoke spreads in the sky (6, 2^{6}). Like the erector of a post (*metṛ*), he supports the sky with his smoke (4, 6^{2}). He touches the ridge of heaven with his crest and mingles with the rays of the sun (7, 2^{1}). He encompasses heaven with his tongue (8, 61^{18}) and goes to the flood of heaven, to the waters in the bright space above and below the sun (3, 22^{3}). The Agni of Divodāsa spread along mother earth towards the gods and stood on the ridge of the sky (8, 92^{2}). 'Smoke-bannered' (*dhūmaketu*) is a frequent epithet exclusively connected with Agni.

Agni is borne on an lightning car (3, 14^{1}), on a car that is luminous (1, 140^{1}), bright (1, 141^{12}), shining (5, 1^{11}), brilliant (10, 1^{5}), golden (4, 1^{8}) or beautiful (4, 2^{4}). It is drawn by two or more horses[4], which are butter-backed (1, 14^{6}), ruddy (*rohita*, *aruṣa*), tawny and ruddy (7, 42^{1}), beautiful (4, 2^{2}), omniform (10, 70^{2}), active (2, 4^{2}), wind-impelled (1, 94^{10}), mind-yoked (1, 14^{6}). He yokes them to summon the gods (1, 14^{12}; 3, 6^{6}; 8, 64^{1}). For he is a charioteer (1, 25^{3} &c.) of the sacrifice (10, 92^{1} &c.). With his steeds he brings the gods on his car (3, 6^{9}). He comes seated on the same car as the gods (3, 4^{11}; 7, 11^{1}) or in advance of them (10, 70^{2}). He brings Varuṇa to the offering, Indra from the sky, the Maruts from the air (10, 70^{11}).

According to the ordinary view of the Vedic poets, Agni's father is Dyaus, who generated him (10, 45^{8}). He is the child (*śiśu*) of Dyaus (4, 15^{6}; 6, 49^{2}) and is said to have been born from the belly of the Asura[5] (3, 29^{4}). He is often called the son of Dyaus and Pṛthivī (3, 2^{2}. 3^{11}. 25^{1}; 10, 1^{2}. 2^{7}.

140^{1}). He is also spoken of as the offspring of Tvaṣṭṛ and the Waters, as well as of Heaven and Earth (10, 2^{7}. 46^{9}), or even simply of Tvaṣṭṛ (1, 95^{4}) or of the Waters (10, 91^{6}; AV. 1, 33^{1}). It is otherwise incidentally said that the Dawns generated Agni as well as the Sun and Sacrifice (7, 78^{3}) or Indra-Viṣṇu generated Agni besides Sun and Dawn (7, 99^{4}), or Indra generated Agni between two stones (2, 12^{3}, cp. 1^{1}). Agni is also described as the son of Iḷā (3, 29^{3}) or as the embryo of the rite (6, 48^{5}). The gods, it is sometimes said, generated him (6, 7^{1}; 8, 91^{17}), as a light for the Āryan (1, 59^{2}), or simply fashioned him for man (10, 46^{9}) or placed him among men (1, 36^{10}; 2, 4^{3}; 6, 16^{1}; 8, 73^{2}). At the same time Agni is the father of the gods (1, 69^{1}, cp. p. 12). The different points of view which give rise to these seemingly contradictory statements, are sufficiently clear.

Owing to his slightly developed anthropomorphism, the myths of Agni have little to say about his deeds, being, outside his main activity as sacrificial fire, chiefly concerned with his various births, forms, and abodes.

The divergent accounts given of the births of Agni are not inconsistent, because they refer to different places of origin. His daily terrestrial birth by friction from the two *araṇīs* or firesticks[6] is often referred to (3, 29^{2}. 23$^{2.3}$; 7, 1^{1}; 10, 7^{9}). In this connexion they are his parents, the upper being the male and the lower the female (3, 29^{3}). Or they are his mothers, for he is said to have two mothers (1, 31^{2})[7]. The two sticks produce him as a new-born infant, who is hard to catch (5, 9$^{3.4}$). From the dry (wood) the god is born living (1, 68^{2}). The child as soon as born devours the parents (10, 79^{4}). He is born of a mother who cannot suckle him (10, 115^{1}). With reference to this production by friction, men are said to have generated him (1, 60^{3}; 4, 1^{1}; 7, 1^{1}), the ten maidens[8] that produce him (1, 95^{2}) being the ten fingers (cp. 3, 23^{3}) employed in twirling the upright drill, which is the upper *araṇī*. *Pramantha*, the name of this fire-drill, occuring for the first time in a late metrical Smṛti work[9], the Karmapradīpa (1, 7^{5})[10] has, owing to a superficial resemblance, been connected with Προμηθεύς[11]. The latter word has, however, every appearance of being a purely Greek formation, while the Indian verb *math*, to twirl, is found compounded only with *nis*, never with *pra*, to express the act of producing fire by friction.

The powerful friction necessary to produce fire is probably the reason why Agni is frequently called the 'son (*sūnu*, *putra*, once *yuvan*) of strength' (*sahasaḥ*)[12]. This explanation is supported by a passage of the RV. stating that Agni 'rubbed with strength (*sahasā*) is produced (*jāyate*) by men on the surface of the earth' (6, 48^{5}). According to a later text, the kindling of Agni by friction must not take place before sunrise (MS. 1, 6^{10}). Being produced every morning for the sacrifice Agni appropriately receives the very frequent epithet, exclusively connected with him, of 'youngest' (*yaviṣṭha*, *yaviṣṭhya*). His new births are opposed to his old (3, 1^{20}). Having grown old he is born again as a youth (2, 4^{5}). In this sense, he does not grow old (1, 128^{2}), his new light being like his old (6, 16^{21}). Like some other gods, Agni is also spoken of simply as 'young'. At the same time he is old. There is no sacrificer older than Agni (5, 3^{5}), for he conducted the first sacrifice (3, 15^{4}). He shone forth after former dawns (1, 44^{10}), and the part played by Agni in the sacrifices of ancestors is often referred to (8, 43^{13} &c.). He is thus sometimes in the same passage paradoxically called both 'ancient' and 'very young' (10, 4$^{1.2}$).

More generally Agni is spoken of as born in wood (6, 3^{3}; 10, 79^{7}), as the embryo of plants (2, 1^{14}; 3, 1^{13}) or as distributed in plants (10, 1^{2}). He is also said to have entered into all plants or to strive after them (8, 43^{9}).

When he is called the embryo of trees (1, 70[4]) or of trees as well as plants (2, 1[1]), there may be a side-glance at the fire produced in forests by the friction of the boughs of trees.

The terrestrial existence of Agni is further indicated by his being called the 'navel of the earth' (1, 59[2]). This expression appears, in the many passages in which it occurs, to allude to the receptacle of the sacrificial Agni on the excavated altar or *vedi*[13]. In the Vedic ritual *nābhi* or 'navel' is the technical term designating the hollow in the *uttarā vedi*, in which Agni is deposited[14]. The earlier use of the term probably suggested the figure, that the gods made Agni the 'navel' or centre of immortality (3, 17[4]). The only two occurrences in the RV. of the attribute *vediṣad*, 'sitting on the altar', refer to Agni.

Agni's origin in the aerial waters is often referred to. The 'Son of waters' has, as has been shown (§ 24), become a distinct deity. Agni is also the 'embryo' (*garbha*) of the waters (3, 1[12, 13]); he is kindled in the waters (10, 45[1]; AV. 13, 1[50]); he is a bull who has grown in the lap of the waters (10, 8[1]); he is ocean-girt (8, 91[5]). He is also said to descend from the *dhanu* or cloud-island (1, 144[5]; 10, 4[5]) and to be the shining thunder dwelling in the bright space (6, 6[2]). In such passages the lightning form of Agni must be meant. Some of the later hymns of the RV. (10, 51—3. 124)[15] tell a legend of Agni hiding in the waters and plants and being found by the gods. This legend is also often related in the Brāhmaṇas[16]. In the AV. the Agnis in the waters are distinguished from those that go on the path of lightning or from the celestial Agni with the lightning (AV. 3, 21[1. 7]; 8, 1[11]) and are said to have dwelt on earth (AV. 12, 1[37]). In one passage of the RV. also it is stated that Agni rests in all streams (8, 39[8], cp. Āp. ŚS. 5, 2[1]); and in the later ritual texts Agni in the waters is invoked in connexion with ponds and water-vessels. Thus even in the oldest Vedic period, the waters in which Agni is latent, though not those from which he is produced, may in various passages have been regarded as terrestrial. OLDENBERG[17] thinks that the terrestrial waters are chiefly meant in this connexion and doubts whether the lightning Agni is intended even in the first hymn of the third book[18]. In any case, the notion of Agni in the waters is prominent throughout the Vedas. Water is Agni's home, as heaven is that of the sun (5, 85[2]: cp. AV. 13, 1[50]; 19, 33[1]). The waters are also often mentioned along with the plants or wood as his abode[19] (2, 1[1] &c.).

Agni's origin in heaven is moreover frequently spoken of. He is born in the highest heavens (1, 143[2]; 6, 8[2]). He existed potentially though not actually in the highest heavens (10, 5[7]), and was brought from heaven, from afar by Mātariśvan (§ 25). In such passages Agni doubtless represents lightning; for lightning is regarded as coming from heaven as well as from the waters (AV. 3, 21[1. 7]; 8, 1[11]), and in a Brāhmaṇa passage (AB. 7, 7[2]) it is spoken of as both celestial (*divya*) and aqueous (*apsumat*). When lightning is mentioned by its proper name *vidyut* (which occurs hardly 30 times in the RV.) along with Agni, it is commonly compared with and thereby distinguished from him[20], doubtless as a concrete phenomenon in contrast with the god. The myth, too, of the descent of fire from heaven to earth, due undoubtedly to the actual observation of conflagrations caused by the stroke of lightning, implies the identity of the celestial Agni and lightning. The heavenly origin of Agni is further implied in the fact that the acquisition of fire by man is regarded as a gift of the gods as well as a production of Mātariśvan; and Agni's frequent epithet of 'guest (*atithi*) of men' may allude to the same notion (5, 1[9] &c.).

In other passages, again, Agni is to be identified with the sun; for the conception of the sun as a form of Agni, is an undoubted Vedic belief. Thus Agni is the light of heaven in the bright sky, waking at dawn, the head of heaven (3, 2^{14}). He was born on the other side of the air and sees all things (10, $187^{4.5}$). He is born as the sun rising in the morning (10, 88^{6})[21]. The AB. (8, $28^{9.13}$) remarks that the sun when setting enters into Agni and is produced from him. The same identification is probably alluded to in passages stating that Agni unites with the light or the rays of the sun (5, 37^{1}; 7, 2^{1}), that when men light Agni on earth, the celestials light him (6, 2^{3}), or that Agni shines in heaven (3, 27^{12}; 8, 44^{29}). Sometimes, however, it is difficult to decide whether lightning or the sun is intended. The solar aspect of Agni's nature is not often mentioned, the sun being too individual a phenomenon to be generally conceived as a form of fire. Agni is usually thought of in his terrestrial form, being compared rather than identified with the sun. Thus the poet says that the minds of the godly are turned to Agni as eyes towards the sun (5, 1^{4}). At the same time there is frequently a side-glance at Agni's other forms, it being therefore in many cases doubtful which of his aspects is intended.

Owing to the diverse births above described, Agni is often regarded as having a triple character[22], which in many passages is expressly referred to with some form of the numeral 'three'. This earliest Indian trinity is important, for on it is based much of the mystical speculation of the Vedic age[23]. Agni's births are three or threefold (1, 95^{3}; 4, 1^{7}). The gods made him threefold (10, 88^{10}). He is threefold light (3, 26^{7}), has three heads (1, 146^{1}), three tongues, three bodies, three stations (3, 20^{2}). The epithet *triṣadhastha*, 'having three stations', is predominantly connected with Agni[24], and the only passage in which the word *tripastya*, 'having three dwellings', occurs (8, 39^{8}), it is an attribute of Agni. The triad is not always understood in exactly the same way or mentioned in the same order. Thus one poet says: 'From heaven first Agni was born, the second time from us (= men), thirdly in the waters (10, 45^{1}, cp. vv. $^{2.3}$). The order of Agni's abodes is also heaven, earth, waters in other passages (8, 44^{16}; 10, 2^{7}. 46^{9}), while one verse (1, 95^{3}) has the variation: ocean, heaven, waters. Sometimes the terrestrial Agni comes first: 'He was first born in houses, at the base of great heaven, in the womb of this atmosphere' (4, 1^{11}); 'the immortals kindled three flames of Agni: of these they placed one with man for use, and two went to the sister-world' (3, 2^{9}). A Sūtra passage (Āp. ŚS. 5, 16^{4}) distinguishes a terrestrial Agni in animals, an aerial one in the waters, and a celestial one in the sun. Occasionally the terrestrial Agni comes third. He is one of three brothers of whom 'the middlemost brother is lightning (*aśnaḥ*) and the third is butter-backed' (1, 164^{1}, cp. 141^{2}). 'Agni glows from the sky, to god Agni belongs the broad air, men kindle Agni, bearer of oblations, lover of ghee' (AV. 12, 1^{20}, cp. 13, 3^{21}; 18, 4^{11}).

The third form of Agni is once spoken of as the highest (10, 1^{3}; cp. 5, 3^{3}; 1, $72^{2.4}$). Yāska (Nir. 7, 28) mentions that his predecessor Śākapūṇi regarded the threefold existence of Agni referred to in 10, 88^{10} as being in earth, air, and heaven, a certain Brāhmaṇa considering Agni's third manifestation, which is in heaven, to be the sun (cp. Nir. 12, 19). This threefold nature of Agni, so clearly recognised in the RV., was probably the prototype not only of the posterior triad of Sun, Wind, Fire (8, 18^{9}), which is spoken of as distributed in the three worlds (10, 158^{1}; AV. 4, 39^{2}) and is implied in another verse (1, 164^{44}), but also of the triad of Sun, Indra, Fire, which though not Rigvedic is still ancient. Here Vāta or Vāyu and Indra have taken the place of Agni Vaidyuta, the lightning Agni, as the Brāhmaṇas and commentators call him. This substitution is perhaps partly due to the transient nature of lightning and partly to the lack of any name other than Agni for the personified lightning, which could therefore be expressed only by epithets or allusions. The triad of Agnis may have suggested and would explain the division of the sacrificial fire into the three sacrificial fires[25] which in the Vedic ritual are kept distinct from the domestic fire[26] and which form an essential feature of the cult in the Brāhmaṇas[27]. The ritual may have then reacted on the myth. At any rate, later Hindu literature took the three fires as representative of the three forms of Agni known to the RV.[28] The three sacrificial fires may go back to the time of the RV., possibly even to an anterior period[29]. Thus Agni is besought to bring the gods and to seat himself in the three receptacles (*yoniṣu*: 2, 36^{4}, cp. 5, 11^{3}; 10, 105^{9}).

Doubtless on the basis of the twofold division of the Universe into heaven and earth, Agni is in several passages said to have two births, being the only single god spoken of as *dvijanman* (1, 60^{1}. 140^{2}. $149^{4.5}$). An upper and a lower birth are mentioned (2, 9^{3}), his abode in lower and upper spheres is referred to (1, 128^{3}), and the opposition is generally between terrestrial and celestial fire (3, 54^{1}; 10, 45^{10}), though in one passage at least (8, 43^{28}) the contrast is between his birth in heaven and in the waters. Agni is summoned from his supreme abode (8, 11^{7}) and comes thence to the lower ones (8, 64^{15}). When he is brought from the highest father he rises into the plants (1, 141^{4}). Here Agni is conceived as coming down in rain and then entering the plants, out of which he is again produced. The fires, like water, after descending to earth again rise to heaven (1, 164^{51}). On this distinction of two forms of fire are based such prayers as that Agni should sacrifice to himself (10, 7^{6}), that he should bring Agni (7, 39^{5}), or that he should descend with the gods to the sacrifice (3, 6^{9} &c.). Allied to this distinction is the notion that Agni was kindled by the gods as contrasted with men[30] (6, 2^{3}). The latter notion is due to the assumption that celestial fires must be kindled by some one and gods must sacrifice like men (cp. AB. 2, 34).

From another point of view, Agni is said to have many births (10, 5^{1}). This multiplicity no doubt primarily refers to the numerous fires kindled on terrestrial altars. For Agni is very frequently said to abide in every family, house, or abode (4, 6^{8}. $7^{1.3}$; 5, 1^{5}. 6^{8} &c.). He is produced in many places (3, 54^{19}) and has many bodies (10, 98^{10}). Scattered in many places, he is one and the same king (3, 55^{4}). Kindled in many places, he is but one (Vāl. 10^{2}). Other fires are attached to him as branches to a tree (8, 19^{33}). Thus he comes to be invoked with the Agnis (7, 3^{1}; 8, 18^{9}. 49^{1}; 10, 141^{6}) or all the Agnis (1, 26^{10}; 6, 12^{6}).

The accounts given of Agni's abodes or birthplaces sometimes involve cross divisions. Thus his brilliance in heaven, earth, air, waters, and plants is referred to (3, 22^{2}) or he is said to be born from the heavens, the waters, stone, woods, and plants (2, 1^{1}). Longer enumerations of a similar kind occasionally occur elsewhere (AV. 3, 21; 12, 1^{19}; Āp. ŚS. 5, 16^{4}). When Agni is said (1, 70^{4}, cp. 6, 48^{5}) to dwell in a rock *(adrau)* the reference is probably to the lightning latent in the cloud (cp. p. 10). The same is probably the case when he is said (2, 1^{1}) to be produced from a stone *(aśmanaḥ)* or to have been generated by Indra between two stones (2, 12^{3}); but here there may lurk an allusion to the production of fire from flint. Animal heat is of course meant when Agni is said to be in the heart of man (10, 5^{1}), or in beasts, horses, birds, bipeds and quadrupeds (AV. 3, 21^{2}; 12, 1^{19}. 2^{33}; TS. 4, 6, 1^{3}). As being the spark of vitality and so widely diffused in nature,

Agni naturally comes to be described as the germ (*garbha*) of what is stationary or moves and of all that exists (1, 70^{3}; AV. 5, 25^{7}).

The triple nature of Agni gave rise to the notion of three brothers (1, 164^{1}); while the multiplicity of sacrificial fires may have suggested the idea of Agni's elder brothers who are spoken of in the plural (10, 51^{6}). The number of these is later stated to be three (TS. 2, 6, 6^{1}). The same are probably meant by the four Hotṛs of the gods, of whom the first three died (Kāṭh. 25, 7)[31]. Varuṇa is once spoken of as Agni's brother (4, 1^{2}). Elsewhere Indra is said to be his twin brother (6, 59^{2})[32]. Indra is indeed oftener associated with Agni than with any other god and is, with two slight exceptions, the only god with whom Agni forms a dual divinity (§ 44). It is doubtless owing to this association that Agni is described as bursting the rock with heat (8, 46^{10}) and vanquishing the unbelieving Paṇis (7, 6^{3}). In one entire hymn (1, 93) Agni is also coupled with Soma (§ 44).

Agni is occasionally identified with other gods, especially with Varuṇa and Mitra[33] (2, 1^{4}; 3, 5^{4}; 7, 12^{3}). He is Varuṇa when he goes to the sacrifice (10, 8^{5}). He is Varuṇa when he is born and Mitra when he is kindled (5, 3^{1}). Agni in the evening becomes Varuṇa, rising in the morning he becomes Mitra; becoming Savitṛ he traverses the air, becoming Indra he illumines the sky in the midst (AV. 13, 3^{13}). In one passage of the RV. (2, 1^{3-7}) he is successively identified with about a dozen gods besides five goddesses. He assumes various divine forms (3, 38^{7}) and has many names (3, 20^{3}). In him are comprehended all the gods (5, 3^{1}), whom he surrounds as a felly the spokes (5, 13^{6}).

What is probably the oldest function of fire in regard to its cult, that of burning and dispelling evil spirits and hostile magic, still survives in the Veda. Agni drives away the goblins with his light (3, 15^{1} &c.)[34] and receives the epithet *rakṣohan*, 'goblin-slayer' (10, 87^{1}). When kindled he consumes with iron teeth and scorches with heat the sorcerers as well as the goblins (10, $87^{2.5.14}$), protecting the sacrifice with keen glance (ib. ^{9}). He knows the races of the sorcerers and destroys them (AV. 1, 8^{4}). Though this function of dispelling terrestrial demons is shared with Agni by Indra (as well as by Bṛhaspati, the Aśvins, and especially Soma), it must primarily have belonged to Agni alone, just as, conversely, that of slaying Asuras or aerial demons is transferred to Agni (7, 13^{1}) though properly peculiar to Indra. This is borne out by the fact that Agni is undoubtedly more prominent as a goblin-slayer than Indra, both in the hymns and in the ritual[35].

Agni is more closely connected with human life than any other god. His association with the dwellings of men is peculiarly intimate. He is the only god to whom the frequent epithet *gṛhapati*, 'lord of the house', is applied. He dwells in every abode (7, 15^{2}), never leaving his home (8, 49^{19}). The attribute 'domestic' (*damūnas*) is generally connected with him (1, 60^{4} &c.). This household deity probably represents an old order of ideas; for in the later elaborate ritual of the three sacrificial fires, the one from which the other two (the *āhavanīya* or eastern and the *dakṣiṇa* or southern) were taken, is called the *gārhapatya* or that which belongs to *gṛhapati*. In this connexion it is interesting to observe that even as early as Rigvedic times there are traces of the sacrificial fire having been transported[36]. For Agni is led round (4, 9^{3}. 15^{1}), strides round the offerings (4, 15^{3}) or goes round the sacrifice three times (4, $6^{4.5}$. 15^{2}); and as soon as he is released from his parents, he is led to the east and again to the west (1, 31^{4}).

He is further constantly designated a 'guest' (*atithi*) in human abodes. He is a guest in every house (10, 91^{2}), the first guest of settlers (5, 8^{2}). For he is an immortal (a term much more commonly applied to Agni than to any other god), who has taken up his abode among mortals (8, 60[1]). He has been established or settled among human habitations (3, 5[1]; 4, 6[2]). It is the domestic Agni who caused mortals to settle (3, 1[17]). He is a leader (3, 2[5]) and a protector of settlers (1, 96[4]), and the epithet *viśpati*, 'lord of settlers' is mainly connected with him.

Thus Agni comes to be called the nearest kinsman of man (7, 15[1]; 8, 49[10]), or simply a kinsman (1, 26[3] &c.) or a friend (1, 75[4] &c.). But he is oftenest described as a father (6, 1[5] &c.), sometimes also as a brother (8, 43[16]; 10, 7[3] &c.), and even as a son (2, 1[9]) or mother (6, 1[5]), of his worshippers. Such terms seem to point to an older order of things, when Agni was less sacrificial and, as the centre of domestic life, produced an intimate relation such as is not easily found in the worship of other gods[17].

The continuity of Agni's presence in the house would naturally connect him more closely than any other god with the past. Hence the ancestral friendship of Agni with his worshipper (1, 71[10]) is probably more typical of him than of any other deity. He is the god whom the forefathers kindled, to whom they prayed. Thus mention is made of an Agni of Bharata (2,7[1]; 7,8[4] &c.), of Vadhryaśva (10,69[1]), of Devavāta (3,23[3]), of Divodāsa (8,92[2]), and of Trasadasyu (8, 19[32])[38]. The names of ancestors sometimes identified with Agni are in part those of families to which composers of the RV. belonged. Some of these, like Vasiṣṭha, seem to have had a historical origin, while others, like Aṅgiras (§ 54) and Bhṛgu (§ 51), are probably mythical (cp. § 58).

Agni is further brought into close relations with the daily life of man in the sacrifice. He is, however, not merely a passive receiver of the offering, but is an intermediary between heaven and earth. He transmits the oblation to the gods, who do not get exhilarated without him (7, 11[1]). On the other hand, he brings the gods (3, 14[2]) to the sacrifice as well as takes it to them (7, 11[5]). He seats them on the strewn grass (1, 31[17]; 8, 44[3]), to eat the offering (5, 1[11] &c.). He goes on the paths leading both to the gods (10,98[11]) and to earth (8, 7[2]), knowing these paths (6, 16[3]). He is therefore constantly and characteristically called a messenger (*dūta*), who knows the paths and conveys the sacrifice (1, 72[7]) or visits all abodes (4, 1[8]); who flies swiftly (10, 6[4]), moving between heaven and earth (4, 7[8]. 8[4]; 10, 4[2]), or the two races, gods and men (4,2[2.3]); who has been appointed by the gods (5,8[6] &c.) and by men (10, 46[10]), to be an oblation-bearer (*havya-vah* or *-vāhana*, terms always connected with Agni) and to announce the hymn of the worshipper (1, 27[4]) or to bring the gods to the place of sacrifice (4, 8[2]). He is the messenger of the gods (6, 15[9]) and of Vivasvat (p. 42); but as knowing the innermost recesses of heaven, as conveying the sacrifice, and bringing the gods (4, 7[8]. 8[4]) he is mainly to be considered the messenger of men. A later text states that Agni is the messenger of the gods, and Kāvya Uśanas or Daivya that of the Asuras (TS. 2, 5, 8[5]. 11[8]). Another describes Agni not as the messenger of, but as the path leading to, the gods, by which the summit of heaven may be reached (TB. 2, 4, 1[6]).

In consequence of his main function in the Veda of officiating at the sacrifice, Agni comes to be celebrated as the divine counterpart of the earthly priesthood. He is therefore often called generically the 'priest' (*ṛtvij*, *vipra*) or specifically the 'domestic priest' (*purohita*), and constantly, more frequently in fact than by any other name, the 'offerer' (*hotṛ*) or chief priest, who is poet and spokesman in one. He is a Hotṛ appointed by men (8, 49[1]; 10, 7[5]) and by gods (6, 16[1]). He is the most adorable, the most eminent of Hotṛs

(10, 2^{1}. 91^{8}). He is also termed an *adhvaryu* (3, 5^{4}) and (like Bṛhaspati, Soma, and Indra) a *brahman* or praying priest (4,9^{4}). He combines in himself the functions, in a higher sense, of the various human priests called by the above and other specific names (1, 94^{6}; 2, 1^{2} &c.). He is constantly invoked to honour or worship the gods (3, 25^{1}; 7, 11^{3} &c.), while they in their turn are said to honour Agni three times a day (3, 4^{2}). He is the accomplisher of the rite or sacrifice (3, 3^{3}. 27^{2}), promoting it by his occult power (3, 27^{7}), making the oblations fragrant (10, 15^{12}), and causing the offering which he protects to reach the gods (1, 1^{4}). He is the father (3,3^{4}), the king (4,3^{1}), the ruler (10, 6^{3}), the superintendant (8, 43^{24}), the banner (3, 3^{3}. 10^{4}; 6, 2^{3}; 10, 1^{5}), of sacrifice. In one hymn (10, 51) it is related that Agni grew weary of the service and refused to fulfil his sacrificial offices, but on being granted the remuneration he required from the gods, continued to act as high priest of men[39]. Agni's priesthood is the most salient feature of his character. He is in fact the great priest, as Indra is the great warrior. But though this phase of Agni's character is so prominent from the beginning to the end of the RV., it is of course from a historical point of view comparatively recent, due to those mystical sacerdotal speculations which ultimately led to the endless sacrificial symbolism of the later ritual texts. From the ordinary sacrificial Agni who conveys the offering (*havya-vah* or *-vāhana*) is distinguished the form of Fire which is called 'corpse-devouring' (*kravyād*: cp. § 71). The VS. distinguishes three forms, as the Agni who devours raw-flesh (*āmād*), the corpse-devouring or funereal, and the sacrificial Agni (VS. 1, 17, cp. 18, 51). The TS. (2, 5, 8^{6}) also distinguishes three, the Agni that bears the oblation (*havyavāhana*), as belonging to the gods, the Agni that bears the funeral offering (*kavyavāhana*), as belonging to the Fathers, and the Agni associated with goblins (*saharakṣas*) as belonging to the Asuras.

Agni is a seer (*ṛṣi*) as well as a priest (9, 66^{20}); he is kindled as an eminent seer (3, 21^{3}); he is the most gracious seer (6, 14^{2}); he is the first seer Aṅgiras (1, 31^{1}). He is the divine one (*asura*) among the sages (3, 3^{4}). Agni knows the sacrifice exactly (10, 110^{11}) and knows all rites (10, 122^{2}). Knowing the proper seasons he rectifies the mistakes which men commit through ignorance of the sacrificial ordinances of the gods (10, $2^{4.5}$) He knows the recesses of heaven (4, $8^{2.4}$). He knows everything (10, 11^{1}) by his wisdom (10,91^{3}). He has all wisdom (3,1^{17}; 10,21^{5}), which he embraces as the felly the wheel (2,5^{3}) and which he acquired as soon as born (1,96^{1}). He is 'all-knowing' (*viśvavid*); and the epithets 'possessed of all knowledge' (*viśvavedas*), 'sage' (*kavi*), and 'possessing the intelligence of a sage' (*kavikratu*) are predominantly applicable to him. He exclusively bears the epithet *jātavedas*, which occurs upwards of 120 times in the RV. and is there (6, 15^{13}) explained as meaning 'he who knows all generations' (*viśvā veda janimā*)[40]. He knows the divine ordinances and the generations of men (1, $70^{1.3}$). He knows and sees all creatures (3, 55^{10}; 10, 187^{4}) and hears the invocations addressed to him (8, 43^{23}). Agni is also a producer of wisdom (8, 91^{8}). Wisdom and prayers arise from him (4, 11^{3}). He is an inspirer (10, 46^{5}), an inventor of brilliant speech (2, 9^{4}), the first inventor of prayer (6, 1^{1}). He is also said to be eloquent (6, 4^{4}) and a singer (*jaritṛ*).

Agni is a great benefactor of his worshippers. He protects them with a hundred iron walls (7, 3^{7}. 16^{10}, cp. 6, 48^{8}; 1, 189^{2}). He preserves them from calamities or takes them across calamities as in a ship over the sea (3,20^{4}; 5, 4^{9}; 7, 12^{2}). He is a deliverer (8, 49^{5}) and a friend of the man who entertains him as a guest (4, 4^{10}). He grants protection to the worshipper who sweats to bring him fuel (4, 2^{6}). He watches with a thousand eyes the man who brings him food and nourishes him with oblations (10, 79[5]). He consumes his worshippers' enemies like dry bushes (4, 4[4]) and strikes down the malevolent as a tree is destroyed by lightning (6, 8[5], cp. AV. 3, 2[1] &c.). He is therefore invoked in battle (8,43[21]), in which he leads the van (8,73[8]). The man whom he protects and inspires in battle wins abundant food and can never be overcome (1,27[7]). All blessings issue from him as branches from a tree (6,13[1]). He gives riches, which he abundantly commands (1,1[3]. 31[10]. 36[4]). All treasures are collected in him (10, 6[6]) and he opens the door of riches (1, 68[10]). He commands all riches in heaven and earth (4, 5[11]) or in earth, heaven, and ocean (7, 6[7]; 10, 91[3]). He gives rain from heaven (2, 6[5]) and is like a water-trough in the desert (10, 4[1]). He is therefore constantly besought to bestow every kind of boon: food, riches, deliverance from poverty, childlessness, enemies, and demons[41]. The boons which Agni bestows are rather domestic welfare, offspring, and prosperity, while Indra for the most part gives power, victory, and glory. Agni also forgives sin[42] committed through folly, makes guiltless before Aditi (4, 12[4]; 7, 93[7], cp. p. 121), and averts Varuṇa's wrath (4, 1[4]). He even frees from guilt committed by a man's father and mother (AV. 5, 30[4]; TB. 3, 7, 12[3. 4])

Agni is a divine (*asura*) monarch (*samrāj*), strong as Indra (7, 6[1]). His greatness surpasses that of mighty heaven (1, 59[5]). He is greater than heaven and earth (3, 6[2]; 10, 88[14]), than all the worlds, which he filled when born (3, 3[10]). He is superior to all the other gods in greatness (1, 68[2]). All the gods fear and do homage to him when he abides in darkness (6, 9[7]). He is celebrated and worshipped by Varuṇa, Mitra, the Maruts, and all the gods (3, 9[8]. 14[4]; 10, 69[9]). Agni performed great deeds of old (7, 6[2]). Men tremble at his mighty deeds (8,92[3]). In battle he procured space for the gods (1, 59[5]) and he delivered them from curse (7, 13[2]). He is a conqueror of thousands (*sahasrajit*: more commonly an attribute of Soma). He drives away the Dasyus from the house, thus creating a wide light for the Ārya (7, 5[6]). He is a promoter of the Ārya (8, 92[1]) and a vanquisher of irreligious Paṇis (7, 6[3]). He receives with some frequency the epithet of 'Vṛtra-slayer', and two or three times that of 'fort-destroyer' (*puraṃdara*), attributes primarily appropriate to Indra (p. 60). Such warlike qualities, though suitable to Agni in his lightning form, are doubtless derived by him from Indra, with whom he is so frequently associated (p. 127).

Although Agni is the son of Heaven and Earth he is nevertheless called the generator of the two worlds (1, 96[4], cp. 7, 5[7]), his ordinance, which does not perish (2, 8[3]), being followed by heaven and earth (7, 5[4]). He stretched them out (3, 6[5]; 7, 5[4]) or spread them out like two skins (6, 8[3]). With his flame or his smoke he supported the vault of heaven (3, 5[10]; 4, 6[2]). He kept asunder the two worlds (6, 8[3]). He supported earth and heaven with true hymns (1, 67[3]). He stands at the head of the world or is the head of the earth at night (10, 88[5. 6]), but he is also the head and summit (*kakud*) of the sky (1, 59[2]; 6, 7[1]; 8, 44[16]). He measured out the air and touched the vault of heaven with his greatness (6, 8[2]). He measured out the aerial spaces and the bright realms of heaven (6, 7[7]). He caused the sun to ascend the sky (10, 156[4]). The notion that the kindling of Agni exercised a magical influence on the sunrise seems not to be entirely absent in the RV.[43]. Such appears to be the meaning of the poet when he exclaims: 'Let us light Agni, that thy wondrous brand may shine in heaven' (5, 6[4]). This notion is clearly stated in a Brāhmaṇa passage: 'By sacrificing before sunrise he produces him (the sun), else he would not rise' (ŚB. 2, 3, 1[5], cp. TS. 4, 7, 13[3]). Otherwise the kindling of Agni and the sunrise are represented merely as simultaneous in the RV.: 'The sun became visible when Agni was born' (4, 3^{11}). This trait of the Agni myth resembles the winning of the sun in the Indra myth, but the original point of view in the two cases is clearly different. Agni is further said to have adorned the sky with stars (1, 68^{5}). He created all that flies, walks, stands, or moves (10, 88^{4}). He placed the germ in these beings (3, 2^{10}), in plants, in all beings, and engendered offspring in the earth and in women (10, 183^{3}). Agni is once spoken of as having generated these children of men (1, 96^{2}); but this is a mere incidental extension of the notion expressed in the same stanza, that he created heaven, earth, and the waters, and cannot be interpreted as a general belief in Agni as father of the human race[44]. Finally, Agni is the guardian (7, 7^{4}) and lord (7, 4^{6}) of immortality, which he confers on mortal men (1, 31^{7}).

Though *agni* is an Indo-European word (Lat. *igni-s*, Slavonic *ogni*), the worship of fire under this name is purely Indian. In the Indo-Iranian period the sacrificial fire is already found as the centre of a developed ritual, tended by a priestly class probably called Atharvan; personified and worshipped as a strong, pure, wise god, giver of food, offspring, intellectual power, fame; friendly to the house, but a destroyer of foes; probably even thought of as having different forms like lightning or the fire produced from wood[45]. The sacrificial fire seems to have been an Indo-European institution also[46], since the Italians and Greeks, as well as the Iranians and Indians had the custom of offering gifts to the gods in fire. But the personification of this fire, if it then existed, must have been extremely shadowy[47].

The word *ag-ni* may possibly be derived from the root which in Sanskrit appears as *aj*[48], to drive (*ájāmi*, Lat. *ago*, Gk. ἄγω); meaning 'nimble', with reference to the agility of the element.

Besides epithets of celestial fire which, like Apāṃ napāt, have become separate names, some epithets of Agni exhibit a semi-independent character. The epithet Vaiśvānara[49], occurring about sixty times in the RV. and with two exceptions restricted to Agni, is, apart from some five detached verses, to be found in fourteen hymns of the RV., in nearly all of which, according to the native tradition of the Anukramaṇī, Agni Vaiśvānara is the deity addressed. The attribute is never in the RV. unaccompanied by the name of Agni. It means 'belonging to all men' and seems to designate 'Universal Agni', fire in all its aspects, celestial as well as terrestrial. Thus the hymns addressed to this form of Agni sometimes refer to the myth of Mātariśvan and the Bhṛgus, which is connected with the descent of celestial fire to earth (3, 2^{4}; 6, 8^{4}), and Agni Vaiśvānara is once even directly styled Mātariśvan (3, 26^{2}). In the Naighaṇṭuka (5, 1) Vaiśvānara is given as one of the names of Agni. Yāska in commenting on the epithet states (Nir. 7, 23) that ancient ritualists (*yājñikāḥ*) took Agni Vaiśvānara to be the sun, while Śākapūṇi considered him to be this Agni[50]. Later on (Nir. 7, 31), he states as his own opinion that the Agni Vaiśvānara who receives praise and sacrifice is this (i. e. terrestrial) Agni, while the two higher (*uttare*) lights (i. e. the aerial and the celestial) only occasionally share this designation. In the ritual texts Vaiśvānara is distinguished as a special form of Agni (ĀSS. 1, 3^{23}; KŚS. 23, 3^{1}; (PB. 21, 10^{11}; ŚB. 1, 5, 1^{10}).

The epithet Tanūnapāt, generally unaccompanied by the name of Agni, occurs eight times in the RV. and, with two exceptions (3, 29^{11}; 10, 92^{2}) always in the second verse of the Āprī hymns, which are liturgical invitations introducing the animal sacrifice and in which fire under various names and forms is invoked[51]. The word occurs as an independent name in the Naighaṇṭuka (5, 2). The explanations given by Yāska (Nir. 8, 5) are artificial and improbable[52]. It seems to mean 'son of himself', as spontaneously generated in wood and cloud. According to BERGAIGNE's interpretation, it signifies 'the bodily (i. e. own) son' of the divine father[53]. Tanūnapāt as contrasted with Mātariśvan and Narāśaṃsa is said to be 'the divine (*āsura*) embryo' (3, 29^{11}). The dawns are said to kiss Agni 'the domestic priest, the Tanūnapāt of the ruddy one' (10, 92^{2}, cp. 5, 58^{6}). Tanūnapāt is beautiful-tongued (10, 110^{2}). He is besought to take the sacrifice to the gods (1, 13^{2}; 10, 110^{2}); he distributes the sacrifice rich in ghee and mead (1, 142^{2}, cp. 188^{2}). The gods honour him three times a day, Varuṇa, Mitra, Agni, every day (3, 4^{2}). HILLEBRANDT[54] (comparing 9, 5^{2}) identifies Agni Tanūnapāt with Agni Somagopā or the lunar Fire, which he assumes to be a special form of Agni[55].

The somewhat more frequent epithet Narāśaṃsa which is given as an independent appellation in the Naighaṇṭuka (5, 3) and is unaccompanied by the name of Agni in the RV., is not restricted to Agni, being twice connected with Pūṣan (1, 106^{4}; 10, 64^{3})[56]. It has the third verse as its fixed place in the Āprī hymns and the second in those which are technically called Āpra. Narāśaṃsa is 'four-limbed' (10, 92^{11}) and is the 'lord of a celestial wife (*gnāspati*: 2, 38^{10}). With honey on his tongue and in his hand, he performs the sacrifice (1, 13^{3}; 5, 5^{2}). Three times a day he besprinkles the sacrifice with honey (1, 142^{3}). He anoints the three heavens and the gods (2, 3^{2}). He comes at the head of the gods and makes the sacrifice pleasant for them (10, 70^{2}). Through his sacrifices worshippers praise the greatness of the gods (7, 2^{2}). Soma is said to go between Narāśaṃsa and the celestial (*daivya*) one (9, 86^{42}), which seems to mean, between the terrestrial and the celestial Agni. As contrasted with Tanūnapāt and Mātariśvan, Agni is called Narāśaṃsa when he is born (3, 29^{11}). In one hymn to Bṛhaspati (10, 182^{2}) Narāśaṃsa is invoked for protection, and in another he is spoken of as the sacrificer of the seat of heaven (1, 18^{9}). He thus seems in these two passages to be identified with Bṛhaspati. The word *nárā-śáṃsa* is apparently an improper compound (in which the *m* of the genitive plural has disappeared), having a double accent and having its parts separated by particles in two passages (9, 86^{42}; 10, 64^{3}). As the expressions *narāṃ śaṃsa* and *devānāṃ śaṃsa* occur (2, 34^{6}; 1, 141^{11}) and a poet once calls Agni *śaṃsam āyoḥ*, 'Praise of Āyu' (4, 6^{11}), Narāśaṃsa appears to mean 'Praise of men' in the sense of 'he who is the object of men's praise'. BERGAIGNE expresses the opinion[57] that the exact aspect of Agni represented by Narāśaṃsa, is that of a god of human prayer, like a second Bṛhaspati.

[1] Muṇd. Up. 1, 2^{4}; cp. ZDMG. 35, 552. — [2] Cp. OLDENBERG, ZDMG. 50, 425—6; SBE. 46, 159. 207. — [3] ORV. 104; SBE. 46, 128. — [4] Cp. BRV. 1, 143; SBE. 46, 144. — [5] BDA. 50—1; OLDENBERG, ZDMG. 39, 69. — [6] SCHWAB, Das altindische Tieropfer 77—8; ROTH, Indisches Feuerzeug, ZDMG. 43, 590—5. — [7] BRV. 2, 52; PVS. 2, 50. — [8] ROTH, Nirukta, Erl. 120; PW. s. v. *yuvati* and *tvaṣṭṛ*; OO. 2, 510. — [9] JOLLY in this Encyclopaedia II, 8, p. 25. — [10] KHF. ed. Schrader (1889) 37—9; cp. ZDMG. 35, 561. — [11] KHF. 18; KRV. note 121; HRI. 107. — [12] ROTH, ZDMG. 43, 593; ORV. 121. — [13] Cp. HVM. 1, 179 note 4. — [14] HAUG, AB. 2, p. 62. — [15] OLDENBERG, ZDMG. 39, 68—72; MACDONELL, JRAS. 26, 16 ff. — [16] LRV. 5, 504. — [17] ORV. 115. — [18] Cp. GVS. 1, 157—70. — [19] ORV. 113 note 2. — [20] Ibid. 112. — [21] Other passages are 3, 14^{4}; 8, 56^{5}; 10, 88$^{11.12}$; AV. 13, 1^{13}; TS. 4, 2, 9^{4}. — [22] OST. 5, 206; BRV. 1, 21—5; MACDONELL, JRAS. 25, 468—70; ORV. 106; SBE. 46, 231. — [23] Cp. HRI. 105. — [24] See GW. s. v. — [25] LRV. 3, 356; BRV. 1, 23. — [26] ORV. 348. — [27] Cp. ŚB. 2, 1 and EGGELING, SBE. 12, 274 ff. — [28] HRI. 106; cp. LRV. 3, 356. — [29] BRV. 1, 23; LRV. 3, 355; OLDENBERG, SBE. 30, x, note 1; 46, 362; ORV. 348. — [30] BRV. 1, 103. — [31] LRV. 5, 504—5. — [32] Cp. Sāyaṇa; ROTH, Nirukta, Erl. 140; MM., LSL. 2, 614. — [33] Cp. BRV. 3, 134 f. — [34] BRV. 2, 217. — [35] ORV. 128. [36] SBE. 46, 361. —

37 ORV. 132—3. — — 38 OST. 1, 348—9; cp. SBE. 46, 123. 211. — 39 MACDONELL, JRAS. 26, 12—22. — 40 WHITNEY, AJP. 3, 409; otherwise PVS. 1, 94 and BLOOMFIELD, JAOS. 16, 16. — 41 OST. 5, 218. — 42 Cp. ORV. 299—300. — 43 Cp. BRV. 1, 140 ff.; ORV. 109; SBE. 46, 330. — 44 The view of KHF. 69 ff. — 45 ORV. 103. — 46 KNAUER, FaR. 64. — 47 ORV. 102. — 48 PW.; MM.PhR. 117 (cp. KIRSTE, WZKM. 7, 97); rejected by BARTHOLOMAE, IF. 5, 222. — 49 BRV. 153—6. — 50 ROTH, Nir. Erl. 7, 19. — 51 ROTH, Nirukta, Introd. 36 f.; Erl. 117—8. 121—4; MM.ASL. 463—6; WEBER, IS. 10, 89—95; GRV. 1, 6. — 52 ROTH, Nir. Erl. 117; cp. OLDENBERG, SBE. 46, 10. — 53 BRV. 2, 99 f. — 54 HVM. 1, 339. — 55 Ibid. 330—6. — 56 ROTH, Erl. 117 f.; cp. Sp.AP. 209 f. — 57 BRV. 1, 305—8.

KHF. 1—105; WHITNEY, JAOS. 3, 317—8; OST. 199—220; LRV. 3, 324—5; KRV. 35—7; BRV. 1, 11—31. 38—45. 70—4. 100—1. 139—45; BRI. 9—11; Sp.AP. 147—53; v. SCHROEDER, KZ. 29, 193 ff. (cp. BB. 19, 230); WZKM. 225—30; MM.PhR. 144—203. 252—302; HVBP. 63—8; ORV. 102—33; HRI. 105—12.

§ 36. **Bṛhaspati.** — This god occupies a position of considerable prominence in the RV., eleven entire hymns being dedicated to his praise. He also forms a pair with Indra in two hymns (4, 49; 7, 97). His name occurs about 120 times and in the form of Brahmaṇas pati about 50 times besides. The two forms of the name alternate in different verses of the same hymn (e. g. in 2, 23). The physical features of Bṛhaspati are few. He is seven-mouthed and seven-rayed (4, 50^{4}), beautiful-tongued (1, 190^{1}; 4, 50^{1}), sharp-horned (10, 155^{2}), blue-backed (5, 43^{12}), and hundred-winged (7, 97^{7}). He is golden-coloured and ruddy (5, 43^{12}), bright (3, 62^{7}; 7, 97^{7}), pure (7, 97^{7}), and clear-voiced (7, 97^{5}). He has a bow, the string of which is the rite (*ṛta*), and good arrows (2, 24^{8}; cp. AV. 5, 18$^{8.9}$). He also wields a golden hatchet (7, 97^{7}) and is armed with an iron axe, which Tvaṣṭṛ sharpens (10, 53^{9}). He has a car (10, 103^{4}) and stands on the car of the rite, which slays the goblins, bursts the cowstalls, and wins the light (2, 23^{3}). He is drawn by ruddy steeds (7, 97^{6}).

Bṛhaspati was first born from great light in the highest heaven and with thunder (*ravena*) drove away darkness (4, 50^{4}; cp. 10, 68^{12}). He is the offspring of the two worlds (7, 97^{8}), but is also said to have been generated by Tvaṣṭṛ (2, 23^{17}). On the other hand, he is called the father of the gods (2, 26^{3}), being said to have blown forth the births of the gods like a blacksmith (10, 72^{2}).

Bṛhaspati is a domestic priest[1] (2, 24^{9}; VS. 20, 11; TS. 6, 4, 10; AB. 8, 26^{4}), a term almost peculiar to Agni (p. 96). The ancient seers placed him at their head (*puro-dhā*) (4, 50^{1}). He is Soma's *purohita* (ŚB. 4, 1, 2^{4}). He is also a *brahman* or praying priest[2] (2, 1^{3}; 4, 50^{8}), once probably in the technical sense (10, 141^{3}). In later Vedic texts Bṛhaspati is the *brahman* priest (in the technical sense) of the gods[3]. He is even called the prayer or devotion (*brahma*) of the gods (TS. 2, 2, 9^{1} &c.) Bṛhaspati promotes the yoking of devotion, and without him sacrifice does not succeed (1, 18^{7}). As a pathmaker he makes good the access to the feast of the gods (2, 23$^{6.7}$). From him even the gods obtained their share of sacrifice (2, 23^{1}). He awakens the gods with sacrifice (AV. 19, 63^{1}). He himself pronounces the hymn in which Indra, Varuṇa, Mitra, Aryaman, the gods take pleasure (1, 40^{5}). He sings chants (10, 36^{5}). His song (*śloka*) goes to heaven (1, 190^{4}) and metre (*chandas*) belongs to him (MS. 1, 9^{2}). He is associated with singers (7, 10^{4}; 10, 14^{3}). He sings with his 'friends that cry like Haṃsas' (10, 67^{3}), by whom the Aṅgirases[4] (§ 54) mentioned in the preceding verse (10, 67^{2}) seem to be meant. He is also said to be accompanied by a singing (*ṛkvat*)[5] host (*gaṇa*: 4, 50^{5}). This is doubtless the reason why he is called *gaṇapati*, 'lord of a host' (2, 23^{1}), a term once applied to Indra also (10, 112^{9}).

As the name Brahmaṇas pati shows, the god is a 'lord of prayer'. He is also described as the supreme king of prayers, the most famous sage of sages (2, 23^{1}). Mounting the car of the rite he conquers the enemies of prayer and of the gods (2, $23^{3.8}$). He is the generator of all prayers (1, 190^{2}). He utters prayer (1, 40^{5}) and communicates prayers to the human priest (10, 98^{27}). Thus he comes later to be called a 'lord of speech', *vācaspati* (MS. 2, 6^{6}, cp. ŚB. 14, 4, 1^{23}), a term specially applied to Bṛhaspati as god of eloquence and wisdom in post-Vedic literature.[6]

There are several passages in which Bṛhaspati appears identified with Agni. Thus 'the lord of prayer, Agni, handsome like Mitra' is invoked (1, 38^{13}). In another passage (2, 1^{3} ff.) Agni, though identified with other gods as well, is clearly more intimately connected with Brahmaṇaspati, as only these two names are in the vocative. In one verse (3, 26^{2}) both Mātariśvan and 'Bṛhaspati the wise priest, the guest, the swiftly-moving' seem to be epithets of Agni, while in another (1, 190^{2}) Mātariśvan seems to be an epithet of Bṛhaspati. Again, by Bṛhaspati, who is blue-backed, takes up his abode in the house, shines brightly, is golden-coloured and ruddy (5, 43^{12}), Agni must be meant. In two other verses (1, 18^{9}; 10, 182^{2}) Bṛhaspati seems to be the same as Narāśaṃsa, a form of Agni (p. 100). Like Agni, Bṛhaspati is a priest, is called 'Son of strength' (1, 40^{2}) and Aṅgiras (2, 23^{18}) as well (the epithet *āṅgirasa* belonging to him exclusively), and burns the goblins (2, 23^{14}) or slays them (10, 103^{4}). Bṛhaspati is also spoken of as ascending to heaven, to the upper abodes (10, 67^{10}). Like Agni, Bṛhaspati has three abodes (4, 50^{1}); he is the adorable one of houses (7, 97^{5}), and 'lord of the dwelling', *sadasas pati*[7] (1, 18^{6}; Indra-Agni are once called *sadaspatī*, 1, 21^{5}). On the other hand, Agni is called *brahmaṇas kavi*, 'sage of prayer' (6, 16^{30}) and is besought (2, 2^{7}) to make heaven and earth favourable by prayer (*brahmaṇā*). But Bṛhaspati is much more commonly distinguished from Agni (2, 25^{3}; 7, 10^{4}; 10, 68^{9}), chiefly by being invoked or named along with him in enumerations (3, 20^{5} &c.)[8].

Like Agni, Bṛhaspati has been drawn into and has obtained a firm footing in the Indra myth of the release of the cows. The mountain yielded to his splendour, when Bṛhaspati, the Aṅgiras, opened the cowstall and with Indra as his companion let loose the flood of water enveloped by darkness (2, 23^{18}, cp. 1, 56^{5}. 89^{9}). Accompanied by his singing host (cp. § 54) he with a roar rent Vala; shouting he drove out the lowing cows (4, 50^{5}). He won treasures and the great stalls full of cows; desiring waters and light, the irresistible Bṛhaspati slays his foe with flames (6, 73^{3}). What was firm was loosened, what was strong yielded to him; he drove out the cows, he cleft Vala with prayer; he covered up the darkness and made heaven visible; the stone-mouthed well filled with honey, which Bṛhaspati pierced with might, that the celestials drank, while they poured out together abundantly the watery fountain (2, $24^{3.4}$). When Bṛhaspati with fiery gleams rent the defences of Vala, he revealed the treasures of the cows; as if splitting open eggs, he drove out the cows of the mountain; he beheld the honey enclosed by the stone; he brought it out, having cloven (Vala) with his roar; he smote forth as it were the marrow of Vala (10, 68^{4-9}). He drove out the cows and distributed them in heaven (2, 24^{14}). Bṛhaspati fetched the cows out of the rock; seizing the cows of Vala, he took possession of them (10, 68^{5}). His conquest of Vala is so characteristic that it became proverbial (AV. 9, 3^{2}). Being in the clouds (*abhriya*) he shouts aloud after the many cows (10, 68^{12}, cp. 67^{3}). These cows may represent the waters, which are expressly mentioned (2, 23^{18}; 6, 73^{3}) or possibly the rays of dawn (cp. 10, 67^{5}. 68^{9}).

In releasing the cows Bṛhaspati seeks light in darkness and finds the light; he found the Dawn, light, and Agni, and dispelled the darkness (10, 68[4.9]). In shattering the fort, he found the Dawn, the Sun, the Cow (10, 67[5]). He hid or dispelled the darkness and made visible the light (2, 24[3]; 4, 50[4]). Bṛhaspati thus comes to acquire more general warlike traits. He penetrated the mountain full of riches and split open the strongholds of Śambara (2, 24[2]). Bṛhaspati Āṅgirasa, the first-born holy one, cleaver of rocks, roars as a bull at the two worlds, slays Vṛtras (*vṛtrāṇi*), shatters forts, overcomes foes (6, 73[1.2]). He disperses foes and wins victory (10, 103[4]). No one can overcome him in great fight or small (1, 40[8]). He vanquishes the enemy in battle (2, 23[11]). He is to be invoked in combats (2, 23[13]) and is a priest much praised in conflict (2, 24[9]).

Being the companion and ally of Indra (2, 23[18]. 24[1]; 8, 85[15]), he is often invoked with that deity (4, 50[10.11] &c.). With Indra he is a soma-drinker (4, 49[1]. 50[10]) and, like him, is styled *maghavan*, 'bountiful' (2, 24[12]). Indra, too, is the only god with whom he forms a pair (2, 24[12]; 4, 49[1–6]). Thus he comes to be styled *vajrin*, 'wielder of the bolt' (1, 40[8]) and to be described as hurling the bolt, the Asura-slaying missile (AV. 11, 10[13]). He is also invoked with the Maruts at the same time as Indra (1, 40[1]) and is once besought to come accompanied by the Maruts, whether he be Mitra, Varuṇa or Pūṣan (10, 98[1]). In one passage he is said to have heard the prayer of Trita buried in a well and to have delivered him (1, 105[17]).

Bṛhaspati favours the man who offers prayer (2, 25[1]) but scourges the hater of prayer (2, 23[4]). He protects the pious man from all dangers and calamities, from curse and malignity, and blesses him with wealth and prosperity (1, 18[3]; 2, 23[4–10]). Possessed of all desirable things (7, 10[4]. 97[4]), he is opulent, a procurer of wealth, and an increaser of prosperity (1, 18[2]). He is a prolonger of life and a remover of disease (1, 18[2]). Having such benevolent traits he is called a father (4, 50[6]; 6, 73[1]).

He is *asurya*, 'divine' (2, 23[2]), belongs to all the gods (3, 62[4]; 4, 50[6]), and is the most god-like of the gods (2, 24[3]). As a god he widely extended to the gods and embraces all things (2, 24[11], cp. 8, 61[18]). Mightily he holds asunder the ends of the earth with his roar (4, 50[1]). It is his inimitable deed that sun and moon rise alternately (10, 68[10]). He is also spoken of as stimulating the growth of plants (10, 97[15.19]). Later Bṛhaspati is brought into connexion with certain stars. Thus in the TS. (4, 4, 10[1]) he is stated to be the deity of the constellation Tiṣya[9], and in post-Vedic literature he is regarded as the regent of the planet Jupiter.

Bṛhaspati is a purely Indian deity. Both forms of the name occur throughout the older as well as the later books of the RV. But since appellations formed with *pati* (like *vācas pati*, *vāstoṣ pati*, *kṣetrasya pati*) to designate deities presiding over a particular domain, must be comparatively recent as products of reflexion[10], this mythological creation can hardly go much further back than the beginning of the Rigvedic period. The accentuation of the word *bṛ́haspáti* shows it to be an improper compound. The prior member might possibly be a neuter noun in *-as*[11], but the contemporaneous form *bráhmaṇas páti*, which is a kind of explanation, indicates that the poets of the RV. regarded it as the genitive[12] of a noun *bṛh*, from the same root as *brahman*.

The evidence adduced above seems to favour the view that Bṛhaspati was originally an aspect of Agni as a divine priest presiding over devotion, an aspect which (unlike other epithets of Agni formed with *pati*, such as *viśām pati*, *gṛhapati*, *sadaspati*) had attained an independent character by the beginning of the Rigvedic period, though the connexion with Agni was not entirely severed. Langlois[13], H. H. Wilson[14], Max Müller[15] agree in regarding Bṛhaspati as a variety of Agni. Roth[16] was of opinion that this sacerdotal god is a direct impersonation of the power of devotion. Similarly Kaegi[17] and Oldenberg[18] think him to be an abstraction of priestly action, which has appropriated the deeds of earlier gods. Weber[19] considers Bṛhaspati to be a priestly abstraction of Indra, and is followed in this by Hopkins[20]. Finally, Hillebrandt[21] holds him to be a lord of plants and a personification of the moon[22], representing predominantly the igneous side of that luminary.

As the divine *brahman* priest, Bṛhaspati seems to have been the prototype of Brahmā, the chief of the Hindu triad, while the neuter form of the word, *brahma*, developed into the Absolute of the Vedānta philosophy[23].

1 Cp. ZDMG. 32, 316. — 2 ORV. 396, note 1; SBE. 46, 190. — 3 ORV. 382. — 4 Roth thinks they are the Maruts: ZDMG. 1, 77. — 5 Stars, HVM. 1, 416; Maruts, Vedainterpretation 10. — 6 ZDMG. 1, 77. — 7 Cp. Hillebrandt, Vedaint. 10. — 8 OST. 5, 283. — 9 Weber, Die Nakṣatra 2, 371. — 10 Roth, ZDMG. 1, 72. — 11 HVM. 1, 409. — 12 Macdonell, KZ. 34, 292—6. — 13 RV. Trans. 1, 249. 254. 578. — 14 RV. Trans. 1, xxxvii. — 15 Vedic Hymns, SBE. 32, 94. — 16 ZDMG. 1, 73; PW. — 17 KRV. 32. — 18 ORV. 66—8. 381—2; SBE 46, 94. 19 Vājapeya 15. — 20 HRI. 136; cp. Wilson, RV. Tr. 2, ix; BDA. xi. — 21 HVM, 1, 404. 418—9 (cp. 277); cp. Oldenberg, ZDMG. 49, 173. — 22 Also HVBP. 46—7. — 23 BRV. 1, 304; HRI. 136.

Roth, ZDMG. 1, 72—80; OST. 5, 272—83; BRV. 1, 299—304; KRV. 73—4; BRI. 15—6; HVM. 1, 404—25; LRF. 97—8; Pischel, GGA. 1894, p. 420.

§ 37. **Soma.** — Since the Soma sacrifice forms the main feature of the ritual of the RV.[1], the god Soma is naturally one of the most important deities of that Veda. All the 114 hymns of the ninth besides 6 in other books, are dedicated to his praise. He is also celebrated in portions of four or five other hymns, and as a dual divinity with Indra, Agni, Pūṣan, or Rudra, in about six more. The name of Soma, in its simple form and in compounds, occurs hundreds of times in the RV. Judged by the standard of frequency, Soma therefore comes third in order of importance among the Vedic gods. Soma is much less anthropomorphic than Indra or Varuṇa, the constant presence of the plant and its juice setting limits to the imagination of the poets who describe its personification. Consequently little is said of his human form or action. The marvellous and heroic deeds attributed to him are either colourless, because common to almost all the greater gods, or else only secondarily belong to him. Like other gods, he is, under the name of Indu as well as Soma, invoked to come to the sacrifice and receive the offerings on the strewn grass[2]. The ninth book mainly consists of incantations sung over the tangible Soma while it is pressed by the stones, flows through the woolen strainer into the wooden vats, in which it is finally offered on a litter of grass to the gods as a beverage, sometimes in fire (1, 94^{14}; 5, 5^{1}; 8, 43^{11} &c.) or drunk by the priests. The processes to which it is subjected are overlaid with the most varied and chaotic imagery and with mystical fancies often incapable of certain interpretation.

In order to make intelligible the mythology of Soma, the basis of which are the concrete terrestrial plant and the intoxicating juice extracted therefrom, it is necessary briefly to describe these as well as the treatment they undergo. The part of the Soma plant which is pressed is called *aṃśu*, 'shoot or stalk' (9, 67^{28}). The shoots swelling give milk like cows with their udders (8, 9^{19}). As distinguished from the stalk, the whole Soma plant seems to be intended by *andhas* (8, 32^{28}; 10, 94^{8} &c.), which is said to have come from heaven (9, 61^{10}) and to have been brought by the eagle (5, 45^{9}; 9, 68^{6}; 10, 144^{5}). The same term is applied to the juice also[3] and is distinguished from Indu the god (9, 51^{3}; 10, 115^{3}). The juice is also designated by *soma* (which means the plant as well) and generally by *rasa*, fluid. In one hymn (1, 187) the juice is called *pitu*, the 'beverage'; and it is often styled *mada*, 'intoxicating draught'[4]. Soma is occasionally also referred to with *anna*, 'food' (7, 98[2]; 8, 4[12]; SB. 1; 6, 4[5]). The term *madhu*, which in connexion with the Aśvins means 'honey' or 'mead', comes to be applied, in the general sense of 'sweet draught', not only to milk (*payas*) and ghee (*ghṛta*), but especially to the Soma juice (4, 27[5]; 8, 69[6]). Mythologically *madhu* is the equivalent of Soma when the latter means the celestial ambrosia (*amṛta*)[5]. Conversely, *amṛta* is frequently used as an equivalent of ordinary Soma (5, 2[3]; 6, 37[3] &c.; VS. 6, 34; SB. 9, 5, 1[8])[6]. King Soma when pressed is *amṛta* (VS. 19, 72). Another expression is *somyam madhu*, 'Soma mead' (4, 26[5]; 6, 20[3]). Figuratively the Soma juice is called *pīyūṣa* (3, 48[2] &c.), milk (9, 107[12]), the wave of the stalk (9, 96[8]) or the juice of honey (5, 43[4]). The most frequent figurative name applied to Soma is *indu*, the 'bright drop', another term of similar meaning, *drapsa*, 'drop', being much less common.

The extraction of the juice is generally described by the root *su*, 'to press' (9, 62[4] &c.), but often also by *duh* 'to milk' (3, 36[6. 7] &c.). The juice is intoxicating (1, 125[3]; 6, 17[11]. 20[6]) and 'honied', *madhumat* (9, 97[14]). The latter expression simply means 'sweet', but as applied to Soma originally seems to have meant 'sweetened with honey', some passages pointing to this admixture (9, 17[8]. 86[48]. 97[11]. 109[20])[7]. As flowing from the press, Soma is compared with the wave of a stream (9, 80[5]) and directly called a wave (9, 64[11] &c.) or a wave of honey (3, 47[1]). With reference to the juice collected in the vat, Soma is spoken of as a sea (*arṇava*: 10, 115[3]) and frequently as an ocean (*samudra*: 5, 47[3]; 9, 64[8] &c.). The heavenly Soma is also called a well (*utsa*), which is in the highest place of the cows (5, 45[8]), which is placed in the cows and guided with ten reins (i. e. fingers: 6, 44[24]), or a well of honey in the highest step of Viṣṇu (1, 154[5]).

The colour of the plant and juice, as well as of the god, is described as brown (*babhru*) or ruddy (*aruṇa*), but most frequently as tawny (*hari*). Thus Soma is the branch of a ruddy tree (10, 94[3]); it is a ruddy milked shoot (7, 98[1]); the tawny shoot is pressed into the strainer (9, 92[1]). The colour of the Soma plant or its substitute prescribed in the Brāhmaṇas is ruddy (SB. 4, 5, 10[1]); and in the ritual the cow which is the price paid in the purchase of Soma, must be brown or ruddy because that is Soma's colour (TS. 6, 1, 6[7]; SB. 3, 3, 1[14])[8].

Soma is described as purified with the hands (9, 86[34]), by the ten fingers (9, 8[4]. 15[8] &c.), or, figuratively, by the ten maidens who are sisters (9, 1[7]. 6[5]), or by the daughters (*naptī*) of Vivasvat (9, 14[5]). Similarly, the maidens of Trita are said to urge on the tawny one with stones as a drop for Indra to drink (9, 32[2]. 38[2]). Soma is also spoken of as purified or brought by the daughter of the sun (9, 1[6]. 72[3]. 113[3])[9]. Sometimes it is said to be purified by prayer (9, 96[13]. 113[5]). The priests who press Soma are Adhvaryus[10] (8, 4[11]).

The shoot is crushed with a stone (9, 67[19]) or pressed with stones (9, 107[10]); the plant is pounded to produce the Soma draught (10, 85[3]). The stones tear its skin (TB. 3, 7, 13[1]). The stones lie on a skin; for they 'chew him on the hide of the cow' (9, 79[4]). They are placed on the *vedi* or altar (5, 31[12]): a practice differing from that of the later ritual[11]. They are held with hands or arms (7, 22[1]; 9, 79[4]; AV. 11, 1[10]). The two arms and the ten fingers yoke the stone (5, 43[4]). Hence the stones are said to be guided by ten reins (10, 94[8]). Being spoken of as yoked, they are compared with horses (10, 94[6]). The usual name for the pressing stones is *adri* (generally used with the verb *su*, to press) or *grāvan* (generally connected with *vad*, to speak, or verbs of cognate meaning, and hence showing a greater tendency to personification[12] than *adri*). Both terms nearly always occur either in the singular or the plural, and not in the dual. The stones are also once respectively called *aśna* (8, 2[2]), *bharitra* (3, 36[7]), *parvata* (3, 35[8]) and *parvatā adrayaḥ* (10, 94[1]). The pressing of Soma by means of stones was the usual method in the period of the RV. But the extraction of the juice by mortar and pestle, which is also sanctioned by the ritual texts, was already known to the RV. (1, 28[1–4]); and as this method is in use among the Parsis, it may go back to the Indo-Iranian age.

The pressed drops are poured upon (9, 63[10] &c.) and pass over the strainer of sheep's wool (9, 69[9]). For it removes Soma's impurity, so that he goes cleansed to the feast of the gods (9, 78[1]). This strainer, which is very frequently mentioned, passes under various names. It is called a skin (*tvac*), hair (*roman*), wool (*vāra*), filter (*pavitra*), or ridge (*sānu*, as the top of the contrivance). All these terms are used with or without an adjective formed from *avi*, sheep. The word *avi* itself is sometimes figuratively employed in this sense. As passing through the strainer Soma is usually called *pavamāna* or *punāna*, 'flowing clear' (from √*pū*). The more general term *mṛj*, 'to cleanse', is not only applied to the purification of Soma with the strainer, but also to the addition of water and milk (9, 86[11]. 91[2]). The purified (unmixed) Soma juice is sometimes called *śuddha*, 'pure', but much oftener *śukra* or *śuci*, 'bright' (8, 2[10]; 9, 33[2]; 1, 5[5]. 30[2]). This unmixed Soma is offered almost exclusively to Vāyu and Indra, the epithet *śucipā*, 'drinking clear (Soma)' being distinctive of Vāyu (p. 82). This agrees with the later ritual, where, in the Grahas or draughts for dual divinities, clear Soma is offered to Vāyu and Indra-Vāyu, but is mixed with milk for Mitra-Varuṇa, and with honey for the Aśvins[13].

After passing the filter, Soma flows into jars (*kalaśa*, 9, 60[3] &c.) or vats (*droṇa*)[14]. The streams of Soma rush to the forest of the vats like buffaloes (9, 33[1]. 92[6]); the god flies like a bird to settle in the vats (9, 3[1]); like a bird sitting on a tree, the tawny one settles in the bowls (*camū*: 9, 72[5]). Soma is mixed with water in the vat. United with the wave, the stalk roars (9, 74[5]). Like a bull on the herd, he rushes on the vat, into the lap of the waters, a roaring bull; clothing himself in waters, Indu rushes around the vat, impelled by the singers (9, 76[5]. 107[26]). The wise milk him into the waters with their hands (9, 79[4]). Having passed over the wool and playing in the wood, he is cleansed by the ten maidens (9, 6[5]). Several other passages refer to the admixture of water with Soma (9, 30[5]. 53[4]. 86[8.25]). The Soma drops are said to spread brightness in the streams (9, 76[1]). Besides the verb *mṛj*, 'to cleanse', which is commonly used to express the admixture of water (e. g. 9, 63[17]), *ā-dhāv*, 'to wash', is also employed (8, 1[17]). In the preparation of Soma, the pressing (√*su*) comes first, then the mixing with water (7, 32[6]; 8, 1[17]. 31[5]; AV. 6, 2[1]), just as in the later ritual the *savana*, 'pressure', precedes the *ādhāvana*, 'washing'. In the bowls Soma is mixed with milk (9, 8[6] &c.)[15], which is said to sweeten it (8,2[3])[16]. In several passages the addition of both water and milk is mentioned. Thus it is said that Soma clothes himself in waters, that streams of water flow after him, when he desires to clothe himself in cows (i. e. milk: 9, 2[3.4]). They press him with stones, they wash him in water, clothing him as it were in cow-garments, men milk him out of the stalks (8, 1[17]; cp. 2, 36[1]; 6, 40[2]; 9, 86[24–5]. 96[19]).

Soma is recognised in the RV. as having three kinds of admixture (*tryāśir*: 5, 27[5]), with milk (*gavāśir*), sour milk (*dadhyāśir*), and barley (*yavā-*

śir). The admixture is figuratively called a garment (*vastra, vāsas, atka*)[17] or a shining robe (*nirṇij*: 9, 14[5]), the latter term being applied to the strainer also (9, 70[7]). Hence Soma is spoken of as decked with beauty (9, 34[4] &c.) and as richly adorned (9, 81[1]). Mention is also made, though rarely, of mixture with ghee (9, 82[2]); but neither this addition nor that of water, is a regular *āśir*[18].

In the ritual there is a ceremony called *āpyāyana* or causing the half-pressed Soma stalks to swell by moistening them with water afresh. The beginnings of it are found in the MS. (4, 5[5]). The verb *ā-pyā*, 'to swell', occurs in the RV. in connexion with Soma (1, 91[16–8]; 10, 85[5])[19]; but here it seems to refer to Soma as identified with the moon. In one other passage, however, (9, 31[4]) it may have a ritual application. Soma is also said in the RV. to swell (*pi, pinv*), like a sea or river (9, 64[8]. 107[12]).

Soma is described in the RV. as pressed three times in the day. Thus the Ṛbhus are invited to the evening pressing (4, 33[11] &c.)[20], Indra to the midday pressing (3, 32[1, 2]; 8, 37[1]), which is his alone (4, 36[7]), while the morning libation is his first drink (10, 112[1]).

The abode (*sadhastha*) of Soma is often referred to[21]; once, however, mention is made of three, which he occupies when purified (9, 103[2]), the epithet *triṣadhastha*, 'having three abodes', being also applied to him in another passage (8, 83[5]). These three abodes may already designate the three tubs used at the Soma sacrifice of the later ritual (TS. 3, 2, 1[2]; KSS. 9, 5[17]. 7[4]; cp. RV. 8, 2[8]); but BERGAIGNE (BRV, 1, 179) regards them as purely mythological. A similar remark applies to the three lakes of Soma which Indra drinks (5, 29[7.8]; 6, 17[11]; 8, 7[10])[22]. The epithet *triprṣṭha*, 'three-backed', is peculiar to Soma. Being applied to the juice at least once (7, 37[1]) it probably refers (as Sāyaṇa thinks) to the three admixtures, much as the Agni's epithet *ghṛtapṛṣṭha* alludes to ghee being thrown on the fire[23].

Based on the mixture of water with the juice, the connexion of Soma with the waters is expressed in the most varied ways. Streams flow for him (9, 31[3]). The waters follow his ordinance (9, 82[5]). He flows at the head of streams (9, 86[12]). He is lord and king of streams (9, 15[5]. 86[33]. 89[2]), lord of spouses (9, 86[32]), an oceanic (*samudriya*) king and god (9, 107[16]). The waters are his sisters (9, 82[3]). As leader of waters, Soma rules over rain (9, 74[3]). He produces waters and causes heaven and earth to rain (9, 96[3]). He streams rains from heaven (9, 8[8]. 49[1]. 97[17]. 108[9.10]). The Soma drops themselves are several times compared with rain (9, 41[3]. 89[1]. 106[9])[24] and Soma is said to flow clearly with a stream of honey like the rain-charged cloud (9, 2[9]). So too the Pavamāna drops are said to have streamed from heaven, from air, on the ridge of earth (9, 63[27]). There are some other passages in which the soma that is milked appears to refer to rain (8, 7[10]; 9, 74[4], cp. 10, 30[4])[25]. The ŚB. (11, 5, 4[5]) identifies the *amṛta* with the waters. This identification may have given rise to the myth of Soma brought down to man by an eagle (p. 111)[26]. But the celestial Soma descending to earth was doubtless usually regarded as only mixed with rain, and not confounded with it[27].

The waters are invoked to set in motion the exhilerating wave, the draught of Indra, the sky-born well (10, 30[9]). Soma is the drop which grows in the waters (9, 85[10]. 89[2]). Hence he is the embryo of the waters (9, 97[41]; ŚB. 4, 4, 5[21]) or their child, for seven sisters as mothers are around the child, the newly born, the Gandharva of the waters (9, 86[36]; cp. 10, 13[5]), and the waters are directly called his mothers (9, 61[4]). Soma is also spoken of as a youth among the waters or cows (5, 45[9]; 9, 9[5]).

The sound made by the Soma juice as it is being purified and rushes into the vats or bowls, is often referred to. It is compared with that of rain (9, 41^{3}). But the language is generally hyperbolical. Thus the sweet drop is said to flow over the filter like the din of combatants (9, 69^{2}). The noise is constantly designated by various verbs meaning to roar or bellow (*krand, nad, mā, ru, vāś*: 9, 91^{3}. 95^{4} &c.). Even the verb *stan*, 'to thunder', is used (9, 86^{9}) and the wise are described as 'milking the thundering unfailing stalk' (9, 72^{6}). Lightning also is in some verses connected with the purification of Soma (9, 41^{3}. 80^{1}. 84^{3}. 87^{8}); this in all probability alludes to the purification of the celestial Soma and may have referred to the phenomena of the thunderstorm[28].

When Soma is said to roar he is commonly compared with or directly called a bull. 'As a bull he bellows in the wood' (9, 7^{3}); 'the tawny bull bellows and shines with the Sun' (9, 2^{6}). As the waters, added with or without milk,[29] are figuratively called cows, the relation of Soma to them is usually that of a bull to cows. He is a bull among the cows (9, 16^{6}. 69^{4}. 96^{7}) or is lord of the cows (9, 72^{4}). He bellows like a bull traversing the cows (9, 71^{9}) or like a bull towards the cows (9, 71^{7}), the cows also bellowing towards him (9, 80^{2} &c.). He is the bull of heaven as well as of the earth and the streams (6, 44^{21}). The impetuosity of Soma is also several times illustrated by comparison with a buffalo (*mahiṣa*). Thus he even comes to be called an animal (*paśu*: 9, 86^{43}). Being a bull among the cow-waters, Soma is the fertilizer of the waters (10, 36^{8}, cp. 9, 19^{5}). He is also (9, 86^{39}) an impregnator (*retodhā*), an epithet especially applied to the moon in the YV. (e. g. MS. 1, 6^{9}). Hence he is a bestower of fertility (9, 60^{4}. 74^{5}). Soma being so frequently called a bull (*ukṣan, vṛṣan, vṛṣabha*) is sharp-horned (*tigmaśṛṅga*), an epithet which in five of its six occurrences in the RV. is accompanied by a word meaning 'bull'. Thus the brewed drink (*mantha*) of Indra is like a sharp-horned bull (10, 86^{15}). Soma is also said (like Agni) to sharpen his horns (9, 15^{4}. 70^{7})[30].

Soma is swift (1, 4^{7}) and, in illustration of the speed with which the pressed juice flows, is very often compared with or designated a steed. Thus the ten maidens are said to cleanse him like a swift steed (9, 6^{5}). The drop which intoxicates Indra is a tawny steed (9, 63^{17}). Soma flowing into the vats is sometimes also compared with a bird flying to the wood (9, 72^{5} &c).

Owing to the yellow colour of the juice, the physical quality of Soma mainly dwelt on by the poets, is his brilliance. His rays are often referred to and he is frequently assimilated to the sun. He shines like or with the sun or clothes himself in its rays (9, 76^{4}. 86^{32}; cp. 71^{9}). He ascends the car of the sun and stands above all beings like the sun[31]. He fills heaven and earth with rays like the sun (9, 41^{5}). When born a bright son, he caused his parents to shine (9, 9^{3}). The daughter of the sun purifies him (9, 1^{6}). Thus it comes to be said of him that he combats the darkness (9, 9^{7}), wards it off with light (9, 86^{22}), or creates bright light, dispelling the darkness (9, 66^{24}. 100^{8}. 108^{12} &c.).

Its mysteriously exhilerating and invigorating action, surpassing that of ordinary food or drink and prompting to deeds beyond the natural powers, led to Soma being regarded as a divine drink which bestows immortal life. Hence it is mythologically called *amṛta*, the draught of immortality. It is an immortal stimulant (1, 84^{4}), which the gods love (9, 85^{2}) and of which, when pressed by men and mixed with milk, all the gods drink (9, 109^{15}); for they hasten to exhileration (8, 2^{18}) and become exhilerated (8, 58^{11}). Soma is immortal (1, 43^{9}; 8, 48^{12}; 9, 3^{1} &c.); and the gods drank him for immortality

(9, 106^{8}). He confers immortality on the gods (1, 91^{6}; 9, 108^{3}) and on men (1, 91^{1}; 8, 48^{3}). He places his worshipper in the everlasting and imperishable world where there is eternal light and glory, and makes him immortal where king Vaivasvata lives (9, 113$^{7.8}$)[32].

Thus Soma naturally has medicinal power also. It is medicine for a sick man (8, 61^{17}). Hence the god Soma heals whatever is sick, making the blind to see and the lame to walk (8, 68^{2}; 10, 25^{11}). He is the guardian of men's bodies and occupies their every limb (8, 48^{9}), bestowing length of life in this world (1, 91^{6}; 8, 48$^{4.7}$; 9, 4^{6}. 91^{6}). The Soma draught is even said to dispel sin from the heart, to destroy falsehood and to promote truth.

When imbibed Soma stimulates the voice (6, 47^{3}; 9, 84^{4}. 95^{5}. 97^{32}), which he impels as the rower his boat (9, 95^{2}). This is doubtless the reason why Soma is called 'lord of speech' *vācas pati*[33] (9, 26^{4}. 101^{5}) or leader of speech, *vāco agriya* or *agre* (9, 7^{3}. 62$^{25-6}$. 86^{12}. 106^{10}). He is also said to raise his voice from heaven (9, 68^{8}). In the Brāhmaṇas *vāc*, 'speech', is described as the price paid by the gods for Soma[34]. Soma also awakens eager thought (6, 47^{3}). So his worshippers exclaim: 'We have drunk Soma, we have become immortal, we have entered into light, we have known the gods' (8, 48^{3}). Thus he is also spoken of as a lord of thought and as a father, leader, or generator of hymns[35]. He is a leader of poets, a seer among priests (9, 96^{6}). He has the mind of seers, is a maker of seers (9, 96^{18}) and a protector of prayer (6, 52^{3}). He is the 'soul of sacrifice' (9, 2^{10}. 6^{8}), a priest (*brahmā*) among the gods (9, 96^{6}), and apportions to them their share of sacrifice (10, 85^{19}). Soma's wisdom thus comes to be predominantly dwelt upon[36]. He is a wise seer (8, 68^{1}). He knows the races of the gods (9, 81^{2}. 95^{2}. 97^{7}. 108^{3}). He is a wise man-seeing wave (9, 78^{2}). Soma with intelligence surveys creatures (9, 71^{9}). Hence he is many-eyed (9, 26^{5}) and thousand-eyed (9, 60^{1}).

Soma stimulated the Fathers to deeds (9, 96^{11}); through him the Fathers found the light and the cows (9, 97^{39}). Soma is also said to be united with the fathers (8, 48^{13}) or to be accompanied by them (AV. 18, 4^{12}; ŚB. 2, 6, 1^{4}, &c.), the Fathers, conversely, being called soma-loving, (*somya:* 10, 14^{6}; AV. 2, 12^{5}).

The exhilerating effect of the draught on man was naturally transferred to the gods, to whom the Soma was offered. The main application of its intoxicating power is its stimulating effect on Indra in his conflict with the hostile powers of the air. That Soma strengthens Indra for the fight with Vṛtra, is mentioned in innumerable passages of the RV. (8, 81^{17} &c.). In the intoxication of Soma Indra slays all foes (9, 1^{10}) and no one can resist him in battle when he has drunk it (6, 47^{1}). Soma is the soul of Indra (9, 85^{3}), the auspicious friend of Indra (10, 25^{9}), whose vigour he stimulates (9, 76^{2}) and whom he aids in slaying Vṛtra (9, 61^{22}). With Soma as a companion Indra made the waters to flow for man and slew the dragon (4, 28^{1}). Thus Soma is sometimes even called the bolt (*vajra*) of Indra (9. 72^{7}. 77^{1} 111^{3}). Soma, Indra's juice, becomes a thousand-winning bolt (9, 47^{3}). It is the intoxicating draught which destroys a hundred forts (9, 48^{2}) and is a Vṛtra-slaying intoxicating stalk (6, 17^{11}). Thus the god Soma is said to be 'like Indra a slayer of Vṛtras and a fort-destroyer' (9, 88^{4}) and comes to receive half a dozen times the epithet *vṛtrahan*, 'Vṛtra-slaying', which primarily belongs to Indra[37].

When drunk by Indra Soma caused the sun to rise in heaven (9, 86^{22}). So this cosmic action comes to be attributed to Soma independently. He caused the sun to shine (9, 28^{5}. 37^{4}), caused the lights of the sky to shine

(9, 85^{9}), and produced the sun in the waters (9, 42^{1})[38]. He caused the sun to rise, impelled it, obtained and bestowed it, and caused the dawns to shine[39]. He makes his worshippers participate in the sun (9, 4^{5}) and finds light for them (9, 35^{1}). He found the light (9, 59^{4}) and wins light and heaven (9, 3^{2}). Just as even the sacrificial butter is spoken of as the 'navel of immortality', on which rests the whole world (4, $58^{1.11}$), the conception of Soma comes to be extended to that of a being of universal dominion (9, $86^{28.29}$), who is 'lord of the quarters' (9, 113^{2}), who performs the great cosmic actions of generating the two worlds (9, 90^{1}), of creating or establishing heaven and earth, of supporting heaven, and of placing light in the sun (6, 44^{23-4}. $47^{3.4}$)[40].

Being so intimately connected with Indra in the conflict with Vṛtra, Soma comes to be spoken of independently as a great fighter. He is a victor, unconquered in fight, born for battle (1, 91^{21}). He is the most heroic of heroes, the fiercest of the terrible, ever victorious (9, 66^{16-7}). He conquers for his worshippers cows, chariots, horses, gold, heaven, water, a thousand boons (9, 78^{4}), and everything (8, 68^{1}). Without reference to his warlike character, he is constantly said to bestow all the wealth of heaven and earth, food, cattle, horses, and so forth (9, 45^{3}. 49^{1}. 52^{1} &c.). Soma himself is occasionally called a treasure (*rayi:* 9, 48^{3}) or the wealth of the gods (ŚB. 1, 6, 4^{5}). Soma can also afford protection from foes (10, 25^{7}). He drives away goblins (9, 49^{5}) and, like some other deities but more frequently, receives the epithet of goblin-slayer (*rakṣohan*). Soma is the only god who is called a slayer of the wicked (9, 28^{6} &c.). In the later Vedic literature the statement occurs that Brāhmans who drink Soma are able to slay at a glance (MS. 4, 8^{2})[41].

Being a warrior, Soma is said to have weapons (9, 96^{16}), which like a hero he grasps in his hand (9, 76^{2}) and which are terrible and sharp (9, 61^{30}. 90^{3}). In one passage he is said to have obtained his weapons by robbing his malignant father of them (6, 44^{22}). He is described as armed with a thousand-pointed shaft (9, 83^{5}. 86^{40}) and his bow is swift (9, 90^{3}).

Soma rides in the same chariot as Indra (9, 87^{9}. 96^{2}. 103^{5}). He is charioteer to the car-fighter Indra (AV. 8, 8^{23}). He drives in a car (9, 3^{5}), which is heavenly (9, 111^{3}). He has light (9, 86^{45}) or a filter for his car (9, 83^{5}). He is the best of charioteers (9, 66^{26}). He has well-winged mares of his own (9, 86^{37}) and a team like Vāyu (9, 88^{3}).

Soma is naturally sometimes connected with Indra's intimate associates, the Maruts. They are said to milk the bull of heaven (9, 108^{11}, cp. 54^{1}) and to adorn the child when born (9, 96^{17}). Like Indra, Soma is attended by the Maruts (6, 47^{5}) or the troop of the Maruts (9, 66^{22}). The Winds, too, are said to be gladdening to Soma (9, 31^{3}) and Vāyu is his guardian (10, 85^{5}). Soma forms a pair with Agni, Pūṣan, and Rudra respectively (p. 128—9). A few times he is mystically indentified with Varuṇa (9, 77^{5}. 95^{4}; cp. $73^{3.9}$; 8, 41^{8}).

The Soma plant is once in the RV. (10, 34^{1}) described as *maujavata*, which according to later statements[42] would mean 'produced on Mount Mūjavat'. Soma is also several times described as dwelling in the mountains (*giriṣṭhā*)[43] or growing in the mountains[44] (*parvatāvṛdh:* 9, 46^{1}). Mountains are also called 'Soma-backed' (AV. 3, 21^{10}), a term which, perhaps by sacrificial symbolism, is applied to the pressing stones (*adrayaḥ*) in RV. 8, 52^{2}. All these terms point to the abode of the Soma plant being on terrestrial mountains (cp. especially 9, 82^{3}). This is confirmed by the statement of the Avesta that Haoma grows on the mountains[45]. Since the Soma plant actually grew on mountains, it is probable that this fact is present to the mind of the poet even when he says that 'on the vault of heaven sweet-tongued friends milk the mountain-dwelling bull' (9, 85[10] cp. 95[4]). Terrestrial hills may also be intended when it is said that 'Varuṇa has placed Agni in the waters, the sun in heaven, and Soma on the rock' (5, 85[2]), or that 'Mātariśvan brought the one (Agni) from heaven, while the eagle carried off the other (Soma) from the rock' (1, 93[6]); but here there is more doubt, as 'mountain' and 'rock' mythologically often mean 'cloud' (p. 10).

Though Soma is a terrestrial plant, it is also celestial (10, 116[3]); in fact its true origin and abode are regarded as in heaven. Thus it is said that the birth of the plant is on high; being in heaven it has been received by earth (9, 61[10]). The 'intoxicating juice' is the 'child of heaven' (9, 38[5]), an epithet frequently applied to Soma. In one passage, however, he is called the offspring (*jāḥ*) of the sun (9, 93[1]) and in another Parjanya is spoken of as the father of the mighty bird (9, 82[3] cp. 113[3]). In the AV. the origin of *amṛta* is also traced to the seed of Parjanya (AV. 8, 7[21]). When Soma is called a child (*śiśu*) simply (9, 96[17]) or a youth (*yuvan*), this is doubtless in allusion to the fact that, like Agni, he is continually produced anew[46]. Soma is the milk (*pīyūṣa*) of heaven (9, 51[2] &c.), is purified in heaven (9, 83[2]. 86[22] &c.). He flows with his stream to the dear places of heaven (9, 12[8]). He runs through heaven across the spaces with his stream (9, 3[7]). He occupies heaven (9, 85[9]), is in heaven (ŚB. 3, 4, 3[13]), or is the lord of heaven (9, 86[11.33]). As bird of heaven he looks down on earth and regards all beings (9, 71[9]). He stands above all worlds like god Sūrya (9, 54[3]). The drops being purified have been poured from heaven, from the air, on the surface of the earth (9, 63[27])[47]; for he is a traverser of space (*rajastur:* 4, 48[4]. 108[7]). Fingers rub him surrounded with milk 'on the third ridge, in the bright realm of heaven' (9, 86[27]). His place is in the highest heaven (3, 32[10]; 4, 26[6]; 9, 86[15]) or in the third heaven (TS. 3, 5, 7[1] &c.)[48]. 'Heaven', however, also seems to be frequently a mystical name of the strainer of sheep's wool[49]. This seems to be the case when Soma is spoken of as being 'on the navel of heaven, on the sheep-filter' (9, 12[4]), as traversing the lights of heaven, the sheep-filter (9, 37[3]), as running with Sūrya in heaven, on the filter (9, 27[5]); or when it is said that 'the bull has occupied heaven, the king goes soaring over the strainer' (9, 85[9] cp. 86[8]). The term *sānu*, 'summit', so frequently applied to the filter, is suggestive of *divaḥ sānu*, 'the summit of heaven'. Such terms would naturally come to be connected with the terrestrial Soma, because heaven is the abode of the celestial Soma or *amṛta* (6, 44[23]).

Soma has been brought from heaven (9, 63[27]. 66[30]). The myth most commonly expressive of this belief is that of Soma and the eagle. It was brought by the eagle (1, 80[2]). The bird brought Soma from that highest heaven (4, 26[6]). The eagle brought the Soma or mead (*madhu*) to Indra (3, 43[7]; 4, 18[13]). The swift eagle flew to the Soma plant (5, 45[9]); the eagle tore off the sweet stalk for Indra (4, 20[6]). The eagle brought it for Indra through the air with his foot (8, 71[9]). Flying swift as thought, the bird broke through the iron castle (cp. 4, 27[1]), going to heaven he brought the Soma for the wielder of the bolt (8, 89[8]). The eagle bore the plant from afar, from heaven (9, 68[6]. 77[2]. 86[24]; 10, 11[4]. 99[8]. 144[4]). The myth is most fully dealt with in RV. 4, 26 and 27[50]. In the Brāhmaṇas it is Gāyatrī, a mystical sacerdotal name of Agni[51], that carries off the Soma. In the RV. the eagle is constantly distinguished from Indra as bringing the Soma to him. There is only one passage (unconnected with this myth) in which Indra seated at the Soma offering is called an eagle (10, 99[8]). 'Eagle of heaven' is an epithet applied to Agni (7, 15[4]: otherwise twice said of the Maruts), the term eagle is connected with Agni Vaidyuta or lightning (TB. 3, 10, 5[1] cp. 12,1[2]), and Agni is often called a bird in the RV. (p. 89). On this evidence BLOOMFIELD, who subjects his predecessors' interpretations of RV. 4, 27 to a searching criticism, with much plausibility explains the carrying off of Soma by the eagle as a mythological account of the simple phenomenon of the descent of lightning, darting from the cloud (i. e. the iron castle) and causing the fall of the ambrosial fluid Soma (i. e. the water of the cloud). At the same time he refers to a passage of the RV. (1, 93[6]) in which the descent of fire and of Soma are mentioned together[52]. A detail of the myth (probably a mere embellishment added by the individual poet) is the trait that as the eagle carried away Soma, the archer Kṛśānu[53] shot at him knocking out a feather (4, 27[3. 4]; cp. AB. 3, 25). This trait is related with greater detail in the Brāhmaṇas. Either a feather or a claw is here stated to have been shot off. Falling to the ground, it became a *parṇa* (*palāśa*) or a *śalyaka* tree. The tree hereby acquired a specially sacred character in connexion with the ritual[54].

Being the most important of herbs Soma is said to have been born as the lord of plants (9, 114[2]), which are also said to have Soma as their king[55] (9, 97[18–9]). He receives the epithet *vanaspati*, 'lord of the wood' (1, 91[6]; 9, 12[7]) and is said to have generated all plants (1, 91[22]). In the Brāhmaṇas plants are connected with Soma, being styled *saumya* (ŚB. 12, 1, 1[2])[56]. Irrespectively of his being lord of plants, Soma is often, like other leading gods, called a king[57]. He is also a king of rivers (9, 89[2]), a king of the whole earth (9, 97[58]), a king or father of the gods (9, 86[10]. 87[2]. 109[4]) a king of gods and mortals (9, 97[24]), and a king of Brāhmans (VS. 9, 40; TS. 1, 8[10]; MS. 2, 6[9]). He is of course often called a god; but in one passage he is described as 'a god pressed for the gods' (9, 3[6. 7]).

In the post-Vedic literature Soma is a regular name of the moon, which is regarded as being drunk up by the gods and so waning, till it is filled up again by the sun. In the Chāndogya Upaniṣad (5, 10[1]) the statement is found that the moon is king Soma, the food of the gods, and is drunk up by them[58]. Even in the Brāhmaṇas the identification of Soma with the moon is already a common-place[59]. Thus the AB. (7, 11) remarks that the moon is the Soma of the gods; the ŚB. (1, 6, 4[5]), that king Soma, the food of the gods, is the moon; and in the Kauṣītaki Br. (7, 10; 4, 4) the sacrificial plant or juice is symbolical of the moon-god. The mythology of the Brāhmaṇas already explains the phases of the moon as due to the gods and Fathers eating its substance, which consists of ambrosia[60]. Soma, as the moon, is in the YV. also conceived as having the lunar asterisms, the daughters of Prajāpati, for his wives[61]. In the AV., moreover, Soma several times means the moon (7, 81[3. 4]; 11, 6[7], &c.). A large number of scholars agree that even in a few of the latest hymns of the RV. (in the first and tenth books) Soma is already identified with the moon[62]. Most of them, however, hold that Soma as a god is celebrated in the Vedic hymns only as a personification of the beverage, regarding his identification with the moon as merely a secondary mythological growth[63]. The most important of the passages in which the identification is generally admitted, is that which describes the wedding of Soma and the sun-maiden Sūryā (10, 85)[64]. Here Soma is spoken of as 'in the lap of the stars', (v.[2]), and it is said that no one eats of that Soma which the priests know and which is contrasted with that which they crush (v. [3]). The Soma nature of the moon being referred to as a secret known to Brāhmans only, shows that it cannot yet have been a popular notion. The process by which the celestial Soma gradually coalesced with the moon is not difficult to understand. Soma is, on the one hand, continually thought of as celestial and bright, sometimes as dispelling darkness and swelling in the waters; on the other hand, it is very often called a 'drop', *indu* (6, 44^{21})[65]. Comparison with the moon would therefore easily suggest itself. Thus Soma in the bowls is said in one passage to appear like the moon in the waters (8, 71^{8}; cp. 1, 105^{1}); and in another, Soma being described as the drop (*drapsa*) which goes to the ocean, looking with the eye of a vulture (10, 123^{8}), is generally admitted to allude to the moon.

HILLEBRANDT, however, in his Vedische Mythologie not only claims this identification for a number of other passages in the RV., but asserts that in the whole of the ninth book Soma is the moon (p. 309) and nowhere the ordinary plant (p. 326), the ninth book in fact being a book of hymns to the moon[66]. Soma, he maintains, means, in the earliest as well as the latest parts of the whole RV., only the Soma plant or juice on the one hand, and, as a deity, only the moon on the other (pp. 274. 340. 450). According to his view, the moon is a receptacle of Soma or *amṛta* and is the god whom the worshipper means when he presses the draught, which is part of the lunar ambrosia. HILLEBRANDT goes even further than this complete identification of Soma and the moon in the RV. He also asserts that the moon-god as Soma forms the centre of Vedic belief and cult (p. 277), being the creator and ruler of the world much more than the sun (p. 313), while Indra is the most popular Vedic god only next to the moon[67] (p. 315).

In opposition to this hypothesis, it has been argued that, in the vast majority of the references to Soma in the RV., the character of the god as a personification of the plant and juice is clear and obvious. On the other hand, while the identification of Soma and the moon is perfectly clear in the later literature, there is in the whole of the RV. no single distinct and explicit instance either of the identification or of the conception that the moon is the food of the gods. It is only in passages where the brilliance of Soma, so constantly connected with the sun, is vaguely expressed, that references to the moon can be found. At the same time it is possible that amid the chaotic details of the imagery of the Soma hymns, there may occasionally lurk a veiled identification of ambrosia and the moon. Here and there passages celebrating the luminous nature of Soma or referring to his swelling (*āpyāyana*), which affords a parallel to the swelling of the moon, may allude to such a notion. But on the whole, with the few late exceptions generally admitted, it appears to be certain that to the seers of the RV. the god Soma is a personification of the terrestrial plant and juice[68]. It is, moreover, hardly conceivable that all the Vedic commentators, in whose day Soma and the moon were believed to be one, should not know that Soma means the moon in the RV. also[69].

It is an undoubted fact that Soma, the Avestan Haoma, was already prepared and celebrated in the Indo-Iranian period. In the RV. Soma is described as growing on the mountains or a particular mountain; in the Avesta it is said to grow on a certain mountain. In the RV. Varuṇa places it on the rock; in the Avesta it is placed on the great mountain Haraiti by a skilful god. In the RV. it is brought by an eagle; in the Avesta it is distributed from its native mountain by certain auspicious birds. In both it is king of plants. In both it is a medicine which gives health, long life, and removes death. As Soma grows in the waters, so Haoma in the waters of Ardvī-sūra[70]. The pressing and offering of Soma was already an important feature of Indo-Iranian worship. But while three daily pressings are referred to in the RV., only two are mentioned in the Avesta (Yasna 10, 2). In both it is stated that the stalks (*aṃśu* = *āsu*) were pressed, that the juice was yellow and was mixed with milk (Yasna 10, 13). In both the celestial Soma is distinguished from the terrestrial, and the beverage from the god. In both the mythical home of Soma is heaven, whence it comes down to earth. In both the Soma draught (like the sacrificial fire) had already become a mighty god and is called a king. As Soma is *vṛtrahan*, so Haoma is *verethrajan* and casts missiles (*vadare* = Vedic *vadhar*). Both are light-winning (*svarṣā* = *hvaresa*) and wise (*sukratu* = *hukhratu*). Both remove the machinations of the wicked, bestow victory over foes, and confer the celestial world. Both grant steeds and excellent children. The RV. and the Avesta even agree in the names of ancient preparers of Soma, Vivasvat and Trita Āptya on the one hand, and Vīvaṅhvant, Āthwya, and Thrita on the other[71]. The belief in an intoxicating divine beverage, the home of which was heaven, may be Indo-European. If so, it must have been regarded as a kind of honey-mead (Skt. *mádhu*, Gk. μέθυ, As. *medu*) brought down to earth from its guardian demon by an eagle (the Soma-bringing eagle of Indra agreeing with the nectar-bringing eagle of Zeus and with the eagle which, as a metamorphosis of Odhin, carried off the mead)[72]. This *madhu* or honey-mead, if Indo-European, was replaced in the Indo-Iranian period by Soma; but may have survived into the Vedic period, by amalgamating with Soma[73].

Etymologically *Soma* = *Haoma* means 'pressed juice', being derived from the root *su* = *hu*, 'to press'.

[1] Oldenberg, ZDMG. 42, 241. — [2] BRV. 1, 182. — [3] HVM. 1, 47. — [4] *Anna* = *surā* ŚB. 12, 7, 3^{8}; cp. HVM. 1, 264. — [5] HVM. 1, 518. — [6] KHF. 128 f.; ZDMG. 32, 301. — [7] HVM. 1, 243—4. — [8] Op. cit. 28. — [9] Op. cit. 468 ff.; ORV. 389. — [10] Hillebrandt, Vedainterpretation 16. — [11] HVM. 1, 182. — [12] Op. cit. 151. — [13] Op. cit. 206—7. — [14] Windisch, FaR. 141. — [15] HVM. 1, 186. — [16] LRV. 3, 378—9. — [17] HVM. 1, 210. — [18] Op. cit. 229. — [19] Op. cit. 195. — [20] Op. cit. 256, note 3. — [21] Op. cit. 189. — [22] LRV. 5, 260. — [23] Otherwise HVM. 1, 392—3. — [24] Windisch, FaR. 140. — [25] PVS. 1, 87—8; KHF. 129. 142. 227; KZ. 1, 521 ff.; GGH. 70. 115; WVB. 1894, 4. 13. — [26] HRI. 123—4. — [27] BRV. 1, 165. — [28] Op. cit. 1, 170; lightning is associated with rain in 1, 399; 5, 84^{3}; 7, 56^{13}; 10, 91^{5} cp. 5, 83^{4}; Bloomfield, AJP. 7, 470. — [29] BRV. 1, 204. — [30] HVM. 1, 340 thinks the horns are those of the moon. — [31] References in HVM. 1, 601. — [32] KRV. note 308; BRV. 1, 192. — [33] BRV. 1, 185; HVM. 1, 349. — [34] Roth, ZDMG. 35, 687; Weber, IS. 10, 360; HVM. 1, 79. — [35] BRV. 1, 300, note 2; HVM. 1, 403. — [36] BRV. 1, 185—6. — [37] KHF. 105; Macdonell, JRAS. 25, 472. — [38] HVM. 1, 387—8. — [39] References in HVM. 1, 388. — [40] Cp Haug, ZDMG. 7, 511. — [41] ZDMG. 7, 331. 375. — [42] VS. 3, 61 and comm., Āp. ŚS. 12, 5, 11; YN. 9, 8; cp. AIL. 29; HVM. 1, 63 ff. — [43] Twice, also said of Viṣṇu, once of the Maruts. — [44] 'Bergfroh', Hillebrandt, Vedainterpretation 15. — [45] On the habitat of the Soma plant, see Roth, ZDMG. 38, 134—9; MM., Biographies of Words (London, 1888) 222—42. — [46] JRAS. 25, 437. — [47] Windisch, FaR. 140. — [48] Also 6, 1, 6^{1}; Kāṭh. 23, 10 in IS. 8, 31; VS. 1, 211; TB. 1, 1, 3^{10}; 3, 2, 1^{1}. — [49] HVM. 1, 361, note 3. — [50] Roth, ZDMG. 36, 353—60. 384; Ludwig, Methode 30. 66; Koulikovski, Revue de linguistique 18, 1—9; BRV. 3, 322 ff.; PVS. 1, 207—16; HVM. 1, 278—9; Bloomfield, FaR. 149—55; ORV. 180—1; WVB. 1894, p. 5. — [51] Cp. ŚB. 3, 9, 4^{10}; KHF. 130 f. 144 f. 172. — [52] Bloomfield, JAOS. 16, 1—24; ORV. 176. 180 thinks there is no reason to see a natural agent in the bird, or to assume any connexion between the Soma and the water of clouds. — [53] Sp.AP. 224. — [54] KHF. 159 f. 170. 209; WVB. 1894, p. 5. — [55] Cp. ZDMG. 25, 647. — [56] HVM. 1, 390, note 4. — [57] Op. cit. 317—8. — [58] Deussen, System des Vedānta 415 ff. — [59] WVB. 1894, p. 16—7. — [60] HVM. 1, 296. — [61] Weber, Nakṣatra 2, 274 ff; Oldenberg, ZDMG. 49, 470; on Soma dwelling with Rohiṇī, cp. Jacobi, FaR. 71, note; R. Brown jr., Academy 42, 439. — [62] HVM. 1, 269. — [63] BRV. 1, 160. — [64] Weber, IS. 5, 178 ff.; WVB. 1894, p. 34; OST. 5, 237; Ehni, ZDMG. 33, 167—8; Jacobi, ib. 49, 227; Oldenberg, ib. 478. — [65] Ehni, l. c. — [66] Cp. Bloomfield, AJP. 14, 491—3; MM.

Fortnightly Review, Oct. 1893, 443 ff. (= Chips 4², 328—67) — 67 GUBERNATIS, Myth. des Plantes 2, 351, Letture sopra la mitol. vedica 106, and PVS. 1, 80 (cp. 2, 242) had called for a complete identification, but without attempting to prove the proposition (cp. GGA. 1889, p. 10). — 68 WHITNEY, PAOS. 1894, p. xcix f.; ORV. 599—612. — 69 HRI. 117. — 70 SPIEGEL, Av. Tr. 2, LXXII f.; DARMESTETER, Ormazd et Ahriman 140. — 71 Yasna IX—X; cp. SP.AP. 172; HVM. 1, 121. 265. 450; ORV. 178; MACDONELL, JRAS. 25, 485. — 72 ORV. 176. — 73 Op. cit. 178.

WINDISCHMANN, Ueber den Somakultus der Arier, Abh. d. Münchner Akad. 1846, p. 127 ff.; KHF. 105 ff.; WHITNEY, JAOS. 3, 299; WEBER, IS. 3, 466; WVB. 1894, p. 3. 13—17; HAUG, AB. Introd. p. 61—2; OST. 5, 258—71; BRV. 1, 148—225 &c.; BRI. 24; ROTH, ZDMG. 35, 680—92; SP.AP. 168—78; HVM. I; ZDMG. 48, 419 f.; E. H. MEYER, IF. 2, 161; KNAUER, Vedische Fragen, FaR. 61—7; HVBP. 68—74.

D. ABSTRACT GODS.

§ 38. Two Classes. — There are in the RV. two classes of deities whose nature is founded on abstraction. The one class consisting of the direct personfications of abstract notions such as 'desire' is rare, occurring only in the very latest hymns of the RV. and due to that growth of speculation which is so plainly traceable in the course of the Vedic age. The other and more numerous class comprises deities whose names primarily either denote an agent, in the form of a noun derived from a root with the suffix *-tṛ*, such as Dhātṛ, 'Creator', or designate some attribute, such as Prajāpati, 'Lord of Creatures'. This class, judged by the evolution of the mythological creations of the Veda, does not represent direct abstractions, but appears in each case to be derived from an epithet applied to one or more deities and illustrating a particular aspect of activity or character. Such epithets gradually becoming detached finally attained to an independent position. Thus Rohita, 'the Red One' (whose female form is Rohiṇī), originally an epithet of the sun, figures in the AV. as a separate deity in the capacity of a Creator[1].

A. Various Agent Gods. — The most important of the gods whose names denote an agent in *-tṛ*, is Savitṛ, who has already been treated among the solar deities (§ 15). Most of the others are of rare occurrence in the RV. Dhātṛ, found in a few passages as an appellative designating priests as 'establishers' of the sacrifice, occurs as the name of a deity about a dozen times and, with the exception of one indefinite mention in company with a number of other gods (7, 35³), only in the tenth book. In one of these passages the name is an epithet of Indra (10, 167³) and in another of Viśvakarman (10, 82²). The frequent ascription of the action of establishing (√*dhā*) the phenomena of the world to different gods, gradually led to the conception of a separate deity exercising this particular activity. Thus Dhātṛ generally has the independent character of a god who creates sun, moon, heaven, earth, and air (10, 190³), and is lord of the world (10, 128⁷). In a hymn to the Sun, Dhātṛ is invoked to grant a clear eye (10, 158³). He is besought with Viṣṇu, Tvaṣṭṛ, Prajāpati, to grant offspring (10, 184¹) and, by himself, to bestow length of days (10, 18⁵). He is also prayed to indefinitely with Viṣṇu and Savitṛ (10, 181¹⁻³) or with Mātariśvan and Deṣṭrī (10, 85⁴⁷). In the Naighaṇṭuka (5, 5) Dhātṛ is enumerated among the gods of the middle region and by Yāska (Nir. 11, 10) explained as the 'ordainer of everything'. In the post-Vedic period, Dhātṛ is the Creator and Preserver of the world, being the equivalent of Prajāpati or Brahmā. The rare name Vidhātṛ, the 'Disposer' is in two passages an epithet, beside Dhātṛ, once of Indra (10, 167³) and once of Viśvakarman (10, 82²); but appears twice in enumerations of deities to have an independent character (6, 50¹²; 9, 81⁵). Dhartṛ, 'Supporter', frequently used (almost exclusively with the genitive of that which is supported) as an epithet of Indra and other gods, occurs once as an independent name along with Dhātṛ and other deities (7, 35[3]). Similarly, Trātṛ, the 'Protector', mostly employed as an epithet of Agni or Indra and, in the plural, of the Ādityas, occurs independently as 'the Protector God' in five passages along with other deities (1, 106[7]; 4, 55[5. 7]; 8, 18[20]; 10, 128[7]). In Roth's opinion, Savitṛ especially and also Bhaga are intended by this god[2]. A 'Leader God' (*deva netṛ*) is invoked two or three times in one hymn (5, 50) as a guide to prosperity in life.

B. **Tvaṣṭṛ.** — The only deity bearing a name of this type, who besides Savitṛ is mentioned with any frequency, is Tvaṣṭṛ. His name occurs about 65 times in the RV., pretty uniformly in the family books (though rarely in the seventh as well as the eighth), but relatively oftenest in the first and tenth. No hymn is, however, devoted to his praise.

No part of Tvaṣṭṛ's physical form is mentioned except his arm or hand, it being characteristic of him to hold an iron axe in his hand (8, 29[3]). He is once described as yoking his two steeds to his chariot and shining greatly (6, 47[19]). Tvaṣṭṛ is beautiful-armed (*sugabhasti*: 6, 49[9]), or beautiful-handed (*supāṇi*: predominantly applied to him and Savitṛ).

He is a skilful workman (1, 85[9]; 3, 54[12]), producing various objects showing the skill of an artificer. He is in fact the most skilful of workmen, versed in crafty contrivances (10, 53[9]). He is several times said (5, 31[4] &c.) to have fashioned (√*takṣ*) the bolt of Indra. He also sharpens the iron axe of Brahmaṇaspati (10, 53[9]). He formed a new cup (1, 20[6]) which contained the food of the *asura* (1, 110[3]) or the beverage of the gods (1, 161[5]; 3, 35[5]). He thus possesses vessels out of which the gods drink (10, 53[9]). The AV. (9, 4[3. 6]) describes him as an old man bearing a bowl of wealth, a cup full of Soma. From Tvaṣṭṛ the swift horse was produced (VS. 29, 9), and he gives speed to the horse (AV. 6, 92[1]).

The RV. further states that Tvaṣṭṛ adorned all beings with form (10, 110[9]). He developes the germ in the womb and is the shaper of all forms, human and animal (1, 188[9]; 8, 91[8]; 10, 184[1]). Similar statements are frequently made in later Vedic texts (AV. 2, 26[1], &c.), where he is characteristically a creator of forms (ŚB. 11, 4, 3[3]; TB. 1, 4, 7[1])[3]. He himself is called omniform (*viśvarūpa*) oftener than any other deity in the RV. As fashioner of living forms, he is frequently described as presiding over generation and bestowing offspring (3, 4[9] &c.). Thus he is said to have fashioned husband and wife for each other from the womb (10, 10[5]; AV. 6, 78[3]). He has produced and nourishes a great variety of creatures (3, 55[19]). Beasts belong to Tvaṣṭṛ (ŚB. 3, 7, 3[11]. 8, 3[11]). He is indeed a universal father, for he produced the whole world (VS. 29, 9).

He is also the ancestor of the human race in so far as his daughter Saraṇyū, wife of Vivasvat, becomes the mother of the primeval twins Yama and Yamī (10, 17[1. 2], cp. 5, 42[13]). Vāyu is once said to be his son-in-law (8, 26[21]). Tvaṣṭṛ begot Bṛhaspati (2, 23[17]). Agni produced by the ten fingers, is the offspring of Tvaṣṭṛ (1, 95[2]), who, along with Heaven and Earth, the Waters, and the Bhṛgus, generated him (10, 2[7]. 46[9]). It is to be inferred that Tvaṣṭṛ was also the father of Indra (p. 57). Tvaṣṭṛ is especially a guardian of Soma, which is called 'the mead of Tvaṣṭṛ' (1, 117[22]). It is in his house that Indra drinks Soma and presumately steals it, even slaying his father in order to obtain it (p. 57). The 'omniform' Tvaṣṭṛ has a son named Viśvarūpa (the Omniform), who is a guardian of cows. The hostility of Indra is directed against the son in order to win these cows, just as against the father in order to gain possession of the Soma. Even Tvaṣṭṛ himself is said to tremble with fear at the wrath of Indra (1, 80^{14}) and is represented as inferior to Indra, inasmuch as not even he was able to perform a feat done by Indra (10, 49^{10}). The TS. (2, 4, 12^{1}) tells a story of how Tvaṣṭṛ, whose son had been slain by Indra, refused to allow the latter to assist at his Soma sacrifice, but Indra came and drank off the Soma by force. The Brāhmaṇas often relate a similar tale (ŚB. 1, 6, 3^{6}, &c.).

Probably because of his creative agency in the womb[4], Tvaṣṭṛ is closely allied with celestial females (*gnāḥ, janayaḥ*) or the wives of the gods, who are his most frequent attendants (1, 22^{9} &c.)[5]. Tvaṣṭṛ is chiefly mentioned with gods of cognate activity, Pūṣan, Savitṛ, Dhātṛ, Prajāpati. 'Savitṛ' is indeed an attribute of Tvaṣṭṛ in two passages (3, 55^{19}; 10, 10^{5}) in which occurs the identical collocation *devas tvaṣṭā savitā viśvarūpaḥ*[6], 'god Tvaṣṭṛ, the omniform vivifier', and in both of which the generative or creative faculty of the deity is referred to. In the Kauśika Sūtra, Tvaṣṭṛ is identified with Savitṛ and Prajāpati[7], and in the Mārkaṇḍeya Purāṇa, with Viśvakarman and Prajāpati. In the later mythology Tvaṣṭṛ is one of the twelve Ādityas and in the Mahābhārata and the Bhāgavata Purāṇa is once or twice a form of the sun.

The RV. adds a few rather indefinite traits, which throw no light on Tvaṣṭṛ's character. He is said to be the first (1, 13^{10}) or the first-born (*agrajā*) and one who goes before (9, 5^{9}). As a companion of the Aṅgirases he knows the region of the gods (10, 70^{9}), goes to the place of the gods (2, 1^{9}) between heaven and earth (MS. 4, 14^{9}). He is a bestower of blessings and is possessed of excellent wealth (10, 70^{9}. 92^{11}). He is supplicated to grant riches to his worshippers and to delight in their hymns (7, 34^{21}). Tvaṣṭṛ also confers long life (10, 18^{6}; AV. 6, 78^{3}).

The word is derived from a rare root *tvakṣ*, of which only one verbal form, besides some nominal derivatives, occurs in the RV., and the cognate of which, *thwakṣ*, is found in the Avesta. It appears to be identical in meaning with the common root *takṣ*, which is used with the name of Tvaṣṭṛ in referring to the fashioning of Indra's bolt. The meaning therefore appears to be the 'Fashioner' or 'Artificer'.

Tvaṣṭṛ is one of the obscurest members of the Vedic pantheon[8]. The obscurity of the conception is explained by KAEGI[9] as due to Tvaṣṭṛ, like Trita and others, having belonged to an earlier race of gods who were ousted by later ones; while HILLEBRANDT thinks Tvaṣṭṛ was derived from a mythical cycle outside the range of the Vedic tribes. Different explanations have been offered of Tvaṣṭṛ's original nature. Owing to Tvaṣṭṛ being called Savitṛ, A. KUHN[10] thought that he meant the sun, but seems later[11] to have withdrawn this view. LUDWIG[12] regards him as a god of the year, while OLDENBERG believes him to be a pure abstraction expressing a definite characteristic activity[13]. HILLEBRANDT holds KUHN's earlier view that Tvaṣṭṛ represents the sun, to be probable[14]. HARDY also considers him a solar deity[15]. It does not indeed seem unlikely that this god, in a period anterior to the RV., represented the creative aspect of the sun's nature. If such was the case the Rigvedic poets themselves were only very dimly conscious of it. The name itself would have encouraged the growth of mythical accretions illustrative of creative skill, the desire to supply the pantheon with a regular divine artificer being natural enough. Much in the same way it was supplied with a divine priest in the person of Bṛhaspati.

The cup of Tvaṣṭṛ has been explained as the 'bowl of the year' or the nocturnal sky. But neither of these could well have been conceived as full of Soma and drunk by the gods. Hillebrandt's interpretation of it as the moon is more plausible (cp. p. 133).

[1] OST. 5, 395—6; V. Henry, Les Hymnes Rohitas, Paris 1891; Bloomfield, AJP. 12, 429—44; HRI. 209, n. 1. — [2] Roth, PW.; cp. GW.; WC. 9—10. — [3] Cp. PW. s. v. *tvaṣṭṛ*. — [4] Ibid. — [5] OST. 5, 229. — [6] Roth, Nir. Erl. 144. — [7] Weber, Omina und Portenta 391—2. — [8] GGH. 113—6. — [9] KRV. note 131. — [10] KZ. 1, 448. — [11] KHF. 109. — [12] LRV. 3, 333—5. — [13] ORV. 233. — [14] HVM. 1, 517. — [15] HVBP. 30—1.

ZDMG. 1, 522; Geiger, Ostiranische Kultur 304; BRI. 22; BRV. 3, 38—64; HVM. 1, 513—35; IF. 1, S; Ehni, Yama 4—16; Oldenberg, SBE. 46, 416 f. 248.

§ 39. **Viśvakarman, Prajāpati.** — A few other abstract deities originating in compound epithets and all representing the supreme god who was being evolved at the end of the Rigvedic period, are found in the RV. As the name of a god **Viśvakarman** occurs only five times in the RV. and always in the tenth book. Two whole hymns (10, 81. 82) are dedicated to his praise. The word also occurs as an attribute once (8, 87^{2}) of Indra and once (10, 170^{4}) of the Sun as the 'all-creating'. It is not uncommon as an adjective in the later Vedas, where it also appears as an attribute of Prajāpati (VS. 12, 61). The two hymns of the RV. describe Viśvakarman thus. He is all-seeing, having eyes, as well as a face, arms, and feet, on every side. (In this the Brahmā of later mythology, who is four-faced and four-armed, resembles him.) He is also provided with wings. He is a seer, a priest, our father. He is a lord of speech (*vācas pati*), swift as thought, beneficent, the source of all prosperity. He knows all places and beings, and he alone gives their names to the gods. He is wise and energetic, the highest apparition (*paramā saṃdṛk*). He is an establisher (*dhātṛ*) and a disposer (*vidhātṛ*), having produced the earth and disclosed the sky. It seems likely that the word was at first attached as an epithet chiefly to the sun-god, but in the later Rigvedic period became one of the almost synonymous names given to the one god (10, 81^{3}) the conception of whom was then being tentatively evolved, and who as Viśvakarman was, owing to the name, mainly thought of in his architechtonic aspect[1]. Viśvakarman in the Brāhmaṇas is expressly identified with the creator Prajāpati (ŚB. 8, 2, 1^{10}. 3^{13}, cp. AB. 4, 22). In post-Vedic times he was conceived as the artificer of the gods.

Prajāpati occurs in one passage of the RV. (4, 53^{2}) as an epithet of Savitṛ, who is spoken of as a supporter of heaven and *prajāpati* of the world[2], and in another, as an epithet of Soma compared with Tvaṣṭṛ and Indra (9, 5^{9}). Otherwise the word is found four times as the name of a distinct deity, always in the tenth book. The god Prajāpati is invoked (10, 85^{43}) to bestow abundant offspring (*prajām*), is besought, along with Viṣṇu, Tvaṣṭṛ, and Dhātṛ, to grant offspring (10, 184^{1}), and is spoken of as making cows prolific (10, 169^{4}). As a protector of generation and living beings Prajāpati is also often invoked in the AV.[3] In the one hymn devoted to his praise in the RV. (10, 121), he is invoked by this name only in the last verse. In this hymn he is celebrated as the creator of heaven and earth, of the waters and of all that lives; who was born (*jāta*) as the one lord (*pati*) of all that is, the one king of all that breathes and moves, the one god above the gods; whose ordinances all beings and the gods follow; who established heaven and earth; who traverses space in the atmosphere; who embraces with his arms the whole world and all creatures. Here Prajāpati is clearly the name of the supreme god. Though only mentioned once in the RV. in this sense, he is commonly in the AV. and VS., and regularly in the Brāhmaṇas, recognized as the chief god. He is the father of the gods (ŚB. 11, 1, 6^{14}; TB. 8, 1, 3^{4} &c.), having existed alone in the beginning (ŚB. 2

2, 4^{1}). He created the Asuras as well (TB. 2, 2, 2^{3})[4]. He is also described as the first sacrificer (ŚB. 2, 4, 4^{1}; 6, 2, 3^{1}). In the Sūtras Prajāpati is identified with Brahmā (AGS. 3, 4, &c.). In the place of this chief god of the later Vedic theology, the philosophy of the Upaniṣads put the impersonal Brahma, the universal soul or the Absolute.

A myth is told in the MS. (4, 2^{12}) of Prajāpati being enamoured of his daughter Uṣas. She transformed herself into a gazelle; whereupon he transformed himself into the corresponding male. Rudra incensed at this aimed his arrow at him, when Prajāpati promised to make him lord of beasts if he did not shoot (cp. RV. 10, 61^{7}). The story is several times referred to in the Brāhmaṇas (AB. 3, 33; ŚB. 1, 7, 4^{1}; PB. 8, 2^{10})[5]. The basis of this myth seem to be two passages of the RV. (1, 71^{5}; 10, 61$^{5-7}$) in which the incest of a father (who seems to be Dyaus) with his daughter (here apparently the Earth) is referred to and an archer is mentioned[6].

In the refrain of the first nine verses of RV. 10, 121 the supreme god is referred to as unknown by the interrogative pronoun *Ka*, Who? The answer given in the tenth verse, is that Prajāpati alone embraces all beings. This later led to the employment of *Ka* not only as an epithet of Prajāpati (AB. 3, 22^{7}), but as a name, used by itself, of the supreme god (MS. 3, 12^{5}). In the TS. (1, 7, 6^{6}) Ka is expressly identified with Prajāpati[7].

In the first verse of RV. 10, 121 the supreme god is referred to as Hiraṇyagarbha, the 'Germ of Gold', the one lord of what exists. This is the only occurrence of the name in the RV., but it is mentioned several times in the AV. and the literature of the Brāhmaṇa period (cp. p. 13). Hiraṇyagarbha is also alluded to in a passage of the AV. (4, 2^{8}) where it is stated that the waters produced an embryo, which as it was being born, was enveloped in a golden covering. In the TS. (5, 5, 1^{2}) Hiraṇyagarbha is expressly identified with Prajāpati. In the later literature he is chiefly a designation of the personal Brahmā[8].

1 OST. 4, 5—11; 5, 354—5; WC. 80—5; SPH. 33—40. — 2 Cp. BLOOMFIELD, AJP. 14, 493. — 3 See PW. s. v. *prajāpati*. — 4 Cp. OST. 5, 80—1. — 5 ASL. 529; OST. 4, 45; SBE. 12, 284, n. 1; DELBRÜCK, FaB. 24; WVB. 1894, p. 34; GELDNER, FaW. 21. — 6 Cp. BRV. 2, 109 f.; OLDENBERG, SBE. 46, 78 f. — 7 SPH. 27, n. 2; ASL. 433; IS. 2, 94; SBE. 12, 8. — 8 ASL. 569 f.; OGR. 295; OST. 4, 15—18; 5, 352. 355; WC. 50—1; HVM. 1, 380, n. 1; HRI. 141—2; GELDNER, l. c.

§ 40. Manyu, Śraddhā &c. — We have yet to deal with the deifications of abstract nouns. Manyu, Wrath, a personification suggested chiefly by the fierce anger of Indra, is invoked in two hymns of the RV. (10, 83. 84). He is of irresistible might and self-existent. He glows like fire, is a god, who is Indra, Varuṇa, Jātavedas. He slays Vṛtra, is accompanied by the Maruts, grants victory like Indra, and bestows wealth. United with Tapas, Ardour, he protects his adorers and slays their foes. One short hymn of the RV. (10, 151) is devoted to the praise of Śraddhā, Faith[1]. She is said to be invoked morning, noon, and night. Through Faith fire is kindled and ghee offered. Through Faith wealth is obtained. In the Brāhmaṇas Śraddhā is the daughter of the Sun (ŚB. 12, 7, 3^{11}) or of Prajāpati (TB. 2, 3, 10^{1}). Her relationships are still further worked out in the Epics and Purāṇas. Anumati, Favour (of the gods), occurs twice as a personification in the RV. She is besought to be gracious and let her worshippers long see the sun (10, 59^{6}) and her protection is referred to (10, 167^{3}). In the AV. and VS. she becomes a goddess of love and presides over propagation. The later ritual connected her with the moon, regarding her as representing the day before full-moon[2]. Aramati, Devotion, Piety, is occasionally personified in the RV. The name has a counterpart in the Avestic Ārmaiti, a genius of earth as well as wisdom[3], but the personification can hardly go back to the Indo-Iranian period. **Sūnṛtā**, Bounty[4], appears to be personified as a goddess two or three times in the RV. (1, 40^{3}; 10, 141^{2}). **Asunīti**, Spirit-life, is personified in one passage of the RV. (10, $59^{5.6}$), being besought to prolong life and grant strength and nourishment[5]. **Nirṛti**, Decease, Dissolution, appears about twelve times in the RV. as a personification presiding over death.

Other personifications appear for the first time in the later Vedas. **Kāma**, Desire, is deified in the AV. (9, 2; 19, 52). Here he is not, as in post-Vedic literature, a god of love, but a deity who fulfils all desires. His arrows, with which he pierces hearts, are already referred to (AV. 3, 25^{1}). He is described as the first who was born (AV. 9, 2^{19}). The origin of the conception is most probably to be traced to the *kāma* 'desire', which in a cosmogonic hymn (p. 13) of the RV. (10, 129^{4}), is called 'the first seed of mind'[6]. **Kāla**, Time, is personified as a cosmogonic force in the AV. (19, 53. 54)[7], and **Skambha**, Support, an abstraction postulated by the speculation of the AV. to uphold the universe created by Prajāpati, comes to be praised as the All-god (AV. 10, 8^{2})[8]. **Prāṇa**, Breath, is also deified and identified with Prajāpati (AV. 11, 4^{12} &c.)[9]. Other personified abstractions of a like nature are to be found in the AV.[10] **Śrī** as a personification of Beauty or Fortune first appears in the ŚB. (11, 4, 3^{1})[11].

1 Cp. OLDENBERG, ZDMG. 50, 450 f. — 2 ZDMG. 7, 608; IS. 5, 229. — 3 ZDMG. 7, 519; 8, 770; 9, 690—2; SP.AP. 151. 200—3; HVBP. 91; HRI. 136. — 4 OLDENBERG, ZDMG. 50, 440. — 5 But cp. MM., JRAS. 2, 460, n. 2. — 6 WEBER, IS. 5, 224; 17, 290; ZDMG. 14, 269; OST. 5, 402; SPH. 76—7. — 7 SPH. 78—82; HVBP. 88. — 8 SPH. 50—9; HRI. 209. — 9 SPH. 35. — 10 SPH. 14. — 11 GGH. 4.

§ 41. **Aditi.** — There is one deity who, if rightly interpreted as the personification of a pure abstraction, like those treated in the preceding paragraph, occupies an anomalous position in the RV. For the name is not limited to the latest portion, but occurs throughout the collection. This would be accounted for by the peculiar manner in which the personification came about, supposing the explanation offered below to be correct. Otherwise this deity would have to be classed with abstractions of the epithet type (§ 39).

The goddess Aditi is not the subject of any separate hymn, but is often incidentally celebrated in the RV., her name occurring nearly eighty times. Very rarely mentioned alone (8, 19^{14}), she is constantly invoked with her sons, the Ādityas.

She has no definite physical features. She is often called a goddess (*devī*), who is sometimes styled *anarvā*, 'intact' (2, 40^{6}; 7, 40^{4}). She is widely expanded (5, 46^{6}), extensive, a mistress of wide stalls (8, 67^{12}). She is bright and luminous, a supporter of creatures (1, 136^{3}: otherwise said of Mitra-Varuṇa only), and belongs to all men (7, 10^{4}: also said of Heaven and Earth). She is invoked at morning, noon, and sunset (5, 69^{3})[1].

Aditi is the mother of Mitra and Varuṇa (8, 25^{3}; 10, 36^{3}. 132^{6}) as well as of Aryaman (8, 47^{9}). Hence she is called the mother of kings (2, 27^{7}, cp. v. [1]), of excellent sons (3, 4^{11}), of powerful sons (8, 56^{11}), of heroic sons (AV. 3, 8^{3}; 11, 1^{11}), or of eight sons (10, 72^{8}; AV. 8, 9^{21}). She is once said to be the mother of the Rudras, being the daughter of the Vasus and (strange to say) sister of the Ādityas (8, 90^{15}), and the AV. (6, 4^{1}) mentions her brothers as well as her sons. In another passage of the AV. (7, 6^{2} = VS. 21, 5) she is invoked as the great mother of the devout, the mistress of *ṛta*, strong in might, undecaying, widely extended, protecting, skilfully guiding. Such passages and the constant invocation of Aditi along with the Ādityas, her sons, show that her motherhood is an essential and characteristic trait. Her epithet *pastyā*, housewife (4, 55^{3}; 8, 27^{5}) may possibly also allude to her motherhood. In the Epic and Purāṇic mythology Aditi is the daughter of Dakṣa and mother of the gods in general, and expressly of Vivasvat, the Sun, and of Viṣṇu in his dwarf incarnation. She is said to be the wife of Viṣṇu in VS. (29, 60 = TS. 7, 5^{14}).

Aditi is several times spoken of as protecting from distress (*aṃhas*), and she is said to grant complete welfare or safety (10, 100; 1, 94^{15}), but she is more frequently invoked to release from guilt or sin. Thus Varuṇa (1, 24^{15}), Agni (4, 12^{4}), and Savitṛ (5, 82^{6}), are besought to free from guilt against Aditi. Aditi, Mitra, and Varuṇa are implored to forgive sin (2, 27^{14}), Aditi and Aryaman, to loosen (the bonds of) sin (7, 93^{7}). Worshippers beseech Aditi to make them sinless (1, 162^{22}); praying that by fulfilling her ordinances they may be without sin towards Varuṇa (7, 87^{7}) and that evildoers may be cut off from Aditi (10, 87^{18}). Hence though other gods, Agni (3, 54^{19}), Savitṛ (4, 54^{3}), Sun, Dawn, Heaven and Earth (10, $35^{2.3}$) are petitioned to pardon sin, the notion of releasing from it is much more closely connected with Aditi and her son Varuṇa, whose fetters that bind sinners are characteristic, and who unties sin like a rope and removes it (p. 26).

This notion is nearly allied to the etymology of the name. The word *aditi* is primarily a noun meaning 'unbinding', 'bondlessness', from *dí-ti* 'binding' (= Gk. δέ-σι-ς), derived from the root *dā*, 'to bind'. The past passive participle of this verb is employed to describe Śunaḥśepa 'bound' (*di-tá*) to the stake (5, 2^{7}). Hence as a goddess Aditi is naturally invoked to release her worshippers like a tied (*baddha*) thief (8, 67^{14}). The original unpersonified meaning of 'freedom' seems to survive in a few passages of the RV. Thus a worshipper exclaims, 'who gives us back to great *aditi*, that I may see father and mother'? (1, 24^{1}). The Ādityas are besought (7, 51^{1}) to 'place the offering in guiltlessness (*anāgāstve*) and freedom (*adititve*)'. The poet perhaps means the same thing when he prays to Heaven and Earth for 'the secure and unlimited gift of *aditi*' (1, 185^{3}). The word *aditi* also occurs several times in the adjectival sense of 'boundless'. It is thus used as an attribute twice of Dyaus (5, 59^{8}; 10, 63^{3}) and more frequently of Agni (1, 94^{15}; 4, 1^{20}; 7, 9^{3}; 8, 19^{14}).

The indefiniteness of the name would easily have lent itself to mystical identifications, and the conception was naturally affected by the theogonic and cosmogonic speculations found in the more recent portions of the RV. Thus the gods are said to have been born from Aditi, the Waters, and Earth (10, 63^{2}; cp. p. 14). In the verse immediately following, the 'boundless' Sky (*dyaur aditi*), their mother, is said to supply the gods with honied milk. Here therefore she appears to be identified with the sky[2]. Elsewhere (1, 72^{9}; AV. 13, 1^{38}) Aditi seems to be identified with the Earth, and this identification is frequent in the TS. and ŚB. In the Naighaṇṭuka the name is given as a synonym of earth, and, in the dual, of Heaven and Earth[3]. In many passages of the RV., however, she is distinguished from Heaven and Earth by being mentioned separately along with them (10, 63^{10} &c.)[4]. In another passage (1, 89^{10}) Aditi represents a personification of Universal Nature: 'Aditi is the sky; Aditi is the air; Aditi is the mother, and father, and son; Aditi is all the gods and the five tribes; Aditi is whatever has been born; Aditi is whatever shall be born' (p. 16; cp. Kaṭha Up. 4, 7).

Though according to the older mythology of the RV. Aditi is the mother of Dakṣa as an Āditya (2, 27^{1}), she is in a cosmogonic hymn (10, $72^{4.5}$) said to be his daughter as well as his mother by the reciprocal generation which is a notion not unfamiliar to the RV. (p. 12; cp. 10, 90[5]). In two other hymns of the tenth book (5[7]. 64[5]) these deities are connected in such a way that Aditi can scarcely be the mother of Dakṣa, but seems rather to be subordinate to him. Though Aditi is the mother of some of the leading deities, she plays an inferior part in a few other passages also. Thus she celebrates, along with her sons Varuṇa, Mitra, Aryaman, the praises of Savitṛ (7, 38[4]) and is said to have produced a hymn for Indra (8, 12[14], cp. 5, 31[5]).

Probably as the mother of the luminous Ādityas, Aditi is sometimes connected with light. She is asked for light (4, 25[3], cp. 10, 36[3]), her imperishable light is celebrated (7, 82[10]), and Dawn is called the face of Aditi (1, 113[19]). Occasionally Aditi is referred to in general terms which might apply to other deities. Thus she is implored to protect or bless her worshippers, their children, and their cattle (8, 18[6. 7]; 1, 43[2]). She is prayed to for wealth (7, 40[2]), her pure, intact, celestial, imperishable gifts are supplicated (1, 185[3]), and the large blessings bestowed by the Maruts are compared with the beneficent deeds of Aditi (1, 166[12]).

In some passages of the RV. (1, 153[3]; 8, 90[15]; 10, 11[1] &c.) as well as in later Vedic texts (VS. 13, 43. 49), Aditi is spoken of as a cow, and, in the ritual, a ceremonial cow is commonly addressed as Aditi[5]. Terrestrial Soma is compared to the milk of Aditi (9, 96[15]); and milk only can be meant[6] by the daughter of Aditi who yields to Soma as he flows to the vat (9, 69[3]). There may be a similar allusion when priests with their ten fingers are said to purify Soma on the lap of Aditi (9, 26[1]. 71[5]).

A review of the evidence indicates that Aditi has two and only two prominent characteristics. The first is her motherhood. She is the mother of a group of gods whose name represents a metronymic formation from hers. Her second main characteristic, in conformity with the etymological meaning of the name, is her power of releasing from the bonds of physical suffering and moral guilt. Mystical speculation on the name would lead to her being styled a cow, as representing boundless plenty, or to her being identified with the boundless earth, heaven, or universe. But how are we to account for so early a personification of such an abstract idea, and in particular for Aditi becoming the mother of the Ādityas? Bergaigne[7] thinks the transition to Aditi's motherhood is to be found in such an expression as *dyaur aditiḥ*, the 'boundless sky', the mother who supplies the gods with milk (10, 63[3]). According to this view, the rare and secondary adjectival meaning 'boundless' would have developed from being an epithet of the sky, otherwise characteristically regarded as a father, into an independent female deity. Nor does this explanation seem to account satisfactorily for the conception of Aditi releasing from bondage. Another explanation is possible. The expression *aditeḥ putrāḥ*, sons of Aditi, several times applied to the Ādityas in the RV., may in the pre-Vedic period have simply meant 'sons of freedom' (like *sahasaḥ putraḥ*, 'son of strength': p. 12) as describing a prominent quality of Varuṇa and cognate gods. Such an expression would easily lead to the personification of Aditi as a mother. Similarly Śavasī was evolved as a name of Indra's mother in the RV. itself from his epithet 'Son of Might' (*śavasaḥ*: p. 12) and Indra's epithet *śacīpati*, 'lord of might', later led to *śacī* being personified as the wife of that god, the compound being interpreted as 'husband of Śacī'. The formation of a metronymic Āditya, son of Aditi, would tend to the limitation of the group comprising her sons. The deified personification would naturally retain a connexion with the original meaning of existence free from all fetters, but would assume a few additional fluctuating attributes, such as brightness, from the Ādityas. As mother of some of the leading gods or of the gods in general, she might occasionally be identified with Heaven and Earth, the universal parents, and the meaning of the word would encourage cosmogonic speculations. Thus Aditi, an entirely Indian goddess, is historically younger than some at least of her sons.

The opinion that Aditi is a personification of the idea of 'freedom from bondage' is favoured by WALLIS[8] and OLDENBERG[9]. MAX MÜLLER[10] thinks that Aditi, an ancient god or goddess, is the earliest name invented to express the infinite as visible to the naked eye, the endless expanse beyond the earth, the clouds, and the sky. ROTH at first[11] interpreted Aditi to mean 'inviolability, imperishableness', denoting as a personification the goddess of eternity. Later he explained her as 'eternity', the principle which sustains the Ādityas, or imperishable celestial light[12]. He regards her not as a definite but only an incipient personification. In the St. Petersburg Dictionary, however, he explains Aditi as a personification of the boundlessness of heaven as opposed to the finite earth. PISCHEL, on the other hand believes Aditi represents the earth[13]. This is also HARDY's opinion[14]. COLINET considers Aditi the female counterpart of Dyaus[15]. The Naighaṇṭuka gives *aditi* as a synonym of *pṛthivī* (earth), *vāc* (speech), *go* (cow), and, in the dual, of *dyāvā-pṛthivī* (heaven and earth). Yāska defines Aditi as 'the mighty mother of the gods'. and following the Naighaṇṭuka (5, 5) locates her in the atmospheric region, while the Ādityas are assigned to the celestial, and Varuṇa to both[16].

1 OST. 5, 36, note 68. — 2 Op. cit. 5, 39, note 73. — 3 According to BRV. 3, 90, Aditi in 4, 55[1b] = 7, 62[4a] is synonymous with dyāvāpṛthivī. — 4 References in OST. 5, 40 f. — 5 ORV. 206 cp. 72. — 6 Otherwise BRV. 3, 94. — 7 BRV. 3, 90. — 8 WC. 45 f. — 9 ORV. 204—7 cp. SBE. 46, 329. — 10 Vedic Hymns, SBE. 32, 241; cp. LSL. 2, 619; HOPKINS, JAOS. 17, 91. — 11 Nirukta, Erl. 150—1. — 12 ZDMG. 6, 68 f.; so also KRV. 59, HILLEBRANDT, Aditi p. 20. — 13 PVS. 2, 86. — 14 HVBP. 94. — 15 Trans. of the 9th Or. Congress 1, 396—410. — 16 ROTH on Nir. 10, 4.

BENFEY, Hymnen des Sāmaveda 218 (= Unteilbarkeit); OST. 1, 26; 5, 35—53. 55; BRV. 3, 88—98; HILLEBRANDT, Ueber die Göttin Aditi, Breslau 1876; BRI. 19; DARMESTETER, Ormazd p. 82; COLINET, Etude sur le mot Aditi, Museon 12, 81—90; ROTH, IS. 14, 392—3; BLOOMFIELD, ZDMG. 48, 552, note 1; HRI. 72—3.

§ 42. Diti. — The name of Diti occurs only three times in the RV., twice along with that of Aditi. Mitra and Varuṇa are said to behold from their car Aditi and Diti (5, 62[8]). Sāyaṇa here explains the two as the indivisible earth and the separate creatures on it, ROTH[1], as 'the eternal and the perishable', and MUIR[2] as 'the entire aggregate of visible nature'. In a second passage (4, 2[11]), Agni is besought to grant *diti* and preserve from *aditi*. Here Sāyaṇa interprets the two words as 'liberal giver' and 'illiberal giver', ROTH as 'wealth' and 'penury'. BERGAIGNE[3] takes the words to designate the goddesses of the previous passage; but it is more likely that they are here quite different words, derived from *dā*, 'to give', and thus meaning 'giving' and 'non-giving'. This view seems to be favoured by both the context and the order in which the words occur. In the third passage (7, 15[12]) Diti is mentioned without Aditi, but along with Agni, Savitṛ, and Bhaga, being said to give (*dā*) what is desirable (*vāryam*). Diti is named along with Aditi as a goddess in the later Saṃhitās also (VS. 18, 22; AV. 15, 18[4]; 16, 6[7]). Her sons are mentioned in AV. 7, 7[1]. These are the Daityas, who in post-Vedic mythology are the enemies of the gods. The name of Diti as a goddess seems to be merely an antithesis to that of Aditi[4], formed from the latter to express a positive sense, as *sura*, 'god', was later (by false etymology) evolved from *asura*, 'demon'.

1 ZDMG. 6, 71. — 2 OST. 5, 42. — 3 BRV. 3, 97. — 4 MM., SBE. 32, 256; cp. WC. 46.

E. GODDESSES.

§ 43. **Goddesses.** — Goddesses occupy a very subordinate position in Vedic belief and worship. They play hardly any part as rulers of the world. The only one of any importance is Uṣas, who judged by the statistical standard ranks as a deity of the third class (p. 20). But, unlike nearly all the gods, she received no share in the Soma offering[1]. Next to her comes Sarasvatī (§ 33), who, however, only ranks with the lowest class of deities. A few other goddesses are praised in one hymn each. Pṛthivī, hardly separable from Dyaus, is praised in one short hymn of three stanzas (§ 34). **Rātrī**, Night, is also invoked in one hymn (10, 127). Like her sister Dawn, she is called the daughter of Heaven. She is not conceived as the dark, but as the bright starlit night. She shines manifoldly with her eyes. Decked with all splendour, she fills the valleys and heights, driving away the darkness with light. At her approach men return home like birds to their nests. She is invoked to keep away the wolf and the thief, guiding her worshippers to safety. Night probably became a goddess by way of antithesis to Dawn, with whom she is invoked in several verses as a dual divinity[2] (pp. 48. 129). **Vāc**, personified Speech, is celebrated in one hymn (10, 125 cp. 71), in which she describes herself. She accompanies all the gods and supports Mitra-Varuṇa, Indra-Agni, and the Aśvins. She bends Rudra's bow against the unbeliever. Her place is in the waters, the sea. She encompasses all beings. In another passage (8, $89^{10.\,11}$) she is called queen of the gods and divine[3]. In the Naighaṇṭuka (5, 5) Vāc is enumerated among the deities of the atmosphere; and thunder, or *mādhyamikā vāc*, 'the voice of the middle region', in the terminology of the commentators (Nir. 11, 27), may have been the starting point of the personification. A legend about Vāc frequently referred to in the Brāhmaṇas is that of Soma being bought back from the Gandharvas at the price of Vāc transformed into a woman (AB. 1, 27). **Puraṃdhi**, whose name occurs about nine times in the RV., is goddess of Plenty[4]. She is nearly always mentioned with Bhaga[5], two or three times also with Pūṣan and Savitṛ, and once with Viṣṇu and Agni. Pārendi, commonly regarded as identical with Puraṃdhi, is generally considered a goddess of riches and abundance (cp. Yaṣt 8, 38) in the Avesta[6]. HILLEBRANDT, however, thinks Puraṃdhi is a goddess of Activity[7]. Another goddess of abundance is **Dhiṣaṇā**, mentioned nearly a dozen times in the RV[8]. **Iḷa**, Nourishment, is the personification (mentioned less than a dozen times in the RV.) of the offering of milk and butter, thus representing plenty derived from the cow. Hence Iḍā is in the Brāhmaṇas frequently connected with, though never an actual name of, the cow; and in the Naighaṇṭuka (2, 11) it occurs as one of the synonyms of cow. Owing to the nature of the offering Iḷa is called butter-handed (7, 16^8) and butter-footed (10, 70^8). As a personification she generally appears in the Āprī hymns, in which she usually forms a triad with Sarasvatī and Mahī or Bhāratī[9]. It is doubtful whether the literal or the personified sense is intended by the phrase *iḷāyās pade*, 'in the place of nourishment' (i. e. of the sacrificial fire). Agni is once called the son of Iḷā, clearly in allusion to the place of his production (3, $29^{9.\,10}$). Purūravas is also said to be her son (10, 95^{18}). She is once called the mother of the herd (*yūtha*) and connected with Urvaśī (5, 41^{19}). She is once mentioned with Dadhikrāvan and the Aśvins in reference to the morning sacrifice (7, 44^2). In the ŚB. she is called the daughter of Manu (1, 8, 1^8; 11, 5, 3^5) as well as of Mitra-Varuṇa (1, 8, 1^{27}; 14, 9, 4^{27}; AŚS. 1, 7^7). The name of the goddess **Bṛhaddivā** occurs four times in hymns to the

Viśvedevas. She is called a mother ($10, 64^{10}$) and is mentioned with Iḷā ($2, 31^{4}$; $5, 41^{19}$), Sarasvatī and Rākā ($5, 42^{11}$). Rākā (probably from √*rā*, to give) is mentioned only twice in the RV. as a rich and bountiful goddess, who is invoked with others ($2, 32^{7}$; $5, 42^{12}$). Sinīvālī is referred to in two hymns of the RV. (2, 32; 10, 184). She is a sister of the gods, broad-hipped, fair-armed, fair-fingered, prolific, a mistress of the family, and is implored to grant offspring. She is invoked with Sarasvatī, Rākā, as well as Guṅgū (who is only mentioned here). In the AV. ($8, 46^{3}$) Sinīvālī is called the wife of Viṣṇu. The later Saṃhitās and the Brāhmaṇas also mention a goddess Kuhū, a personification of the new moon[10]. Rākā and Sinīvālī are in later Vedic texts connected with phases of the moon, the former being the presiding deity of the actual day of full moon, and the latter, of the first day of new moon. There is nothing to show that any such connexion is to be found in the RV[11].

A few other goddesses occasionally mentioned in the RV. have already been incidentally referred to. Pṛṣni, the mother of the Maruts (p. 78) presumably represents the mottled storm-cloud[12]. The word is also used as an adjective in the sense of speckled (cp. $7, 103^{6. 10}$), in the singular as an attribute of both bull and cow, and in the plural, of the cows which milk Soma for Indra ($1, 84^{10. 11}$; $8, 6^{19}. 7^{10}. 58^{3}$). It thus came to mean 'speckled cow', and finally 'speckled cloud'. Saraṇyū occurs once in the RV. ($10, 17^{2}$) as the name of Tvaṣṭṛ's daughter, wedded to Vivasvat. The most likely interpretation seems to be that which identifies her with the sun-maiden Sūryā or Uṣas, the Dawn[13]. The word also occurs four times as an adjective in the RV. meaning 'swift'. It is an ordinary Sanskrit formation, derived with the suffix *-yu* from *saraṇa*, speed (√*sṛ*, to run), like *caraṇ-yu* and others.

Goddesses as wives of the great gods similarly play an insignificant part in the Veda. They are altogether without independent character, simply representing the spouses whom such gods as Indra must have had. Hardly anything about them is mentioned but their names, which are simply formed from those of the gods with the feminine suffix *-ānī*. Thus *Indrāṇī* is simply 'wife of Indra'[14]. Varuṇānī and Agnāyī also occur in the RV., but rarely. Rudrāṇī is not found till the Sūtras, but she plays a decidedly more important part in the cult than any of the other goddesses in *-ānī*[15]. The wife of the Aśvins is once in the RV. called Aśvinī (= Sūryā: p. 51)[16]. The 'wives of the gods' (*devānāṃ patnīḥ*) occasionally mentioned in the RV. have in the Brāhmaṇas an established place assigned to them in the cult apart from the gods (SB. $1, 9, 2^{11}$)[17].

[1] BERGAIGNE, Recherches sur l'histoire de la liturgie védique, p. 9. — [2] OST. 5, 191; HRI. 79 f. — [3] WEBER, IS. 9, 473 ff.; BRI. 16; OLDENBERG, ZDMG. 39, 58—9; WC. 85—6; HRI. 142—3. 226. — [4] PVS. 2, 202—16; BLOOMFIELD, JAOS. 16, 19; ORV. 63. — [5] Cp. OLDENBERG, SBE. 46, 190. — [6] DARMESTETER, Ormazd et Ahriman 25; SBE. 4, LXX; 23, 11; MILLS, SBE. 31, 25; PVS. 1, 202; SP.AP. 207—9; COLINET, BOR. 2, 245; 4, 121; Trans. Or. Cong. 1892, 1, 396—420. — [7] HILLEBRANDT, WZKM. 3, 188—94. 259—73; cp. also V. HENRY, Vedica, 1re série, p. 1 ff., Mémoires de la Société de ling. 9. — [8] PVS. 2, 82 ff.; OLDENBERG, SBE. 46, 120—2. — [9] WEBER, IS. 1, 168—9; BRV. 1, 325; GGH. 51; ORV. 238. 326; SBE. 46, 11. 156. 191. 288; BAUNACK, KZ. 34, 563. — [10] ZDMG. 9, LVIII. — [11] IS. 5, 228 ff. — [12] Cp. ROTH on Nir. 10, 39, p. 145. — [13] BLOOMFIELD, JAOS. 15, 172—88, where the opinions of his predecessors are stated. — [14] ORV. 172; cp. LEUMANN, KZ. 32, 299. — [15] ORV. 219. — [16] KRV. n. 148; on Sūryā and the Aśvins cp. WEBER, IS. 5, 178—89; BRV. 2, 486; PVS. 1, 13—29; OLDENBERG, GGA. 1889, 7—8; ORV. 241. — [17] On female divinities cp. HOPKINS, PAOS. 1889, p. CLXII; on Saramā (above pp. 63—4) see below, § 62.

F. DUAL DIVINITIES.

§. 44. A peculiar feature of Vedic mythology is the celebration in pairs of a number of deities whose names are joined in the form of a special kind of dual compound in which both members are dual, accented, and occasionally separable[1]. About a dozen gods are thus conjointly praised in at least sixty hymns of the RV. The name of Indra enters into seven or more than half of these combinations, but by far the largest number of hymns — twenty-three, and parts of several others — is addressed, to the pair *Mitrā́váruṇā*. Eleven are dedicated to *Indrāgnī́*, nine to *Índrā-váruṇā*, about seven to *Índra-vāyū́*, six to *Dyā́vā-pṛthivī́*, two each to *Índrā-sómā* and *Índrā-bṛ́haspátī*, and one each to *Índrāvíṣṇū*, *Índrā-pūṣáṇā*, *Somā-pūṣáṇā*, *Somā-rudrā*, and *Agnī́-ṣómā*. A few other couples, including the names of nine or ten deities not mentioned above, are invoked in detached verses. These are *Indra-nāsatyā*, *Índrā-parvatā*, *Índrā-marutaḥ*, *Agnī-parjanyā*, *Parjányā-vā́tā* (once *Vā́tā-parjanyā́*), *Uṣā́sānáktā* or (less often) *Náktoṣā́sā*, *Sū́ryā-mā́sā or Sūryā-candramā́sā.*

There can be little doubt that the analogy for this favourite formation was furnished by Dyāvāpṛthivī, Heaven and Earth[2], the pair which to early thought appeared so indissolubly connected in nature, that the myth of their conjugal union is found widely diffused among primitive peoples[3] and has therefore probably come down to the Veda from a period anterior to that immediately preceding the separation of the Indo-European nations. In the RV. itself this couple is so closely associated that while they are invoked as a pair in six hymns, not one is devoted to the praise of Dyaus alone and only one of three verses to that of Pṛthivī. So hard was it for the poets to dissociate the two, that even in this hymn Pṛthivī is praised for sending the rain of heaven from her cloud (5, 84^{3}). The dual compound, moreover, occurs much more frequently than the name of Dyaus as a god. It occurs, including the comparatively rare synonyms *Dyā́vākṣā́mā* and *Dyā́vābhū́mī*, about a hundred times, or more frequently than the name of any other pair. Heaven and Earth are also called *rodasī*, the two worlds (spoken of as sisters, 1, 185^{5}, owing to the gender of the word), an expression occurring at least a hundred times in the RV. Heaven and Earth are parents, being often styled *pitarā*, *mātarā*, *janitrī*, and also separately addressed as father and mother (1, 159$^{1-3}$. 160^{2}). They are primeval parents (7, 53^{2}; 10, 65^{8}). Their marriage is referred to in the AB. (4, 27$^{5-6}$)[4]. They have made and sustain all creatures (1, 159^{2}. 160^{2}. 185^{1}). Though themselves footless, they support much offspring with feet (1, 185^{2}). They are the parents of the gods also; for to them exclusively belongs the epithet *devóputre*, 'having the gods as sons'. They are in particular said to be the parents of Bṛhaspati (7, 97^{8}) and, with the Waters and Tvaṣṭṛ, to have begotten Agni (10, 2^{7}). At the same time they are in different passages spoken of as themselves created by individual gods. Thus a poet observes that he who produced heaven and earth must have been the most skilful artisan of all the gods (1, 160^{4}; 4, 56^{3}). Indra is said to have generated or fashioned them (6, 30^{5}; 8, 36^{4}; 10, 29^{6}. 54^{3}). Viśvakarman produced them (10, 81^{2} cp. AV. 12, 1^{60})[5]. They received their forms from Tvaṣṭṛ (10, 110^{9}). They sprang from the head and feet of Puruṣa (10, 90^{14}). But one poet is puzzled as to how they were produced and which of the two first came into being (1, 185^{1}; cp. p. 13)[6]. Many of the epithets applied to Dyāvāpṛthivī are suggested by their physical characteristics. The one is a prolific bull, the other a variegated cow (1, 160^{3}). They are both rich in seed (1, 159^{2}; 6, 70$^{1.2}$). They yield milk, ghee, and honey abundantly

(6, 70^{1-5}), and produce *amṛta* (1, 159^{2}. 185^{6}). They never grow old (6, 70^{1}). They are great (1, 159^{1}) and wide-extended (1, 160^{2}). They are broad and great abodes (1, 185^{6}). They are fair-faced, wide, manifold, with ends which are far away (1, $185^{6.7}$). Sometimes, however, moral qualities are attributed to them. They are wise and promote righteousness (1, 159^{1}). As father and mother they guard beings (1, 160^{2}) and protect from disgrace and misfortune (1, 185^{10}). They grant food and wealth (6, 70^{6}; 1, 159^{5}) or bestow great fame and dominion (1, 160^{5}). They are sufficiently personified to be called leaders of the sacrifice and to be conceived as seating themselves around the sacrifice (4, $56^{2.7}$), as coming to their worshippers along with the heavenly folk (7, 53^{2}), or taking the sacrifice to the gods (2, 41^{20}). But Heaven and Earth never attained to a living personification or importance in worship. These two deities are quite coördinate. But in most of the other couples one of the two greatly predominates, his characteristic qualities being shared by his companion. Thus Indra-Agni are conjointly called 'wielders of the bolt' and 'Vṛtra-slayers'. Occasionally an attribute of the lesser deity is predicated of both. Thus Indra-Viṣṇu are together said to have taken wide strides (6, 69^{5}). Frequent association of this kind may lead to a deity receiving by himself an epithet to which he originally had no right. Thus Agni when mentioned alone is often called a 'Vṛtra-slayer'. The characteristics of each member of the pair are, however, in some passages distinguished[7].

Next to Heaven and Earth, the pair most frequently named is **Mitra-Varuṇa**. These two deities are invoked conjointly in many more hymns than are dedicated to their separate praise. As Mitra has hardly any individual traits, the same attributes and functions belong to the pair conjointly as to Varuṇa alone. Scarcely anything need therefore be here added to what has already been said about Varuṇa. The couple are conceived as young men (3, 54^{10}; 7, 62^{5}). Like various other gods, they are spoken of as shining (*candra*), bright (*śuci*), sunlike (*svardṛś*), ruddy (*rudra*), and terrible (*ghora*). The priority of the name of Mitra in the compound might seem to indicate that he was originally the more important deity; it is, however, probably due simply to the tendency to make the shorter word the first member of a compound. This dual invocation goes back to the Indo-Iranian period, for Ahura and Mithra are thus coupled in the Avesta[8].

Indra-Varuṇa, the two universal monarchs (1, 17^{1}), hollowed out the channels of the waters and set the sun in motion in the sky (7, 82^{3}). They are vanquishers of Vṛtra (6, 68^{2}), aid in battle (4, 41^{11}), and grant victory (1, 17^{7}). They cast their mighty bolt against the wicked (4, 41^{4}). They bestow protection and prosperity (1, $17^{7.8}$), fame, wealth, and abundance of steeds (4, $41^{2.10}$; 6, 68^{8}). They are drinkers of the pressed Soma, their car comes to the sacrifice, and they are invoked to exhilerate themselves seated on the sacrificial grass (6, $68^{10.11}$). In some passages the characteristics of each member of the pair are distinguished. Thus Varuṇa is besought to divert his wrath from his worshippers, and Indra to procure them wide space (7, 84^{2}). Indra is contrasted as the warlike god who slays Vṛtra, with Varuṇa who supports men in peace and wisdom (6, 68^{3}; 7, $82^{5.6}$. 85^{3}). The association of the couple **Indra-Agni**[9] is very intimate; for Indra is invoked conjointly with Agni in more hymns than with any other deity[10], while Agni is otherwise addressed as a dual divinity only in one hymn and two detached verses with Soma and in one verse with Parjanya. Indra-Agni, the best of Soma-drinkers (1, 21^{1}), come on their car to drink Soma (1, 108^{1}), and are invited together to come and drink it (7, 93^{6}; 8, $38^{4.7-9}$), to sit down on the sacrificial grass at the offering, and to exhilerate themselves with the pressed draught (1, 109[5]). They are often called Vṛtra-slayers. They are armed with the bolt (6, 59[3] &c.), and their lightning is sharp (5, 86[3]). They are fort-destroyers who aid in battle (1, 109[7,8]). They together demolished the 99 forts of the Dāsa (3, 12[6]) and are invincible in battle (5, 86[2]). They released the rivers from their imprisonment (8, 48[8]) and accomplished heroic deeds together (1, 108[5]). They are bountiful (5, 86[3]). All these are traits characteristic of Indra. Indra-Agni are also called the two priests of sacrifice (8, 38[1]), and are wise (8, 40[3]). They are lords of the abode (*sadaspatī*) and drive away the goblins (1, 21[5]). These features are more appropriate to Agni. The two gods are twin brothers who have one father (6, 59[2]). They are once called Aśvins[11] (1, 109[4]), possibly in allusion to this close relationship. They bestow food, wealth, strength, cattle, steeds (4, 60[13—14]). They are greater than heaven and earth, rivers, and mountains (1, 109[6]). The two gods are once contrasted, though not when addressed as a pair; Indra being said to slay, but Agni to burn, the Dasyus (6, 28[4]). The two hymns (4, 49; 7, 97) addressed to Indra-Bṛhaspati consist chiefly of invitations to drink Soma and of prayers to bestow great wealth abounding in steeds and to promote devotion. Indra-Vāyu are constantly invited to come and drink Soma (1, 23[1—2] &c.), little else being said about them. They come to the offering with their teams (4, 47[2—4]) or in their golden-seated car (4, 46[4]) and seat themselves on the sacrificial litter (7, 91[4]). They are thousand-eyed, lords of devotion (*dhiyas patī:* 1, 23[3]), and lords of might (*śavasas patī*: 4, 47[3]). They help in battle (7, 92[4]) and bestow wealth in steeds, cattle, and gold (7, 90[6]). Indra-Soma perform the warlike exploits characteristic of Indra or the great cosmic actions so often ascribed to him. They made the waters flow for man, released the seven rivers, slew the dragon, depressed the wheel of the sun (4, 28[1.2]; 6, 72[3]). The true work of the two bountiful gods was that they destroyed their foes and broke open what was enclosed in the rock (4, 28[4.5]). They performed the first great deeds in finding the sun and light, dispelling the darkness, causing the sun to shine, supporting heaven, and spreading out the earth (6, 72[1.2]). They too placed ripe milk in the raw bodies of cows (ib.[4]). They grant victorious might to men (ib.[5]). Indra-Viṣṇu, who are receptacles of Soma, lords of intoxication (*madapatī*), are invited to come with their steeds, to drink Soma, and to fill their belly with it. The two gods strode out widely in the intoxication of Soma, made the air broader, and spread out the spaces for existence. Ever victorious, they grant wealth, and conduct safely across dangers. As generators of all prayers, they are besought to hear the invocations of their worshippers (6, 69)[12]. Indra-Pūṣan are invoked conjointly in only one short hymn (6, 57), and their names form a dual compound only twice. When Indra made the great waters flow, Pūṣan was his companion. With him as a friend, Indra slays Vṛtras (6, 56[2]). One of them drinks Soma and is drawn by two steeds with which he slays Vṛtras, while the other desires gruel (*karambha*) and is drawn by goats. Mention is once (1, 162[2]) made of the abode (*pāthas*) of Indra-Pūṣan, to which a goat conducts the sacrificial horse. The two gods are as usual also besought to confer welfare and booty.

Soma-Pūṣan (2, 40) drive away darkness and are invoked to quicken the seven-wheeled five-reined car, yoked by thought, which measures out space. They are generators of wealth, of heaven and earth, and protectors of the world (cp. 10, 17[3]), whom the gods made the centre of immortality. For them Indra is invoked to produce ripe milk in the raw cows. Together they bestow victory over foes and grant abundance of wealth and food.

But they are also contrasted. One of them has made his abode high in heaven, while the other dwells on earth and in air; one generated all beings, while the other moves seeing everything[13]. Soma-Rudra (6, 74) are invoked to drive away sickness and decay from the house, to place all remedies in the bodies of their worshippers, to remove from them all sin, and to free from the fetter of Varuṇa. Wielding sharp weapons, they are besought to have mercy and are implored for prosperity to man and beast. Agni-Soma are celebrated together for having released the confined streams, obtained the light, and set the luminaries in the sky. At the same time they are distinguished, Mātariśvan being said to have brought the one from heaven, and the eagle the other from the rock (1, 93). Their joint help and protection are invoked, and they are besought to grant cattle, horses, offspring, health, happiness, and wealth (10, 19[1]. 66[7]). This pair is mentioned several times in the AV. In the MS. (3, 7[1]) they are spoken of as 'two eyes'. The ŚB. refers to them as brothers (11, 1, 6[19]), also stating that the sun belongs to Agni and the moon to Soma (1, 6, 3[24]). In the ritual Agni-Soma seem never to receive a share in the Soma offering, but only cakes and animal sacrifices. It is somewhat remarkable that the two great ritual deities, who form a very frequent couple in the sacrificial literature, should, outside the one hymn (1, 93) devoted to their praise, be mentioned only twice as a pair, and that only in the most recent part of the RV.[14]

A few other pairs are invoked in detached verses only. Agni-Parjanya are mentioned in one passage (6, 52[16]). They are together besought to bestow food and progeny, but are at the same time contrasted, the one being said to have produced the oblation (*iḷām*) and the other offspring (*garbham*). Parjanya-Vāta are invoked in four passages. As bulls of earth they are besought (6, 49[6]) to impel the watery vapours (*purīṣāṇi*). Along with Indra-Vāyu and other gods, they are invoked as vaporous (*purīṣiṇā*) bulls (10, 65[9]). In another enumeration they are entreated to bestow abundant food (6, 50[12]). They are also once (10, 66[10] cp. Nir. 7, 10) invoked as connected with 'the thundering buffalo' (probably Dyaus[15]). Dawn and Night are invoked several times. They are mentioned almost exclusively in Viṣvedeva or Āprī hymns. They are rich goddesses (2, 31[5]; 10, 70[6]), divine maidens (7, 2[6]; 10, 110[6]), daughters of heaven (5, 41[7]; 10, 70[6]). They are like two wives (1, 122[2]) and abound in milk (2, 3[6]). Changing their colour they suckle a single child who beams between heaven and earth (1, 96[5]). They are two sisters who are of one mind but of different colour, whose path is the same and endless, who, taught by the gods, move alternately and never clash or stand still (1, 113[3]). They are the shining mothers of order (1, 142[7]); they conduct with bright rays every offering (5, 41[7]) and weave the web of sacrifice (2, 3[6]). They are bountiful, much invoked, and sit on the sacrificial grass (7, 2[6]). They are great and well-adorned (10, 36[1]. 110[6]; 1, 13[7]. 142[7]). Appearing alternately they arouse all living things (2, 31[5])[16]. Sun and Moon are mentioned five times in the form of *sūryāmāsā* and three times in that of *sūryācandramásā*. These are the only dual compounds formed with the name of Sūrya[17]. In most cases the concrete luminaries only are meant. Thus they are said to move alternately so that we may see (1, 102[2]). It is the act of Bṛhaspati that sun and moon rise alternately (10, 68[10]). The Creator fashioned sun and moon (10, 190[3]). A poet says, 'let us go on our path like sun and moon' (5, 51[15]). There is, however, an incipient personification when the pair is invoked with other deities (10, 64[3]. 92[12]. 93[5]). In a few passages sun and moon, though not expressly mentioned, are evidently thought of in their dual character. 'The two go round the sacrifice like playing children; the one surveys all beings, the other is born again, ordering the seasons' (10, 85[18]). There is no doubt that they are meant by the two bright eyes of Varuṇa (8, 41[9]) and by the two eyes of heaven made by the immortals (1, 72[10]).

[1] KHF. 161 f.; OGR. 297 f.; HVM. 1, 98. — [2] SP.AP. 159; cp. ORV. 93. 240. — [3] TYLOR, Primitive Culture 322—8 (Chapter on Mythology). — [4] HAUG Translation of the AB., vol. 2, 308. — [5] Cp. ibid. 2, 299. — [6] Cp. Nirukta 3, 22; MM., LSL. 2, 606. — [7] RV. 2, 40[4. 5]; 6, 52[10]. 57[2]. 68[3]; 7, 36[2]. 82[5. 6]. 83[9]. 84[2]. 85[3]. — [8] OST. 5, 70; EGGERS, Mitra 29—31; OLDENBERG, ZDMG. 50, 46. — [9] OST. 5, 220; MACDONELL, JRAS. 25, 470. — [10] Cp. FAY, AJP. 17, 14. — [11] LSL. 2, 614. — [12] MACDONELL, JRAS. 27, 175. — [13] OST. 5, 180; HVM. 1, 456. — [14] OLDENBERG, Die Hymnen des Rigveda I, 267; HILLEBRANDT, GGA. 1890, p. 401; HVM. 1, 458—61. — [15] Cp. LRV. 4, 228. — [16] KRV. 52; OLDENBERG, ZDMG. 39, 89; HRI. 79. — [17] OLDENBERG, ZDMG. 50, 63.

G. GROUPS OF GODS.

§ 45. The mythology of the Veda recognised a certain number of more or less definite groups of divine beings, generally associated with some particular god. The largest and most important of these, the **Maruts**, whose number in the RV. is variously stated to be 21 or 180 (p. 78), is, as has been shown, constantly described as attending Indra in his warlike exploits (p. 57). The same group under the name of **Rudras** is occasionally associated with their father Rudra (7, 10[4]. 35[6]). The number of the Rudras, treated as a separate class in the Brāhmaṇas, is stated to be eleven in the AB. and ŚB. (p. 19) but is thirty-three in the TS. (1, 4, 11[1]). The smaller group of the **Ādityas**, whose number in two passages of the RV. is seven or eight (p. 43) and in the Brāhmaṇas becomes twelve, is in the RV. constantly associated either with their mother Aditi (7, 10[4] &c.) or with their chief Varuṇa (7, 35[6] &c.). This group is more definite than that of the Maruts inasmuch as its members have separate names. A third group frequently mentioned in the RV. is more vague than the other two, for they are neither characterized nor is their number mentioned. That they were conceived as specially connected with Indra, is shown by two passages in which Varuṇa or Aditi with the Ādityas, Rudra with the Rudras and Indra with the Vasus, are invoked (7, 10[4]. 35[6]). But in later Vedic texts Agni is the leader of the Vasus[1]. They are regarded as eight in number in the AB. and ŚB. (p. 19), but in the TS. (5, 5, 2[5]) become 333. The three groups of the Ādityas, Rudras and Vasus are invoked together in a few passages of the RV. (2, 31[1]; 10, 66[12] cp. 7, 10[4]. 35[6])[2]. The Brāhmaṇas distinguish, as three kinds of gods, the Vasus of earth, the Rudras of air, and the Ādityas of heaven (ŚB. 1, 3, 4[12]; 4, 3, 5[1]). In the Chāndogya Upaniṣad (3, 6—10) five groups are mentioned, the Vasus being connected with Agni, the Rudras with Indra, the Ādityas with Varuṇa, the Maruts with Soma, and the Sādhyas with Brahmā (cp. RV. 10, 97[16])[3]. There is besides the group of the semi-divine **Aṅgirases** who are chiefly connected with Bṛhaspati (§§ 36, 54) and the small one of the three **Ṛbhus** who are nearly always associated with Indra (§ 46). Finally, a comprehensive group is formed of the **Viśvedevāḥ** or All-gods, who occupy an important position in the sacrifice, for at least forty entire hymns of the RV. are devoted to their praise. It is a factitious sacrificial group meant to represent all the gods in order that none should be excluded in laudations intended to be addressed to all. But the All-gods are sometimes conceived as a narrower group, being invoked with other groups, such as the Vasus and Ādityas (2, 3[4])[4].

[1] IS. 5, 240; BRV. 2, 370; BLOOMFIELD, FaR. 151. — [2] LRV. 6, 147; cp. PERRY, JAOS. 16, 178. — [3] WEBER, IS. 9, 6; SPH. 23. — [4] HRI. 137. 143, note 1. 182.

H. LOWER DEITIES.

§ 46. Ṛbhus. — Besides the higher gods of the Veda there are a number of mythical beings not regarded as having the divine nature fully and originally. The most important of these are the Ṛbhus. They are celebrated in eleven hymns of the RV. and are mentioned by name over a hundred times. They form a triad. Their individual names, which often occur, are Ṛbhu or less commonly Ṛbhukṣan ('chief of the Ṛbhus'), Vāja, and Vibhvan. These three names are several times mentioned together, sometimes only two of them, while occasionally Ṛbhu is referred to alone. They are most often spoken of in the plural as *ṛbhavaḥ*, but the plural of each of their names may designate the triad. Sometimes the plurals of all three (4, 36[3]; 8, 48[1]) or of only two (*Vājā Ṛbhukṣaṇaḥ* or *Vājā Ṛbhavaḥ*) appear to be used together pleonastically to indicate the trio. Once the combination *Vājo Vibhvāṅ Ṛbhavaḥ* occurs (4, 36[6]). Occasionally an indefinite group seems to be meant, as all (*viśve*) the Ṛbhus (7, 51[3]), or Ṛbhu with the Ṛbhus, Vibhvan with the Vibhus (7, 48[2]) are invoked. In the latter passage Ṛbhu and Vibhvan are evidently thought of as chiefs of groups of the same name. The three Ṛbhus are once distinguished as eldest, younger, and youngest (4, 33[5]).

The Ṛhbus are about a dozen times called by the patronymic name of Saudhanvana, sons of Sudhanvan, 'the good archer'. They are also once collectively addressed as the son (*sūno*) of Indra (4, 37[4]). In the same verse they are invoked as 'children of might' (*śavaso napātaḥ*), as if a play on the meaning of *napāt* (also 'grandson') were intended, in contrast with the epithet 'son of might' (*śavasaḥ sūnu*), which is applied exclusively to Indra. The epithet *śavaso napātaḥ* is almost peculiar to them, being applied to them five times and otherwise only once to Mitra-Varuṇa. In one passage (3,60[3]) they are spoken of as 'children of Manu' (*manor napātaḥ*) and their parents (*pitarā*) are several times mentioned. In one hymn they address Agni as their brother (1, 161[1. 3]).

They are very frequently invoked to come to the sacrifice (4,34[1.3]. 37[1]) and to drink the Soma juice (4, 34[4]. 36[2]; 7, 48[1]). Being high in heaven they are besought to come to the Soma in the lower abodes (4, 37[3]). In this they are generally associated with Indra (3, 60[4–6]; 4, 33[3]. 34[6]. 35[7]), a few times with the Maruts (1, 20[5]. 111[4]; 4, 34[11]), and once with the Ādityas, Savitṛ, Mountains, and Rivers (4,34[8]). In other respects also they are closely connected with Indra. They are Indra-like (4,37[5]) and Ṛbhu is like a new Indra (1,110[7]). With Indra they help mortals to victory (4, 37[6]) and are invoked with him to crush foes (7, 48[3]). They are said to have obtained the friendship of Indra by their skilful work (3, 60[3]; 4, 35[7. 9]); for it is they who fashioned his steeds. In the hymns devoted to their praise, they are rarely invoked with gods other than Indra, there being only one such passage (4, 34[8]) in which Indra is not mentioned as well. Indra's connexion with them is indeed so characteristic, that he is, like the eldest of the triad, called 'chief of the Ṛbhus' (*ṛbhukṣan*), a term also two or three times applied to Indra's associates, the Maruts. In some of the Viśvedeva hymns they are brought into connexion with a few other gods, chiefly Tvaṣṭṛ.

The references to the physical aspect or the equipment of the Ṛbhus are scanty. They are of sunlike appearance (1, 110[4]). They have a car (1,161[7]), which is drawn by steeds (7, 48[1]). Their car is bright, their steeds are fat; they wear metal helmets and fair necklaces (4, 37[4]). Ṛbhu is a possessor of steeds (*aśvin*: 4, 37[5]). The Ṛbhus are characteristically deft-handed (*suhastāḥ*) and skilful (*apás, suapas*: 4, 33[1. 8] &c.), their skilful deeds being incomparable (3, 60[4]). They are frequently said to have acquired the rank of gods in consequence of their marvellous skill. Through their wondrous deeds they obtained divinity (3, 60[1]). By their skilful deeds they became gods and immortal, alighting like eagles in heaven (4, 35[8]). They are men of the air who by their energy mounted to heaven (1, 110[6]). For their skilful services they went the path of immortality to the host of the gods (4, 35[3]), obtaining immortality among the gods and their friendship (4, 33[3. 4]. 35[3]. 36[4]). But they were originally mortals, children of Manu, who by their industry acquired immortality (3, 60[3]; 1, 110[4]). The AB. (3, 30[2]) speaks of them as men who by austerity (*tapas*) obtained a right to partake of Soma among the gods. The gods rejoiced so greatly in their work, that Vaja became the artificer of the gods, Ṛbhukṣan of Indra, and Vibhvan of Varuṇa (4, 33[9]). They went to the gods and obtained the sacrifice, or a share of the sacrifice, among the gods through their skilful work (1, 20[1. 8]. 121[6. 7]). Thus the third or evening pressing or libation (*savana*) belongs to them, they having obtained it by their skilful work (1, 161[8]; 4, 33[11]. 34[4]. 35[9]). They are thus sometimes expressly invoked as gods (4, 36[5]. 37[1]).

Like the higher gods, they are besought to give prosperity and wealth (4, 33[8]. 37[5]), in cattle, horses, heroes (4, 34[10]), and to grant vigour, nourishment, offspring, dexterity (1, 111[2]). They grant treasures to the Soma presser (1, 20[7]; 4, 35[6]). He whom they help is invincible in fight (4, 36[6]), and Ṛbhu and Vāja are besought to give aid and booty in battle (1, 115[5]).

The same verb *takṣ*, to fashion, is generally used with reference to the manual skill of the Ṛbhus as to that of Tvaṣṭṛ. The five great feats of dexterity by which they became gods, are spoken of with pretty uniform frequency and are all or most of them mentioned in nearly every hymn dedicated to their praise. They fashioned or made a car (1, 111[1]. 161[3]; 4, 33[8]. 36[2]), which is horseless, reinless, three-wheeled, and traverses space (4, 36[1]). The car which goes round they fashioned for the Aśvins (1, 20[3]. 161[6]; 10, 39[12]). When in a verse (4, 34[9]) which enumerates each of their feats with a single word, they are said to have fashioned the Aśvins themselves, this appears to be only a loose way of referring to the same exploit.

For Indra they fashioned the two bay steeds (*harī*) which waft him (4, 33[10] &c.). It appears to be only a varied reference to the same feat when the Ṛbhus are represented as desiring to make a horse or as having made one horse after another (1, 161[3. 7]).

They further fashioned or made a cow (1, 161[3]; 4, 34[9]), which yields nectar (1, 20[3]) and is all-stimulating and omniform (4, 33[8]). This cow they formed out of hide (1, 110[8]) or extracted (*ariṇīta*) from a hide (1, 161[7] &c.). They guarded her and formed her flesh (4, 33[4]). That they formed this cow for Bṛhaspati may be inferred from a verse (1, 161[6]) which states that Indra yoked the two bay steeds and the Aśvins the car, while Bṛhaspati drove up the omniform (cow). A minor feat, only twice referred to and perhaps connected with the foregoing one, consists in their having re-united the mother with her calf (1, 110[8]. 111[1]).

The Ṛbhus also rejuvenated their parents (1, 20[4]. 111[1]; 4, 35[5]), who were frail and lay like decaying posts (1, 110[8]; 4, 33[2. 3]). They made the two who were old young again (1, 161[3. 7]). When in the brief enumeration of their feats already referred to (4, 34[9]), they are simply said to have fashioned their parents, the same feat is doubtless meant. It was their laudable fame among the gods, that they made their frail and very old parents young again so as to walk (4, 36[3]). In the first verse of the same hymn it is said to have been the great proclamation of their divine power, that they made heaven and earth to thrive. The latter thus seem to be intended by their parents.

The exhibition of skill which is most frequently mentioned and appears to have been thought the greatest, as showing the Ṛbhus in the character of successful rivals of Tvaṣṭṛ, consists in their having made the one cup, the work of Tvaṣṭṛ, into four (1, 20^{6}. 110^{3}; 4, $35^{2.3}$. 36^{4}). This cup is the drinking vessel of the gods (1, 161^{5}; 4, 35^{5}) or of the Asura (1, 110^{3}). The Ṛbhus were commissioned by the gods through their messenger Agni, to make the one cup, which was of wood, into four, promising as a reward that they should receive worship equally with the gods (1, $161^{1.2}$). Tvaṣṭṛ praised (*panayat*) the proposal of the Ṛbhus to make two, three, or four cups, and acquiesced (*avenat*) when he saw the four shining cups (4, $33^{5.6}$). But in another passage it is said that Tvaṣṭṛ, on seeing the four cups, hid himself among the females and desired to kill the Ṛbhus for desecrating the drinking vessel of the gods (1, $161^{4.5}$), though the Ṛbhus in a previous verse of the same hymn (v. ^{1}) disclaim any wish to desecrate it. They are described as measuring out like a field the one wide drinking vessel (*pātra*), desiring fame among the immortals (1, 110^{5}). The same feat is less definitely referred to when they are said to have formed or fashioned cups (1, 161^{9}; 3, 60^{2} cp. 4, 35^{5}).

The skill of the Ṛbhus is incidentally exemplified by the statement that they fashioned prayer (10, 80^{7}), sacrifice (3, 54^{12}), and the two worlds (4, 34^{9}), or that they are supporters of the sky (10, 66^{10}).

Another myth connects the Ṛbhus with Savitṛ. They are said to have been round the sky, wind-sped, in swift course (4, 33^{1} cp. 1, 161^{12}). After much wandering they came to the house of Savitṛ, who conferred immortality on them when they came to Agohya (1, $110^{2.3}$). When, slumbering for twelve days, they had rejoiced in the hospitality of Agohya, they made fair fields and directed the streams, plants occupied the arid ground and waters the lowlands (4, 33^{7}). By their skill they made grass on the heights and waters in the depths, when they slumbered in the house of Agohya (1, 161^{11}). Having slept, they asked Agohya as to who had awakened them; in a year they looked around (ib. ^{13}).

The word *ṛbhu* is apparently derived from the root *rabh*, to grasp (cp. 2, 3^{8})[1], thus meaning 'handy', 'dexterous'. It frequently occurs in the RV. as an adjective and is several times thus used as an attribute of Indra, Agni, and the Ādityas. It seems to be identical with the German *elbe* and the English *elf*[2]. Vāja (from the root *vaj*) means the 'vigorous one'[3], and Vibhvan[4] (from *vi* and the root *bhū*), 'the eminent' (artist). Thus both the name of the Ṛbhus and the account given of them in the RV. indicate that their essential character is that of skilful artificers.

It is clear that they were regarded as not having been gods from the beginning. Whether their close connexion with Indra has in any way to do with their original nature is doubtful. It is also uncertain who is meant by their patronymic Saudhanvana, since the word *sudhanvan* occurs only twice in the RV. as an attribute of Rudra and of the Maruts. It is, however, most probable that their parents who are mentioned so often, represent heaven and earth[5]. The notion that they produce fertility is connected with their sojourn of twelve days in the house of Savitṛ or Agohya, the sun 'who cannot be concealed'[6]. They have therefore by various scholars[7] been taken to be genii of the three seasons[8], which are at a stand-still during the twelve days of the winter solstice. The cup of Tvaṣṭṛ possibly represents the moon, and the four into which it was transformed by the Ṛbhus, its four phases. On the whole it seems probable that the Ṛbhus were originally terrestrial or aerial elves, whose dexterity gradually attracted to them various myths illustrative of marvelous skill. But the evidence furnished by the RV. is hardly sufficient to warrant any certain conclusion.

[1] Cp. WACKERNAGEL, Altind. Gr. p. 70. — [2] BRUGMANN, Grundriss 2, 298; cp. A. KUHN, KZ. 4, 103—20; WACKERNAGEL, KZ. 24, 297. — [3] 'Riches' according to BRV. 2, 407. — [4] Cp. OLDENBERG, SBE. 46, 191. — [5] A. KUHN, Entwicklungsstufen 134; AIL. 366. — [6] WVB. 1894, 37, note 3; according to BRV. 3, 52, 'from whom nothing is concealed'. — [7] AIL. l. c.; LRV. 3, 335; KRV. 53—4; HVM. 1, 515; HVBP. 100. — [8] According to WEBER, l. c., they are genii of creative time, past, present, and future; according to BRV. 2, 412, three ancient skilful sacrificers who acquired immortality and whose number is connected with the triad of sacrificial fires.

NÈVE, Essai sur le Mythe des Ribhavas, Paris 1847; cp. ROTH, ZDMG. 2, 126; OST. 5, 226—7; GKR. 119; GRV. 1, 103; BRV. 2, 403—13; 3, 51—5; GGH. 108. 110; WC. 24—6; E. H. MEYER, Germanische Mythologie 124; Anzeiger für deutsches Altertum 13, 31—5; ORV. 235—6 (cp. L. V. SCHROEDER, WZKM. 9, 253).

§ 47. The Apsarases. — Apsaras denotes a kind of nymph that even in the RV. appears almost completely separated from her physical basis. The information there obtainable is very scanty, as the name occurs only five times. The Apsaras smiles at her beloved (the Gandharva mentioned in the preceding verse) in the highest heaven (10, 123⁵). Vasiṣṭha was born of the Apsaras (7, 33¹²) and the Vasiṣṭhas are said to have sat close to the Apsarases (ibid. ⁹). The Apsarases of the sea are described as flowing to Soma (9, 78³), with reference to the water which is mixed with the juice. The long-haired ascetic with semi-divine powers is spoken of as able to move on the path of the Apsarases and the Gandharvas (10, 136⁶). The Apsaras is also doubtless meant by the aqueous nymph (*apyā yoṣā*), the wife of the Gandharva in the waters (10, 10⁴).

More is said about the Apsarases in the AV. Their abode is in the waters, whence they come and go in a trice (AV. 2, 2³); and they are besought to depart from the vicinity of men to the river and the bank of the waters (AV. 4, 37³). The goddesses accompanying the Gandharva Viśvāvasu are described as connected with clouds, lightning, and stars (AV. 2, 2⁴). They are expressly called wives of the Gandharvas (AV. 2, 2⁵), and their connexion with the latter has assumed the character of a formula in the later Saṃhitās (VS. 30, 8; AV. 8, 9⁹, &c.)[1]. In the ŚB. (11, 5, 1⁴) the Apsarases are described as transforming themselves into a kind of aquatic bird (*ātayaḥ*: cp. RV. 9, 5⁹). In the post-Vedic literature they are very often spoken of as frequenting forest lakes and rivers, espescially the Ganges, and they are found in Varuṇa's palace in the ocean[2]. The etymological meaning of the word is most probably 'moving in the waters'[3].

The above evidence indicates that the oldest conception of the Apsaras is that of a celestial water nymph, already regarded in the RV. as the consort of a genius named Gandharva. In the later Saṃhitās the sphere of the Apsarases extends to the earth and in particular to trees. They are spoken of as inhabiting banyans (*nyagrodha*) and sacred fig-trees (*aśvattha*), in which their cymbals and lutes resound (AV. 4, 37⁴). Elsewhere the same trees as well as other varieties of the fig-tree (*udumbara* and *plakṣa*) are said to be the houses of Gandharvas and Apsarases (TS. 3, 4, 8¹). The Gandharvas and Apsarases in such trees are entreated to be propitious to a passing wedding procession (AV. 14, 2⁹)[4]. In the ŚB. (11, 6, 1) the Apsarases are described as engaged in dance, song, and play. Post-Vedic texts even speak of mountains, both mythical and actual, as favourite resorts of these two classes of beings[5]. The AV. adds the traits that the Apsarases are fond of dice and bestow luck at play (AV. 2, 2[5] &c.), but that they are feared especially as causing mental derangement, magic therefore being employed against them (AV. 2, 3[5] &c.).

The love of the Apsarases, who are of the great beauty[6] (cp. ŚB. 13, 4 3[7. 8]), is enjoyed not only by the Gandharvas, but occasionally even by men (cp. 10, 95[9]). A myth turning on such a union is related of at least one individual Apsaras in Vedic literature. The names only of several other Apsarases are there mentioned. The AV. refers to three, Ugrajit, Ugraṃpaśyā, and Rāṣṭrabhṛt (AV. 16, 118[1. 2]), while the VS., among several others, speaks of Urvaśī and Menakā (VS. 15, 15—19). The ŚB. (3, 4, 1[22]) also specifies Śakuntalā, the ancestress of the royal family of the Bharatas[7] (ŚB. 13, 5, 4[13]), as well as Urvaśī (ŚB. 11, 5, 1[1]).

The only one of these names occurring in the RV. is that of Urvaśī. That she was there regarded as an Apsaras, appears from the fact that Vasiṣṭha is said in one verse to have been born of Urvaśī and, in the next, of an Apsaras (7, 33[11. 12]). She is once invoked with the streams (5, 41[19]). Her name is otherwise only mentioned[8] twice in a late and obscure hymn (10, 95[10. 17]), which consists of a dialogue between her and her lover Purūravas, son of Iḷā. She is there described as aqueous (*āpyā*), as filling the atmosphere, and traversing space (the latter expression is also applied to the celestial Gandharva in 10, 139[5]). She is said to have spent four autumns among mortals (v. [16]) and is besought to return (v. [17]). The request is apparently refused; but Purūravas receives the promise that his offspring shall worship the gods with the offering, while he himself shall enjoy bliss in heaven (*svarga*: v. [18]). Several verses of this hymn find their setting in a continous story told in the ŚB. (11, 5, 1), which fills in details partly based on a misunderstanding of the text of RV. It is there related that the Apsaras Urvaśī joins herself with Purūravas, son of Iḷā, in an alliance, the permanence of which depends on the condition that she shall never see him naked. The Gandharvas by a stratagem produce a noise during the night. Purūravas springs up naked, when he is seen by Urvaśī illuminated by a flash of lightning. Urvaśī vanishes forthwith. Purūravas wanders about in search of her, till he at last observes her swimming in a lotus lake with other Apsarases in the form of an aquatic bird. Urvaśī discovers herself to him and, in response to his entreaties, consents to receive him for one night a year later[9]. He returns at the appointed time, and on the following day the Gandharvas grant him the boon of becoming one of themselves by producing fire in a particular way. Excepting 10, 95, the name of Purūravas, which means 'calling aloud', occurs only in one passage of the RV. (1, 31[4]), where Agni is said to have caused the sky to thunder (*vāśaya*) for the righteous man (*manave*) Purūravas. The word may here, however, have the adjectival sense. Purūravas and Urvaśī have by some scholars[10] been interpreted as sun and dawn.

1 See PW. s. v. *gandharva*. — 2 HOLTZMANN, ZDMG. 33, 635. 641. — 3 Explained by YN. 5, 13 by *ap-sāriṇī*; cp. MEYER, Indogermanische Mythen 1, 183; GGH. 10; PVS. 1, 79 cp. 183 ff.; LUDWIG, Methode 91; otherwise WEBER, IS. 13, 135, GW., BURY, BB. 7, 339. — 4 HAAS, IS. 5, 394; 13, 136; E. H. MEYER, op. cit. 13. — 5 HOLTZMANN, ZDMG. 33, 640 f.; v. SCHROEDER, op. cit. 67; MANNHARDT, Wald- und Feldkulte 1, 99 ff. — 6 In the Epic period the Apsarases have become regular celestial courtesans. — 7 Cp. WEBER, IS. 1, 198—201; HOLTZMANN, ZDMG. 33, 635 f.; LEUMANN, ZDMG. 48, 80—2; v. BRADKE, ibid. 498 ff. — 8 Cp. OLDENBERG, SBE. 46, 323. — 9 They have a son named Āyu: cp. KHF. 65. 71;

IS. 1, 197; GVS. 1, 283; BRV. 2, 324; Oldenberg, SBE. 46, 28. — [10] Weber, IS. 1, 196; MM., Oxford Essays p. 61; Essays 1, 408—10; Chips 4[2], 109 f.

Lassen, Indische Alterthumskunde 1, 432, note 2; KHF. 71—8; Roth, Nirukta 155—6; GRV. 2, 488; BRV. 2, 90—6; v. Schroeder, op. cit. 1, 23—39 (cp. WZKM. 9, 253); Oldenberg, ZDMG. 37, 81; 39, 52 n. 4. 73—6; GGA. 1890, 420 ff.; GVS. 1, 243—95; Siecke, Die Liebesgeschichte des Himmels, Strassburg 1892 (Urvaśī = moon); HRI. 137.

§ 48. Gandharvas. — With the Apsaras or Apsarases are associated even in the RV., as has been shown, a male being or beings named Gandharva. Of the twenty occurrences of the word in the RV. only three are in the plural, while of the thirty-two occurrences in the AV. half are in the plural. The name is found a few times in the Avesta as Gandarewa[1] (a dragon-like monster) and only in the singular. This points to the Gandharvas as a class having been gradually developed from a single being. In the later Saṃhitās they are spoken of as forming a distinct class by the side of Gods, Fathers and Asuras (AV. 11, 5[2]; TS. 7, 8, 25[1]). Their number is fixed as 27 in some Yajus texts and is even said to be 6333 in the AV. (11, 5[2])[2]. The fact that the conception goes back to the Indo-Iranian period, accounts to some extent for its obscurity. The evidence of the RV. is, moreover, so scanty and vague that no certain result as to its definite original character is attainable. It is worthy of note that the name is found only once in books II to VII, while in book VIII it occurs twice as that of a being hostile to Indra. The word seems sometimes to be only an appellative[3]. It is occasionally accompanied by the epithet *viśvāvasu*, 'possessing all goods' (9, 86[36]; 10, 139[4. 5]; AV. 2, 2[4]; VS. 2, 3). This epithet is in one hymn used alone to designate Gandharva (10, 85[21. 22] cp. [40. 41]); and in the later Saṃhitās, the Brāhmaṇas, and the post-Vedic literature, it frequently occurs as the name of an individual Gandharva.

In the RV. Gandharva seems to be localized in the high region of air or sky. He is a measurer of space (10, 139[5]). He is found in the fathomless spaces of air (8, 66[5]). He is heavenly (*divya*) and stands erect on the vault of heaven (10, 123[7]). He is the lover on whom the Apsaras smiles (ib. [5]). His abode is in heaven (AV. 2, 2[1. 2]) and the Blest live with the Gandharvas (AV. 4, 34[3]). In several passages Gandharva is closely connected with some form of celestial light. Thus he is brought into relation with the sun, 'the golden-winged bird, the messenger of Varuṇa' (10, 123[6]), with the sun-bird (10, 177[2]), with the sun-steed (1, 163[2]), with Soma likened to the sun (9, 85[12]). He is further connected with the 27 stars of the moon's orbit (VS. 9, 7) and in particular with Rohiṇī (AV. 13, 1[23]). He is possibly also associated with the rainbow[4] in one hymn of the RV. (10, 123). In the VS. (18, 38 ff.) the Gandharvas are enumerated with Agni, Sun, Moon, and Wind. In post-Vedic literature one of the names of the mirage is 'city of the Gandharvas'[5].

Gandharva is, moreover, in the RV. often associated (chiefly in the ninth book) with Soma. He guards the place of Soma and protects the races of the gods (9, 83[4] cp. 1, 22[14]). Observing all the forms of Soma, he stands on the vault of heaven (9, 85[12]). Together with Parjanya and the daughter of the sun, the Gandharvas cherish Soma (9, 113[3]). Through Gandharva's mouth the gods drink their draught (AV. 7, 73[3]). The MS. (3, 8[10]) states that the Gandharvas kept Soma for the gods, but having allowed it to be stolen, were as a punishment excluded from the Soma draught. Doubtless owing to this association with Soma, Gandharva is described as knowing plants (AV. 4, 4[1]). It is probably as a jealous guardian of Soma that Gandharva in the RV. appears as a hostile being, who is pierced by Indra in the regions of air (8, 66^{5}) or whom Indra is invoked to overcome (8, 1^{11}). For in a later text Soma is besought to elude the Gandharva Viśvāvasu in the form of an eagle (TS. 1, 2, 9^{1}). Soma is further said to have dwelt among the Gandharvas or to have been stolen by the Gandharva Viśvāvasu, but to have been bought from the Gandharvas, as they were fond of females, at the price of the goddess Vāc (AB. 1, 27; TS. 6, 1, 6^{5}; MS. 3, 7^{3}). The trait of hostility appears to be old, for in the Avesta (Yt. 5, 38) the hostile Gandarewa, dwelling in the sea Vourukaṣa, the abode of the white Haoma, is fought with and overcome by Keresāspa. Moreover, the archer Kṛśānu, who shoots at the eagle that carries off the Soma (RV. 4, 27^{3}), appears to be a Gandharva[6], being expressly said to be one in TA. 1, 9^{3}.

Gandharva is sometimes connected with the waters. 'Gandharva in the waters' and the 'aqueous nymph' are alluded to as the parents of Yama and Yamī (10, 10^{4}). Soma poured into water is called 'the Gandharva of the waters' (9, 86^{36}). Gandharva, connected with the Apsarases, is also said to dwell in the waters in the AV. (2, 2^{3}; 4, 37^{12}). In the Avesta Gandarewa is a lord of the abyss who dwells in the waters (Yt. 15, 28).

The union of Gandharva with the water nymph is typical of marriage. He is therefore connected with the wedding ceremony, and the unmarried maiden is said to belong to Gandharva as well as to Soma and Agni (10, 85^{40-1}). The Gandharva Viśvāvasu in the first days of wedlock is regarded as a rival of the husband (ib. ^{22}), and the Gandharvas' love of women is prominent in later texts (cp. MS. 3, 7^{3}). The Gandharvas and Apsarases thus preside over fertility and are prayed to by those who desire offspring (PB. 19, 3^{2}).

Of the conception of the Gandharvas being celestial singers, which appears in the Epics and later, there seems to be no distinct trace in the RV. (cp. 10, 177^{2}. 11^{2}).

There are only two or three references to their physical appearance in the RV. They are wind-haired (3, 38^{6}) and Gandharva has brilliant weapons (10, 123^{7}). The AV. is more definite (especially 4, 37; 8, 6^{1} ff.). Here they are said to be shaggy and to have half animal forms, being in many ways dangerous to men. Elsewhere, however, they are spoken of as handsome (ŚB. 13, 4, $3^{7.8}$). The RV. adds the touch that Gandharva wears a fragrant (*surabhi*) garment (10, 123^{7}), while in the AV. (12, 1^{23}) the odour (*gandha*) of the earth is said to rise to the Gandharvas.

This suggests the derivation from *gandha* as possible. But such an etymology, even if true, would seem to shed no light on the original conception. The name has even been identified with Κένταυρος; but in order to justify this equation the aid of popular etymology has to be called in[7] as well as the doubtful epenthesis of *u* assumed in the Greek word[8]. The two conceptions, moreover, appear to have nothing in common. The utmost, from a review of the evidence, it seems possible to say about the original nature of the Gandharva is, that he was a bright celestial being, sometimes thought of as dwelling in the waters with his spouse the Apsaras. Various conjectures have, however, been made by different scholars. Some regard the Gandharvas as wind-spirits[9], others think that Gandharva represents the rainbow[10], or a genius of the moon[11], or Soma[12], or the rising sun[13], or a cloud-spirit[14].

[1] Yasht 5, 37; 19, 41; cp. SP AP. 276; BARTHOLOMAE, ZDMG. 42, 158. — [2] WVB. 1894, p. 34. — [3] HVM. 1, 427. — [4] Disputed by BERGAIGNE and HILLEBRANDT; cp. ORV. 246, note 1. — [5] See PW. s. v. *gandharva-nagara*, *-pura*. — [6] KHF. 151—2; WVB. 1894, 7—9 (cp. 1888, p. 13, n.); as to Kṛśānu, cp. also WEBER, IS. 2, 313—4; KUHN in KZ. 1, 523; ROTH, ZDMG. 36, 359; BRV. 3, 30 ff.; SP.AP. 223—4; BLOOMFIELD, JAOS. 16, 20; ORV. 181. — [7] v. SCHROEDER, GGH. 73;

MEYER, Indog. Mythen 164 f. — 8 Cp. BRUGMANN, Grundriss 1, 481. — 9 MANNHARDT 201; MEYER, op. cit. 1, 219 f.; v. SCHROEDER, op. cit. 71; HVM. 1, 446. — 10 ROTH, Nir. Erl. 145; GRV. 2, 400; DPV. 253; KIRSTE, WZKM. 9, 164. — 11 PW.; LRV. 4, 158; HRI. 157. — 12 BRV. 2, 38 ff. — 13 WC. 34. 36 cp. LRF. 101. — 14 KHF. 153.

A. KUHN, KZ. 1, 513 ff.; WEBER, IS. 1, 90; 5, 185. 210; 13, 134 f.; MEYER, op. cit. 11—2. 16—8. 23. 55. 179; BRV. 3, 64—7; PVS. 1, 77—81; SP.AP. 210—15; HVM. 1, 427—66; ORV. 244—9; ZDMG. 49, 178—9.

§ 49. Tutelary Deities. — The name of Vástoṣ páti occurs only seven times in the RV., and one hymn of three stanzas (7, 54) is devoted to his praise. He is there invoked to grant a favourable entry, to remove disease, to bless man and beast, to confer prosperity in cattle and horses, and always to afford protection. In the first verse of the hymn immediately following (7, 55[1]) he is described as a destroyer of disease, who assumes all forms. He is once (7, 54[2]) identified with Soma, being addressed as Indu. In a verse of a hymn to the All-gods (5, 41[8]) he is invoked in immediate juxtaposition with Tvaṣṭṛ and is perhaps identified with him as the great artificer. In another verse (8, 17[14]) he is called a firm pillar, a cuirass of Soma-pressers, and seems to be identified with Indra. In the only passage of the tenth book which mentions him, he is spoken of as the observer of ordinances who, along with prayer (*brahma*), was fashioned by the gods (10, 61[7]). According to GELDNER[1] Rudra is here meant, Vāstoṣpati being an epithet of that god in TS. 3, 4, 10[3]. Though identified with various deities in the above passages, there seems no sufficient reason to suppose that the name was originally attached to any one particular greater deity as an epithet (like *gṛhapati* to Agni). The Gṛhya Sūtras (ĀGS. 2, 9[9]; ŚGS. 3, 4; PGS. 3, 4[7]) prescribe that Vāstoṣpati is to be propitiated when a new house is to be entered. This, together with the contents of the hymn devoted to his praise, points to his having been simply a tutelary deity of the house[2], as the name itself 'Lord of the dwelling' implies. He thus seems to be one of the lower order of deities which in primitive beliefs animate, inhabit, or preside over natural objects such as trees and mountains.

To the same order belongs Kṣetrasya pati the tutelary deity of the field. He is invoked, in the first three verses of 4, 57, to grant cattle and horses as well as to fill heaven and earth, plants and waters with sweetness[3]. In a verse of a hymn to the All-gods (7, 35[10]) he is besought, along with Savitṛ, the Dawns, and Parjanya, to bestow prosperity. In a similar hymn (10, 66[13]), worshippers express a desire to have him as a neighbour. The Gṛhya Sūtras state that he is sacrificed to or worshipped when a field is ploughed (AGS. 2, 10[4]; ŚGS. 4, 13[5]). In one verse of a hymn addressed to agricultural deities (4, 57[6]) Sītā, the Furrow, is invoked to grant rich blessings and crops. Sītā later appears (PGS. 2, 17[9]) as the wife of Indra (perhaps because that god is once in the RV. called *urvarāpati*, 'lord of the field': 8, 21[3] cp. 4, 57[7]) and bears the patronymic Sāvitrī (TB. 2, 3, 10[1]). In the Sūtra passage just mentioned the blessings of Urvarā, the arable Field, described as 'having a garland of threshing-floors', are invoked.

1 FaW. 21; V. = Agni, WC. 22. — 2 Cp. BLOOMFIELD, SBE. 42, 343—4. — 3 PERRY, DRISLER Memorial 241, thinks Pūṣan is probably meant. Cp. WINDISCH, Berichte der k. sächs. Gesellschaft 1892, p. 174; ORV. 254—5.

IV. MYTHICAL PRIESTS AND HEROES.

§ 50. Manu. — As the appellation Manu or Manus is often used in the sense of 'man', there is sometimes an uncertainty as to when it has the value of a proper name in the RV. It appears to have the latter signification nearly twenty times in the form of Manu and almost as often in that of Manus. Manu is five times styled a father, and in two of these passages more definitely as 'our father' (2, 33[13] &c., cp. § 9). Sacrificers are spoken of as the people (*viśaḥ*) of Manus (4, 37[1] &c.) and Agni is said to abide among the offspring of Manu (1, 68[4]). Manu was the institutor of sacrifice. For when he had kindled the fire, he presented the first offering with the seven priests to the gods (10, 63[7]). The sacrifice of Manu is the prototype of the present sacrifice. For the latter is compared to the sacrifice which Manus offered to the gods (1, 76[5]). Such comparisons are frequently made with the adverb *manuṣvat*, 'like Manus'. Worshippers make Agni the accomplisher of sacrifice, as Manus did (1, 44[11]). They kindle Agni like Manus (5, 21[1] &c.). Like Manus, they invoke Agni who was kindled by Manu (7, 2[3]). They offer Soma as Manus did (4, 37[3]). Soma is prayed to flow as he once flowed for Manu (9, 96[12]). Manu established Agni as a light for all people (1, 36[19]). Manu is also mentioned with other ancient sacrificers, with Aṅgiras and Yayāti (1, 31[17]), with Bhṛgu and Aṅgiras (8, 43[13]), with Atharvan and Dadhyañc (1, 80[16]), with Dadhyañc, Aṅgiras, Atri and Kaṇva (1, 139[9]). The gods (1, 36[10]), Mātariśvan (1, 128[2]), Mātariśvan and the gods (10, 46[9]), and Kāvya Uśanā[1] (8, 23[17]) are said to have given Agni to Manu or to have instituted him a sacrificer for Manu. In the last four passages the word has perhaps only the appellative meaning of 'man'.

Indra is said to have drunk Soma beside Manu Vivasvat (Vāl. 4[1]) or Manu Sāṃvaraṇi (Vāl. 3[1]), and to have drunk the Soma of Manus, three lakes, to strengthen himself for the Vṛtra-fight (5, 29[7]). Soma is said to have been brought to Manu by the bird (4, 26[4]). In the TS. and the ŚB. Manu is also frequently described as a celebrator of religious ceremonies.

Manu appears to have been regarded as the son of Vivasvat even in the RV.; for he is once (Vāl. 4[1] cp. 3[1]) called Manu Vivasvat (cp. p. 42). In the AV. (8, 10[24]) and the ŚB. (13,4,3[3]), as well as in post-Vedic literature, he bears the regular patronymic Vaivasvata. Yama also is a son of Vivasvat, and the first of mortals. Manu is thus a doublet of Yama as ancestor of the human race[2]. But Manu is regarded as the first of men living on earth, while Yama, as first of men who died, became the king of the dead in the other world. Hence in the ŚB. (13, 4, 3[3—5]) Manu Vaivasvata is described as ruler of men, and Yama Vaivasvata as ruler of the Manes. Yāska (Nir. 12, 10) explains Manu to be the son of Vivasvat, the sun (*Āditya*), and of Savarṇā the substitute of Saraṇyū (cp. 10, 17[2]; p. 125), counting him (Nir. 12, 34) among the divine beings of the celestial region (Naigh. 5, 6).

The ŚB. (1, 8, 1[1—10]) relates a legend of how Manu was saved in a ship from a deluge, which swept away all other creatures, by a fish (in post-Vedic mythology an Avatār of Viṣṇu). Manu is then said to have become the progenitor of mankind through his daughter Iḍā, who was produced from his offerings. That the story of the flood was known as early as the time of the AV. is implied in a passage of that Saṃhitā (19, 39[8])[3]. The myth of the deluge occurs in the Avesta also, and may be Indo-European[4]. It is generally regarded as borrowed from a Semitic source[5], but this seems to be an unnecessary hypothesis[6].

[1] An ancient sage and sacrificer, see § 58B. — [2] Possibly ancestor of the Āryans only, as he is in several passages contrasted with Dasyus, cp. OST. 1, 174; SP.AP. 272. — [3] HRI. 160. — [4] LINDNER, Die iranische Flutsage, FaR. 213—6. — [5] BURNOUF, Bhāgavata Purāṇa, preface, LI—LIV; WEBER, IS. 1, 160 ff.; SP.AP. 271—4; ORV. 276 note. — [6] MM., India 133—8; HRI. 160.

KHF. 21; KZ. 4, 91; CORSSEN, KZ. 2, 32; WEBER, IS. 1, 194; ZDMG. 4, 302; 18, 286; ROTH, ZDMG. 4, 430; ZDMG. 5, 525 ff.; KZ. 12, 293; 19, 156; ASCOLI,

KZ. 17, 334; Muir, JRAS. 1863, 410—16; 1865, 287 ff.; OST. 1, 162—96; BRV. 1, 62—70; ORV. 275—6; HRI. 143.

§ 51. Bhṛgus. — Bhṛgu is a name met with twenty-one times in the RV., besides two occurrences in the adverbial form *bhṛguvat*. It is found only once in the singular; and appears therefore to have properly designated a group of mythical beings. Mentioned twelve times in Agni hymns, they are chiefly connected with the communication of fire to men. Mātariśvan brought Agni as a treasure to Bhṛgu (1, 60[1]) or kindled the hidden Agni for[1] the Bhṛgus (3, 5[10]). Mātariśvan and the gods fashioned Agni for Manu, while the Bhṛgus with might produced him (10, 46[9]). The Bhṛgus found Agni lurking in the waters (10, 46[2]); worshipping him in the waters, they placed him in the abodes of Āyu or man (2, 4[2] cp. [4]). They established Agni like a friend well-deposited in the wood (6, 15[2]) or as a treasure among men (1, 58[6]). For Agni is the Bhṛgus' gift (3, 2[4]). Rubbing him they invoked him with prayer (1, 127[7]). With songs of praise they caused him to shine forth (10, 122[5]) in wood (4, 7[1]). They brought him to the navel (cp. p. 92) of the earth (1, 143[4]). While Atharvan established rites with sacrifices, the Bhṛgus showed themselves as gods with their dexterity (10, 92[10]). Their skill, primarily manifested in producing fire, is incidentally spoken of as artistic. For worshippers make a prayer for Indra or the Aśvins as the Bhṛgus (made) a car (4, 16[20]; 10, 39[14]).

They are an ancient race. For sacrificers speak of them, together with the Aṅgirases and Atharvans, as their Soma-loving fathers (10, 14[6]) and invoke Agni as the Bhṛgus (*bhṛguvat*), the Aṅgirases, and Manu did (8, 43[13]). They implore Indra to hear their prayer like those of the Yatis and Bhṛgus (8, 6[18]), or to aid them as he did the Yatis, Bhṛgus, and Praskaṇva (8, 3[9]). The Bhṛgus are mentioned, along with the Druhyus and Turvaśa, as the foes of king Sudās (7, 18[6]). In the last three passages their name appears in the historical character of the designation of a tribe. The Bhṛgus are invoked to drink soma with all the thirty-three gods, the Maruts, the Waters, the Aśvins, Uṣas, and Sūrya (8, 35[3]). They are compared with suns and said to have gained all their desires (8, 3[16]). In one passage (9, 101[13]) they are connected with an unknown myth, when worshippers express a wish to drive away the niggardly, as the Bhṛgus the demon (*makham*).

Thus the Bhṛgus never designate actually existing priests in the RV., but only a group of ancient sacrificers and ancestors, to which Bhṛgu bears the relation of chief, just as Aṅgiras does to the group of the Aṅgirases, or Vasiṣṭha to that of the Vasiṣṭhas.

The myth of the descent of fire and its communication to man is chiefly connected with Mātariśvan and the Bhṛgus. But while Mātariśvan brings it from heaven as lightning, the Bhṛgus do not fetch it, but are rather regarded as kindling it for the establishment and diffusion of the sacrifice on earth.

In the later Vedic literature Bhṛgu occurs as the name of a seer representing a tribe (AV. 5, 19[1]; AB. 2, 20[7]). He arises as a spark from Prajāpati's seed and being adopted by Varuṇa receives the patronymic Vāruṇi (AB. 3, 34[1] cp. PB. 18, 9[1]) and is expressly called a son of Varuṇa (ŚB. 11, 6, 1[1])[2].

Etymologically the word *bhṛgu* means 'shining' from the root *bhrāj*, 'to shine'. Bergaigne[3] thinks there can hardly be a doubt that *bhṛgu* was originally a name of fire, while Kuhn[4] and Barth[5] agree in the opinion that the form of fire it represents is lightning. Kuhn[6] and Weber[7] further identify the Bhṛgus as fire-priests with the Greek φλεγύαι.

[1] Cp. Oldenberg, SBE. 46, 243. — [2] Weber, ZDMG. 9, 240 ff. — [3] BRV. 1,

52—6; cp. HOPKINS, JAOS. 16, 280. — [4] KHF. 9—14. — [5] BRI. 10. — [6] KHF. 21—2. — [7] ZDMG. 9, 242. — OST. 1, 170; ORV. 123; HRI. 168.

§ 52. **Atharvan.** — The name of Atharvan occurs fourteen times in the RV., thrice in the plural, and is also several times found in the AV. Atharvan generally appears in the character of an ancient priest. He rubbed Agni forth (6, 16[13]) and priests rub Agni as Atharvan did (6, 15[17]). Agni produced by Atharvan became the messenger of Vivasvat (10, 21[5]). Atharvan first established (order) by sacrifices, while the Bhṛgus showed themselves gods by their skill (10, 92[10]). By sacrifices Atharvan first extended the paths; then the sun was produced (1, 83[5]). Atharvan along with Father Manu and Dadhyañc practised devotion (1, 80[16]). Indra is the helper of Atharvan as well as of Trita, Dadhyañc and Mātariśvan (10, 48[2]). The goblin-destroying Agni is invoked to burn down the fool with divine flame like Atharvan (10, 87[12]). The AV. adds some further traits. Atharvan brought a cup of Soma to Indra (AV. 18, 3[54]). A miraculous cow was given to him by Varuṇa (AV. 5, 11; 7, 104). Atharvan is a companion of the gods, is related to them, and dwells in heaven (AV. 4, 1[7], &c.). In the ŚB. Atharvan is spoken of as an ancient teacher (14, 5, 5[22]. 7, 3[28]).

In the plural the Atharvans are enumerated as Fathers along with the Aṅgirases, Navagvas, and Bhṛgus (10, 14[6]). They dwell in heaven and are called gods (AV. 11, 6[13]). They destroy goblins with a magical herb (AV. 4, 37[7]).

In a few passages of the RV. the word *atharvan* appears to have the appellative meaning of 'priest'. Thus it is an attribute of Bṛhaddiva, the composer of a hymn (10, 120[9] cp. [8]). In this sense it seems to be an epithet of Agni, when a seer is described as pouring the libation on the Atharvan (8, 9[7]). The word also means priest when it is said that the Atharvans mix Soma (9, 4[2]) or that they receive a hundred cows from a patron (6, 47[24]). That this is the original sense is borne out by the fact that the cognate Avestan word *āthravan* signifies 'fire-priest', which is also the etymological sense; for *ātar* (for *āthar*), fire, is the same as the Vedic *athar-*[1], which also occurs in *athar-yú*, flaming (said of Agni, 7, 1[1]). This old name must then have been mythologically applied to designate an ancient priestly race of a semi-divine character, generally represented in the singular by their chief.

[1] BRUGMANN, Grundriss 2, 360; cp. BLOOMFIELD, SBE. 42, XXIII, n. 2; BARTHOLOMAE, IF. 5, 221, rejects the connexion of *ātar* with *atharvan*. — Cp. also LASSEN, Indische Alterthumskunde 1, 523; KHF. 10; IS. 1, 289 ff.; OST. 1, 160; BRV. 1, 49; HRI. 160, n. 1.

§ 53. **Dadhyañc.** — Dadhyañc, who is the son of Atharvan (6, 16[14]; 1, 116[12]. 117[22]), is mentioned nine times in the RV. and, with one exception, only in the ninth, the tenth, and especially the first book. He is a seer who kindled Agni (6, 16[14]) and is mentioned with Atharvan, Aṅgiras, Manu, and other ancient sacrificers (1, 80[16]. 139[9]).

The Aśvins gave a horse's head to Atharvan's son Dadhyañc, who then proclaimed to them the (place of the) mead (*madhu*) of Tvaṣṭṛ (1, 117[22]). With the head of a horse Dadhyañc proclaimed to the Aṣvins the (place of the) mead (1, 116[12]). The Aśvins won the heart of Dadhyañc; then the horse's head spoke to them (1, 119[9]). Indra is also connected with this myth. For it is said that, when seeking the head of the horse hidden in the mountains, he found it in Śaryaṇāvat and slew with the bones of Dadhyañc ninety-nine Vṛtras (1, 84[13. 14]). Indra, besides producing cows from the dragon for Trita, gave cowstalls to Dadhyañc (and) Mātariśvan (10, 48[2]). These are probably the cowstalls which Dadhyañc opens by the power of

Soma (9, 108[4]). It is noteworthy that in the only older passage (6, 16[14]) in which the name of Dadhyañc occurs, he is the son of the ancient fire-priest Atharvan and is himself a kindler of fire. Otherwise he is chiefly connected with the secret abode of Soma and with Indra in the release of the cows. Owing to his horse's head and his name he can hardly be altogether dissociated from the steed Dadhikrā. The etymological sense of *dadhi-añc*, 'curd-ward' might signify either 'possessing'[1] or 'fond of' 'curdled milk'. In BERGAIGNE's opinion Dadhyañc does not differ essentially in origin from Soma[2]. The evidence is, however, insufficient to justify any certain conclusion. But it does not seem an altogether improbable conjecture that Dadhyañc originally represented the lightning form of fire. The horse's head would indicate its speed, the voice with which it speaks, the thunder, its bones, the thunderbolt. His connexion with the secret abode of Soma, would resemble that of the eagle with the celestial Soma. The name, too, suggests the curdling effect of the thunderstorm. In post-Vedic literature the name generally occurs in the form of Dadhīca, and in the Mahābhārata the thunderbolt for slaying Vṛtra is said to have been fashioned out of his bones[3].

[1] 'Uni au lait', BRV. 2, 457. — [2] BRV. 2, 458. — [3] PW. s. v. — Cp. also BRV. 2, 456—60; GRV. 2, 84; PERRY, JAOS. 11, 138; LRF. 120—2; OERTEL, JAOS. 18, 16—18.

§ 54. **Aṅgirases.**[1] — Of the more than sixty occurrences of this name in the RV. about two-thirds are in the plural. Derivatives of the word are also found there about thirty times. The whole of one hymn (10, 62) is voted to the praise of the Aṅgirases as a group.

The Aṅgirases are sons of heaven[2] (3, 53[7]; 10, 67[2] cp. 4, 2[15]). They are seers who are sons of the gods (10, 62[4]). A single Aṅgiras being regarded as their ancestor, they are also termed 'sons of Aṅgiras' (10, 62[5]). Poets speak of them as 'fathers' (ib. [2]), 'our fathers' (1, 71[2]), or 'our ancient fathers' (1, 62[2]). They are once mentioned as fathers with the Atharvans and Bhṛgus (10, 14[6]), being especially associated with Yama (ib.[3—5]). They are also in a more general way connected with other groups of divine beings, the Ādityas, Vasus, Maruts (7, 44[4]; 8, 35[14]), or the Ādityas, Rudras, Vasus, as well as the Atharvans (AV. 11, 8[13]). Soma is offered to them (9, 62[9]), and they are invoked like gods (3, 53[7]; 10, 62). They are *brahman* priests (7, 42[1]). They found Agni hidden in the wood (5, 11[6]) and thought of the first ordinance of sacrifice (10, 67[2]). It is by sacrifice that they obtained immortality as well as the friendship of Indra (10, 62[1]).

With the latter deity the Aṅgirases are closely associated. To them Indra disclosed the cows (8, 52[3]), for them he opened the stall (1, 51[3]. 134[4]), and drove out the cows which were hidden, casting down Vala (8, 14[8]). Accompanied by them Indra pierced Vala (2, 11[20]) and drove out the cows (6, 17[6]). As their leader Indra is twice called *aṅgirastama*, chief Aṅgiras (1, 100[4]. 130[3]). Soma (as inspiring Indra) is also once said to have opened the cowstall for the Aṅgirases (9, 86[23]). In connexion with the myth of the deliverance of the cows the song of the Aṅgirases is characteristic. Praised by them Indra pierced Vala (2, 15[8]), and burst the cowstalls (4, 16[18]), slew Vala and opened his citadels (6, 18[5]), or dispelled the darkness, spread out the earth, and established the lower space of heaven (1, 62[5]). So characteristic is their singing that the Maruts with their varied songs are said to be like the Aṅgirases (10, 78[5]), and the gods are invoked to the offering with the chants of the Aṅgirases (1, 107[2]). Hymns addressed by actual priests to Indra are also several times compared with those of the Aṅgirases (1, 62[1, 2] &c). Incidentally Indra assumes a less prominent position than the Aṅgirases in the myth of the cows. Thus the Aṅgirases are said to have emptied the stall containing cows and horses, with Indra as their companion (10, 62[7]). Here we have the transition to the omission of Indra altogether, his characteristic action being directly attributed to the Aṅgirases themselves. By the rite they drove out the cows and pierced Vala (ib. [2]), caused the sun to mount the sky, and spread out mother earth (ib. [3]). By the rite they cleft the rock and shouted with the cows (4, 3[11]). Singing they found the cows (1, 62[2]). They burst the rock with their songs and found the light (1, 72[2]). The Aṅgirases are further connected with the finding of the cows of the Paṇis for Indra by Saramā (10, 108[8. 10]), who is said to have assisted Indra and the Aṅgirases in tracking them (1, 62[3] cp. 72[8]). The Aṅgirases are also described alone as having found the cows and steeds of Paṇi (1, 83[4]). Bṛhaspati, who is connected with the same myth (10, 108[6. 11]), receives the epithet *Āṅgirasa* when piercing the rock and capturing the cows (6, 73[1]) or giving cows like Bhaga (10, 68[2]).

Bṛhaspati is even directly called Aṅgiras when he drives out the cows and releases the waters with Indra (2, 23[18]). Otherwise in nearly all the occurrences of the word in the singular, Aṅgiras is an epithet of Agni, who is the first seer Aṅgiras (1, 31[1]), the ancient Aṅgiras (10, 92[15]) or the oldest (1, 127[2]) and the most inspired (6, 11[3]) of the Aṅgirases. Agni is several times also called the chief Aṅgiras (1, 75[2] &c.). This term is, however, once or twice applied to Indra, Uṣas, and Soma. Sometimes Aṅgiras only designates an ancient priest without direct allusion to Agni, as when 'the ancient Aṅgiras' is mentioned in an enumeration of ancestors (1, 139[9]) or when the context shows that in the form *aṅgirasvat* the singular sense 'like Aṅgiras' is meant (1, 45[3]). In one passage (1, 31[17]), in which the poet exclaims, 'O Agni, come to us as to Manus, as to Aṅgiras, o Aṅgiras', the name designates both the ancestor and Agni.

According to the tradition found in the Anukramaṇī of the RV., the Aṅgirases must have been regarded as an actual priestly family, as the composition of the ninth book is attributed to members of it[3]. Priestly families also seem to be alluded to in the compound Atharva-aṅgirasaḥ, which occurs as a designation of the AV. in that Veda itself (AV. 10, 7[20]) and later (ŚB. 11, 5, 6[7] &c.)[4].

On the whole it seems probable that the Aṅgirases were originally conceived as a race of higher beings intermediate between gods and men, as attendants of Agni, who is so often described as a messenger between heaven and earth (p. 96), and that their priestly character was a later development[5]. They may possibly have been personifications of the flames of fire as messengers to heaven (cp. RV. 7, 3[3]). This view is borne out by the etymological connexion of *aṅgiras* with the Greek ἄγγελος, 'messenger'[6]. WEBER, however, is of opinion that they were originally priests of the Indo-Iranian period[7].

[1] KHF. 10; OST. 5, 23; GW.; BRV. 1, 47—8; 2, 308—21; WC. 69—72; ORV. 127—8. — [2] Cp. BDA. 45. — [3] Cp. WEBER, History of Ind. Lit., Engl. tr. p. 31. — [4] Cp. BLOOMFIELD, JAOS. 17, 180—2; SBE. 42, XVII—XXVII. — [5] Cp. ROTH, PW.; BRV. 2, 309; cp. HVBP. 109; ORV. 127. — [6] BRUGMANN, Grundriss 2, 188; HRI. 167. — [7] IS. 1, 291 ff.

§ 55. A. Virūpas[1]. — Closely connected with the Aṅgirases are the Virūpas, whose name is mentioned three times in the plural. The Aṅgirases, the Virūpas, are sons of heaven (3, 53[7]). The Virūpas are seers, sons of Aṅgiras, born from Agni, from heaven (10, 62[5. 6]). Virūpa once occurs as the name of a single being, who sings the praises of Agni, in a stanza (8, 64[6]) immediately following one in which Aṅgiras is invoked. The name also has the singular sense in the adverb *virūpavat*, 'like Virūpa', as is indicated by the occurrence in the same stanza (1, 45[3]) of *Priyamedhavat, Atrivat,* besides *Aṅgirasvat.* The word once occurs in its patronymic form in a verse (10, 14[5]) in which Yama is invoked with the Aṅgirases and the Vairūpas. As the word is most usually a simple adjective meaning 'of variable form' and, when a name, is always found in company with that of Aṅgiras or the Aṅgirases, it would seem to have been hardly more than an epithet of the latter.

B. Navagvas[2]. The name of these beings occurs altogether fourteen times in the RV., six times in association with that of the Aṅgirases. The Navagvas are spoken of as 'our ancient fathers' (6, 22[2]), or as 'our fathers' along with the Aṅgirases, the Atharvans, and the Bhṛgus (10, 14[6]). Like the Aṅgirases, they are connected with the myth of Indra, Saramā, and the cows of the Paṇis (1, 62[3.4]; 5, 45[7]; 10, 108[8]). Indra with the Navagvas as his friends sought the cows (3, 39[5]). Pressing Soma they laud Indra with songs: they broke open the stall of the cows (5, 29[12]). In one hymn they are described as having sung with the pressing stones for ten months (5, 45[7.11]). In two of its occurrences in the plural the word *navagva* is a simple adjective, being in one of these cases an attribute of the rays of Agni (6, 6[3]). It is also found three times in the singular, when it appears to be an epithet of Aṅgiras (4, 51[4]; 10, 62[6]) or of Dadhyañc (9, 108[4]). It apparently means 'going in (a company of) nine'[3], designating as a plural noun a group of nine ancient priestly ancestors.

C. Daśagvas[2]. This name occurs seven times in the RV., three times in the singular, and only twice unassociated with that of the Navagvas. The Daśagvas were the first who offered sacrifice (2, 34[12]). Indra with the Navagvas sought the cows and with the ten Daśagvas found the sun (3, 39[5]). With the Navagvas and the Daśagvas Indra rent the rock and Vala (1, 62[4]). The Navagvas and Daśagvas praise Indra and broke open the stall of the cows (5, 29[12]). The dawns shine on the Navagva Aṅgira and the seven-mouthed Daśagva (4, 51[4]). Daśagva, mentioned with Navagva, is once spoken of as chief Aṅgiras (10, 62[6]). Daśagva is described in one passage as having been succoured by Indra (8, 12[2]). The name, being merely a numerical variation of Navagva, was most probably suggested by the latter.

D. The seven Ṛṣis[4]. The ancient seers are represented by a definite numerical group as 'the seven Ṛṣis', who are, however, only mentioned four times in the RV. One poet speaks of them as 'our fathers, the seven seers' (4, 42[8]). They are called divine (10, 130[7]), and in another passage (10, 109[4]) the 'seven ancient seers' are associated with the gods. The number may have been suggested by that of the seven technical priests (enumerated in 2, 1[2]), of whom they would, in that case, have been regarded as the prototypes. In the ŚB. they become individualized by each receiving a name (ŚB. 14, 5, 2[6]; Bṛhadār. Up. 2, 2[6]). In the same Brāhmaṇa (2, 1, 2[4] cp. 8, 1, 10) they are also regarded as the seven stars in the constellation of the Great Bear and are stated to have been originally bears[5]. This identification is doubtless due partly to the sameness of the number in the two cases and partly to the similarity of sound between *ṛṣi*, 'seer', and *ṛkṣa*, which in the RV. means both 'star' (1, 24[10]) and 'bear' (5, 56[3]).

Probably the same ancient sacrificers are referred to as the seven priests (*viprāḥ*) who with the Navagvas praise Indra (6, 22[2] cp. 3, 31[5]; 4, 2[15]), or the seven Hotṛs[6] with whom Manu made the first offering to the gods (10, 63[7]). Similarly the 'two divine Sacrificers' (*daivyā hotārā*) mentioned nearly a dozen times in the RV. seem to have been the celestial counterpart of two technical priests[7].

[1] GW. s. v. *virupa*; BRV, 2, 307, note 4. — [2] BRV. 2, 145—6. 307—8. —

3 Cp. YN. 11, 19; BRV. 2, 145: 'having nine cows'. — 4 ROTH, PW.; OLDENBERG, ZDMG. 42, 236; ORV. 276—8. — 5 WEBER, IS. 1, 167; EGGELING, SBE. 12, 282, n. 2. — 6 Cp. HOPKINS, JAOS. 16, 277; ORV. 383—4; SBE. 46, 189. 322. — 7 ORV. 391; SBE. 46, 11; cp. BRV. 1, 234—5.

§ 56. Atri. — This is one of the seers of ancient days most frequently mentioned in the RV. The name occurs there about forty times in the singular and six times in the plural as a designation of his descendants. Atri is spoken of as a seer belonging to the five tribes (1, 117[3]) and is mentioned along with Manu and other ancestors of the human race (1, 39[9]).

Agni is said to have helped Atri (7, 15[5]) as a well as other ancient seers (1, 45[3]; 10, 150[5]). Indra also heard the prayer of Atri (8, 36[7]) and opened the cowstall for him and the Aṅgirases (1, 51[3]). Atri is, however, chiefly represented as the protégé of the Aśvins, and the characteristic myth about him is connected with them. They delivered Atri from the darkness (6, 50[10]; 7, 71[5]). They rescued him out of a chasm (5, 78[4]) with all his host (1, 116[8]. 117[3]), when they destroyed the wiles of the malignant demon (1, 117[3]). The chasm into which he has fallen and from which they deliver him is a burning one, but they gave him a strengthening draught (1, 116[8]. 118[7]). They made the burning chasm (*ṛbīsa*) or his abode (*gṛha*) agreeable for him (10, 39[9]; 8, 62[7]); they prevent the fire from burning him (8, 62[8]). They rescued Atri who was in the heat (10, 80[3]), they protected him from the heat with coolness (1, 119[6]; 8, 62[3]), and made the burning heat agreeable for him (1, 112[7]). Once they are said to have rejuvenated Atri, who had grown old (10, 143[1. 2]).

In one hymn Atri is said to have found the sun when it was hidden by the demon Svarbhānu and to have placed it in the sky (5, 40[6. 8]). But in the very next verse (9) this deed is attributed to the Atris collectively. The AV. also refers to Atri finding and placing the sun in the sky (AV. 13, 2[4. 12. 36]). In the ŚB. Atri is a priest who dispelled darkness (4, 3, 4[21]), originated from Vāc (1, 4, 5[13]), and is even identical with her (14, 5, 2[5]).

The plural form of the name in the RV. regularly occurs in the last or one of the last verses of a hymn. The Atris here designate the family of seers who are the composers of the hymns (5, 39[5] &c.). The whole of the fifth book is attributed to the family of the Atris, and about one-fourth of the occurrences of the name in the singular or plural are found in that book.

The name is perhaps derived from the root *ad*, to eat, in the sense of 'devouring', as the cognate word *atrin*, a frequent adjective in the RV. used to describe demons, seems to have this meaning. The word *atri*[1] itself is once employed as an attribute of Agni, probably with this signification (2, 8[5]). BERGAIGNE[2] is even of opinion that, though Atri has become a priest, he originally represented some form of Agni. The name of Atri is four times accompanied or, in the next verse, followed by that of Saptavadhri. The latter is a protégé of the Aśvins, a seer whom they are invoked to release from captivity (5, 78[5. 6]), and who is said to have sharpened the blade of Agni with his prayer (8, 62[8]). For Atri Saptavadhri the Aśvins made the burning chasm agreeable (10, 39[9]). The two are therefore probably identical[3].

1 Cp. OLDENBERG, SBE. 46, 35. 214. — 2 BRV. 2, 467—72. — 3 Op. cit. 467; BAUNACK, ZDMG. 50, 266. — Cp. also PW., s. v. Atri; OLDENBERG, ZDMG. 42, 213; BAUNACK, ZDMG. 50, 266—87.

§ 57. Kaṇva &c. — The name of Kaṇva occurs about sixty times in the RV. as that of an ancient seer and of his descendants, the occurrences in the singular and plural being nearly equally divided. Kaṇva is spoken of as the son of Nṛṣad (10, 31[11]) and bears the patronymic Nārṣada (1, 117[8];

AV. 4, 19[1]). He is mentioned in an enumeration of ancient ancestors such as Manu and Aṅgiras (1, 139[9]). The gods gave Agni to Kaṇva and others, who kindled him and were blessed by him (1, 36[10. 11. 17]). Agni helped Kaṇva, as well as Atri, Trasadasyu, and others, in battle (10, 50[5]), and is spoken of as a friend and chief of the Kaṇvas (10, 115[5]). Indra conferred gold and cattle on Kaṇva, Trasadasyu, and others (Vāl. 1[10]. 2[10]). The Maruts bestowed wealth on Kaṇva along with Turvaśa and Yadu (8, 7[18]). The Aśvins are several times said to have helped Kaṇva (1, 47[5]. 112[5]; 8, 5[25]. 8[20]). He was blind when succoured by the Aśvins (8, 5[23]), who restored his sight (1, 118[7]).

Most of the hymns of the eighth book of the RV. are attributed to the family of Kaṇva, and poets there speak of themselves as Kaṇvas. The name as that of a family is therefore historical. But the ancestor whose name was transferred to them in reality[1] never appears in the RV. as that of a contemporary. ROTH thinks his origin may have been mythical like that of Aṅgiras[2]; and BERGAIGNE is of opinion that the blind Kaṇva represents the sun during the night or, more generally, the hidden Agni or Soma[3].

Medhyātithi, a descendant of Kaṇva, being called by the patronymic Kāṇva (8, 2[40]), is mentioned nine times in the RV., occasionally with Kaṇva in enumerations of ancestors (1, 36[10. 11. 17]). The name seems to mean 'he who has a sacrificial guest (i. e. Agni)'. Priyamedha, whose name occurs four or five times and is found beside that of Kaṇva (8, 5[25]), belongs to the past, but his descendants often speak of themselves in the plural as Priyamedhas[4].

[1] OLDENBERG, ZDMG. 42, 216—7. — [2] PW. s. v. Kaṇva. — [3] BRV. 2, 465. — [4] OLDENBERG, ZDMG. 42, 217.

§ 58. A. Kutsa[1]. This warlike hero belonging to the Indra myth is mentioned nearly forty times in the RV. The name occurs only once in the plural as a designation of a family of singers who address a hymn to Indra (7, 25[5]). Kutsa is four times called by the patronymic Ārjuneya, son of Arjuna (1, 112[23] &c.). Mention is made of a son of his, whom Indra aided in fight against a Dasyu (10, 105[11]). Kutsa is young and brilliant (1, 63[3]). He is a seer, who called upon Indra for aid when plunged in a pit (1, 106[6]). Kutsa rides on the same car as Indra (4, 16[11]; 5, 29[9]), who wafts him (5, 31[8]; 8, 1[11]) or takes him as his charioteer (2, 19[6]; 6, 20[5]). Kutsa is similar to Indra (4, 16[10]) and is even invoked with him in a dual compound as *Indrākutsā*, the pair being besought to come on their car (5, 31[9]).

The foe against whom Kutsa is associated with Indra is Śuṣṇa. Indra smote Śuṣṇa for Kutsa (1, 63[3]. 121[9]; 4, 16[12]; 6, 26[3]), aided Kutsa against Śuṣṇa (1, 51[6]), subjected Śuṣṇa to him (7, 19[2]), or, associated with Kutsa and the gods, vanquished Śuṣṇa (5, 29[9]). Indra is invoked to fight with Kutsa against Śuṣṇa (6, 31[3]) or to bring Kutsa as a slayer of Śuṣṇa (1, 175[4]). Indra fights for Kutsa even against the gods (4, 30[2—5]) or against Gandharva (8, 1[11]). The conflict with Śuṣṇa results in the stealing of the wheel of the sun (1, 175[4]; 6, 31[3]). For Kutsa pressed by his foes Indra tore off the wheel of the sun (4, 30[4]) while the other he gave to Kutsa to drive on with (5, 29[10]). This miracle of stopping the sun (cp. 1, 121[10]; 10, 138[3]) seems to be a transference of the myth of Indra gaining the sun for human happiness, to the reminiscence of a semi-historical battle. In winning the sun Indra is said to have made wide space for his charioteer Kutsa (6, 20[5]). He is invoked to crush the fiends with Kutsa and to roll forward the wheel of the sun (4, 16[12]). In one passage Indra is said to have subjected other foes than Śuṣṇa to Kutsa, viz. Tugra, Smadibha, and the Vetasus (10, 49[4]).

Kutsa, whom Indra aided and loved (1, 33[14]), nevertheless sometimes appears as his enemy. Thus Indra struck down the heroes of Kutsa, Āyu, and Atithigva (2, 14[7]), harassed Āyu, Kutsa, and Atithigva (Vāl. 5[2]), delivered these three into the hand of the young king Tūrvayāṇa (1, 53[10]), or smote them to the earth for him (6, 18[13]). This seems to indicate the historical character of Kutsa. For a deity of light would naturally have been regarded by the Vedic poets as always a friend, and a demon of darkness always as a foe. Tradition also attributes a number of the hymns of the first and ninth book of the RV. to a seer Kutsa of the family of the Aṅgirases. BERGAIGNE, however, thinks that Kutsa is purely mythical, originally a form of Agni (or Soma), sometimes seeming to represent the sun. In the Naighaṇṭuka (2, 20) *kutsa* appears as one of the synonyms of thunderbolt (*vajra*).

B. Kāvya Uśanā[2]. The ancient seer Uśanā is mentioned eleven times in the RV. He is twice called a sage (*kavi*) and five times receives the epithet Kāvya. He is characteristically wise; for Soma uttering wisdom is compared (9, 97[7]) and, owing to his wisdom, is identified with Uśanā (9, 87[3]). Kāvya Uśanā established Agni as the *hotṛ* of sacrifice (8, 23[17]). He is said to have driven hither the cows, in the same verse in which Atharvan, the institutor of sacrifice, is referred to as having prepared the path of the sun (1, 83[5]). He was a protégé of Indra (6, 20[11]), who rejoiced with him (1, 51[11]) and who is represented as identifying himself with Uśanā as well as Kutsa and others (4, 26[1]). He was associated with Indra when the latter, along with Kutsa, vanquished Śuṣṇa (5, 29[9]). Uśanā also fashioned for Indra the bolt for slaying Vṛtra (1, 121[12]; 5, 34[2] cp. 1, 51[10]).

C. Several other ancient seers of a historical or semi-historical character are mentioned in the RV. Such are Gotama, Viśvāmitra, Vāmadeva, Bharadvāja and Vasiṣṭha[3] to whom, or to whose families, the composition of the second, third, fourth, sixth, and seventh books are respectively attributed. Agastya is another seer mentioned several times in the RV.[4]. More or less historical warriors of the olden time are king Sudās, Purukutsa and his son Trasadasyu, as well as Divodāsa Atithigva[5].

Even the most mythical of the ancestors of man or of particular families treated of in this chapter seem, with perhaps two or three exceptions, to have been either actual men of bygone days or to have been projected into the past to represent the first progenitors of actually living men. The deeds attributed to them are partly historical reminiscences, partly aetiological myths, and partly poetical creations. By association with the gods they are often drawn into participation in the mythological actions, such as the winning of the sun, on which the order of nature is founded. Most of what is told about the priestly ancestors, is intended to furnish evidence of sacerdotal art and power, which are therefore treated supernaturally. It is not likely that they represent powers of nature and are faded gods come down to earth[6].

[1] KHF. 54 ff.; BRV. 2, 333—8; PERRY, JAOS. 11, 181; PVS. 1, 24; GVS. 2, 35. 163 ff.; ZDMG. 42, 211; ORV. 158—60; JAOS. 18, 31—3. — [2] BRV. 2, 338—41; SP.AP. 281—7. — [3] Cp. BRV. 1, 50—2; OLDENBERG, ZDMG. 42, 203 ff.; OERTEL, JAOS. 18, 47—8. — [4] Cp. ZDMG. 34, 589 ff.; 39. 65—8. — [5] OLDENBERG, ZDMG. 42, 199—247; HRI. 111. — [6] Cp. GRUPPE, Die griechischen Culte 1, 298 ff.; ORV. 273—4.

V. ANIMALS AND INANIMATE OBJECTS.

§ 59. General Traits. — Animals enter to a considerable extent into the mythological creations of the Veda. There are still numerous traces surviving from a more primitive age, when the line dividing men from animals was not definitely drawn (§ 65) and gods might be conceived as having animal forms also. The higher Vedic gods themselves being anthropomorphic in character, the supernatural beings of the Veda which have an animal form belong to a lower order, being semi-divine only or demoniac according as the animal is useful to man, as the cow, or injurious, as the serpent. Moreover, just as man has attached to him various animals which are serviceable to him, so the great anthropomorphic gods are naturally surrounded by a celestial animal world of a similar character. Lastly, actual animals are in the ritual connected with mythological conceptions of the gods. They are symbolical representatives intended only as an instrument for the time being to influence the gods they in some respect resemble. This fetishistic point of view is probably the faded remnant of a more primitive identification of gods with visible objects. The part which such animal fetishes play in Vedic times is, however, no longer great, since the representation of deities by animals conflicted with the higher conception prevailing of the gods as mighty men dwelling in heaven and coming invisibly to the sacrifice.

§ 60. The Horse[1]. — A. Dadhikrā. Besides the celestial horses which draw the cars of the gods, various individual divine steeds occur in Vedic mythology. One of the most notable of these is Dadhikrā, who is celebrated in four rather late[2] hymns of the RV. (4, 38—40; 7, 44). The name is mentioned there twelve times, interchanging with the extended form Dadhikrāvan, which is found ten times. The name hardly ever occurs in other Vedic texts. Dadhikrā is so characteristically a steed that the word is given in the Naighaṇṭuka (1, 14) as a synonym of horse. He is swift (4, $38^{2.9}$. 39^{1}), being the first steed at the head of chariots (7, 44^{4}) and a vanquisher of chariots (*rathatur*), who speeds like the wind (4, 38^{3}). The people praise his swiftness and every Pūru praises him as he runs on a precipice as it were (ib. $^{9.3}$). He bounds along the curves of the paths (4, 40^{4}). He is also conceived as winged. For he is called bird-like, his wing being compared with that of a bird and of a speeding eagle (4, $40^{2.3}$). He is likened to a swooping eagle and even directly called an eagle (4, $38^{5.2}$). In one passage (4, 40^{5}) he is spoken of as the swan (*haṃsa*) dwelling in light, as well as the Vasu in the air, the priest at the altar, the guest in the house — all epithets appropriate to various forms of Agni.

Dadhikrā is a hero, smites the Dasyus, and is victorious (4, $38^{1-3.7}$). His adversaries fear him as the thunder of heaven, when he fights against a thousand; he wins booty in combats and the tribes cry after him in contests (ib. $^{8.5.4}$). Making himself (*kṛṇvāna*) a garland, he tosses the dust and scatters it from his brows (ib. $^{6.7}$). He belongs to all the tribes, pervades the five tribes with his power, as Sūrya the waters with his light, and observes the assemblies (ib. $^{2.10.4}$). Mitra-Varuṇa gave him, the victorious steed, like shining Agni, to the Pūrus (4, 39^{2} cp. $38^{1.2}$); they gave us the horse Dadhikrā as a blessing for the mortal (ib. ^{5}).

The steed Dadhikrāvan is praised when Agni is kindled at the dawning of Uṣas (4, 39^{3}). He is invoked with the Dawns (ib.^{1}. 40^{1}), who are prayed to turn to the sacrifice like Dadhikrāvan (7, 41^{6}). He is regularly invoked with Uṣas, nearly as often with Agni, less frequently with the Aśvins and Sūrya, sometimes with other deities also (3, $20^{1.5}$; 7, 44^{1-4}; 10, 101^{1}); but Dadhikrā is invoked first (7, 44^{1}).

The etymological meaning, being uncertain[3], cannot be said to throw any additional light on the original nature of Dadhikrā. The second part of the compound may be a by-form of the root *kṛ*, 'to scatter', and the word would then mean 'scattering curdled milk', in allusion to the dew or rime appearing at sunrise, according to ROTH and GRASSMANN[4], who both think that Dadhikrā represents in the form of a steed the circling ball of the sun. This view is supported by the fact that the deity with whom Dadhikrā is most closely connected is Uṣas, that the sun is often conceived as a steed or bird (p. 31) and that he is sometimes regarded as warlike (ib.). The statement that Dadhikrā was given by Mitra and Varuṇa might be connected with the notion of the sun being the eye of those deities. BERGAIGNE thinks that the name of Dadhikrā refers rather to lightning, but that he represents Agni in general, including his solar and lightning forms[5]. LUDWIG[6], PISCHEL[7], v. BRADKE[8], and OLDENBERG[9], however, agree in the opinion that Dadhikrā was not a deity, but an actual horse, famous as a racer or charger, which received divine honours.

It has already been remarked (p. 142) that Dadhyañc is allied to Dadhikrā in name, and possibly in nature, since he is spoken of as having a horse's head.

B. **Tārkṣya.** Nearly related to Dadhikrā is Tārkṣya, whose name is mentioned only twice in the RV. (1, 89^{6}; 10, 178^{1}). One late hymn, consisting of three stanzas (10, 178), is devoted to his praise. He is there described as a god-impelled mighty steed (*vājin*), a vanquisher of chariots (cp. 6, 44^{4}), swift, and speeding to battle. He is invoked as a gift of Indra. In the identical words applied to Dadhikrā (4, 38^{10}), he is said to have pervaded the five tribes with his power, as Surya the waters with his light. That he was primarily conceived as a steed is shown (v. ^{2}; 1, 89^{6}) by his epithet *ariṣṭanemi*, 'whose fellies are intact' (which in VS. 15, 18 appears as an independent name beside Tārkṣya and Garuḍa). In the Naighaṇṭuka (1, 14) the word *tārkṣya* occurs as a synonym of 'horse'. In one or two later Vedic texts Tārkṣya is, however, referred to as a bird; and in the Epic and subsequent literature, he is identical with the swift bird Garuḍa, the vehicle of Viṣṇu. It seems on the whole probable that Tārkṣya originally represented the sun in the form of a divine steed[10]. The word seems to be derived from Tṛkṣi, the name of a man, with the patronymic Trāsadasyava, once mentioned in the RV. (8, 22^{7}). This derivation leads FOY[11] to believe that Tārkṣya was an actual race horse (like Dadhikrā), belonging to Tṛkṣi of the family of Trasadasyu.

C. **Paidva.** Another mythical steed is that which the Aśvins are said to have brought to Pedu (1, 119^{10}; 7, 71^{5}) and which is therefore called Paidva (1, 116^{6}; 9, 88^{4}). The object of the gift was to replace an inferior horse, as may be inferred from the description of Pedu as *aghāśva*, 'he who has a bad horse' (1, 116^{6}). This steed is several times spoken of as 'white', *śveta* (1, 116^{6}, &c.). He is praiseworthy (1, 119^{10}; 10, 39^{10}; cp. 4, 38^{2}) and is to be invoked (1, 116^{6}) by men, like Bhaga (10, 39^{10}). He is compared with Indra (1, 119^{10}) and is called a 'dragon-slayer', *ahihan* (1, 117^{9}. 118^{9} cp. 9, 88^{4}), an epithet otherwise peculiar to Indra. He is a conqueror invincible in battles, seeking heaven (1, 119^{10}). Here again the evidence, as far as it goes, appears to favour the interpretation of the steed of Pedu as symbolical of the sun[12].

D. **Etaśa.** The word *etaśa*, which occurs a few times as an adjective meaning 'swift', more frequently signifies 'steed' in the RV. In the plural it designates the horses of the sun (7, 62^{2}; 10, 37^{3}. 49^{7}). It occurs about a dozen times as a proper name in the singular, always connected with the sun, often with reference to the wheel of the sun. Savitṛ is the steed (*etaśa*) who measured out the terrestrial regions (5, 81^{3}). The swift god Etaśa draws the bright form of the sun (7, 66^{14}). Yoked to the pole, Etaśa moves the wheel of the sun (7, 63^{2}); he brought the wheel of the sun (1, 121^{13}; 5, 31^{11}). Indra urged on the steed (*etaśa*) of the sun (8, 1^{11} cp. 9, 63^{8}). Indra helped Etaśa contending in a race with Sūrya (1, 61^{15}). It may be gathered from stray references to this mythical contest, that Etaśa being at first behind takes up the lost wheel of the sun and fixes it to the car of Sūrya; he has now gained the lead, and in the end Sūrya seems to concede to him the place of honour before his own car[13]. It appears to be impossible to suggest any satisfactory interpretation of this myth. It can, however, hardly be doubted that Etaśa represents the steed of the sun.

E. The Horse symbolical of Sun and Fire. That the horse is symbolical of the sun, is indicated by a passage of the RV. in which Dawn is said to lead a white steed (7, 77^{3}), and is suggested by another (1, 163^{2}) in which the sacrificial steed is said to have been fashioned by the gods out of the sun[14]. In a particular form of the Soma ritual, the horse also appears to be symbolical of the sun[15].

Agni, the swift and agile god, is often, as has been shown (p. 89), spoken of as a steed. In the ritual the horse is symbolical of Agni. A horse is stationed so as to look at the place where fire is produced by friction. When the fire is borne towards the east, it is deposited in the track of the horse which goes in front[16]. In the ceremony of piling the fire-altar, the horse is addressed with the verse: 'In heaven is thy highest birth, in air thy navel, on earth thy home' (VS. 11, 12). Such a rite is explained in the ŚB. as bringing Agni together with himself[17]. The same Brāhmaṇa speaks of lightning as a horse descended from the waters or the clouds (ŚB. 5, 1, 4^{5}; 7, 5, 2^{18}).

[1] Cp. Gubernatis, Zoological Mythology 1, 283 ff. — [2] E. V. Arnold, KZ. 34, 303. — [3] Cp. Wackernagel, Altind. Gr. p. 15. — [4] Roth, PW.; GW. s. v.; cp. HRI. 55, note 5. — [5] BRV. 2, 456–7; cp. Macdonell, JRAS. 25, 471; MM., SBE. 46, 282. — [6] LRV. 4, 79. — [7] PVS. 1, 124; cp. Hillebrandt, Vedainterpretation 17—18. — [8] ZDMG. 42, 447—9. 462—3. — [9] ORV. 71; SBE. 46, 282. — [10] PW.; BRV. 2, 498; Hirzel, Gleichnisse und Metaphern im RV. (1890) 27. 62–3; Griffith, Transl. of SV. 69, note 1. — [11] KZ. 34, 366—7. — [12] Cp. BRV. 2, 51—2. — [13] BRV. 2, 330 — 3; ORV. 169 f.; cp. PVS. 1, 42; GVS. 2, 161 ff. [14] Cp. AB. 6, 35 &c.; KHF. 52; Weber, IS. 13, 247, n. 3; Die Nakṣatra 2, 270. – [15] ORV. 81. — [16] ORV. 77. — [17] ORV. 80.

§ 61. A. The Bull. — Indra is in the RV. constantly designated a bull, a term applied much less frequently to Agni, and occasionally to other gods, such as Dyaus (p. 22). In the AV. (9, 4^{9}) a bull is addressed as Indra, and in the ŚB. (2, 5, 3^{18}) the bull is stated to be Indra's form[1]. In the Avesta the bull appears as one of the incarnations of Verethraghna, the Avestan Indra[2]. In one of the sacrifices of the Vedic ritual, a bull also represents the god Rudra[3]. A bull plays a part in the obscure and much discussed myth of Mudgala and Mudgalānī (RV. 10, 102)[4].

B. The Cow. — Owing to its great utility on earth, the cow naturally enters largely into the conceptions of Vedic mythology. The beams of Dawn are personified as cows[5], which draw her car (p. 47). The rain-cloud is personified as a cow, the mother of a (lightning) calf (pp. 10. 12). This cloud-cow is individualized as Pṛśni[6], the mother of the Maruts (VS. 2, 16), her milk (6, 48^{22}) and udder being several times referred to (cp. p. 125). The bountiful clouds are doubtless the prototypes of the many-coloured cows which yield all desires (*kāmadughā*) in the heaven of the Blest (AV. 4, 34^{8}) and which are the forerunners of the Cow of Plenty (*kāmaduh*) so often mentioned in post-Vedic poetry[7]. Iḍā, the personification of the offering of milk and butter, has a tendency to be regarded as a cow (p. 124). Aditi also is sometimes spoken of as a cow (p. 122). The gods are sometimes called cow-born, *gojātāḥ*. The most frequent application of the cow is, however, in the myth of the kine released from the rock by Indra (pp. 59. 61).

The terrestrial cow herself has already acquired a certain sanctity in the RV., being addressed as Aditi and a goddess, while the poet impresses on his hearers that she should not be killed (8, $90^{15.16}$ cp. VS. 4, 19. 20). The inviolability of the cow is further indicated by her designation *aghnyā*, 'not to be slain', which occurs sixteen times in the RV. (the corresponding masculine form *aghnya* being found only three times). In the AV. the worship of the cow as a sacred animal is fully recognised (AV. 12, 4. 5.)[8]. In the ŚB. (3, 1, 2^{21}) he who eats beef is said to be born again (on earth) as a man of evil fame; though beef is allowed to be cooked for guests (ŚB. 3, 4, 1^{2})[9].

[1] Cp. MS. 1, 10^{16}; TB. 1, 6, 7^{4}; Āp. ŚS. 8, 11^{19}. — [2] ORV. 76, note 2. — [3] ORV. 82. — [4] Last treated of by V. HENRY (with reference to his predecessors) in JA. 1895 (6), 516–48. — [5] Cp. GRUPPE, op. cit. 1, 77. — [6] Cp. ROTH, Nir. Erl. 145; PW. s v. — [7] KHF. 188. — [8] HRI. 156; cp. BLOOMFIELD, SBE. 42, 656. — [9] WVB. 1894, p. 36; HRI. 189; cp. WINTERNITZ, Hochzeitsrituell 33.

§ 62. **The Goat** &c. — In the RV. the goat is specially connected with Pūṣan as drawing his car (p. 35). It also appears there as a divine being in the form of Aja ekapād, the one-footed Goat (§ 27)[1]. In the the later Vedic literature the goat is several times connected or identified with Agni[2].

The **ass** appears in Vedic mythology mainly as drawing the car of the Aśvins (p. 50)[3].

The **dog**[4] is found in the RV. mythologically in the form of the two brindled hounds of Yama, called Sārameya (p. 173). This name indicates that they were regarded as descendants[5] of Saramā[6] (p. 63), the messenger of Indra. There is nothing in the RV. directly showing that Saramā was there conceived as a bitch, though in the later Vedic literature she is regarded as such and by Yāska (Nir. 11, 25) is described as the 'bitch of the gods' (*devaśunī*).

The **boar** occurs in the RV. as a figurative designation of Rudra, the Maruts, and Vṛtra[7]. In the TS. and TB. this animal appears in a cosmogonic character as the form assumed by the Creator Prajāpati when he raised the earth out of the waters. A later development of it is the boar incarnation of Viṣṇu[8].

In the later Saṃhitās the **tortoise** is raised to a semi-divine position as 'lord of waters' (VS. 13, 31)[9], or, as Kaśyapa, often appears beside or identical with Prajāpati in the AV., where he receives the epithet *svayambhū*, 'self-existent' (AV. 19, 53^{10})[10]. In the AB. (8, 21^{10}) the earth is said to have been promised to Kaśyapa by Viśvakarman. In the ŚB. Prajāpati is described as changing himself into a tortoise (7, 4, 3^{5}), in which form he produced all creatures (7, 5, 1^{1})[11]. This assumed form of the creator became in post-Vedic mythology the tortoise incarnation of Viṣṇu[12]. In the TS. (2, 6, 3^{3}) the sacrificial cake (*puroḍāśa*) is said to become a tortoise.

A **monkey** appears in a late hymn of the RV. (10, 86) as Indra's favourite, who is expelled for his mischievousness by Indrāṇī, but is finally restored to favour (§ 22, p. 64).

Frogs awakened by the rains are in RV. 7, 103 the objects of a panegyric as bestowing cows and long life, and seem to be conceived as possessing magical powers[13]. This hymn has, however, been interpreted by MAX MÜLLER[14] as a satire on Brahmans. BERGAIGNE interprets the frogs as meteorological phenomena[15].

[1] ORV. 72; SBE. 46, 62; Bloomfield, SBE. 42, 625. 664, who thinks Aja ekapād is undoubtedly the Sun, with reference to TB. 3, 1, 2^{8} ('Aja ekapād has risen in the east', &c.), a passage which, however, is not cogent for the Rigvedic conception. — [2] ORV. 78. — [3] WVB. 1894, p. 26, n. 2. — [4] Cp. Hopkins, The Dog in the RV., AJP. 1894, 154—5; Bloomfield, SBE. 42, 500. — [5] Cp. Whitney, Sanskrit Grammar², 1216. — [6] Op. cit. 1166 b; Wackernagel, Altind. Gr. § 52 a.; KRV. n. 149; ZDMG. 13, 493—9; 14, 583. — [7] Cp. KHF. 177—8; Entwicklungsstufen 136; IS. 1, 272, note; Hopkins, JAOS. 17, 67. — [8] Macdonell, JRAS. 27, 178—89. — [9] Cp. IS. 13, 250. — [10] Cp. SPH. 81. — [11] Cp. IS. 1, 187. — [12] Macdonell, JRAS. 27, 166—7. — [13] ORV. 70; Bloomfield, JAOS. 17, 173—9. — [14] ASL. 494—5; cp. OST. 5, 436. — [15] BRV. 1, 292 &c.; cp. HRI. 100—1.

§ 63. The Bird. — Birds figure largely in Vedic mythology. Soma is often compared with or called a bird[1] (p. 106). Agni in particular is frequently likened to or directly designated a bird[2], once being spoken of as the eagle of the sky (p. 89)[3]. The sun is also sometimes conceived as a bird (p. 31)[4], twice under the name of *garutmat*[5]. The fact that Viṣṇu's vehicle in post-Vedic mythology is Garuḍa, the chief of the birds, is probably based on the same notion (cp. p. 39). The main application of the bird in the Veda is as the eagle which carries off the Soma for Indra and which appears to represent lightning[6]. In the Kāṭhaka it is Indra himself who in the form of an eagle captures the Soma or *amṛta*. Similarly in the Avesta, Verethraghna assumes the form of Vāraghna, the swiftest of birds, and in Germanic mythology, the god Odhin transforming himself into an eagle, flies with the mead to the realm of the gods (p. 114)[7].

Ominous birds as well as beasts are occasionally connected with certain gods by whom they are supposed to be sent. Thus in the RV. the owl and the pigeon are spoken of as messengers of Yama (§ 77)[8]. In the Sūtras the owl is 'the messenger of evil spirits'; while the beast of prey besmeared with blood and the carrion vulture are called messengers of Yama[9]. In the RV. a bird of omen is once invoked to give auspicious signs (2, 42^{43}).

[1] Cp. Benfey, SV. glossary, s. v. *śyena*. — [2] Bloomfield, FaR. 152. — [3] KHF. 29. — [4] v. Bradke, ZDMG. 40, 356. — [5] GW.; HRI. 45. — [6] BRI. 11. — [7] ORV. 75. — [8] Cp. ZDMG. 31, 352 ff.; Bloomfield, SBE. 42, 474. — [9] ORV. 76.

§ 64. Noxious Animals. — These generally appear as demons or show demoniac traits. Demons are sometimes in the RV. referred to with the generic term *mṛga*, 'wild beast' (1, 80^{7}; 5, 29^{4}. 32^{3}). One demon who is mentioned three times (2, 11^{18}; 8, 32^{26}. 66^{2}) is called Aurṇavābha, 'Spider-brood'; another referred to only once (2, 14^{4}) is named Urana, 'Ram'.

The most common animal form applied in this way is the serpent[1] (*ahi* = Av. *azhi*)[2]. This is generally only another designation of the demon Vṛtra, who probably received his name (cp. § 68) as a formidable enemy of mankind enveloping his prey like a serpent in his coils[3]. The Vṛtra-slayer Indra, who is also called the serpent-slayer, is said to have slain the serpent (8, 82^{2} cp. 4, 17^{1}); the identity of Ahi and Vṛtra is clear where the terms interchange (1, $32^{1.2.7-14}$); and by the 'first-born of the serpents' (ib.$^{3.4}$) no other can be meant than 'Vṛtra, the most Vṛtra' (ib.^{5}). In several passages, too, the words are in apposition and may be translated 'the serpent Vṛtra'[4]. When Ahi is mentioned alone, the results of Indra's victory over him are the same as in the case of Vṛtra, the god causing the waters to flow, delivering the seven streams, or winning the cows[5]. The waters are also described as encompassed by the serpent, the action being expressed by the root *vṛ* (2, 19^{2}) among others. They are similarly said to be swallowed (√*gras*) by the serpent (4, 17^{7}; 10, 111^{9}). Ahi is armed with lightning thunder and hail (1, 32^{13}). He is bright, for the Maruts are called *ahibhānavaḥ*, 'shining like Ahi' (1, 172^{1}); and the term *ahi* is applied to Agni, who is described as a 'raging serpent, like the rushing wind' (1, 79[1])[5]. Soma is once besought to deliver an enemy to Ahi (7, 104[9]). The plural of the word is occasionally used to express a race of demons (9, 88[4]; 10, 139[6]), of whom *the* Ahi is the first-born (1, 32[3. 4]).

The serpent, however, also appears as a divine being in the form of Ahi budhnya (§ 26), who seems to represent the beneficent side of the character of Ahi Vṛtra.

In the later Saṃhitās the serpents (*sarpāḥ*) are found as a class of semi-divine beings beside the Gandharvas and others. They are spoken of as being in earth, air, and heaven (VS. 13, 6; cp. TB. 3, 1, 1[7]). They are often mentioned in the AV.[6], one hymn of which (11, 9) is sometimes interpreted as an invocation of certain serpent divinities[7]. In the Sūtras offerings to the serpents of earth, air, and heaven (AGS. 2, 1[9]; PGS. 2, 14[9]) are prescribed; serpents are satiated along with gods, plants, demons, &c. (SGS. 4, 9[3]. 15[4]; AGS. 3, 4[1]), and blood is poured out for them (AGS. 4, 8[27]). In this worship the serpent, owing to its hurtfulness, is naturally regarded as having a demoniac nature, which has to be propitiated. In a similar sense offerings are sometimes made to ants (KS. 116).

[1] Cp. BENFEY, GGA. 1847, p. 1484; GUBERNATIS, Zoological Mythology 2, 392—7; WINTERNITZ, Der Sarpabali, Vienna 1888. — [2] SP.AP. 257. — [3] Cp. SP.AP. 261. — [4] BRV. 2, 204. — [5] GRIFFITH, RV. Transl. 1, 133, note 1; MACDONELL, JRAS. 25, 429. — [6] WEBER, Jyotiṣa 94; PW. s. v. *sarpa*. — [7] Cp. BLOOMFIELD, SBE. 42, 631—4.

§ 65. **Survival of prehistoric notions.** — The primitive conception that man does not differ essentially from beast, has left a few traces in the form of a belief in beings of the werewolf order. These are represented by the man-tigers (VS. 30, 8; SB. 13, 2, 4[2])[1] and by the Nāgas, human beings in appearance but in reality serpents, which are first mentioned under this name in the Sūtras[2] (AGS. 3, 4[1]). It does not seem likely that the later serpent worship had any connexion with the myth of the Vṛtra serpent, but its development was probably due rather to the influence of the aborigines. For on the one hand there is no trace of it in the RV., and on the other it has been found prevailing very widely among the non-Aryan Indians. The Aryans doubtless found the cult extensively diffused among the natives when they spread over India, the land of serpents[3].

Similarly, there are possibly in the RV. some survivals of totemism or the belief in the descent of the human race or of individual tribes or families from animals or plants. Kaśyapa, 'Tortoise', the name of a seer (9, 114[2]) and of a priestly family (AB. 7, 27), is also frequently found in the AV. and the later Vedic literature[4] as that of a cosmogonic power nearly related to or identified with the Creator Prajāpati. In a passage of the SB. (7, 5, 1[5]) Prajāpati appears in the form of a tortoise (*kūrma*). Here it is remarked that, as *kūrma* is identical with *kaśyapa*, 'therefore men say: all beings are the children of the tortoise (*kaśyapa*)'. The RV. (7, 18[6. 19]) mentions as tribal names the Matsyas (Fishes)[5], the Ajas (Goats), and the Śigrus (Horse-radishes). As names of Vedic priestly families also occur the Gotamas[6] (Oxen), the Vatsas (Calves), the Śunakas (Dogs), the Kauśikas (Owls), and Māṇḍukeyas[7] (Frog-sons). The father of Saṃvaraṇa (a name occurring in RV. 5, 53[10]), from whom the kings of the Kurus claimed descent, is in the Epic called Ṛkṣa (Bear)[8]. HOPKINS, however, expresses a doubt whether the names of animals ever point to totemism in the RV.[9]

[1] Cp. the Man-lion incarnation of Viṣṇu. — [2] Cp. WINTERNITZ, Sarpabali 43. — [3] ORV. 69, note 2. — [4] PW. s. v.; IS. 3, 457. 459. — [5] Also mentioned in

Manu 2, 19. — 6 Superlative of *go*. — 7 See PW. sub vocibus. — 8 ORV. 85—6; BLOOMFIELD, JAOS. 15, 178, note. — 9 PAOS. 1894, p. CLIV.

§ 66. Deified Terrestrial Objects. — A. Besides the phenomena and forces of nature, mostly aerial and celestial, and the earth itself (§ 34), various natural features of the earth's surface, as well as artificial objects, are treated as deities in the RV. It is the worship of inanimate things chiefly regarded as useful to man[1]. It is not pantheistic, since each object is regarded as a separate divinity[2], but is rather fetishistic in its character.

Rivers personified as goddesses have already been dealt with (§ 33).

Mountains (*parvata*) are often in the RV. conceived as divinely animate, being invoked as deities nearly twenty times in the plural and four times in the singular. In this capacity they never appear alone, but only with other natural objects such as waters, rivers, plants, trees, heaven and earth (7, 34[23], &c.), or with gods like Savitṛ, Indra, and others (6, 49[14], &c.). They are invoked as manly, firmly fixed, rejoicing in plenty (3, 54[20]). Parvata is even three times lauded with Indra in the dual compound *Indrāparvatā* (1, 122[3]. 132[6]). The pair are spoken of as driving in a great car and are besought to come to the offering (3, 53[1]). Here Parvata seems to be a mountain god, conceived anthropomorphically as a companion of Indra.

Plants (*oṣadhi*) are also personified as divine. The whole of a long hymn of the RV. (10, 97)[3] is devoted to their praise, mainly with reference to their healing powers[4]. They are called mothers and goddesses (v. [4]), and Soma, to whom trees are subject, is described as their king. In another text a herb to be used medicinally is spoken of as a 'goddess born on the goddess earth' (AV. 6, 136[1]). An animal sacrifice is even offered to plants in order to remove their obstruction to the attainment of offspring (TS. 2, 1, 5[3]).

Large trees, called *vanaspati*, 'lord of the forest', are a few times addressed as deities either in the plural (7, 34[23]; 10, 64[8]) or the singular (1, 90[8]; Vāl. 6[4]), chiefly along with Waters and Mountains. Later texts refer to the adoration paid to large trees passed in marriage processions[5] (cp. p. 134).

The forest as a whole appears as a deity under the name of Araṇyānī, the jungle goddess, who is invoked in RV. 10, 146. Here she is called the mother of beasts, abounding in food without tillage; and the various uncanny sounds heard in her dark solitudes are weirdly described. The plant, tree, and forest deities, however, play a very insignificant part not only in the RV., but even in the AV. and in the ritual of the lesser domestic sacrifices; while in the Buddhist literature they seem to have been more closely connected with human life than any other lower deities[6].

B. Implements. Another group of inanimate objects susceptible of personification and worship is formed by various implements of sacrifice. The deification of these is by BARTH[7] called by the rather misleading name of ritualistic pantheism[8]. The most important of these objects is the sacrificial post, which under the name of *vanaspati* and *svaru* is deified and invoked in RV. 3, 8. The tree is here described as well-lopped with the axe, as anointed and adorned by priests; and the posts set up by priests are gods, and as gods go to the gods (vv. [6. 9]). In the tenth or eleventh verses of the Āprī hymns[10], the post is described as thrice anointed with ghee and being set up beside the fire is invoked to let the offering go to the gods. In other verses of the same hymns the sacrificial grass (*barhis*) is twice (2, 3[4]; 10, 70[4]) addressed as a god, and more frequently the doors leading to the place of sacrifice, as goddesses (*devīr dvāraḥ*).

The pressing stones (*grāvan*, also *adri*) are deified in three hymns (10, 76. 94. 175). They are spoken of as immortal, unaging, and more mighty even than heaven[11]. When pressing they are like steeds or bulls and the sound of their voice reaches to heaven. They are invoked to drive away demons and destruction, and to bestow wealth and offspring. In two verses of the RV. (1, $28^{5.6}$) the mortar and pestle are invoked to resound aloud and to press Soma for Indra.

The AV. ascribes divine power of the highest order to Ucchiṣṭa, the 'remnant' of the sacrifice (AV. 11, 7)[12] as well as to different sacrificial ladles[13].

Agricultural implements named Śuna and Sīrā, probably the ploughshare and the plough, are invoked in a few verses of the RV. (4, 57^{5-8}), and a cake is assigned to them at the sacrifice in the ritual (ŚB. 2, 6, 3^5).

Weapons, finally, are sometimes deified. The whole of RV. 6, 75 is devoted to the praise of various implements of war, armour, bow, quiver, and arrows. The arrow is adored as divine and is besought to grant protection and to attack the foe (vv. $^{11.15.16}$). The drum (*dundubhi*) is invoked to drive away dangers, foes, and demons (vv. $^{29-31}$); and a whole hymn of the AV. (5, 20) celebrates its praises[14].

C. Symbols. Material objects are occasionally mentioned in the later Vedic literature as symbols representing deities. Something of this kind (possibly an image) must be meant even in a passage of the RV., in which the poet asks, 'Who will buy this my Indra for ten cows? When he has slain his foes he may give him back to me' (4, 24^{10}; cp. 8, 1^5). References to idols[15] begin to appear in the later additions to the Brāhmaṇas and in the Sūtras[16].

The wheel is in various ritual performances employed as a symbol of the sun, as representing both its shape and its motion. It is thus used in the Vājapeya sacrifice[17], in the ceremony of laying the sacrificial fire, and at the solstitial festival[18]. In post-Vedic mythology, moreover, one of the weapons of Viṣṇu is a wheel (*cakra*)[19].

Gold or a firebrand was employed as a symbol of the sun, when drawing water after sunset (ŚB. 3, 9, 2^9); gold served the same purpose when the sacrificial fire was made up after sunset instead of before (ŚB. 12, 4, 4^6); and in piling the fire-altar, a disc of gold was placed on it to represent the sun (ŚB. 7, 4, 1^{10})[20].

A symbol must have been used, as at a later period, in the phallic worship which was known in the earliest Vedic period, as is shown by the occurrence in two passages of the word *śiśnádevāḥ*, 'those who have a phallus for their deity'. Such worship was, however, repugnant to the religious ideas of the RV.; for Indra is besought not to let the *śiśnadevāḥ* approach the sacrifice (7, 21^5), and he is said to have slain the *śiśnadevāḥ*, when he won the treasure of the hundred-gated fort (10, 99^3). In the post-Vedic period the phallus or *liṅga* became symbolical of Śiva's generative power and its worship is widely diffused in India even at the present day[21].

1 HRI. 166. — 2 HRI. 135. — 3 Cp. ROTH, ZDMG. 25, 645—8. — 4 Cp. DARMESTETER, Haurvatāt et Ameretāt 74—6. — 5 ORV. 252; tree-worship also appears in the Sūtras, where a newly married couple are said to bring offerings to the *udumbara* and to invoke its blessing: WINTERNITZ, Hochzeitsrituell 101—2. — 6 ORV. 259—61. — 7 BRI. 37, note. — 8 HRI. 135. — 9 Cp. OLDENBERG, SBE. 46, 12. 253—5. — 10 Cp. ROTH, Nir. XXXVI, Erl. 117—8. 121—4; ASL. 463—6; WEBER, IS. 10, 89—95; GRV. 1, 6; KRV. n. 126; OLDENBERG, SBE. 46, 9—10. — 11 HVM. 1, 151. — 12 OST. 5, 396; SPH. 87—8. — 13 OST. 5, 398. — 14 ROTH, FaB. 99. — 15 The allusion to idols of Agni, seen in RV. 1, $145^{4.5}$ by BOLLENSEN (ZDMG. 47, 586), is inconclusive. — 16 WEBER, Omina und Portenta 337. 367 f.; IS. 5, 149; KRV. note 79a; HRI. 251. — 17 WEBER, Vājapeya 20. 34 f. — 18 ORV. 88, note 4. — 19 v. BRADKE, ZDMG. 40, 356. — 20 ORV. 255—61. 87—92. — 21 v. SCHROEDER WZKM. 9, 237; HRI. 150.

VI. DEMONS AND FIENDS.

§ 67. A. Asuras. — Opposed to the beneficent gods is a body of malevolent beings called by various designations. Asura is throughout the Vedic literature the name of the celestial demons who are regarded as the regular adversaries of the gods in their mythical conflicts and who only rarely appear as present foes of men (e. g. AV. 8, 6⁵; KS. 87¹⁰; 88¹). The term, however, occurs only a few times in the RV. with the later sense of demon. It is there found only four times in the plural with this meaning. Indra is invoked to scatter the godless Asuras (8, 85⁹). Otherwise they are only mentioned in the tenth book, always as opposed to the gods in general. The gods, it is said, smote the Asuras (10, 157⁴). Agni promises to devise a hymn by which the gods may vanquish the Asuras (10, 53⁴). The gods are even said to have placed faith in the formidable Asuras (10, 151³). The word also occurs three times as the designation of an individual demon. Bṛhaspati is besought to pierce with a burning stone the heroes of the wolfish Asura (2, 30⁴). Indra shattered the forts of the crafty Asura Pipru (10, 138³) and Indra-Viṣṇu smote the 100000 heroes of the Asura Varcin (7, 99⁵). The sense of 'demon' is also found in the epithet *asurahan*, 'Asura-slayer', which occurs three times and is applied to Indra (6, 22⁴), to Agni (7, 13¹), and to the Sun (10, 170²). The older Rigvedic notion of the conflict of a single god with a single demon, mainly exemplified by Indra and Vṛtra, gradually developed into that of the gods and the Asuras in general being arrayed against each other in two hostile camps. This is the regular view of the Brāhmaṇas. A new and frequent feature of the conflicts constantly described in these works is that the gods are worsted at the outset and only win by artifice. The most notable illustration of this notion is the myth of Viṣṇu taking his three strides in the form of a dwarf on behalf of the gods[1].

In the Brāhmaṇas the Asuras are associated with darkness (ŚB. 2, 4, 2⁵)[2]. Day belongs to the gods, night to the Asuras (TS. 1, 5, 9²). They are, however, constantly spoken of as being the offspring of Prajāpati and as having originally been equal to and like the gods[3]. It is perhaps for this reason that malignant spirits are sometimes included by the term *deva* (TS. 3, 5, 4¹; AV. 3, 15⁵).

In the AV. and later *asura* means 'demon' only; but in the RV. the word is predominantly a designation of gods, and in the Avesta Ahura (= *asura*) is the name of the highest god. Thus the sense of 'god' is clearly the older. An attempt has been made to explain the transition from this meaning to that of 'devil', from national conflicts in consequence of which the Asuras or gods of extra-Vedic tribes became 'demons' to the Vedic Indian[4]. There is, however, no traditional evidence in support of this view. The explanation seems rather to be found in the following development within the Veda itself[5]. *Asura* as compared with *deva* has in its older sense a peculiar shade of meaning. It is especially applied to Varuṇa or Mitra-Varuṇa[6], whose *māyā* or 'occult power' is particularly dwelt upon[7]. But the word *māyā* in the sense of 'craft' is also applied to hostile beings[8] and is closely connected with the bad sense of *asura* (10, 124⁵. 138³)[9]. To the Vedic poets *asura* must therefore have meant 'possessor of occult power'[10] and as such would have been potentially applicable to hostile beings. In one hymn of the RV. (10, 124) both senses seem to occur[11]. Towards the end of the Rigvedic period the application of the word to the gods began to fall into disuse. This tendency was perhaps aided by the want of a general word to denote the higher hostile demoniac power and by an incipient popular etymology[12] recognising a negative in the word and leading to the invention of ***sura***, 'god' (first found in the Upaniṣads)[13].

B. **Paṇis**. — A group of demons of the upper air, primarily the enemies of Indra (6, 20[1]. 39[2]), secondarily also of his allies Soma, Agni, Bṛhaspati, and the Aṅgirases, are the Paṇis. In nearly all the passages in which these demons are named, their cows are either expressly mentioned (10, 108; 6, 39[2]) or alluded to as the treasure or wealth of the Paṇis (2, 24[6]; 9, 111[2]). There is a similar reference when Agni is said to have opened the doors of the Paṇis (7, 9[2]). In one passage the gods are described as having found in the cow the ghee hidden by the Paṇis (4, 58[4]). The Paṇis are comparatively powerful, for they are said to be surpassed in might by Indra (7, 56[10]) and not to have attained to the greatness of Mitra-Varuṇa (1, 151[9]).

The name occurs in the RV. about sixteen times in the plural, but is also found four times in the singular as representative of the group. Thus Indra or Agni-Soma are described as having robbed the cows from Paṇi (10, 67[6]; 1, 93[4]), or Soma is invoked to strike down the voracious Paṇi who is a wolf (6, 51[14]).

The word *paṇi* occurs with considerably greater frequency, and here oftener as a singular than a plural, in the sense of 'niggard', especially with regard to sacrificial gifts. From this signification it developed the mythological meaning of demons similar to those who primarily withhold the treasures of heaven[14].

C. The word *dāsa* or its equivalent *dasyu*, is also used to designate atmospheric demons. Its history is the converse of that of Vṛtra (§ 68). Primarily signifying the dark aborigines of India contrasted with their fair Aryan conquerors, it frequently rises to mythological rank in the RV. as the line between what is historical and mythical is not clearly drawn. This is especially the case with individual Dāsas, some of whose names even (e. g. Suṣṇa) lend themselves to a mythological interpretation, though others seem to be those of non-Aryan men (e. g. Ilībiśa)[15].

Thus both the singular (2, 12[10], &c.) and (mostly of *dasyu*) the plural (1, 101[5]) are frequently used to designate foes vanquished by Indra, sometimes beside the name of Vṛtra (6, 23[2], &c.). Hence Indra is sometimes called *dasyuhan*, 'Dasyu-slayer' (1, 100[12], &c.) and the combat is several times referred to as *dasyuhatya* (1, 51[5. 6], &c.). In favour of individual protégés Indra 'sent to sleep' (i. e. slew) 30000 Dāsas (4, 30[21]), bound a thousand Dasyus (2, 13[9]), or won cowstalls from the Dasyus for Dadhyañc (and) Mātariśvan (10, 48[2]). When Indra's aid is invoked against both Ārya and Dāsa foes (10, 38[3], &c.) or when he is spoken of as discriminating between Āryas and Dasyus or Dāsas (1, 51[8]; 10, 86[19]), terrestrial foes are undoubtedly meant. This is probably also the case when Indra fights against the Dasyus in favour of the Āryas (6, 18[3]. 25[2]). Owing to the Dāsas being so frequently taken captive by the conquering Aryans, the word *dāsa* comes to be used two or three times in the RV. (7, 86[7]; Vāl. 8[3]) in the sense of 'servant', 'slave', its ordinary meaning in post-Vedic Sanskrit[16]. On the other hand, the Dasyus who endeavouring to scale heaven are cast down by Indra (8, 14[14] cp. 2, 12[12]), the Dasyu whom he burnt down from heaven (1, 33[7]), whom he vanquished from birth (1, 51[6]; 8, 66[1–3]), or against whom he aids the gods (10, 54[1]), must be demons. This is also the case, when Indra attacks the Dasyu, scattering the mist and darkness (10, 73[5]), or wins the sun and the waters after slaying the Dasyus (1, 100[18]), and when the gods and the Dasyus are contrasted as foes (3, 29[9]). A demon must be meant by the Dāsa who is the husband of the waters (1, 32^{11}; 5, 30^{5}; 8, 85^{18}), which by his victory Indra makes the wives of a noble husband (10, 43^{8}). The seven forts of the Dāsas, which, like those of Vṛtra (1, 174^{2}), are called autumnal (6, 20^{10} cp. 7, 103^{9}), are doubtless atmospheric.

As the words *dāsa* and *dasyu* primarily mean 'malignant foe' and then 'demon'[17], it seems convenient to render them by 'fiend'. They are frequently added as a generic term to the names of individual fiends combated by Indra, being most commonly thus applied to Namuci (5, 30^{7-9}, &c.), Śambara (4, 30^{14}, &c.), Suṣṇa (7, 19^{2}, &c.), sometimes to Pipru (8, 32^{2}; 10, 138^{3}), Cumuri and Dhuni (2, 15^{9}; 7, 19^{4}), Varcin (4, 30^{15}; 6, 47^{21}), Navavāstva (10, $49^{6.7}$), once to Tvāṣṭra (2, 11^{19}) and to the dragon Ahi (2, 11^{2}).

1 MACDONELL, JRAS. 27, 168–77. — 2 HRI. 187. — 3 OST. 4, 52. 58—62; 5, 15. 18. 22. 230. — 4 Cp. BDA. 109. — 5 Otherwise BDA. 106. — 6 Op. cit. 120 ff. — 7 BRV. 3, 81 cp. GVS. 1, 142. — 8 BRV. 3, 80. — 9 AV. passim; cp. ORV. 164, note 2. — 10 ORV. 162—5; cp. DARMESTETER, Ormazd et Ahriman 269 f. The Indo-Iranian meaning was according to BDA. 86 'Herr' (lord). — 11 OLDENBERG, ZDMG. 39, 70, note 2. — 12 On the etymology cp. v. BRADKE, ZDMG. 40, 347—9. — 13 Cp. PW. s. v. *sura*. — 14 Cp ORV. 145; otherwise HVM. 1, 83 ff. — 15 Cp. WACKERNAGEL, Altindische Grammatik 1, XXII. — 16 Cp. 'Slave', originally = 'captive Slav'. — 17 Cp. AIL. 109—13.

§ 68. A. Vṛtra[1]. — Of the individual atmospheric demons by far the most important and the most frequently mentioned is Vṛtra, who is the chief adversary of Indra and for whose slaughter that deity is said to have been born or grown (8, 78^{5}; 10, 55). Hence the most distinctive epithet of Indra is *vṛtrahan*, 'Vṛtra-slayer'. This compound is analyzed in two passages of the RV.: 'May the Vṛtra-slayer slay Vṛtra' (8, 78^{3}) and 'Vṛtra-slayer, slay the Vṛtras' (8, 17^{9}). Indra's conflict with Vṛtra is also frequently referred to with *vṛtrahatya*, 'slaughter of Vṛtra' and sometimes with *vṛtratūrya*, 'conquest of Vṛtra'.

It has already been shown that Vṛtra is conceived as having the form of a serpent (§ 64). Hence he is without feet or hands (1, 32^{7}; 3, 30^{8})[2]. His head, which Indra pierces, is mentioned several times (1, 52^{10}; 8, 6^{6}. 65^{2}), as well as his jaws, into which Indra strikes his bolt (1, 52^{6}). His hissing or snorting is sometimes referred to (8, 85^{7}; 5, 29^{4} cp. 1, 52^{10}. 61^{10}; 6, 17^{10}). He has thunder at his disposal (1, 80^{12}), as well as lightning, mist, and hail (1, 32^{13}).

Vṛtra's mother is called Dānu and is compared with a cow (1, 32^{9}). This name seems to be identical with the word *dānu*, which is several times used as a neuter meaning 'stream' and once as a feminine to designate the waters of heaven[3]. The same term is applied as a masculine, apparently in the sense of a metronymic, to Vṛtra or the dragon (2, 12^{11}; 4, 30^{7}), as well as to the demon Aurṇavābha (2, 11^{18}), and to seven demons slain by Indra (10, 120^{6}). The regular metronymic Dānava is used five times to designate a demon combated by Indra and doubtless identical with Vṛtra. Indra cast down the wiles of the wily Dānava (2, 11^{10}), he struck down the snorting Dānava (5, 29^{4}), to release the waters (5, 32^{1}).

Vṛtra has a hidden (*ninya*) abode, whence the waters, when released by Indra, escape overflowing the demon (1, 32^{10}). Vṛtra lies on the waters (1, 121^{11}; 2, 11^{9}) or enveloped by waters at the bottom (*budhna*) of the *rajas* or aerial space (1, 52^{6}). He is also described as lying on a summit (*sānu*), when Indra made the waters to flow (1, 80^{5}), or as having been cast down by Indra from lofty heights (8, 3^{19}). Vṛtra has fortresses, which Indra shatters when he slays him (10, 89^{7}) and which are ninety-nine in number (7, 19^{5}; 8, 82^{2}).

There can be no doubt that the word *vṛ-tra* is derived from the root *vṛ*, 'to cover or encompass'[4]. Poets several times speak of Vṛtra as having encompassed the waters, *apo vavrivāṃsam* (2, 14[2], &c.) or *vavrī* (1, 52[6]), or as being an encompasser of rivers, *nadī-vṛt* (1, 52[2]; 8, 12[26] cp. 6, 30[4]; 7, 21[3]). These are clearly allusions to the etymology of the name. There is also evidently a play on the derivation when it is said that Indra 'encompassed the encompasser', *vṛtram avṛṇot* (3, 43[3]), or that in slaying Vṛtra he uncovered (*apa vṛ*) the prison of the waters (1, 32[11]. 51[4]). A similar notion is implied in a passage in which the (cloud) mountain (*parvata*) is described as being within the belly of Vṛtra and Indra strikes the streams, placed in a covering (*vavri*), down declivities (cp. 1, 57[6]). Vṛtra is also said to be an encloser (*paridhi*) of the streams (3, 33[6]).

It has been shown above that Indra's epithet *vṛtrahan* was understood by the Vedic poets to mean not only 'slayer of Vṛtra' but also as 'slayer of Vṛtras'. This plural, which is of frequent occurrence in the RV. and is always neuter, sometimes appears in passages mentioning the names of various individual fiends (7, 19[4]; 10, 49[6]). The result of Indra's conflict with the Vṛtras is the release of the waters (7, 34[3]) or of the rivers (8, 85[18]) which are 'encompassed', *vṛtān* (4, 42[7]). It is the Vṛtras which, as well as the fiends, he is to smite as soon as born (6, 29[6]) and to destroy which he has been produced by the gods (3, 49[1]). With the bones of Dadhyañc he slew 99 Vṛtras (1, 84[13]) just as he shatters the ninety-nine forts of Vṛtra (7, 19[5]).

The term Vṛtras, which is regularly employed with the verb *han*, 'to slay', also refers to terrestrial foes, as when Āryas and Dāsas are distinguished as two kinds of Vṛtras (6, 22[10]. 33[3]). There are, moreover, many passages in which it is quite as applicable to human enemies as to celestial demons. Then, however, it does not mean simply 'enemy', which is *amitra* (= *inimicus*) or *śatru* (cp. 6, 73[2]), but is employed with a side-glance at the demon Vṛtra, much as the English word 'fiend' in its present use, when applied to men, is suggestive of 'devil'. This relation of meaning is the converse of that in *dāsa* or *dasyu*, which first meant 'foe' and then 'fiend'. The use of *vṛtra* in the plural, as it is then always neuter, can hardly be derived from a generalization of the proper name Vṛtra, but must be based on an earlier meaning such as 'obstruction', then 'obstructor'. In the Avesta *verethra* means 'victory', which is, however, a secondary development of 'obstruction'.

In the Brāhmaṇas Vṛtra is interpreted as the moon, which is swallowed by Indra identified with the sun, at new moon[5].

B. Vala[6]. This word occurs about twenty-four times in the RV. and is regularly connected with the release of the cows by Indra or his allies, especially the Aṅgirases (§ 54). Vala is a guardian of cows, whom Indra rent when he robbed Paṇi of his cows (10, 67[6] cp. 6, 39[2]). He laments for his cows when taken by Bṛhaspati (10, 68[10] cp. 67[6]). He has castles which were forced open by Indra (6, 18[15]), fences which were pierced by Indra (1, 52[5]), and an unbroken summit which was broken by Indra (6, 39[2]). The TS. (2, 1, 5[1]) speaks of Indra having opened the hole (*bila*) of Vala and cast out the best beast in it, a thousand others following. There are, however, several passages in which the word is still unpersonified. The primary meaning in these cases seems to have been 'covering' or 'cave' (from the root *vṛ*, to cover). Thus the word is twice (1, 62[4]; 4, 50[5]) used in apposition with *phaliga*, the receptacle of the (atmospheric) waters (8, 32[25]) and appears in the Naighaṇṭuka (1, 10) as a synonym of *megha*, 'cloud'. Indra is said to have driven out the cows and opened (*apa var*) the *vala* (2, 14[3]) or to have opened (*apāvar*) the aperture (cp. 1, 32[11]) of the *vala* containing cows (1, 11^{5}). The PB. (19, 7) speaks of the cave (*vala*) of the Asuras being closed with a stone. In several passages the word may have either the primary or the personified sense (1, 52^{5}; 2, 12^{3}; 3, 34^{10}). It has probably the latter in Indra's epithet *valamruja*, 'breaker of Vala', which occurs immediately after *vṛtrakhāda*, 'destroyer of Vṛtra' (3, 45^{2} cp. 2, 12^{3}). The transition to the personified meaning appears in a passage (3, 30^{10}) in which Vala is spoken of as the stable (*vraja*) of the cow and as having opened (*vi āra*) for fear before Indra strikes. That the personification is not fully developed, is indicated by the action of Indra and others, when they attack Vala, being generally expressed by *bhid*, 'to pierce', sometimes by *dṛ*, 'to cleave', or *ruj*, 'to break', but not (as in the case of Vṛtra) by *han*, 'to slay'. The connexion of the verb *bhid* with the name of Vala is preserved in *valabhid*, which is a frequent epithet of Indra in post-Vedic literature. Here Vala is regarded as the brother of Vṛtra, and the two are associated in Indra's compound epithet *vala-vṛtra-han*, 'Slayer of Vala and Vṛtra'.

C. Other demon foes of Indra. Arbuda is mentioned seven times (twice oxytone, five times proparoxytone) in the RV., always as an adversary of Indra. He is a wily beast, whose cows Indra drove out (8, 3^{19}). Indra cast him down (2, 11^{20}. 14^{4} cp. 8, 32^{3}), trod him down with his foot (1, 51^{6}), pierced him with ice (8, 32^{2}) or struck off his head (10, 67^{12}). He is mentioned two or three times with Vṛtra (or Ahi) and appears to be cognate in nature to him[7].

Viśvarūpa[8], the son of Tvaṣṭṛ, is a three-headed demon slain by both Trita and Indra, who seize his cows (10, $8^{8.9}$). He is mentioned simply by his patronymic Tvāṣṭra in two or three other passages, in which he is described as rich in horses and cattle (10, 76^{3}) and is said to have been delivered over by Indra to Trita (2, 11^{19}; cp. pp. 61. 67). In the TS. (2, 5, 1^{1}) Viśvarūpa, though related to the Asuras, is spoken of as Purohita of the gods[9]. In the Mahābhārata (5, 22 f.) the three-heated son of Tvaṣṭṛ and Vṛtra are identical.

Svarbhānu[10] is a demoniac (*āsura*) being mentioned four times in one hymn of the RV. (5, 40). He is described as eclipsing the sun with darkness. Indra fought against his wiles and Atri put the eye of the sun (back) in heaven. This demon is also mentioned several times in the Brāhmaṇas. In post-Vedic mythology his place is taken by Rāhu. The name appears to mean 'withholding the light of the sun'.

Urana, a demon slain by Indra and described as having ninety-nine arms, is mentioned only once (2, 14^{4}).

1 BREAL, Hercule 87—99; BRV. 2, 196—208; ORV. 135—6; ZDMG. 50, 665 f. — 2 Cp. Agni in 4, 1^{11} cp. 2, 2^{3}. — 3 BRV. 2, 220; cp. OLDENBERG, SBE. 46, 123; according to PW. and GW. the words are distinct. — 4 Cp. PERRY, JAOS. 11, 135; Vṛtra = 'Restrainer' HRI. 94. — 5 HRI. 197. — 6 PW.; GW. s. v. *vala*; BRV. 2, 319—21. — 7 Cp. GW. — 8 Cp. HVM. 1, 519. 531—2. — 9 Cp. OST. 5, 230—2. — 10 IS. 3, 164 f.; LRV. 5, 508; BRV. 2, 468; OLDENBERG, ZDMG. 42, 213; HVM. 1, 464. 507, n. 1; LANMAN, FaR. 187—90.

§ 69. Individual Dāsas. — A. Śuṣṇa[1]. This fiend, who is mentioned about forty times in the RV., is the chief enemy of Kutsa, for or with whom Indra vanquishes him (4, 16^{12}; 5, 29^{9}, &c.). He is horned (1, 33^{12}). He has eggs (8, $40^{10.11}$), i. e. a brood (cp. 10, 22^{11}), from which it may be inferred that he is a serpent. He is described as hissing (*śvasana*: 1, 54^{5})[2]. He is six times spoken of as *aśuṣa*, a term which is otherwise only once applied to Agni and perhaps means 'devouring'[3]. He has strong forts (1, 51^{11}) or a fort (4, 30^{13}), which is moving (8, 1^{28}). Indra releases the waters in shattering Śuṣṇa's forts (1, 51^{11}), obtains the receptacle of waters (*krivi*) in smiting

Śuṣṇa (Vāl. 3[8]), or wins heavenly (*svarvatīḥ*) waters when he destroys the brood of Śuṣṇa (8, 40[10]). The name of Śuṣṇa is four times accompanied by the epithet *kuyava*, 'causing bad corn or harvest'. In the two passages in which this word is used independently as the name of a demon (1, 103[8]. 104[3]), it may refer to Śuṣṇa. The result of the conflict between Indra and Śuṣṇa is not always the release of the waters, but is also the finding of the cows (8, 85[17]), or the winning of the sun (cp. § 58). Śuṣṇa in his conflict with Indra moves in darkness, is a 'son of mist', *miho napat*, and a Dānava (5, 32[4]). In the Kāṭhaka (IS. 3, 466) Śuṣṇa is called a Dānava who is in possession of the *amṛta*.

The above evidence seems to point to Śuṣṇa having been a demon of drought from the beginning rather than a reminiscence of some historical human foe. This view is supported by the etymological meaning which must be either 'hisser' (from the root *śvas*, *śuṣ*) or 'scorcher' (from *śuṣ*, 'to dry').

B. Śambara. The name of this fiend occurs about twenty times in the RV. He is mentioned along with others, chiefly Śuṣṇa, Pipru (1, 101[2]. 103[8]; 2, 19[6]; 6, 18[8]), and Varcin. Indra was re-inforced by the Maruts in the fight against the dragon and Śambara (3, 47[4]). Indra shook the summit of heaven when he cut down Śambara (1, 54[4]). He found Śambara dwelling in the mountains (2, 12[11]) and struck him down from the mountain (1, 130[7]; 6, 26[5]). He struck down from the great mountain the Dāsa Śambara, the son of Kulitara (4, 30[14]). He struck down from the height Śambara, who thought himself a little god (7, 18[20]). Śambara is often said to have forts, ninety (1, 130[7]), generally ninety-nine (2, 19[6], &c.), or a hundred (2, 14[6], &c.). The word *śambara* once occurs in the neuter plural, meaning 'the forts of Śambara'[4]. These Bṛhaspati is said to have cleft and then to have entered the mountain rich in treasure (2, 24[2]). Indra vanquishes Śambara in the interest of Atithigva (1, 51[6]), but generally of Divodāsa (2, 19[6], &c.), and sometimes of both (1, 130[7]; 4, 26[3]). The two names are usually thought[5] to refer to the same person, but this is doubted by BERGAIGNE[6].

C. Pipru. This fiend, mentioned eleven times in the RV., is the enemy of Indra's protégé (Vāl. 1[10]) Ṛjiśvan, who offers Soma to Indra and is aided by him in the conflict (5, 29[11]; 10, 99[11]). Indra with Ṛjiśvan (1, 101[1. 2]; 10, 138[3]) or for him (4, 16[13]; 6, 20[7]) conquered Pipru. The fiend, who has the wiles of Ahi, possesses forts which are shattered by Indra (1, 51[5]; 6, 20[7]). When Indra slew the Dāsa Pipru as well as some other rarely mentioned beings, he shed the waters (8, 32[2]). When the sun unyoked his chariot in the midst of the sky, the Aryan found a match for the Dāsa: Indra acting with Rijiśvan, shattered the strong forts of the wily Asura Pipru (10, 138[3]). He delivered the wild beast (*mṛgaya*) Pipru to Ṛjiśvan, overthrew 50 000 blacks, and rent the forts (4, 16[13]). With Ṛjiśvan he drove out those who have a black brood[7] (1, 101[1]). Since Pipru is called an Asura as well as a Dāsa, it is doubtful whether he represents a human foe with a historical foundation, as some scholars think[8]. The name has the appearance of a Sanskrit word as a reduplicated derivative of the root *par* or *pṛ* (like *si-ṣṇ-u* from √*san*)[9], possibly meaning 'resister', 'antagonist'.

D. Namuci[10] is mentioned nine times in the RV. besides several times in the VS., TB., and ŚB. He once receives the epithet *āsura*, 'demoniac', in the RV. (10, 131[4]; ŚB. 12, 7, 1[10]) and is called an Asura in later Vedic texts. He is also spoken of as a Dāsa in three or four passages of the RV. (5, 30[7. 8], &c.) and once as 'wily' (1, 53[7]). In vanquishing Namuci Indra is twice associated with Namī Sāpya as his protégé (1, 53[7]; 6, 20[6]). Namuci is slain like several other demons (2, 14[5]; 7, 19[5]) or struck down (1, 53[7]) by

Indra. Indra destroyed a hundred castles, slaying Vṛtra and Namuci (7, 19^{5}). The characteristic feature about the conflict is that Indra twirls (√*math*) off the head of Namuci (5, 30^{8}; 6, 20^{6}), while he is said to pierce √*bhid*) that of Vṛtra. Otherwise Indra is described as having twisted (*vartaya*) the head of Namuci (5, 30^{7}) or to have twisted it off with the foam of water (8, 14^{13}). The Brāhmaṇas also refer to Indra's cutting off Namuci's head with the foam of the waters[11]. In one passage of the RV. (10. $131^{4.5}$) Indra is described as having drunk wine beside the demoniac Namuci, when the Aśvins aided and Sarasvatī cured him (cp. p. 87).

The etymology of the name is according to Pāṇini (6, 3, 75) *na-muci*, 'not letting go'. In that case it would mean 'the demon withholding the waters'[12].

E. Dhuni and Cumuri[13]. The Dāsa Cumuri is mentioned six times, with one exception always along with Dhuni. The closeness of the association of these two is shown by their names once appearing as a dual compound (6, 20^{13}). Indra sent them to sleep (2, 15^{9}; 6, 20^{13}; 7, 19^{4}), the same being said of Cumuri alone (6, 26^{6}). Along with Sambara, Pipru, Śuṣṇa, they were crushed by Indra, so that their castles were destroyed (6, 18^{8}). They were sent to sleep or overcome by Indra (10, 113^{9}) in favour of Dabhīti, who pressed Soma for him (6, 20^{13}) and who was rewarded by the god for his faith (6, 26^{6}). Without any mention of the two fiends, Indra is also said to have sent to sleep for Dabhīti 30000 Dāsas (4, 30^{21}) and to have bound the Dasyus for him without cords (2, 13^{9}).

Dhuni means 'Roarer' (√*dhvan*), the word being frequently also used in the RV. as an adjective in the sense of 'roaring, raging'. Cumuri on the other hand looks like a borrowed aboriginal name[14].

F. Varcin and others. Varcin is mentioned four times, always with Śambara. He is called an Asura (7, 99^{5}), but he and Śambara together are termed Dāsas (6, 47^{21}). Indra is said to have shattered the hundred forts of Śambara and to have dispersed or slain the 100000 warriors of the Dāsa Varcin (2, 14^{6}; 4, 30^{15}). The name appears to mean 'shining', from *varcas*, 'brilliance'.

Several others, whose names occur only once, are mentioned, along with Vala, Śuṣṇa, Namuci and other fiends, as vanquished by Indra. Such are Dṛbhīka, Rudhikrā (2, $14^{3.5}$), Anarśani[15], Sṛbinda (8, 32^{2}), and Ilībiśa (1, 33^{12}). They probably preserve a historical reminiscence of prominent terrestrial foes. For the last two of these names have an un-Aryan appearance; nor does it seem likely that original individual demons should have received names which do not designate a demoniac attribute like the appellations Vṛtra, Vala, and Śuṣṇa.

[1] KHF. 52 ff.; BRV. 2, 333—8; GVS. 2, 163 ff.; HVM. 1, 516; ORV. 155. 158—61. — [2] Cp. √*śvas* and *śvasatha* applied to Vṛtra. — [3] Cp. ORV. 159. — [4] Perhaps through the influence of the neut. pl. *vṛtrāṇi*. — [5] PW., GW., Oldenberg, ZDMG. 42, 210. — [6] BRV. 2, 342—3. — [7] Acc. pl. fem.: = waters, GW. s. v. *kṛṣṇagarbha*. — [8] LRV. 3, 149; BDA. 95; ORV. 155. — [9] BRV. 2, 349, but with the sense of 'filler' or 'rescuer'. — [10] LRV. 5, 145; BRV. 2, 345—7; Lanman, JAS. Bengal 58, 28—30; Sanskrit Reader 375b; Bloomfield, JAOS. 15, 143—63; Oldenberg, Göttinger Nachrichten 1893, 342—9; ORV. 161. — [11] Bloomfield, JAOS. 15, 155—6. — [12] Cp. Kuhn, KZ. 8, 80. — [13] BRV. 2, 350; ORV. 157. — [14] Wackernagel, Altind. Gr. 1, xxii. — [15] Cp. Johansson, IF. 2, 45; Perry, who treats of all the demons combated by Indra, JAOS. 11, 199—205.

§ 70. A. Rakṣases. — By far the most frequent generic name in the RV. for terrestrial demons or goblins[1], enemies of mankind, is *rakṣas*. It is mentioned (upwards of fifty times) both in the singular and plural, nearly always in connexion with a god, who is invoked to destroy or praised for having destroyed these demons. In two hymns of the RV. (7, 104; 10, 87) which deal with the Rakṣases, the much less common terms *yātu* or *yātudhâna* (strictly speaking 'sorcerer')[2] alternate with, and in some verses appear to be used in the same sense as, *rakṣas*. As the latter word designates evil spirits in general (especially in the YV.), *rakṣas* here perhaps expresses the genus and *yātu* the species[3].

These demons have the form of dogs, vultures, owls, and other birds (7, 104.[20–24]). Becoming birds they fly about at night (ib. [18]). Assuming the form of a brother, husband, or lover, they approach women and desire to destroy their offspring (10, 162[5]). They also lie in wait for women in the shape of a dog or an ape (AV. 4, 37[11]). Thus they are dangerous during pregnancy and childbirth (AV. 8, 6). They prowl around the bride at weddings, and little staves are therefore shot into the air to pierce the eye of the Rakṣases (MGS. 1, 10). The AV. gives the most detailed account of the appearance of the Rakṣases. They have mostly human form, their head, eyes, heart, and other parts being mentioned; but they have frequently some kind of monstrous deformity, being three-headed, two-mouthed, bear-necked, four-eyed, five-footed, fingerless, with feet turned backwards, or with horns on their hands (AV. 8, 6; HGS. 2, 3[7]). Blue and yellow or green demons are also spoken of (AV. 19, 22[4.5])[4]. They are further described as male and female, having families and even kings (AV. 5, 22[12]; HGS. 2, 3[7]); and they are mortal (AV. 6, 32[2] &c.).

The Yātudhānas eat the flesh of men and horses, and drink up the milk of cows (10, 87[16.17]). In order to satisfy their greed for flesh and blood the Rakṣases attack men, usually by entering them. Agni is besought not to let the Rakṣas enter (*ā viś*) into his worshippers (8, 49[20]), and the AV. describes a demon of disease, which flies about, as entering into a man (AV. 7, 76[4]). These evil spirits seem chiefly to have been regarded as entering by the mouth, especially in the process of eating and drinking (AV. 5, 29[6–8]), but also by other entrances (AV. 8, 6[3]). When once within they eat and lacerate a man's flesh and cause disease (AV. 5, 29[5.10]). The Rakṣases are also said to produce madness and take away the power of eloquence (AV. 6, 111[3]; HGS. 1, 15[5]). Human dwellings are invaded by them (KS. 135[9]). Some of these spirits are described as dancing round houses in the evening, braying like donkeys, making a noise in the forest, laughing aloud, or drinking out of skulls (AV. 8, 6[10.11.14]; HGS. 2, 3[7]).

The time of the Rakṣases is the evening or night (7, 104[18]).[5] In the east they have no power, because they are dispersed by the rising sun (TS. 2, 6, 6[3]). A falling meteor is regarded as an embodiment of a Rakṣas (KS. 126[9]). It is especially the dark time of new moon that belongs to evil spirits, as to the souls of the dead (AV. 1, 16[1]; 4, 36[3]).

The sacrifice is peculiarly exposed to their attacks. Thus the RV. speaks of Rakṣases that have produced taints in the divine sacrifice and of Yātus that throw the offering into confusion (7, 104[18.21]). They are haters of prayer (10, 182[3]). Agni is besought to burn them in order to protect the sacrifice from curse (1, 76[3]). The AV. contains a spell meant to nullify the sacrifice of an enemy through the wiles of Yātudhānas and of the Rakṣas (AV. 7, 70[2]). These evil spirits also obtrude themselves at the sacrifice to the dead in the form of the souls of ancestors (AV. 18, 2[28] cp. VS. 2, 29)[6]. In post-Vedic literature this notion of the Rakṣases (there often also called *rākṣasa*) disturbing the sacrifice is still familiar.

Agni, being the dispeller of darkness as well as the officiator at the sacrifice, is naturally the god who is oftenest opposed to them and who is frequently invoked to burn, ward off or destroy them (10, 87[3, 6], &c.)[7]. In this capacity he (as well as some other deities) receives the epithet of ***rakṣohan***, 'Rakṣas-slayer'.

These evil spirits injure not only spontaneously but also at the instigation of men. Thus the RV. speaks of the 'yoker of Rakṣases', *rakṣoyuj* (6, 62[9]), and refers to the Rakṣas and the Yātu of sorcerers (7, 104[25]; 8, 60[20]). One suffering from hostile sorcery drives away the Rakṣases by sacrificing to Agni Yaviṣṭha (TS. 2, 2, 3[2]), and in a hymn of the AV. (2, 24) demons are called upon to devour him who sent them.

As a designation of demons *rakṣas* is both masculine as an oxytone and neuter as paroxytone (in the latter case meaning also 'injury'). It may be derived from the root *rakṣ* to injure[8], which occurs in only one verbal form in the AV. (cp. also *ṛkṣa*, 'injurious'). It is, however, possibly connected with the ordinary root *rakṣ* to protect[9]. In this case it must have meant 'that which is to be warded off'. Bergaigne, however, thinks it may originally have signified (avaricious) 'guardian' of celestial treasure.

B. Piśācas. A third and important class of goblins are the Piśācas. The name occurs only once in the RV. as a singular in the form of *piśāci* (1, 133[5]). Indra is here invoked to crush the yellow-peaked (*piśaṅgabhṛṣṭim*) watery (*ambhṛṇam*) Piśāci and to strike down every Rakṣas. In the TS. (2, 4, 1[1]) the three hostile groups of Asuras, Rakṣases, and Piśācas are opposed to the three classes of gods, men, and Pitṛs. The Piśācas would therefore seem to have been specially connected with the dead. They are frequently spoken of as *kravyād*, eaters of raw flesh or corpses (AV. 5, 29[9] &c.), a term which may be regarded as a synonym of Piśāca[10]. Agni is besought to restore to the sick man the flesh which the Piśācas have eaten away (AV. 5, 29[5]). They were thus apparently a kind of ghoul. Piśācas are also spoken of as shining in water (AV. 4, 20[9]. 37[10])[11], or infesting human dwellings and villages (AV. 4, 36[8]).

A lesser group of demons, mentioned about a dozen times in the RV. and frequently in later Vedic texts, are the Arātis[12], a personification of illiberality (*a-rāti*) and, owing to the gender of the word, always feminine. A group of 'injurious' demons, the Druhs, both male and female, is referred to about twelve times in the RV. They are Indo-Iranian, their name occurring in the Avesta as *druj* (§ 5, p. 8).

Goblins of various kinds are usually conceived as forming an indefinite crowd, but are sometimes thought of as pairs. The latter constitute a class named Kimīdin, already mentioned in the RV. (7, 104[23]; 10, 87[24])[13].

The nature of the spirits which surround the everyday life of man consists in injury, and that of their various species in a particular kind of injury usually indicated by their names. They are as a whole unconnected with phenomena or forces of nature, seeming partly at least to be derived from the spirits of dead enemies[14]. Less personal than the demons mentioned above and probably due to a more advanced order of thought, are the hostile powers which are conceived as a kind of impalpable substance of disease, childlessness, guilt, and so forth, which flying about in the air produce infection, and to deflect which to enemies is one of the chief tasks of sorcery[15].

Some of these terrestrial spirits are, however, not injurious, but are regarded as helping at the harvest or weaving long life for the bride, while others, with Arbudi at their head, assist in battle by striking terror into the foe (AV. 3, 24. 25[1]; 14, 1[45]; 11, 9[12]).

1 BRV. 2, 216—19; ORV. 262—73. — 2 *Yātu* in the Avesta = 'sorcery' and 'sorcerer': Sp.AP. 218—22. — 3 Cp. ORV. 263, note 1. — 4 Hopkins, AJP. 1883,

p. 178. — [5] ORV. 269. — [6] Cp. CALAND, Altindischer Ahnencult, Leiden 1893, p. 3. 4. — [7] Cp. HILLEBRANDT, ZDMG. 33, 248—51. — [8] PW., GW. — [9] Cp. BRV. 2, 218; WHITNEY, Sanskrit Roots, s. v. *rakṣ* — [10] ORV. 264 note. — [11] Cp. ROTH, FaB. 97—8. — [12] Cp. HILLEBRANDT, l. c. — [13] WEBER, IS. 13, 183 ff. — [14] ORV. 60—2; cp. ROTH, FaB. 98. — [15] Cp. RV. 10, 103^{12}; KS. 14, 22; IS. 17, 269.

VII. ESCHATOLOGY.

§ 71. Disposal of the Dead. — In the Vedic hymns there is little reference to death. When the seers mention it, they generally express a desire that it should overtake their enemies, while for themselves they wish long life on earth. It is chiefly at funerals that the future life engages their thoughts. Burial and cremation were concurrent. One hymn of the RV. (10, 16) describes a funeral by burning, and part of another (10, 18^{10-13})[1], one by burial. The 'house of clay' is also once spoken of (7, 89^{1}). Fathers burnt with fire and those not burnt with fire (i. e. buried) are referred to (10, 15^{14}; AV. 18, 2^{34}). But cremation was the usual way for the dead to reach the next world. The later ritual (cp. AGS. 4, 1) practically knew only this method; for besides the bones and ashes of adults, only young children and ascetics were buried[2].

With the rite of cremation therefore the mythology of the future life was specially connected. Agni takes the corpse to the other world, the fathers, and the gods (10, 16^{1-4}. 17^{3}). He places the mortal in the highest immortality (1, 31^{7}). Through Agni, the divine bird, men go to the highest place of the sun, to the highest heaven, to the world of the righteous, whither the ancient, earliest-born seers have gone (VS. 18, 51—2). Agni Gārhapatya conducts the dead man to the world of righteousness (AV. 6, 120^{1}). Agni burns his body and then places him in the world of the righteous (AV. 18, 3^{71}). The Agni that devours the body (*kravyād*) is distinguished from the Agni that takes the offering to the gods (10, 16^{9}). Agni is besought to preserve the corpse intact and to burn the goat (*aja*)[3] which is his portion (10. 16^{4}). A goat is also immolated with the sacrificial horse to go before, as the first portion for Pūṣan, and announce the offering to the gods ere it reaches the highest abode (1, $162^{2.4}$. $163^{12.13}$). In the ritual (AGS. 4. 2; KSS. 25, 7^{10}) the corpse is laid on the skin of a black goat, and when an animal is sacrificed, it is a cow or a goat[5]. During the cremation Agni and Soma are also prayed to heal any injury that bird, beast, ant, or serpent may have inflicted on it (10, 16^{6}).

The dead man was supposed to go with the smoke to the heavenly world (AGS. 4, 4^{7})[6]. The way thither is a distant path on which Pūṣan protects and Savitṛ conducts the dead (10, 17^{4}). The sacrificial goat which precedes and announces the deceased to the fathers, passes through a gulf of thick darkness before reaching the third vault of heaven (AV. 9, $5^{1.3}$; cp. 8, 1^{8}).

The dead man was provided with ornaments and clothing for use in the next life, the object of the custom being still understood in the Veda (AV. 18, 4^{31}). Traces even survive (RV. 10, $18^{8.9}$) which indicate that his widow and his weapons were once burnt with the body of the husband[7]. A bundle of faggots (*kūdī*) was attached to the corpse of the departed to wipe out his track and thus to hinder death from finding its way back to the world of the living (AV. 5, 19^{12} cp. RV. 10, 18^{2}. 97^{10})[8].

[1] ROTH, ZDMG. 8, 467—75; cp. BRI. 23—4; v. SCHROEDER, WZKM. 9, 112—3; HOPKINS, PAOS. 1894, p. CLIII; CALAND, Die altindischen Todten- und Bestattungs-

gebräuche, Amsterdam 1896, § 49—50. — [2] ROTH, ZDMG. 9, 471; MAX MÜLLER, ibid. I—LXXXII; HRI. 271—3. — [3] *Aja* is by some taken to mean the 'unborn' (*a-ja*) part. — [4] HILLEBRANDT, ZDMG. 37, 521. — [5] MM., ZDMG. 9, IV. V. XXX. XXXII. — [6] Cp. Chānd. Up. 5, 10^3; Bṛhadār. Up. 6, 1^{19}. — [7] WEBER, IStr. 1, 66; HILLEBRANDT, ZDMG. 40, 711; ORV. 586—7. — [8] ROTH, FaB. 98—9; BLOOMFIELD, AJP. 11, 355; 12, 416.

§ 72. The Soul. — Fire or the grave are believed to destroy the body only. But the real personality of the deceased is regarded as imperishable. This Vedic conception is based on the primitive belief that the soul was capable of separation from the body, even during unconsciousness, and of continued existence after death. Thus in a whole hymn (10, 58), the soul (*manas*) of one who is lying apparently dead is besought to return from the distance where it is wandering. There is no indication in the Vedas of the later doctrine of transmigration; but in a Brāhmaṇa the statement occurs that those who do not perform rites with correct knowledge, are born again after their decease and repeatedly become the food of death (ŚB. 10, 4, 3^{10}). Besides *prāṇa*, 'respiration', and *ātman*, 'breath' (several times the express parallel of *vāta*, 'wind'), the usual terms denoting the animating principle are *asu*, 'spirit', expressing physical vitality (1, 113^{16}. 140^{8}), even of animals (AB. 2, 6), and *manas*, 'soul', as the seat of thought and emotion, which already in the RV. (8, 89^5) seems to be regarded as dwelling in the heart (*hṛd*)[1]. Many passages, especially in the AV., show that life and death depend on the continuance or departure of *asu* or *manas*; and the terms *asunīti*, *asunīta*, 'spirit-leading' refer to the conduct by Agni of the souls of the dead on the path between this and the other world (10, 15^4. 16^2)[2]. Funeral ritual texts never invoke the *asu* or *manas* of the deceased, but only the individual himself as 'father', 'grandfather', and so forth. Hence the soul is not a mere shadow, but is regarded as retaining its personal identity. Though men obtain immortality only after parting from the body (ŚB. 10, 4, 3^{9}), the corpse plays an important part in the myth of the future state, which is corporeal. For the body shares in the existence of the other world (10, 16^5; AV. 18, 2^{26}). A body, however, from which all imperfections are absent (AV. 6, 120^3), can hardly have been regarded as a gross material body, but rather as one refined by the power of Agni (cp. 10, 16^6), something like the 'subtile' body of later Indian speculation. An indication of the importance of the corpse in connexion with the future life, is the fact that the loss of a dead man's bones, which according to the Sūtras were collected after cremation, was a severe punishment (ŚB. 11, 6, 3^{11}; 14, 6, 9^{28}). In one passage of the RV. (10, 16^3) the eye of the dead man is called upon to go to the sun and his breath (*ātmā*) to the wind. But this notion, occurring in the midst of verses which refer to Agni as conducting the deceased to the other world, can only be an incidental fancy, suggested perhaps by the speculations about Puruṣa (10, 90^{13}), where the eye of the latter becomes the sun and his breath the wind. In the same passage (also in 10, 58^7) the soul is spoken of as going to the waters or the plants, a conception which perhaps contains the germ of the theory of metempsychosis[3].

Proceeding by the path which the fathers trod (10, 14^7), the spirit of the deceased goes to the realm of eternal light (9, 113^7), being invested with lustre like that of the gods (AV. 11, 1^{37}), in a car or on wings (AV. 4, 34^4), on the wings with which Agni slays the Rakṣases (VS. 18, 52). Wafted upward by the Maruts, fanned by soft breezes, cooled by showers, he recovers his ancient body in a complete form (AV. 18, 2^{21-6}), and glorified meets with the fathers who revel with Yama in the highest heaven (10, $14^{8.10}$. $154^{1.5}$). This is spoken of as a return home (*astam*: 10, 14^8). From Yama he obtains a resting place (10, 14^{7}), when recognized by Yama as his own (AV. 18, 2^{37}).

According to the ŚB., the ordinary belief is that the dead leaving this world pass between two fires, which burn the wicked but let the good go by[4]. The latter proceed either by the path leading to the Fathers or by that leading to the sun (ŚB. 1, 9, 3^{2}, &c.)[5]. In the Upaniṣads there are two paths for those who know the Absolute, the one (as a consequence of complete knowledge) leading to Brahma, the other to the world of heaven, whence after the fruit of good works has been exhausted, the spirit returns to earth for rebirth. Those ignorant of the 'Self', on the other hand, go to the dark world of evil spirits or are reborn on earth like the wicked[6].

[1] ORV. 525. — [2] The AV. is already acquainted with the breaths or vital airs familiar to post-Vedic literature: HRI. 153. — [3] BRI. 23. — [4] Cp. KUHN, KZ. 2, 318. — [5] WEBER, ZDMG. 9, 237; IStr. 1, 20—1; OST. 5, 314—5; SVL. 121; HRI. 206. — [6] HRI. 227.

§ 73. Heaven. — The abode where the Fathers and Yama dwell, is situated in the midst of the sky (10, 15^{14}), in the highest heaven (10, 14^{8}), in the third heaven, the inmost recess of the sky, where is eternal light (9, 113^{7-9}). The AV. also speaks of it as the highest (11, 4^{11}), luminous world (4, 34^{2}), the ridge of the firmament (18, 2^{47}), the third firmament (9, $5^{1.8}$; 18, 4^{3}), and the third heaven (18, 2^{48}). In the MS. (1, 10^{18}; 2, 3^{9}) the abode of the Fathers is said to be the third world[1]. The abode of the Fathers is in the RV. also spoken of as the highest point of the sun (9, 113^{9}). The Fathers are united with or guard the sun (10, 107^{2}. 154^{5}), or are connected with the rays of the sun (1, 109^{7}; cp. ŚB. 1, 9, 3^{10})[2], and suns shine for them in heaven (1, 125^{6}). They are connected with the step of Viṣṇu (10, 15^{3}), and pious men are said to rejoice in the dear abode, the highest step of Viṣṇu (1, 154^{5}). As Viṣṇu took his three steps to where the gods are exhilerated[3], so the sun follows the Dawn to where pious men offer sacrifice[4].

Stars are also said to be the lights of virtuous men who go to the heavenly world (TS. 5, 4, 1^{3}; ŚB. 6, 5, 4^{8}), and ancient men, especially the seven Ṛṣis, besides Atri and Agastya, are said to have been raised to the stars (TA. 1, 11, 1^{2})[5].

The RV. mentions a tree beside which Yama drinks with the gods (10, 135^{1}). This according to the AV. (5, 4^{3}) is a fig-tree where the gods abide in the third heaven (no mention being made of Yama).

[1] PVS. 1, 211. — [2] JAOS. 16, 27. — [3] Cp. MACDONELL, JRAS. 27, 172. — [4] WINDISCH, FaB. 118. — [5] WEBER, Nakṣatra 2, 269; KRV. note 286.

§ 74. The most distinct and prominent references to the future life are in the ninth and tenth books of the RV., but it is also sometimes referred to in the first. Heaven is regarded as the reward of those who practise rigorous penance (*tapas*), of heroes who risk their lives in battle (10, 154^{2-5}), but above all of those who bestow liberal sacrificial gifts (ib.[3]; 1, 125^{5}; 10, 107^{2}). The AV. is full of references to the blessings accruing to the latter.

In heaven the deceased enter upon a delectable life (10, 14^{8}. 15^{14}. $16^{2.5}$), in which all desires are fulfilled (9, $113^{9.11}$), and which is passed among the gods (10, 14^{14}), particularly in the presence of the two kings Yama and Varuṇa (10, 14^{7}). There they unswervingly overcome old age (10, 27^{21}). Uniting with a glorious body they are dear and welcome to the gods (10, 14^{8}. 16^{5}. 56^{1}). There they see father, mother, and sons (AV. 6, 120^{3}), and unite with wives and children (AV. 12, 3^{17}). The life is free from imperfections and bodily frailties (10, 14^{8}; AV. 6, 120^{3}). Sickness is left behind and limbs are not lame or crooked (AV. 3, 28^{5}). It is often said in the AV. and ŚB. that the deceased are in that world complete in body and limbs[1].

The dead are in the RV. often spoken of in general terms (*madanti, mādayante*) as enjoying bliss (10, 14^{10}. 15^{14}, &c.). The most detailed account of the joys of the life in heaven is given in RV. 9, 113^{7-11}. There are eternal light and swift waters; there movement is unrestrained (cp. TB. 3, 12, 2^{9}); there is spirit food and satiety; there joy, glee, gladness, and the fulfilment of all desires. The joys here indefinitely referred to, are later explained to be those of love (TB. 2, 4, 6^{6} cp. ŚB. 10, 4, 4^{4}); and the AV. (4, 34^{2}) states that in the heavenly world there is abundance of sexual gratification. According to the ŚB. the joys of the Blest are a hundred times as great as the highest on earth (14, 7, 1^{32-3}). In the heaven of the Blest, the RV. further says, the sound of the flute and of songs is heard (10, 135^{7})[2]; Soma, ghee, and honey flow for them (10, 154^{1}). There are ponds filled with ghee and streams flowing with milk, honey, and wine (AV. 4, $34^{5.6}$; ŚB. 11, 5, 6^{4}). There are at hand bright, many-coloured cows yielding all desires (*kāmadughāḥ*: AV. 4, 34^{8}). There are neither rich nor poor, neither powerful nor oppressed (AV. 3, 29^{3}). To the celestial life of the Blest in the Saṃhitās and Brāhmaṇas corresponds in the Upaniṣads the lower and transient bliss of the heaven of the gods which is followed by rebirth, only those who know the truth attaining to immortality and the changeless joy of unending peace by absorption into the world-soul[3]. Thus the life of the righteous dead in heaven was clearly regarded as one of indolent, material bliss, in which freed from all frailties they were united with the gods, and which was devoted to music, drinking, and sensual joys (such as the gods themselves are occasionally alluded to as indulging in: cp. 3, 53^{6}).

Heaven is a glorified world of material joys as pictured by the imagination not of warriors but of priests[4]. It is the world of the righteous (10, 16^{4}), where righteous and godly men, familiar with rites (*ṛta*) dwell in bliss[5]. There they are united with what they have sacrificed and given (*iṣṭāpūrta*)[6], especially reaping the reward of their pious gifts to priests (10, 154^{3} &c.)[7]. In the Brāhmaṇas it is said that those who sacrifice properly above all attain union and identity of abode with the sun (*āditya*) and with Agni, but also with Vāyu, Indra, Varuṇa, Bṛhaspati, Prajāpati and Brahmā (ŚB. 2, 6, 4^{8}; 11, 4, 4^{21}. 6, $2^{2.3}$; TB. 3, 10, 11^{6}). A certain sage is described as having through his knowledge become a golden swan, gone to heaven, and obtained union with the sun TB. (3, 10, 9^{11}). In the TS. (6, 6, 9^{2}) the notion occurs that a man by the performance of certain rites can reach heaven without dying (*jīvan*)[8].

One who reads the Veda in a particular way is said to be freed from dying again and to attain identity of nature (*sātmatā*) with Brahmā (ŚB. 10, 5, 6^{9}). As a reward for knowing a certain mystery a man is born again, in this world (ŚB. 1, 5, 3^{14}). Thus we have in the ŚB. the beginnings of the doctrine of retribution and transmigration. That doctrine (as well as the doctrine of hell) is not only to be found in the earliest Sūtras[9], but appears fully developed in the later Brāhmaṇa period, that is to say, in the oldest Upaniṣads, the Chāndogya, the Bṛhadāraṇyaka, and especially the Kaṭha Upaniṣad[10]. In the latter Upaniṣad the story is related of Naciketas, who pays a visit to the realm of Death and is told by the latter, that those who have not sufficient merit for heaven and immortality, fall again and again into the power of death and enter upon the cycle of existence (*saṃsāra*), being born again and again with a body or as a stationary object. He who controls himself reaches Viṣṇu's highest place. On the other hand, there is no hell for those not found worthy[11].

[1] References in OST. 5, 315; cp. AIL. 411; HRI. 205. — [2] At the sacrifice to the Manes music was performed, lutes (*vīṇā*) being played (KS. 84, 8). — [3] HRI. 239. — [4] ORV. 532. — [5] 1, 115^{2}. 154^{5}; 10, 15^{1}. 17^{4}. 154$^{2-5}$; AV. 6, 95^{1}. 120^{3}; VS. 15, 50. — [6] WINDISCH, FaB. 115—8. — [7] For references to the same idea in the AV. see OST. 5, 293, note 433; cp. IStr. 1, 20 ff. — [8] WEBER, ZDMG. 9, 237 ff.; OST. 5, 317; HRI. 204. — [9] HRI. 175. — [10] HRI. 145, note 4; cp. v. SCHROEDER, Indiens Litt. u. Kultur 245; GARBE in this encyclopedia 3, 4, p. 15. — [11] Origin of the myth, TB. 3, 11^{8}; cp. SVL. 10, n. 1; BRI. 78.

§ 75. **Hell.** — If in the opinion of the composers of the RV. the virtuous received their reward in the future life, it is natural that they should have believed at least in some kind of abode, if not in future punishment,[1] for the wicked, as is the case in the Avesta[2]. As far as the AV. and the Kaṭha Upaniṣad are concerned, the belief in hell is beyond doubt. The AV. (2, 14^{3}; 5, 19^{3}) speaks of the house below, the abode of female goblins and sorceresses, called *nāraka loka*[3], in contrast with *svarga loka*, the heavenly world, the realm of Yama (12, 4^{36}). To this hell the murderer is consigned (VS. 30, 5). It is in the AV. several times described as 'lowest darkness' (8, 2^{24} &c.), as well as 'black darkness' (5, 30^{11}) and 'blind darkness' (18, 3^{3}). The torments of hell are also once described in the AV. (5, 19) and with greater detail in the ŚB. (11, 6, 1)[4]; for it is not till the period of the Brāhmaṇas that the notion of future punishment appears plainly developed[5]. The same Brāhmaṇa further states that every one is born again after death and is weighed in a balance[6], receiving reward or punishment according as his works are good or bad (ŚB 11, 2, 7^{33}; cp. 12, 9, 1^{1}). This idea is also Iranian.[7] ROTH[8] favours the view that the religion of the RV. knows nothing of hell, the wicked being supposed to be annihilated by death. Evidence of the belief in some kind of hell is, however, not altogether wanting in the RV. Thus, 'this deep place' is said to have been produced for those who are evil, false, and untrue (4, 5^{5}). Indra-Soma are besought to 'dash the evil-doers into the abyss (*vavre*), into bottomless darkness, so that not even one of them may get out' (7, 104^{3}); and the poet prays that 'she (the demoness) who malignantly wanders about like an owl concealing herself, may fall into the endless abysses' (ib. ^{17}), and that the enemy and robber may lie below all the three earths (ib.^{11}). But such references are few and the evidence cannot be said to go beyond showing belief in a hell as an underground darkness. The thoughts of the poets of the RV., intent on the happiness of this earth, appear to have rarely dwelt on the joys of the next life, still less on its possible punishments[9]. The doctrine of the Brāhmaṇas is that after death, all, both good and bad, are born again in the next world and are recompensed according to their deeds (ŚB. 6, 2, 2^{27}; 10, 6, 3^{1}), but nothing is said as to the eternity of reward or punishment[10]. The notion also occurs there that those who do not rightly understand and practise the rites of sacrifice, depart to the next world before the natural term of their terrestrial life (ŚB. 11, 2, 7^{33}).

The idea of a formal judgment to which all the dead must submit, seems hardly traceable to the Vedic period. One or two passages of the RV. in which reference to it has been found[11], are too indefinite to justify such an interpretation. In the TA. (6, 5^{13}) it is said that the truthful and untruthful are separated before Yama, but that he acts in the capacity of a judge, is not implied[12].

That the belief in a hell goes back even to the Indo-European period, has been argued by WEBER[13] on the strength of the equation Bhṛgu = φλεγύαι[14] and the fact that the former is described in the ŚB. as sent by his father Varuṇa for pride to see the tortures of hell, and the latter are condemned for pride to undergo severe tortures in hell. But the similarity of the two legends is probably only a coincidence, as belief in the torments of hell seems to be a later development in India[15].

[1] Zimmer and Scherman, but Hopkins considers this conclusion pedantic. — [2] Roth, JAOS. 3, 345; Geldner, FaW. 22, thinks that hell is directly referred to in RV. 10, 10^{6} by the word *vṛci*. — [3] *Naraka* in AV. and Brāhmaṇas: Whitney, JAOS. 13, civ. — [4] Weber, ZDMG. 9, 240 ff. — [5] HRI. 175. — [6] Weber, ZDMG. 9, 238; OST. 5, 314—5. — [7] Jackson, Trans. of the 10th Or. Congress 2, 67—73. — [8] Roth, JAOS. 3, 329—47; cp. also Weber, ZDMG. 9, 238 f. — [9] Cp. AIL. 418 ff.; Scherman, Romanische Forschungen 5, 569 ff.; SVL. 122 ff.; KRV. n. 287a; ORV. 538 ff.; HRI. 147. — [10] Weber, ZDMG. 9, 237—43. — [11] SVL. 152—3. — [12] ORV. 541—2. — [13] ZDMG. 9, 242. — [14] KHF. 23; WVB. 1894, p. 3. — [15] Cp. Jaiminīya Br. ed. Burnell 1, 42—4; Oertel, JAOS. 15, 234—8; SVL. 5—8; Spiegel, Eranische Altertumskunde 1, 458; HRI. 206.

§ 76. The Pitṛs. — The blessed dead who dwell in the third heaven are called Pitṛs or Fathers. By this term are generally meant the early or first ancestors (10, $15^{8. 10}$), who followed the ancient paths, seers who made the paths by which the recent dead go to join them (10, $14^{2. 7. 15}$). They are connected with the (third) step of Viṣṇu (10, 15^{3} cp. 1, 154^{5}). Two hymns of the RV. are devoted to their praise (10, 15. 54).

Their different races are mentioned by name as Navagvas, Vairūpas, Aṅgirases, Atharvans, Bhṛgus, Vasiṣṭhas (10, 14^{4-6}. 15^{8}), the last four being identical with the names of priestly families, to whom tradition attributed the composition of the AV.[1] and of books II and VII of the RV. Among these the Aṅgirases are particularly associated with Yama (10, $14^{3. 5}$). The Pitṛs are spoken of as lower, higher, and middle, as earlier and later, and though not all known to their descendants, they are known to Agni (10, $15^{1. 2. 13}$). The AV. speaks of the Pitṛs as inhabiting air, earth, and heaven (AV. 18, 2^{49} cp. RV. 10, 15^{2}).

The ancient fathers themselves once offered the Soma libation (10, 15^{8}). They revel with Yama (10, 14^{10} cp. 135^{1}; AV. 18, 4^{10}), and feast with the gods (7, 76^{4}). Leading the same life as the gods, they receive almost divine honours. They come on the same car as Indra and the gods (10, 15^{10}). They are fond of Soma (*somya*: 10, $15^{1. 5}$ &c.) and sitting on the sacrificial grass to the south, they drink the pressed draught (ib.$^{5. 6}$). They thirst for the libations prepared for them on earth, and are invited to come with Yama, his father Vivasvat, and Agni, and to eat the offerings along with Yama (ib. $^{8-11}$. $14^{4. 5}$). Arriving in thousands they range themselves in order on the sacrificial ground (10, $15^{10. 11}$). When the Pitṛs come to the sacrifice, evil spirits sometimes intrude into their society in the guise of friends according to the AV. (18, 2^{28}).

The Fathers receive oblations as their food, which in one passage (10, 14^{3}) is referred to with the term *svadhā* as contrasted with *svāhā*, the call to the gods[2]; so too in the later ritual the portion of the gods at the daily pressings was strictly distinguished from that of the Pitṛs (ŚB. 4, 4, 22). They receive worship, are entreated to hear, intercede for and protect their votaries, and invoked not to injure their descendants for any sin humanly committed against them (10, $15^{2. 5. 6}$ cp. 3, 55^{2}). Their favour is implored along with that of the dawns, streams, mountains, heaven and earth, Pūṣan and the Ṛbhus (6, 52^{4}. 75^{10}; 7, 35^{12}; 1, 106^{3}). They are besought to give riches, offspring, and long life to their sons (10, $15^{7. 11}$; AV. 18, 3^{14}. 4^{62}), who desire to be in their good graces (10, 14^{6}). The Vasiṣṭhas collectively are called upon to help their descendants (7, 33^{1} cp. 10, 15^{8}); and individual ancestors, as Turvaśa, Yadu, and Ugrādeva, are invoked (1, 36^{18}).

The Fathers are immortal (AV. 6, 41^{3}) and are even spoken of as gods (10, 56^{4})[3]. In the Aṅgirases and similar groups the divine character is combined with that of ancient priests. Cosmical actions like those of the gods are sometimes attributed to the Fathers. Thus they are said to have adorned the sky with stars and placed darkness in the night and light in the day (10, 68^{11}), to have found the hidden light and generated the dawn (7, 76^{4} cp. 10, 107^{1}), and in concert with Soma to have extended heaven and earth (8, 48^{13}).

Just as the corpse-devouring Agni is distinguished from the Agni who wafts the sacrifice to the gods (10, 16^{9}), so the path of the Fathers is distinguished from that of the gods (10, 2^{7}. 18^{1} cp. 88^{15})[4]. Similarly in the ŚB. the heavenly world (*svarga loka*) is contrasted with that of the fathers (*pitṛloka*), the door of the former being said to be in the north-east (ŚB. 6, 6, 2^{4}), and that of the latter in the south-east (13, 8, 1^{5})[5]. The fathers are also spoken of as a class distinct from men, having been created separately (TB. 2, 3, 8^{2}).

[1] The attribution of the AV. to fire-priests, the Atharvans and Aṅgirases, is historically justified, as the cult of fire is still associated with the AV. in the epic: cp. WEBER, History of Ind. Lit. 148; HRI. 159. — [2] HAUG, GGA. 1875, 94; SBE. 42, 660; OLDENBERG, SBE. 46, 162. — [3] Otherwise HRI. 145, n. 1. — [4] Cp. Hiraṇyakeśi Pitṛmadhhsūtra, ed. CALAND, Leipzig 1896, p. 55; HRI. 145, n. 4. — [5] The South is in general the quarter of the Manes (ŚB. 1, 2, 5^{17}): this is Indo-Iranian, cp. KERN, Buddhismus 1, 359; CALAND, Altindischer Ahnencult, Leiden 1893, p. 178. 180; ORV. 342, n. 2; ZDMG. 49, 471, n. 1; HRI. 190.

§ 77. Yama. — The chief of the blessed dead is Yama. Reflexion on the future life being remote from the thoughts of the poets of the RV., only three hymns (10, 14. 135. 154) are addressed to Yama. There is besides one other (10, 10) consisting of a dialogue between Yama and his sister Yamī. Yama's name occurs about 50 times in the RV. but almost exclusively in the first and (far oftener) in the tenth book.

He revels with the gods (7, 76^{4}; 10, 135^{1}). Individual gods with whom he is referred to, are Varuṇa (10, 14^{7}), Bṛhaspati (10, 13^{4}. 14^{3}), and especially Agni, who as conductor of the dead would naturally be in close relations with him. Agni is the friend (*kāmya*) of Yama (10, 21^{5}) and his priest (10, 52^{3}). A god (10, 51^{1}) and Yama (who by implication are identical) found the hiding Agni (ib.^{3}). Agni, Yama, Mātariśvan are mentioned together as the names of the one being (1, 164^{46}). Yama is also mentioned in enumerations of gods including Agni (10, 64^{3}. 92^{11}).

Thus it is implied that Yama is a god. He is, however, not expressly called a god, but only a king (9, 113^{8}; 10, 14 passim), who rules the dead (*yamárājñaḥ*: 10, 16^{9}). Yama and god Varuṇa are the two kings whom the dead man sees on reaching heaven (10, 14^{7}). Throughout one of the hymns devoted to his praise (10, 14) he is associated with the departed fathers, particularly with the Aṅgirases (vv.$^{3.5}$). With them he comes to the sacrifice and is exhilerated (vv. $^{3.4}$. 15^{8}). Later texts (TA. 6, 5^{2}; Āp. SS. 16, 6) make mention of the steeds of Yama, which are described as golden-eyed and iron-hoofed. He is a gatherer of the people (10, 14^{1}), gives the dead man a resting place (10, 14^{9}; AV. 18, 2^{37}) and prepares an abode for him (10, 18^{13}).

Yama's dwelling is in the remote recess of the sky (9, 113^{8}). Of the three heavens two belong to Savitṛ and one to Yama[1] (1, 35^{6} cp. 10, 123^{6}), this being the third and highest (cp. § 73). The VS. (12, 63) speaks of him along with Yamī as being in the highest heaven. In his abode (*sádana*[1]) which is the home of the gods (*devamána*) Yama is surrounded by songs and the sound of the flute (10, 135^{7}).

Soma is pressed for Yama, ghee is offered to him (10, $14^{13.14}$), and he is besought to come to the sacrifice and place himself on the seat (10, 14^{4}). He is invoked to lead his worshippers to the gods and to prolong life (10, 14^{14}).

His father is Vivasvat (10, 14^{5}) with whom Saraṇyū is mentioned as his mother (10, 17^{1}). He is also several times called by the patronymic Vaivasvata (10, 14^{1}, &c.). This trait is Indo-Iranian, for in the Avesta Vivaṅhvant, as the first man who pressed Soma, is said to have received Yima as a son[3] in reward. In the AV. (18, 2^{32} cp. 3^{61-2}) Yama is described as superior to Vivasvat, being himself surpassed by none.

In their dialogue in the RV. (10, 10^{4}) Yama and Yamī call themselves children of Gandharva and the water nymph (*apyā yoṣā*)[4]. Yamī further speaks of Yama (v. 3) as the 'only mortal'. In another hymn Yama is said to have chosen death and abandoned his body (10, 13^{4})[5]. He passed[6] to the other world, finding out the path for many, to where the ancient fathers passed away (10, $14^{1.2}$). He was the first of mortals that died (AV. 18, 3^{13}). Here 'mortals' can only mean 'men', though later even gods are spoken of as mortal[7]. As first and oldest of the dead he would easily be regarded as the chief of the dead that followed him[8]. He is called 'lord of settlers' (*viśpati*)[9], 'our father' (10, 135^{1}). Through Yama men come in later texts to be described as descendants of Vivasvān ādityaḥ[10] (TS. 6, 5, 6^{2} cp. ŚB. 3, 1, 3^{4}; RV. 1, 105^{9}). Even in the RV. Yama seems to be connected with the sun; for the heavenly courser (the sun) 'given by Yama' probably means the solar abode granted by Yama to those who become immortal (1, 163^{2} cp. 83^{5}).

Death is the path of Yama (1, 38^{5}) and once (1, 165^{4}; cp. MS. 2, 5^{6}; AV. 6, 28^{3}. 93^{1}) he appears to be identified with death (*mṛtyu*)[11]. Yama's foot-fetter (*paḍbīśa*) is spoken of as parallel to the bond of Varuṇa[12] (10, 97^{16}). Owing to such traits and also to his messengers, Yama must to a certain extent have been an object of fear in the RV. But in the AV. and the later mythology Yama, being more closely associated with the terrors of death, came to be the god of death (though even in the Epic his sphere is by no means limited to hell)[13]. In the later Saṃhitās Yama is mentioned beside Antaka, the Ender, Mṛtyu, Death (VS. 39, 13), and Nirṛti, Decease (AV. 6, 29^{3}; MS. 2, 5^{6}), and Mṛtyu is his messenger (AV. 5, 30^{12}; 18, 2^{27}, &c.). In the AV. Death is said to be the lord of men, Yama of the Manes (AV. 5, 24^{13-4}), and Sleep comes from Yama's realm (19, 56^{1} &c.).

The word *yamá* has also the appellative meaning of 'twin'[14], in which sense it occurs several times in the RV. (generally in the dual masculine or feminine), while *yáma*, which is found a few times in the RV., means 'rein' or guide'. Yamá actually is a twin with Yamī in the RV. (10, 10)[15]. The sense of 'twin' also seems to belong to Yima in the Avesta (Yasna 30, 3). A sister of Yima is mentioned, not in the Avesta, but in the later literature[16] only, as Yimeh, who with her brother produces the first human couple. At a later period of Indian literature, when Yama had become the god of death who punishes the wicked, the name was understood to be derived from *yam*, 'to restrain'[17], but this derivation is not in keeping with the ideas of the Vedic age.

A bird, either the owl (*ulūka*) or the pigeon (*kapota*), is said to be the messenger (10, 165^{4} cp. 123^{6})[18] of Yama apparently identified with death. The messenger of Yama and of death would therefore appear to be the same (AV. 8, 8^{11}). Yama's regular messengers, however, of whom a fuller account is given (10, 14^{10-12}), are two dogs. They are four-eyed, broad-nosed, brindled (*śabala*), brown (*udumbala*), sons of Saramā (*sārameya*). They are guardians that guard the path (10, 14^{11}) or sit on the path (AV. 18, 2^{12}). The dead man is exhorted to hasten straight past these two dogs and to join the fathers who rejoice with Yama (10, 14^{10}); and Yama is besought to deliver him to them and to grant him welfare and freedom from disease. Delighting in lives (*asutṛp*) they watch men and wander about among the peoples as Yama's messengers. They are entreated to grant continued enjoyment of the light of the sun. Their functions therefore seem to consist in tracking out among men those who are to die, and in keeping guard on the path over those who enter the realm of Yama. In the Avesta a four-eyed yellow-eared dog keeps watch at the head of the Cinvaṭ bridge[19], which leads from this world to the next, and with his barking scares away the fiend from the souls of the holy ones, lest he should drag them to hell[20]. There does not seem to be sufficient evidence for supposing that the two dogs of Yama were regarded as keeping out the souls of the wicked, though it is quite possible that they were so regarded[21]. If, however. RV. 7, 55^{2-5} is rightly interpreted by AUFRECHT[22], the object of the dogs was to exclude the wicked. In the AV. the messengers of Yama, sent by him among men, are spoken of both in the plural (AV. 8, 2^{11}. 8^{11}) and the dual (AV. 5, 30^{6}). Of the two dogs one is described as *śabala*, 'brindled' and the other as *śyāma*, 'dark' (AV. 8, 1^{9}). The word *śabala* has been identified with Κέρβερος[23], but this equation has been called in question[24]. BERGAIGNE (1, 93) thinks the two dogs are simply another form of Yama (as fire) and Yamī; and the trait of the later mythology, which represents Yama as coming to fetch the dead himself, is regarded by him as primary (1, 92). BLOOMFIELD[25] identifies Yama's two dogs with sun and moon[26].

The most probable conclusion to be drawn from all the available evidence seems to be, that Yama represents a mythological type found among the most diverse peoples, that of the chief of the souls of the departed. This would naturally follow from his being the mythical first father of mankind and the first of those that died. The myth of the primeval twins that produced the human race, Yama and Yamī = Yima and Yimeh[27], seems to be Indo-Iranian. The attempt to clear Yama of the guilt of incest in RV. 10, 10, shows that the belief in that incest already existed[28]. Yama himself may have been regarded in the Indo-Iranian period as a king of a golden age, since in the Avesta he is the ruler of an earthly[29], and in RV. that of a heavenly paradise. That Yama was originally conceived as a man, is the view of ROTH and other scholars[30]. E. H. MEYER, thinking Yamī to be a later creation like Indrāṇī and others, believes that Yama, the twin, originally represented the soul as the *alter ego*[31]. A number of other scholars believe that Yama originally represented a phenomenon of nature. Some think he was a form of Agni[32], the sun[33], the parting day[34], or the setting sun and thus god of the dead[35]. HILLEBRANDT[36] thinks Yama is the moon, in which dying is typical, and thus the mortal child of the sun and closely connected with the Manes. He considers him, however, to have been a moon-god in the Indo-Iranian period only, but no longer so in either the Avesta or the Veda, where he is merely king of a terrestrial paradise or of the realm of the Blest.

[1] By LRV. 4, 134 regarded as a hell. — [2] This abode (also AV. 2, 12^{7}; 18 2^{56}. 3^{70}), which seems always to mean the world of Yama or the place of burial TA. 6, 7, 2^{c} cp. RV. 10, 18^{13}) is understood by PVS. 1, 242 to refer to a 'chapel of Yama'. A *harmya* of Yama, spoken of in AV. 18, 4^{55}, is understood by EHNI

to mean 'tomb' (cp. SVL. 138). — [3] Cp. Roth, ZDMG. 2, 218. — [4] MM., with Sāyaṇa, regards these two as identical with Vivasvat and Saraṇyū. — [5] The interpretation is doubtful, cp. SVL. 146. — [6] Cp. Roth, Nir. Erl. 138; SVL. 113. — [7] HRI. 128. — [8] KHF. 21; SVL. 137. — [9] *Viśpati* is often said of Agni, once or twice of Indra and Varuṇa. — [10] Cp. Roth, IS. 14, 393. — [11] But the passage may mean 'Yama (and) Death'. — [12] Cp. Bloomfield, AJP. 11, 354 5. — [13] SVL. 155. — [14] Op. cit. 142, note 1. — [15] Yama and Yamī mentioned together as in heaven: TS. 4, 2, 5[3]; VS. 12, 63; ŚB. 7, 2, 1[10]; TA. 6, 4[2]. — [16] Spiegel, Eranische Altertumskunde 1, 527. — [17] This is also the explanation of Grassmann, KZ. 11, 13; Leumann, KZ. 32, 301. — [18] SVL. 130, note 3. — [19] There is no reason to assume such a bridge in RV. 9, 41[2] (cp. SVL. 110) nor a river (Weber, Indische Skizzen 10) in RV. 10, 63[10] (cp. SVL. 111). — [20] SBE. 4[2], lxxiv. — [21] AIL. 419; SVL. 127. 152; ORV. 538. — [22] IS. 4, 341 ff.; cp. AIL. 421; KRV. note 274. — [23] Benfey, Vedica und Verwandtes 149—64; Kuhn, KZ. 2, 314; Weber, IS. 2, 298; MM., Chips 4[2], 250; LSL. (1891), 2, 595; Selected Essays (1881), 1, 494; KRV. note 274a; van den Gheyn, Cerbère, Brussels 1883. — [24] Cp. Rohde, Psyche 1, 280, note 1. — [25] JAOS. 1893, p. 163—72. — [26] Kaṭh. 37, 14 (MS. p. 101, note 2), Kauṣīt. Br. 11, 9 (= day and night); ŚB. 11, 1, 5[1] (moon a heavenly dog); on the dogs of Yama cp. also Rājendralāla Mitra, PRASB. May 1881, pp. 94. 96; Indo-Aryans, Calcutta 1881, 2, 156—65; Sp.AP. 230—40; HVM. 1, 225. 510—1; Casartelli, Dog of Death, BOR. 4, 269 f. — [27] Sp.AP. 246. — [28] Roth, JAOS. 3, 335; Darmesteter, Ormazd et Ahriman 106. — [29] Roth, ZDMG. 4, 420; on traces of Yima having been the first man in the Avesta, cp. SVL. 148 n. 1. — [30] Roth, ZDMG. 4, 425 ff.; IS. 14, 392; Scherman, Festschrift für K. Hofman, Erlangen 1890, p. 573 ff.; Hopkins, PAOS. May 1881. — [31] Indogermanische Mythen 1, 229. 232. — [32] KHF. 208; BRV. 1, 89; cp. Weber, Rājasūya 15, n. 1; YN. 12, 10 (Yama = lightning Agni, Yamī = voice of thunder); SVL. 132, n. 2. — [33] BRI. 22—3; Ehni, Die urspr. Gotth. d. ved. Yama, p. 26 &c. — [34] WVB. 1894, p. 1 (Yamī = night). — [35] MM., LSL. 2, 634—7; India 224; AR. 297—8; Bergaigne, Manuel Védique 283 (sun that has set). — [36] HVM. 1, 394 ff.; IF. 1, 7; also HVBP. 43.

On this chapter cp. also Roth, ZDMG. 4, 417—33; JAOS. 342—5; Whitney, JAOS. 3, 327—8; 13, ciii—viii; OLS. 1, 46—63; Westergaard, IS. 3, 402—40; OST. 5, 284—335; Donner, Piṇḍapitṛyajña, 10—14. 28; AIL. 408—22; BRV. 1, 85—94; 2, 96; KRV. 69—71; Sp. AP. 243—56; Lanman, Sanskrit Reader 377—85; SVL. 122—61; HVM. 1, 489—513; ZDMG. 48, 421; Ehni, Der vedische Mythus des Yama, Strassburg 1890; Die ursprüngliche Gottheit des vedischen Yama, Leipzig 1896; Hopkins, PAOS. 1891, xciv—v; HRI. 128—50. 204—7; MM., PsR. 177—207; ORV. 524—43; SBE. 46, 29; Jackson, JAOS. 17, 185.

LIST OF ABBREVIATIONS.

AB. = Aitareya Brâhmaṇa.
AF. = Arische Forschungen.
AGS. = Âśvalâyana Gṛhya Sûtra.
AIL. = ZIMMER's Altindisches Leben.
AJP. = American Journal of Philology.
Âp. = Âpastamba.
AR. = MAX MÜLLER's Anthropological Religion.
ASL. = MAX MÜLLER's History of Ancient Sanskrit Literature.
AŚS. = Âśvalâyana Śrauta Sûtra.
AV. = Atharvaveda.
BB. = BEZZENBERGER's Beiträge.
BDA. = BRADKE, Dyaus Asura.
BOR. = Babylonian and Oriental Record.
Br. = Brâhmaṇa.
BRV. = BERGAIGNE, La Religion Védique.
Dh. S. = Dharma Sûtra.
DPV. = DEUSSEN, Philosophie des Veda.
FaB. = Festgruss an BÖHTLINGK.
FaR. = Festgruss an ROTH.
FaW. = Festschrift an WEBER (Gurupûjâkaumudî).
GGA. = Göttinger Gelehrte Anzeigen.
GGH. = SCHROEDER's Griechische Götter und Heroen.
GKR. = GELDNER, KAEGI, ROTH, Siebenzig Lieder des Rigveda.
GRV. = GRASSMANN's Translation of the Rigveda.
GS. = Gṛhya Sûtra.
GVS. = GELDNER, Vedische Studien.
GW. = GRASSMANN, Wörterbuch (Rigveda Lexicon).
HGS. = Hiraṇyakeśi Gṛhya Sûtra.
HRI. = HOPKINS, Religions of India.
HVBP. = HARDY, Vedisch-brahmanische Periode.
HVM. = HILLEBRANDT, Vedische Mythologie.
IF. = Indogermanische Forschungen.
IS. = Indische Studien.
IStr. = Indische Streifen.
JA. = Journal Asiatique.
JAOS. = Journal of the American Oriental Society.
JRAS. = Journal of the Royal Asiatic Society.
Kauś. S. = Kauśika Sûtra.
KHF. = KUHN, Herabkunft des Feuers und des Göttertranks.
KRV. = KAEGI, Der Rigveda (quoted from ARROWSMITH's translation).
KS. = Kauśika Sûtra.
KŚS. = Kâtyâyana Śrauta Sûtra.
KZ. = KUHN's Zeitschrift.
LRF. = LUDWIG, Ueber die neuesten arbeiten auf dem gebiete der Ṛgveda-forschung (1893).
LRV. = LUDWIG, Rigveda Translation.
LSL. = MAX MÜLLER's Lectures on the Science of Language (ed. 1891).
MGS. = Mânava Gṛhya Sûtra.
MM. = MAX MÜLLER.
MS. = Maitrâyaṇî Saṃhitâ.
NR. = MAX MÜLLER's Natural Religion.
Nir. = Nirukta.
OGR. = MAX MÜLLER's Origin and Growth of Religion.
OLS. = WHITNEY's Oriental and Linguistic Studies.
OO. = BENFEY's Orient und Occident.
ORV. = OLDENBERG, Die Religion des Veda.
OST. = MUIR's Original Sanskrit Texts.
PAOS. = Proceedings of the American Oriental Society.
PB. = Pañcaviṃśa Brâhmaṇa (= TMB.)
PGS. = Pâraskara Gṛhya Sûtra.
PhR. = MAX MÜLLER's Physical Religion.
Ps.R. = MAX MÜLLER's Psychological Religion.
PRASB. = Proceedings of the Royal Asiatic Society of Bengal.
PVS. = PISCHEL, Vedische Studien.
PW. = Petersburger Wörterbuch (BÖHTLINGK and ROTH's larger Sanskrit Dictionary).
RV. = Rigveda.
ŚB. = Śatapatha Brâhmaṇa.
SBE. = Sacred Books of the East.
Sp.AP. = SPIEGEL, Die Arische Periode.
SPH. = SCHERMAN, Philosophische Hymnen.
SV. = Sâmaveda.
SVL. = SCHERMAN, Visionslitteratur.
ŚŚS. = Śâṅkhâyana Śrauta Sûtra.
TA. = Taittirîya Âraṇyaka.
TB. = Taittirîya Brâhmaṇa.
TMB. = Tâṇḍya Mahâbrâhmaṇa (= PB).
TS. = Taittirîya Saṃhitâ.
Up. = Upaniṣad.
Vâl. = Vâlakhilya.
VS. = Vâjasaneyi Saṃhitâ.
WC. = WALLIS, Cosmology of the Rigveda.
WVB. = WEBER, Vedische Beiträge (Sitzungsberichte der Berliner Akademie).
WZKM. = Wiener Zeitschrift für die Kunde des Morgenlandes (Vienna Oriental Journal).
YN. = YÂSKA's Nirukta.
YV. = Yajurveda.
ZDA. = Zeitschrift für deutsches Altertum.
ZDMG. = Zeitschrift der Deutschen Morgenländischen Gesellschaft.
ZVP. = Zeitschrift für Völkerpsychologie.

N.B. The figures in parentheses without an added abbreviation refer to the Rigveda.

CONTENTS.

NB. The Manuscript was sent in on September 23, 1896.

ADDENDA AND CORRIGENDA.

P. 1, ast line, *for* Oxford Essays II *read* Oxford Essays, 1856 (= Chips 4[2], 1–151). — P. 2, l. 1 *add* Contributions to the Science of Mythology, 2 vols. London, 1897. P. 5, l. 5 from below *for* pove *read* prove. — P. 8, l. 4 *for* Verethragna *read* Verethraghna. — P. 12, l. 7 from below, for *viśvarupa* read *viśvarūpa*; l. 23: on this paradox cp. WC. 41. — P. 15, l. 10 from below *for* Prajanya *read* Parjanya. — P. 17, l. 14 from below *add*: The notion of an infinite number of cosmic ages is already to be found in the AV. (10, 8[39-40]), cp. JACOBI, GGA. 1895, p. 210; GARBE in this Encyclopedia 3, 4 p. 16. — P. 21, note [22] *for* fournished *read* furnished. — P. 22, l. 14 *asanimat*: cp. PAOS. 1895, p. 138. — P. 28, note [2] *add* but cp. RV. 10, 127[1] and BLOOMFIELD, JAOS. 15, 170; SBE. 42, 391. — P. 29, note [21] *add* JOH. SCHMIDT writes to the effect that till the relation of the Aeolic ὄρανος and ὤρανος to οὐρανός has been determined, it is impossible to say whether Varuṇa is connected with οὐρανός or not. — P. 29, § 13, l. 4 for *bruvānah* read *bruvāṇaḥ*. — P. 33, l. 25 *for* stimultae *read* stimulate. — P. 38, l. 4 *add* BLOOMFIELD, AJP. 14, 493. — P. 37, § 16, last line of notes, *after* PERRY *add* JAOS. 11, 190–1. — P. 39, l. 19 *for* mythology *read* mythology[11]. — P. 41, l. 28 *for* IS. XI *read* IS. XII. — P. 42, l. 5, note [4] *add* cp. MACDONELL, GGA. 1897, p. 47–8. P. 42, l. 17 *add* On Viṣṇu's obscure epithet *sipiviṣṭa* cp. OST. 4, 87 f.; LRV. 1, 102; 4, 153; KRV. note 214. — P. 44, l. 6: On Sūrya and Savitṛ as an Āditya cp. JAOS. 18, 28. — P. 44, l. 21 *for* Adityas *read* Ādityas. — P. 46, note 9 *add* Cp. WURM, Gesch. d. ind. Rel. p. 29. — P. 46, l. 5 *for* feast' *read* feast. — P. 50, *delete* note 9. P. 54, note [22] *add* cp. JAOS. 16, 21–2; l. 33 *add* HOPKINS, PAOS. 1894, CXLIX–CL. P. 55, l. 15: On Indra's weapons cp. PERRY, JAOS. 11, 138–198. — P. 55, l. 21: on *arara* cp. OLDENBERG, SBE. 46, 278. — P. 66, note [11] *add* cp. LRF. 142–3; note [33] *add* cp. WINTERNITZ, Hochzeitsrituell 43. 46; OERTEL, JAOS. 18, 26–31; note 3 *add* BRV. 3, 200–7; note [42] *add* cp. ZDMG. 9, 687. — P. 69, note [10] *add* cp. HILLEBRANDT, Vedainterpretation 13. 19; and two lines below before LRV. 3, 355–7 *add* WESTERGAARD, IS. 3, 414–24. — P. 80, l. 9 *for* Marudvṛddhā *read* Marudvṛdhā (also p. 88, note 4). — P. 84, l. 8 from below: On points of resemblance between Indra and Parjanya cp. HOPKINS, PAOS. 1894 (Dec.), 36–9. — P. 85, note 4 *add* JOH. SCHMIDT writes that he regards the equation Parjanya = Perkúnas as quite wrong, since Lith. *ū* can only correspond to Sansk. *ū*. LESKIEN also considers this equation untenable (communication through BÖHTLINGK). It is, however, accepted by WACKERNAGEL, Altindische Grammatik §§ 52. 100 b. — P. 88, note [11] *add* cp. BOLLENSEN, ZDMG. 41, 499. — P. 114 *delete* note 41. — P. 169, note [6] *add* HAUG, GGA. 1875, p. 96.

CPSIA information can be obtained
at www.ICGtesting.com
Printed in the USA
BVHW040452301220
596440BV00005B/467

9 781497 973107